THE OLD TESTAMENT

ITS ORIGINS AND
COMPOSITION

CURT KUHL

THE OLD TESTAMENT

ITS ORIGINS AND COMPOSITION

Translated by
C. T. M. HERRIOTT

JOHN KNOX PRESS
RICHMOND, VIRGINIA

Published in Great Britain by Oliver and Boyd Ltd, Edinburgh and London, and in the United States of America by John Knox Press, Richmond, Virginia.

Library of Congress Catalog Card Number 61-7885

A translation of *Die Entstehung des Alten Testaments*, by Curt Kuhl, lic. theol., Dr. phil., D. theol. h.c., published in 1953 by A. Francke A.G., Bern, as Bd. xxvi of the Sammlung Dalp.

The Scripture quotations in this book are from the Revised Standard Version of the Bible, copyrighted 1946 and 1952 by the Division of Christian Education of the National Council of the Churches of Christ in the United States of America, and used by permission.

ENGLISH EDITION
Second printing 1962

PRINTED IN GREAT BRITAIN FOR OLIVER AND BOYD LTD
BY THE KYNOCH PRESS, BIRMINGHAM

Dedicated to

The Reverend Harold H. Rowley, D.D.

Professor at the University of Manchester

as a mark of the author's
high esteem and gratitude

CONTENTS

CHAPTER I

INTRODUCTION

The Authority of the Old Testament

THE COLLECTION of Holy Scriptures generally described as the Old Testament, in accordance with II Cor. III. 14, contains the religious testimony of two basically different religions. On the one hand it is the Holy Scripture of the Jews, "the Law," and as such has a binding and directive significance for the life and moral conduct of believers. At their services the community of the faithful draw on this book for prayer and edification; from it they derive their strength and their comfort. For it speaks to them of what God did for their ancestors: it tells of men's obedience to their faith, but also of human weakness and unfaithfulness; of God's love and of His wrath, of His gracious guidance and of His punitive judgments, His self-revelation, in the story of the patriarchs and in the destinies of His chosen people, with might and majesty as "the Lord of History."

In addition, however, the Old Testament is most intimately bound up with Christianity. Long before the New Testament existed and before the Gospels and the apostolic writings had been gathered together into a special Christian scripture, the Christian community, from its very beginning, valued and honoured the Old Testament as its own Holy Scripture. It was the Bible of Jesus, in which He was at home and dwelt throughout the whole of His earthly ministry: beginning with the story of His temptation, when He rejected each of the three promptings of the devil with a quotation from Deuteronomy,[1] and ending with His last word from the Cross.[2] In the Old Testament He received the voice of His Father, and from it He derived His consciousness of His special mission. Whenever men came to Him, driven by some inner need, like the scribe or

---

[1] Mt. IV. 1–11: vs. 4, cf. Deut. VIII. 3; vs. 7, cf. Deut. VI. 16; vs. 10, cf. Deut. VI. 13.

[2] Lk. XXIII. 46: Ps. XXXI. 5.

the rich young man, Jesus referred them to what was written
in the Law;[3] and there is certainly a particular intention
behind His allusion to the Old Testament in His conversation
with Nicodemus,[4] and the fact that His sermon in His native
town was based on the words of the prophet Isaiah.[5] The old
words of the Law are given their proper meaning and a deeper
significance for the first time in His sermon on the mount
(Mt. v. 21 ff.) when He made that telling and impressive
comparison between what "was said to the men of old" and
what "I say to you." On the other hand, we should note that
Jesus, recalling God's ordinance at the creation, took issue
against the Law of Moses, which allowed divorce "for your
hardness of hearts" (Mt. xix. 8). We should also remember
His deprecating criticism of the dietary laws (Mt. xv. 11), and
His violation of that most sacred commandment of the Jews,
observance of the Sabbath (Mt. xii. 6–8), above which He is
exalted by reason of His special divine authority: "I tell you,
something greater than the temple is here. . . . For the Son of
man is Lord of the Sabbath." On these same lines are His
words that "the law and the prophets were until John: since
then the good news of the kingdom of God is preached"
(Lk. xvi. 16). These words are taken from His dispute with
the Pharisees, whom He was trying to show that God's
standards are different from man's, and that the time of
personal righteousness, which man could attain by compliance
with the Law, was now past. Though Jesus admittedly used
the sharpest of words against that form of righteousness which is
attached merely to the letter of the Law without embracing
its spirit, He equally certainly saw that it was His duty not to
undermine the Law and the prophets: "I have come not to
abolish them but to fulfil them" (Mt. v. 17 ff.). Add to this
evaluation of the Old Testament Jesus's further words: "Today
this scripture has been fulfilled in your hearing" (Lk. iv. 21).

These words teach us to understand the great value which
the early Christians placed on the Old Testament. For the
Apostles and the Evangelists there was a close connexion
between the Old Testament and the glad tidings of Christ;

[3] Lk. x. 26–7; Deut. vi. 5; Lk. xviii. 20: Ex. xx. 12–16.
[4] Jn. iii. 5: Ezek. xxxvi. 25–7.
[5] Lk. iv. 17–19: Is. lxi. 1–2.

an interaction in as much as the new covenant was concealed
in the old, and the old was fulfilled and perfected in the new.
Christ is the end of the Law (Rom. x. 4): He is its fulfilment
and the goal towards which the Old Testament was striving.
Their experience was something wholly new and unique:
salvation in Christ granted them by the grace of God (II Cor.
v. 19). But this new thing in its turn is closely bound up with
the Old Testament, for it is the continuation and fulfilment of
all the pious yearnings and divine promises contained in the
Old Testament. The old hopes pinned on the divinely appointed and anointed one, the Messiah, have now become
reality. So it is no coincidence, but rather in keeping with the
whole religious outlook of primitive Christianity and the
apostolic period, that the books of the New Testament contain
about 250 quotations, some of them fairly extensive, and in
individual expressions and turns of speech more than 900
allusions to the Old Testament. There is no need to draw
special attention to the Epistle to the Hebrews, which is deeply
rooted in the Old Testament and offers proof by its abundant
Old Testament citations that fulfilment is coming "now,"
and that salvation has appeared and become a reality in
Christ. Let us but mention how Matthew[6] in particular, and
also John,[7] establish a close connexion between the whole
life and passion of Jesus and the Old Testament by the reminder: "that the scripture might be fulfilled." Thus Peter quotes
the words of Psalm cxviii as proof of his salvation through
Christ (Acts iv. 10 f.), and at the Feast of Pentecost he acknowledges the crucified and risen Lord by recalling the words of
the Old Testament.[8] Similarly Stephen testifies before the
Council with a grand review of the course of the history of
salvation from Abraham to Solomon and from the prophets to
Christ (Acts vii. 2 ff.); and the Apostle Philip (Acts viii. 30 ff.)
explains Is. liii to the Ethiopian eunuch as the gospel of Jesus
Christ. In the Epistle to the Romans Paul expounds the
gospel from the faith of Abraham, and points to the evidence of
the scriptures for the Lord's crucifixion and resurrection from

[6] Mt. i. 22, ii. 15, 17, 23, iv. 14, viii. 17, xii. 17, xiii. 35, xxi. 4, xxvi. 54, 56, xxvii. 9, 35.
[7] Jn. xii. 38, xiii, 18, xv. 25, xvii. 12, xix. 24, 28, 36 f.
[8] Acts ii. 14 ff.: Joel iii. 28–32; Ps. xvi. 8–11, cx. 1.

the dead.[9] In this typological interpretation Adam is Paul's "type of the one who was to come" (Rom. v. 14), and what happened to "our fathers under the cloud" as they passed through the wilderness "are warnings for us."[10] Furthermore, he defines the significance of the Law as having brought the children up towards Christ (Gal. III. 24): and he proceeds to prove, from the example of Hagar and Sarah, that we are the children of promise and therefore "not children of the slave," but "of the free woman."[11] Thus the basic attitude of the Evangelists and Apostles towards the Old Testament can be summed up in the words of Paul, that in Jesus Christ all the promises of God are Yes and Amen (II Cor. 1. 20).

Hence the fact that Christianity, whose followers at that time were opposed and persecuted by the Jews, is based not only on the gospels but also on the Jewish scriptures. Not that it simply appropriates the Old Testament and makes it a religious book of its own, as the Jews regarded and esteemed it. Christianity gives it a new meaning and a new content foreign to Judaism: it is only by reference to Christ that the veil covering the Old Testament is removed, revealing it in its true meaning as a history of salvation. Contrasted with "Israel after the flesh" (1 Cor. x. 18 A.V.) is the true Israel, "the Israel of God" (Gal. VI. 16); and God's promise at the making of the covenant at Sinai (Ex. XIX. 6) is valid not only for the Jews but for those who have come to believe in Christ. Hence the triumphant message for Christendom: "But you are a chosen race, a royal priesthood, a holy nation, God's own people" (1 Pet. II. 9).

But if Christ is the end of the Law, this fact must have a retrospective effect on the authority of the Law, and hence on the authority of the Old Testament as a whole. This is largely compensated for by adopting from the Jews the method of allegorical interpretation of the scriptures: in Beroea, for example, Paul's sermons were examined daily by the listening Jews to see whether they were in accordance with the scriptures (Acts XVII. 11). By virtue of its secure standing the Old Testament rendered a significant service to the young Christian community; for with the development of gnosticism it formed

[9] 1 Cor. xv. 3–4: Is. LIII. 8–9; Ps. xvi. 10.
[10] 1 Cor. x. 6: Ex. XIII. 21, XIV. 22; Num. XI. 4, 34, XIV. 23, 30.
[11] Gal. IV. 28, 31: Gen. XVI. 15, XXI. 2.

the dam which prevented the Christian faith from being swamped by Greek thought (Hellenism). The fact that the Old Testament was criticised and rejected by the adherents of gnosticism was of no very great significance so far as the further development of Christianity and its own authority were concerned: neither were the efforts of the Jewish Christian Ebionites, who deprecated the allegorical method of interpretation because they held that the true Old Testament religion was essentially in agreement with the Christian faith. The fact that they were unwilling to recognise any prophet between Aaron and Jesus necessarily led them to reject the Old Testament prophets. Their counterpart is found in the medieval sects of Bogomils and Cathari who for their part rejected the Law but upheld the prophets and the psalms.

More important and more serious by far was the attack made on the Old Testament in the second century A.D. by Marcion,[12] a distinguished member of the Christian community in Rome; an attack the more significant because it was launched not for intellectual reasons, as in the case of the gnostics, but in the interests of faith. Marcion's guiding principle was the unique greatness and significance of Christ's act of redemption, which demands belief in the grace of God in Christ. On the basis of this Pauline doctrine he regarded every connexion between the Christian faith and Old Testament religion as a retrograde step from the great law of love to the law of commandments and ceremonies; and at the same time he rejected allegorical interpretation of the Old Testament as forced. Paul's great antitheses between law and gospel, anger and mercy, works and faith, sin and righteousness, flesh and spirit, death and life, led him to the point where he no longer (as was customary) saw the one great unity, finally crowned by the fact that the God who revealed Himself in the Old Testament is at the same time the Father of Jesus Christ (and therefore of us all). Marcion on the contrary made a clear distinction between the angry and jealous God of the Old Testament, who at the same time is the (inferior) creator of the world—the tendency to gnosticism is evident here—and

[12] See A. von Harnack, *Marcion: das Evangelium vom fremden Gott*, 2nd edn., Texte und Untersuchungen zur Geschichte des altchristlichen Literatur, VOL. XLV, Leipzig 1924; id., *Neue Studien zu Marcion*, Leipzig 1923.

the God unknown in the time before Christ who is all love and compassion. Thus he completely rejected the Old Testament, and replaced it as the Holy Scripture with something like his own canon, comprising Gospel (a shortened Luke's gospel) and Epistle (the letters of Paul without Timothy and Titus). Marcion could not get his ideas put into force, and in A.D. 144 he broke away from the Rome community. He travelled all over the Roman Empire and founded his own communities (Marcionites) everywhere he went: these proved to be vigorous and long-lived. Their remnants revived in the seventh century as Paulicians under Constantine Silvanus, and created work for the Byzantine Church into the ninth century and even longer in Armenia. It is impossible to say whether, and if so how far, the medieval Albigenses, who recognised only those parts of the Old Testament which are quoted in the New, came under Marcionite influence; but in any case they were severely put down by the Church. Seen as a whole, none of these endeavours was successful: the Old Testament remains immovably a permanent component of the Holy Scripture of the Christian Church, firmly established by the formation of the Canon, and protected by the principles laid down by Origen and Augustine as the standards for the interpretation and exposition of the Bible.

Even the Reformation carefully and loyally maintained this authority of the Old Testament and indeed increased it still further, in contrast with general opinion. In the Church there ruled above all else the tradition which dates back to the Apostles and is therefore older than the scriptures contained in the New Testament canon. The apostolic tradition was held to be continued through and handed down by the bishops, and in the early Middle Ages this authority took concrete shape in the Papacy and the General Councils. This helps us to understand Calvin's use of the word of God as the criterion by which to judge papal dispensations, and Luther's declaration before the Diet at Worms that he believed "in nothing, not even in Councils, but only in the word of God." In equating the word of God with the Bible the Reformers' urgent concern was to acknowledge the Holy Scriptures of the Old and New Testaments as the single source of the Christian faith. Since God Himself gives His testimony in the Holy Scriptures, their absolute authority was the starting-point and prerequisite for Calvin's doctrinal system; and this led him, as a logical consequence, to renew even the strictness of the Old Testament Law. In his view the tension between Law and Gospel was removed by the expectation of eternity, by the hope of perfection in the world to come. The tension flared up again, however, for a short time in the Lutheran era in the so-called Antinomian controversy, in which Melanchthon represented the opinion that any preaching of the faith must be preceded by the preaching of repentance for sins in accordance with the Old Testament Law. In opposition, Johannes Agricola stressed the view that the Decalogue was legislation and not preaching; Jesus was being erroneously represented as a second Moses, the Law was merely an unsuccessful attempt on God's part to lead mankind by the use of threats. These ideas, if logically developed, would necessarily have endangered the authority of the Old Testament; but this was avoided, for Agricola recanted in 1537.

Certainly Luther, in his struggle against Karlstadt and the Zwickau prophets, was approaching the thought of Agricola when he said: "Let Moses be the law code of the Jews but do not involve us heathen"; certainly he spoke many a hard and sharp word against the Jews; but just as certainly did the Old Testament remain in his opinion the absolute and unshakeable authority. The asperity of the statement in his preface to the Psalms: "When the Old Testament can be explained by human reason, without the New [Testament], then will I say that the New Testament is given us in vain," is due to the particular circumstances of the case and is rightly corrected in his other observation that "all psalms must be related to Christ, our Lord, unless the text makes it quite clear that something else is meant." But the statement may be indicative of the close links which, in his opinion, bind the two parts of the Bible together. Luther considered that the primary function of the Old Testament is "to teach the law, to denounce sin, to promote good," while the New Testament is "a public preaching and proclamation of the statements contained in the Old Testament and fulfilled by Christ." For him, then, the Old and New Testaments together formed a unity, for both are the word of God, and both embrace the complete content of the divine word, viz. Law and Gospel. He differentiated between the two only in so far as the Old Testament contains command-ments, and the New promises "in plenty," and in so far as God's act of redemption is promised in the one, and certified as fulfilled in the other.[13] In his interpretation of the Old Testa-ment, Luther very soon outgrew the medieval idea, current in his day, of the fourfold meaning of the scriptures.[14] In particular he rejected allegory as arbitrary, even although he himself never could quite get away from it. Since in his eyes the Old Testament contained evangelical doctrine and was inter-spersed throughout with references to Christ, Luther produced a new type of scriptural interpretation by explaining the Old Testament as referring prophetically to Christ.[15] So far as he was concerned, then, the authority of the Old Testament was absolutely self-evident.

In the post-Reformation period the doctrine of the verbal inspiration of Holy Scripture by God grew up in the Protestant Churches. That is to say, from the statement that "all scripture is inspired by God" (II Tim. III. 16) there developed the doctrine that Scripture is the word of God, dictated by God through the Holy Spirit to the individual authors. This means that the authors of the various books of the Bible were nothing more than scribes, merely instruments used by God to write down His word. As a result of their divine origin it was considered that the Scriptures had four special attributes: (a) *auctoritas*, authority in matters of faith, teaching how to distinguish between true and false; (b) *perspicuitas*, superlative clearness of meaning; (c) *perfectio* or *sufficientia*, completeness, being in themselves sufficient for the recognition of the Good, and (d) *efficacia*, effectiveness, in that God uses them to achieve the conversion of mankind. The individual ideas in this doctrine were not new, but can be traced here and there in the ancient Church or in the Middle Ages. Here, however, they

---

[13] H. Bornkamm, *Luther und das Alte Testament*, Tübingen 1948, p. 73.

[14] The fourfold meaning of the scriptures: 1. "Littera gesta docet," the literal historical meaning; 2. "quid credas allegoria," the allegorical interpretation, especially as referring to the Church, its history and possessions; 3. "moralis quid agas," the moral interpretation for the life of the individual; 4. "quid tendas anagogia," the eschatological interpretation.

[15] Cf. Bornkamm, *Luther und das Alte Testament*, pp. 74 ff., esp. pp. 84–5, Luther's interpretation of Ps. CXVII.

were systematically gathered together. And it goes without saying that this doctrine, which was firmly held into the eighteenth century and, we must add, has still not completely died out among Christians even today, was perhaps the most suitable weapon with which to safeguard and enhance the authority of the Scriptures and hence of the Old Testament. In the long run, however, it could render no useful service either to the Scriptures or to the Church: indeed, it is precisely to the extent that the Church held the doctrine of verbal inspiration that the authority of the Scriptures, in particular of the Old Testament, has been so severely shaken by the new knowledge about Israel in all its aspects, archaeological, literary, historical, cultural, and religious, derived from modern research into the Ancient Near East.

CRITICISM OF THE OLD TESTAMENT

If the Holy Scripture was the word of God in the sense that God Himself had given it to man in this form, then indeed it was elevated above all criticism. Up till now any criticism that has been made within the confines of the Church has always been restricted to textual criticism, such as Origen's fundamental and valuable attempt with his *Hexapla*; and the intention has always been not to criticise the word of God, but rather to get closer to the true Word. True, it was criticism—even if it was not felt to be such—which in the end led to the formation of the Canon, but in this case it was not so much criticism of the Holy Scripture itself as an assessment of the individual books, the values of which were controversial in any case.

Apart from Marcion, the definite beginnings of Old Testament criticism are not found until the Reformation. In Calvin they occur only occasionally, but Karlstadt questioned the Mosaic authorship of the Pentateuch in a pamphlet in 1520. Although he had the support of the well-known Catholic jurist Andreas Masius (d. 1573), these preliminary attempts bore no further fruit. More important was the attitude of Luther as shown in his "Prefaces"; he spoke of "Jew-extolling writing" with reference to the Book of Esther; of the threefold laws of Moses (civil laws, ceremonial laws, laws of faith and love); and of the fact that "the prophecy of Hosea is not completely recorded, but a few fragments and statements are

B

taken from his preaching and put together into a book."
These and similar comments on the other prophetic books
already show a tendency towards criticism. Luther wrote of
Ecclesiastes that "it has been collated by others and in addition
the teaching and statements of some other wise men have been
included," while the Song of Solomon is "a fragmentary book,
taken by others from Solomon's mouth." In trying to test the
other books of the Bible to see how far they "deal with Christ,"
Luther was using a standard worthy of consideration, in that it
made it possible to compare the value of, and hence to grade,
the individual books. This principle, however, was far in advance of contemporary developments, and had as little practical
result as Luther's occasional critical observations.

Critical evaluation of the Old Testament in the true sense
was first initiated at the beginning of the Enlightenment.
Under the influence of this movement, churchmen tried to
break away from the prevailing doctrine of inspiration. Their
aim was to render the Church a service by leading the way to a
better and more correct understanding of the scriptures. The
French Oratorian priest Richard Simon entitled his great
work, directed against Spinoza, *Histoire critique du Vieux
Testament* (1678); the Protestant Jean Leclerc laid down in 1685
critical principles for the understanding of the individual
scriptures, which he said should be considered and treated as
literature in the same way as Greek authors. This demand was
repeated, with great emphasis, by Jean Alphonse Turretini
(1728). All these efforts on the part of the Church were
strongly influenced by philosophy, which was responsible for
shaking the foundations of the existing conception of the written
idea. Thomas Hobbes in his *Leviathan* (1651) had already
demanded that, as principles of research, the age and where
possible the author of each book should be examined. The
decisive influence, however, finally emanated from the famous
Dutch philosopher Baruch Spinoza, who in his *Tractatus
theologico-politicus* (1670) was the first to provide a critical
review of the Old Testament as a national and literary product.
In this book he applied a critical, historical, and philosophical
method and wished to be able to differentiate between the
history of the language, the text, the canon, the composition of
each individual book and the range of ideas of its author.

Following upon Spinoza, and largely influenced by him, the English Deists sharply criticised the Old Testament: William Whiston (1722) went so far as to assert that in the second century A.D. the Jews corrupted the text of the Old Testament in order to shake the prophetic evidence of the Christians. Thomas Morgan, who combined ideas derived from the Reformed critics with those of Spinoza, should also be mentioned here, for his book *Moral Philosophers* (1737) was not without influence on Lessing and Reimarus. However, there is no need to pursue this line. Spinoza's demands were of fundamental importance. They changed the old conception of the authority of Scripture and especially the idea of inspiration: henceforth not the thing, but the men, the biblical writers, were held to be inspired. The Bible remains, it is true, the word of God, but now in the different sense that it is bound up with man, experienced and proclaimed by man, at the most diverse times and under the most diverse conditions. The authors as persons are considered to be inspired, intimately linked with God by their piety and speaking and writing on His behalf: the books of the Bible are no longer regarded as self-revelation by God, but as historical records of revelation experienced by man or, better, as testimonies of revelation.

The middle of the eighteenth century saw the beginning of scholarly criticism of the Old Testament, the aim of which was not to destroy what was already in existence or to diminish its importance for the Faith, but to penetrate more deeply into the Old Testament with all the available means of scholarship, and to make it more easily understood. At first it took the form of historico-critical research and turned its attention to textual and literary criticism, producing a rich harvest in working out the individual sources of the Pentateuch.[16] In addition an attempt was made to reach a form of text as definitive as possible: comparison of texts and consultation of ancient versions of the Old Testament were very helpful in this direction,[17] but where these methods failed, there was no alternative, since the texts had been handed down badly in many ways, but to fall back on surmise and conjecture. This textual

[16] On the development and history of Pentateuchal criticism cf. Chapter II, notes 10 and 12.
[17] For the significance of the old translations cf. below, pp. 16 ff.

work is necessary and in future will have to be considered as
the basis of all Old Testament scholarship: but lest it should
open the doors to subjective judgments and caprice, objective
criteria are being sought and attempts made to work out rules
and principles for the development of the text handed down to
us.[18] Since the nineteenth century archaeological research,
particularly in Babylon and Egypt, has brought to light a vast
store of material, including papyri and cuneiform tablets which
are largely older than the oldest written memorials of the Old
Testament. So far they have thrown abundant light on our
understanding of the Old Testament,[19] which is now taken out
of its formerly isolated position and placed within the context of
the ancient Near East of which it forms a part. The cultural,
religious, and literary connexions are now shown to have been
very close in some respects, so much so that from time to time at
the beginning of this century there was a dangerous tendency to
derive each and every feature of the Old Testament from
Assyria-Babylonia.[20] This Panbabylonism, however, was soon
overcome. Important as it is to draw attention to points of
contact, to establish what the peoples of the ancient Near East
had in common, one is nevertheless aware that it is equally
important to recognise the individual characteristics, the
peculiarities which distinguished Israel from her neighbours.
In particular, scholars of the history of religion,[21] starting in
the 1880's, have made many valuable contributions to our
understanding of the Old Testament by investigating foreign

---

[18] Cf. F. Delitzsch, *Die Lese- und Schreibfehler im Alten Testament*, henceforth cited
as *Lese- und Schreibfehler*, Berlin 1920; H. W. Hertzberg, *Die Nachgeschichte alttestamentlicher Texte innerhalb des Alten Testaments*, henceforth cited as *Nachgeschichte*,
Beihefte zur *Zeitschrift für die alttestamentliche Wissenschaft*, henceforth cited as
Beihefte z. *Z. alttest. W.*, No. 66, Berlin 1936, pp. 110–21; G. Fohrer, "Die
Glossen im Buche Ezechiel," henceforth cited as "Ezechielglossen," in *Zeitschrift
für die alttestmentlicher Wissenschaft*, henceforth cited as *Z. alttest. W.*, XIII (1951),
pp. 33–53.

[19] The main excavations in more recent times are those of Boghazkoi, Ras-
Shamra (Ugarite), and Mari.

[20] H. Winckler and his school, the last product being A. Jeremias, *Das Alte
Testament im Lichte des Alten Orients*, 2nd edn., Leipzig 1906, and *Handbuch der
altorientalischen Geisteskultur*, Leipzig 1913. Cf. also H. Gressmann, *Altorientalische
Texte und Bilder zum Alten Testament*, 2 vols., 2nd edn., Berlin 1926–7; *Ancient Near
Eastern Texts relating to the Old Testament*, ed. J. B. Pritchard, 2nd edn., Princeton
and London 1955.

[21] The main representatives for the Old Testament are H. Gunkel, H. Gressmann, S. Mowinckel, and W. Baumgartner.

influences on it.[22] Progress in ancient Near Eastern studies gave rise to another method of looking at the Old Testament—from the aspect of literary history. The starting-point here is oral tradition, based on a varied social life, which is older than the written form of the Old Testament—in which indeed it is not immediately recognisable. This methodology follows up the smallest "units," examines them for form, language, and style, and then proceeds on the basis of a large quantity of comparative material to pick out various classes of material,[23] pointing out their *Sitz im Leben* and meaning, as well as their transformation in the hands of editors and compilers. Research into the history of the material is further concerned with detecting similar or related material in the hope of gaining a better understanding of the individual literary genres. The aim of all the work done by literary historians is to present the writings handed down in the Old Testament in the form of a history of literature.[24] More recently these attempts have been joined by research concerned with the historical development of religious belief: this work examines the origin and development of individual religious ideas and expressions of piety, and investigates any changes they may have undergone. Those concerned with the history of tradition are interested in the prehistory of the books of the Bible and examine the various individual sources of material before they were committed to writing in the Old Testament. Finally, there is research into the history of the cult: this follows up the cultic legends attaching to individuals, sanctuaries, and feasts, and sees in them points on

[22] Fundamental works here are H. Gunkel, *Schöpfung und Chaos in Urzeit und Endzeit*, 2nd edn., Göttingen 1921, and H. Gressmann, *Der Ursprung der israelitisch-jüdischen Eschatologie*, Göttingen 1905, as well as the great biblical work which these two published in company with W. Staerk, P. Volz, H. Schmidt, and M. Haller, *Die Schriften des Alten Testaments in Auswahl*, 7 vols., 2nd edn., Göttingen 1921–5.

[23] Cf. particularly H. Gunkel and J. Begrich, *Einleitung in die Psalmen*, Göttingen 1933.

[24] Cf. H. Gunkel, "Die israelitische Literatur," in *Kultur der Gegenwart*, PT. I, sect. vii, 2nd edn., Leipzig 1925; J. Hempel, *Die althebräische Literatur und ihr hellenistisch-jüdisches Nachleben*, henceforth cited as *Althebräische Literatur*, Potsdam-Wildpark 1930; A. Lods, *Histoire de la littérature hébraïque et juive des origines à la ruine de l'etat juif*, henceforth cited as *Histoire de la littérature*, Paris 1950. A presentation of this nature remains difficult in so far as it necessarily presupposes that the questions will be dealt with in the order of development and date of starting of the individual sections gathered together in the Old Testament.

which further growth of the written tradition crystallised.[25] Last but not least, mention must be made of archaeological studies in Palestine, which have become very intensive, particularly in the last generation, and have led to excellent and very informative results on many points.[26] Even this very sketchy outline reveals the profusion of tasks which must be mastered by a modern critical research programme in any attempt to bring about a better understanding of the Old Testament.

Among the critics of the Old Testament we must include Schleiermacher, who, at the beginning of the nineteenth century, wanted to see the close bond between the Old and New Testaments removed, because Jesus had brought a new awareness of God, and because the only thing Christianity had in common with the Old Testament was the messianic prophecies. Schleiermacher derived this attitude from his assumption that the relationship between Christianity and Judaism is the same as that between Christianity and heathendom. But this is a false argument, for Schleiermacher's conception of Judaism was far too narrow; by it he understood only the "Mosaic institutions." In evaluating the Old Testament he moreover stated expressly that "it does not follow therefrom that the Bible should be split in two, for it is an historical result: it is such an old-established fact that the Church has combined both parts, that there is no cause to abandon this now." These words show that, although he set little value on the Old Testament, he did not intend to remove it from the Canon.

The first to advocate this step was Adolf von Harnack, who, in his outstanding book on Marcion, described as "religious and ecclesiastical paralysis" the fact that "the Old Testament is still, in the nineteenth century, preserved as a canonical document." Unfortunately Harnack was here advancing a thesis rather than establishing a truth, so that it is difficult to recognise the motives which gave rise to such a statement. It is certain, however, that he did not intend to propose that

---

[25] Cf. especially the works of M. Noth and G. von Rad (see below).

[26] The best review is contained in the popular book by W. F. Albright, *The Archaeology of Palestine*, Harmondsworth 1949. Cf. also id., *Recent Discoveries in Bible Lands*, 2nd edn., New York 1955; A. Jirku, *Die Ausgrabungen in Palästina und Syrien*, Halle 1956.

the Old Testament should be rejected: he rather inclined to the view that the Old Testament, and especially the prophets, could only be properly appreciated for its own sake if it was stripped of canonical authority. In the light of Harnack's thesis one must certainly ask whether the development of learned Old Testament research is sufficiently appreciated.

The attitude of the Orientalist Friederich Delitzsch was quite different. About the turn of the century he questioned the revelatory character of the Old Testament and of Israelite religion as a whole in his famous "Babel and Bible" lectures. Then in his two-volume work *Die grosse Täuschung* (The Great Deception, 1920–21) he prepared to launch a general attack on the Old Testament, reviving Marcion's old ideas on the contrast between the Jewish national God and the Father of Jesus Christ. His reasoning, however, especially when it involves the prophets, reveals only too clearly his lack of understanding of history and his domination by the old, long-abandoned doctrine of verbal inspiration. In spite of their special presentation the effect of these two books fell far short of that of his sensational "Babel and Bible" lectures. This may have been largely due to the fact that other developments meanwhile had put all previous threats to the Old Testament completely in the shade.

This was the great attack aimed against the Old Testament by the racial and national movement in Germany. Its roots stretch back to Count von Gobineau (1816–82), founder of modern racial teaching; Richard Wagner (1813–83), who raised the old Marcionite reproach against the Christian idea of God; Paul de Lagarde (1827–91) with his *Deutsche Schriften*, whose aim was the Germanisation of Christianity; and Houston Stewart Chamberlain (1855–1927), who in his famous *Grundlagen des neunzehnten Jahrhunderts* (Greek art, Roman law, and the coming of Jesus Christ, who, as a Galilean, was probably Aryan) attacked the Jews and the Old Testament from the standpoint of racial purity. Prepared by the German Church movement[27] (Kurd Niedlich, 1884–1928) and the Tannenbergbund[28] (Mathilde Ludendorff), there grew up within the

---

[27] Cf. G. Gloege, "Die Deutschkirche," in *Die Nation vor Gott*, edd. W. Kinneth and H. Schreiner, Berlin 1933, pp. 321–43.

[28] Cf. K. Witte, "Der Tannenbergbund," in *Die Nation vor Gott*, pp. 344–92.

Third Reich a dangerous threat to the Old Testament as well as to the New, and indeed to Christianity as a whole, whose "oriental origin" was increasingly treated as alien. National individuality was stressed, Nordic blood acclaimed, and the goal set of a Nordic religion built up on the old traditions of the Icelandic sagas and the Edda. Bound up with an ever-increasing hatred of the Jews, expressed both in word and deed, the "Nordic man of the present" conducted a bitter war against every hint of infiltration by Semitic influences. A profusion of literature plugged these ideas, while attempts to prove their falsity were more and more often banned by Goebbels. We will not go into details here: the facts are only too well known and no longer require discussing. Rosenberg's *Mythus des zwanzigsten Jahrhunderts* became the cultural bible of the Third Reich, and penetrated into the broadest strata of the nation, becoming the common property of the masses who, without criticising, mechanically repeated and handed on whatever cheap slogans were set before them. This avalanche has since crashed terrifyingly into the abyss, dragging with it on its downward course an infinite amount of material now buried beneath it in the depths. If we ask what significance this period through which we have passed has had for the Church, we may certainly say that it has been beneficial: beneficial in so far as it has compelled the Church to examine seriously its own position and to consider anew the sources of its faith, which is based on the revelation of God in the Holy Scriptures and therefore also on the Old Testament.

THE TRANSMISSION OF THE OLD TESTAMENT

The Old Testament is not a book of revelation which descended from Heaven, as it were, as a whole and was thus presented by God to mankind. Written by men, it contains a collection of the most heterogeneous writings, which in our Bible are grouped together, in accordance with the New Testament arrangement, as books of history, instruction, and prophecy. The very name "Old Testament" is taken from the New (II Cor. III. 14), and means something like "old covenant" in contrast to and as distinct from the new covenant made in Christ.[29] The

---

[29] Jer. XXXI. 31; Mt. XXVI. 28; II Cor. III. 6; Heb. VIII. 8, IX. 15, XII. 24.

names "Holy Scripture" or simply "Scripture"[30] or "Law" are more often used in the New Testament: St Paul cites (I Cor. XIV. 21) words from Isaiah XXVIII as being written in the Law. The most common designation seems to have been "the Law and the Prophets," or "Moses and the Prophets."[31] In the case of quotations we find that simply "Moses" is cited instead of the "Law." In one place we find the classification "Law, prophets, and psalms" (Lk. XXIV. 44). The oldest evidence for the dividing up of the Old Testament is provided by the preface to Jesus ben Sirach's (c. 130 B.C.) translation of his grandfather's sayings from Hebrew into Greek, in which he speaks of "Law, prophets, and other books of our ancestors." And so the Old Testament in its original text is divided to this day into the Law (five books of Moses; Hebrew, Torah; Greek, Pentateuch), the Prophets (Hebrew, Nebiim) subdivided into Former (Joshua, Judges, Samuel, Kings) and Latter (Isaiah, Jeremiah, Ezekiel, and Hosea–Malachi); and the Writings (Hebrew, Ketubim; Greek, Hagiographa) which covers the remainder.

Altogether we count thirty-nine books, while the original text restricted their number to twenty-four (II Esdras XIV. 45) and the Jewish writer Josephus (*Contra Apionem*, I. 8) to twenty-two. It would be wrong, however, to conclude from this variation in numbers that certain books have been omitted: the extent is exactly the same. The differences are explained by the fact that according to ancient Jewish calculations the twelve minor prophets, the two books respectively of Samuel, Kings, and Chronicles, as well as Ezra and Nehemiah, are each considered as one book; while Josephus further reduced the total by including Ruth with Judges, and Lamentations with Jeremiah.

The language in which the Old Testament is written belongs to the West Semitic group and is Hebrew, "the language of Canaan" or "the language of Judah"[33]: only in isolated

[30] "Holy scripture," Rom. I, 2; II. Tim. III. 15. "Scripture," Mt. XXI. 42, XXII. 29; Lk. XXIV. 32; Jn. V. 39, XIX. 37.
[31] Law and prophets: Mt. V. 17; Acts XXIV. 14, XXVIII. 23; Rom. III. 21. Moses and the prophets: Lk. XVI. 29, XXIV. 27; Jn. I. 45; Acts XXVI. 22.
[32] Mt. XXII. 24; Mk. XII. 26; Acts XV. 21; Rom. X. 5; II Cor. III. 15.
[33] Is. XIX. 18; II Kings XVIII. 26, 28; Neh. XIII. 24.

places do we find Aramaic.[34] The books are written in an
alphabetical script from right to left; this, at least in the case of
the older books, was the older Hebrew writing as it occurs
elsewhere in various inscriptions.[35] After the Exile, the so-
called Hebrew quadrat script—also called Assyrian script
because it was brought back from the Exile—appeared:
according to the Jewish tradition Ezra introduced this script
for the Torah,[36] and it was thereafter regularly used for the
Hebrew Bible.

The individual books, very probably because of their size,
were not, like the oldest documents, carved in stone (Ex. XXXI.
18; XXXIV. 1) or engraved on tablets (Isaiah XXX. 8; Hab. II. 2)
of clay or lead (Job XIX. 24), but were written in parallel
columns from right to left on book rolls[37] with a pen (Ps. XLV. 1)
and ink (Jer. XXXVI. 18), the scribe carrying an inkhorn at his
belt (Ezek. IX. 2). How vividly the story is told (Jer. XXXVI.
21 ff.) of King Jehoiakim sitting by the hearth in his winter
palace listening to the words dictated by the prophet Jeremiah:
each time three or four columns had been read he slashed them
off with his penknife and threw them on the fire, until finally
the whole roll had been burned. This, together with available
Egyptian information, leads to the conclusion that the material
used was Egyptian papyrus, made from the stems of the papyrus
plant: these stems were worked into sheets which were glued
together to form a strip, written upon, and then rolled round
two sticks, to be unrolled from left to right when the document
was being read. Papyrus was later replaced by leather or
parchment, which from about the second or third century A.D.
was folded in book form: in the worship of the Synagogue,
however, the roll form is retained to this day—at least for the
Torah and the Book of Esther. Such documents could not last
very long, for book rolls of this type would naturally wear out
very easily with use.

For this reason it was necessary, since no duplicating

[34] Gen. XXXI. 47; Jer. X. 11; Dan. II. 4–7, 28; Ezra IV. 8–VI. 18, VII. 12–26.

[35] Mention need only be made of the Mesa tablet (c. 840 B.C.), jug handles, and
numerous written fragments (ostraca) from Samaria (9th cent.) and Lachish (6th
cent.) and the Siloah inscription (c. 715 B.C.).

[36] From Mt. V. 18, where the jot is described as the smallest letter, we may
conclude that in Jesus' day the Law was available in this script.

[37] Jer. XXXVI. 2 ff.; Ezek. II. 9, III. 1 ff.; Zech. V. 1–2; Ps. XL. 8.

process was as yet known, for new copies to be always in the course of preparation, and this involved much painstaking and protracted work. The writing material was costly and therefore had to be used sparingly. All available space had to be utilised, and thus often things appeared together on one roll which originally had no connexion with one another. True, the Talmud[38] demanded that a space of four lines, and in the case of the minor prophets three lines, be left free between items. But in the course of repeated copying this provision could be overlooked, especially when one book ended at the foot of a column and the next began at the top of the following one. This is particularly evident in the case of the prophet Isaiah, who until quite recently was considered to be the author of a much later nameless prophecy of the exilic period which had been appended to his book.

Because of the cost of the writing material the scribes were also at pains to write as small as possible. Jerome, a Father of the Church *Hieronymus* (*d.* A.D. 420), occasionally complained that this made Hebrew writing very difficult to read. One should remember, moreover, that words were not always (as in the older documents) carefully divided but were sometimes combined, that individual sentences were not always clearly separated from one another, that the texts consisted only of consonants, all vowels being omitted: all these are sources of danger, giving rise only too easily to errors in copying which would be faithfully repeated in the next transcription and so preserved and maintained in copy after copy. It must be assumed that the copyists worked with the most painstaking accuracy; but however great the care, human fallibility makes it impossible altogether to exclude slips of the pen. And possibilities of error are many: single letters or words can be confused or omitted or written twice;[39] where similar phrases occur the scribe's eye may only too easily jump over what lies between, with the result that he leaves out parts of sentences, or even whole ones (*homoioarkton* and *homoioteleuton*).

[38] Menahot III fol. 30; L. Goldschmidt, *Der babylonische Talmud neu übertragen*, henceforth cited as *Talmud*, Berlin 1930–6, VOL. X, p. 490.
[39] Cf. F. Delitzsch, *Lese- und Schreibfehler;* H. Junker, *Konsonantenumstellungen als Fehlerquelle und textkritisches Hilfsmittel im Alten Testament*, Beihefte z. *Z. alttest. W.*, No. 66, Berlin 1936, pp. 162–74.

In addition many scribes added explanatory notes of one kind or other (glosses) in the margin, and these were only too easily incorporated into the text by their successors. So, to cite an example, one of the copyists noted beside the name of the Egyptian town Sin (= Syene) "an Egyptian fortress," and this note has penetrated into the wording of the text (Ezek. xxx. 15).[40] While in this case the observation was pertinent, there are numerous other glosses which have contributed to the text a meaning not originally intended, in some cases even the opposite meaning. Thus, for example, in Isaiah xxix. 10, the "eyes" and the "rulers" were later interpreted as prophets and seers.[41] Or the continuity may be completely broken by insertions into the text, as, for example, by the rules for kings in i. Sam. viii. 10–21.[42] Also on occasion there are deliberate changes in places where the religious sensibilities of the scribe took exception to the wording.[43] The Hebrew scribe was afraid of writing down anything disrespectful to God: "to refuse God" (Job i. 5) was a thought utterly intolerable to him. Since this expression is synonymous with "cursing" or "blaspheming," he replaced it in the text with the totally unsuitable word "blessing." Or he disliked compound names including the heathen god's name "Baal," and so he changed this "Baal" to "Bosheth" (= shame).[44] However, all honour to the transmitted text, we must say that such conscious corrections on the part of the scribe are not over-frequent, even if their number exceeds the modest list of eighteen drawn up by the Masoretes.

This leads us to the question how far the Hebrew text in use today can lay claim to originality and reliability. One has only to compare such portions as occur twice over in the Old Testament (e.g. Ps. xviii and ii Sam. xxii) to appreciate the full significance of this question. Once the Hebrew Canon had been fixed (see below), a task which for the most part was

[40] Cf. also Fohrer, "Ezechielglossen."

[41] Hertzberg, *Nachgeschichte.*

[42] Cf. C. Kuhl, "Die Wiederaufnahme—ein literarkritisches Prinzip?" in *Z. alttest. W.*, LXIV (1952), pp. 1–11.

[43] Cf. Job i. 5, ii. 5; i Kings xxi. 10; Ps. x. 3.

[44] Thus, for example, Jerubbaal (Jg. vi. 32); Jerubbesheth (ii Sam. xi. 21); Esh-baal (i Chron. ix. 39): Ish-bosheth (ii Sam. ii. 8); Merib-baal (i Chron. viii. 34); Mephibosheth (ii Sam. iv. 4).

completed before Josephus (c. A.D. 100), respect for the various texts transmitted naturally increased. The scholars (Soferim) in the Rabbinic schools put much effort into ensuring and establishing an irreproachable text. The result was the Masorah (tradition) which at first was transmitted orally, but was committed to writing from the third century onwards. There is no need to go into detail here about the work of the Masoretes, which extended over centuries, their various schools in the east (Babylon; Sura, Nehardea and, after the latter's destruction in A.D. 259, Pumbedita) and in the west (Galilee, especially Tiberias), and their mutual relationships. Suffice it to say that they succeeded in laying down an authentic text, which of course represented a compromise between several transmitted versions. They introduced the very important division of words and provided the text with vowels (punctuation): in the course of this work several systems evolved, the one which finally prevailed being the interlinear system from Tiberias. For reading the texts aloud they introduced stresses, which were also given the significance of punctuation marks; and for liturgical purposes they divided the text into sections according to sense. They did what they could to make the text secure, issuing detailed instructions for the scribes and adding at the end of each book a note of the number of verses it contains (e.g. Genesis, 1,534). This work provided a good foundation for further transmission and for the Hebrew printing of the Bible which started in 1488.

While Luther still relied on Gerson ben Mose's edition of the text (Venice, 1494), that of Jacob ben Chajim achieved considerable importance: the latter appeared from Bomberg in Venice 1525–26 as the so-called Second Rabbinic Bible. It is based on manuscripts of the thirteenth and fourteenth centuries and was held until recently to be the best edition. Now, however, it has been overtaken by the *Biblia Hebraica*, the combined effort of many scholars, which presents the ben Ascher text, older by several centuries, according to a Leningrad Bible manuscript.[45] This manuscript itself goes back to the Specimen Code of ben Ascher, which was protected with

---

[45] The research and discoveries of P. Kahle are fundamental to our knowledge of ben Ascher text; cf. literature quoted in the prefaces to the *Biblia Hebraica*, henceforth cited as *B. Heb.*, 7th edn., ed. R. Kittel, Stuttgart 1951.

great care from the eyes of strangers in the Synagogue of the
Soferim at Aleppo, but was said to have been destroyed during
the riots of 1847. Nevertheless, the Jerusalem scholar U.
Cassuto (d. 1951) was fortunate enough to inspect it and to
assess the value of its variants for the new Jerusalem edition
(1953) of the text.

With regard to number and age of manuscripts the Old
Testament unfortunately compares badly with the New. The
regrettable reason for this is the Jewish habit of storing synagogue rolls which are no longer in use in the lumber rooms of
the synagogue (geniza), and later destroying them in order to
prevent the desecration of the holy texts. By a particularly
lucky chance a walled-up, and therefore forgotten, geniza was
found during restoration work to the Old Cairo Synagogue
around 1890. Its treasures, in the form of rolls of text dating
from the sixth to the ninth century A.D., are today housed in
various libraries in Europe and America. The ideal goal
remains the finding of a pre-Masoretic text, or manuscripts
which at least approximate thereto. The discovery of the
Papyrus Nash (published 1902), the date of which is generally
estimated as second century A.D., was only a very modest step
in this direction; for it contains only the Ten Commandments
(Deut. v. 6–21) and the "Hear, O Israel" (Deut. vi. 4–5).
More important was the sensational discovery made by
Bedouin in 1947 in a very inaccessible cave a little north of
Chirbet Qumran north-west of the Dead Sea. This comprised
several book rolls wrapped in linen, protected against damp by
means of pitch, and stored in jars[46] (cf. Jer. XXXII. 14). These
contain, to name only the most important, the prophet Isaiah,
parts of Daniel, a commentary on Habakkuk, and also a
number of non-biblical writings like the Manual of Discipline,
and date from pre-Masoretic, indeed very probably even from
pre-Christian times to judge by the manner of writing. A
renewed search of the cave in 1949 produced a further (incomplete) book roll and hundreds of fragments, particularly from
the Books of Moses, Judges, and Daniel. Since then the whole
surrounding area has been systematically searched, with the
result that the contents of ten more caves in the region of the

---

[46] For literature on the Dead Sea Scrolls see the Bibliography.

first, and of others on the slope of the Wadi Murabba'at
(twelve miles south of Qumran), in the Chirbet Mird (seven
miles south-east of Qumran) and elsewhere have been brought
to light. Besides two copper rolls containing remarkable
details regarding hidden treasures, and a few *ostraca*, a whole
series of manuscripts of biblical books was found on papyrus
and leather fragments, in particular commentaries on Isaiah,
the Psalms and the minor prophets, but also manuscripts of the
Apocrypha. In addition there are letters, marriage agreements,
contracts, and other writings which may throw light on even
less well-known periods of Jewish history. The yield of fragments in Hebrew, Aramaic, Arabic, Nabataean, and Greek is so
tremendous that, according to a statement by D. Lancaster
Harding, the Jordan Director of Antiquities, a whole generation of Bible experts will be kept busy evaluating the texts. A
few texts have been published in New Haven and Jerusalem.
Now the work of deciphering and editing is organised by
D. L. Harding and Père de Vaux in the Palestine Archaeological
Museum in Jerusalem and is published by the Oxford University Press as a collection "Discoveries in the Judaean Desert."
Comparison of the Isaiah text with the help of photo-copies
reveals numerous differences in vocabulary, spelling, and
grammar; but there are no very great differences in the
text, either by additions, omissions or transpositions.[47] And
this in addition to the great age of the documents is particularly
significant, for it is proof of the reliability of the textual transmission as a whole.

For the rest, our knowledge of the pre-Masoretic text
depends on inferences: these are made possible by the ancient
translations of the Old Testament made in the pre-Masoretic
period. We will restrict ourselves here to the most important
points only, so as not to burden the reader unnecessarily with
these very complicated matters. A certain knowledge of them
is, however, essential if we are to understand what the work of
the textual critics means for the Old Testament as a whole. A
valuable aid for the Torah is the Holy Scripture of the Samaritans, the Hebrew Samaritan Pentateuch of the fourth century

---

[47] Cf. O. Eissfeldt, "Variae lectiones rotulorum manu scriptorum," etc., i
B. Heb., PT. XVII.

B.C., which exists in a multitude of manuscripts.[48] It contains
about 6,000 deviations from the Masoretic text, mostly of a
stylistic or orthographic nature. Of particular significance for
textual criticism is the fact that approximately one-third of
these agree with the Septuagint, the Greek translation of the
Old Testament. According to Aristea's letter (probably first
century B.C.), Ptolemy II Philadelphus (285–247 B.C.) ordered
a translation of the Torah for his library from the High Priest
Eleazar. Eleazar had the work done in Alexandria by seventy-
two scholars (six from each of the twelve tribes) in seventy-two
days. This account, which tries to explain the name Septuagint
(= seventy), is largely legendary. It is fairly certain that the
translation was made to meet the needs of the Greek-speaking
Jewish Diaspora in Alexandria. What is historical about the
legend is the date, and the fact that the translation is not a
single piece of work but the effort of many hands: indeed, even
within individual books there are indications that several
translators were involved. The lack of uniformity is evident
in the whole style of the translation, which is most accurate
with the Pentateuch but very uneven in the case of the other
books, poor of Isaiah and the Psalms, and so free in the case of
Daniel that it was later replaced by the Theodotion translation.
The translation of Jeremiah is a round seventh, and that of
Job almost one-quarter shorter than the Hebrew text. In
some cases the rendering of words is quite different. For
example, the Hebrew Zebaoth is given in 1 Samuel and Isaiah
as Sabaoth, in the Psalms as "of hosts," and in Jeremiah it is
either not translated at all or replaced by the word "Almighty."
The translation of the Torah dates from the third century
B.C., the other books are later; but both Prophets and Writings
must have been available in Greek to the grandson of ben
Sirach (c. 130 B.C.), since he mentions them in his preface. A
profusion of Septuagint manuscripts has been preserved, some
of them, most important textual witnesses, reaching back as
far as the fourth (Codex Vaticanus and Sinaiticus) or the fifth
century A.D. (Codex Alexandrinus). Some isolated fragments,

---

[48] A. von Gall, *Der hebräische Pentateuch der Samaritaner*, Giessen 1914–18. In this
and in the following connexion cf. M. Noth, *Die Welt des Alten Testaments*, Berlin
1940, pp. 200–33; B. J. Roberts, *The Old Testament Text and Versions*, Cardiff 1951,
pp. 101–269.

the Oxyrhynchus and Chester Beatty Papyri, date even from the third and second centuries A.D., while the Papyrus Rylands Greek No. 458 is of pre-Christian origin. Many problems still remain in Septuagint research, not only on the arrangement and combination of the individual manuscripts into groups and on the possibility of ascertaining the original form of the text;[49] there is also the sequence of the books, which is different from the Hebrew, and the translation of writings which are not preserved for us in Hebrew and are therefore not in the Canon. Since the Christians used the Septuagint as their written evidence, it was quickly discredited by the Jews and was replaced by other Greek translations—the rigid verbatim translation of Aquila (middle of the second century) and the translations, in better Greek, of Theodotion and Symmachus from the middle of the second and the beginning of the third centuries A.D. Of particular importance is the great work of Origen with its textual criticism, the Hexapla (= the sixfold), which is preserved, unfortunately, only in a few fragments.[50] This presents (1) the Hebrew original text in Hebraic conso-nants; (2) its transcription into Greek letters; and the texts (3) of Aquila; (4) of Symmachus, (5) of the Septuagint, and (6) of Theodotion. The Tetrapla (= the fourfold), also by Origen, prepares the ground for the Hexapla but leaves out the first two columns.[51] Nevertheless the Septuagint column has been used by the Church since the fourth century, and it has been preserved for us to a large extent in its Syriac translation (A.D. 616–17) made by Bishop Paul of Tela. A further aid is the Peshitta (= the simple, given this name later, no doubt

---

[49] Cf. the critical reviews "Septuaginta-Probleme," by G. Bertram in *Theologische Rundschau*, henceforth cited as *Th.R.*, III (1931), pp. 283–96, V (1933), pp. 173–86, X (1938), pp. 69–80, 133–59; J. W. Wevers, "Septuaginta-Forschungen," in *Th.R.*, XXII (1954), pp. 85–138, 171–90. In addition to the great English edition of the Septuagint by A. E. Brooke and N. McLean (since 1917), which is not yet completed, the Septuagint workers of the Göttingen Gesellschaft der Wissenschaft are publishing (from 1936) a large, complete, critical edition. Independently of this A. Rahlfs, the leader of these workers for many years, published a two-volume pocket edition in 1935: this is restricted to the three great sources of textual evidence Vaticanus, Sinaiticus, and Alexandrinus.

[50] These fragments, called after their discoverer G. Mercati, cover a few parts of the Psalms and contain the last five columns of the Hexapla.

[51] Cf. O. Procksch, "Tetraplarische Studien," in *Z. alttest. W.*, LIII (1935), pp. 240–69, LIV (1936), pp. 61–90.

C

in contrast to the Hexapla), the Syriac translation which was probably made soon after the founding of the Syrian Christian community (*c.* A.D. 150). But although the manuscripts go back to the middle of the fifth century A.D., it follows the Septuagint so closely in many parts, particularly in Isaiah, the Minor Prophets, and the Psalms, that it is not clear whether the translator actually used the Septuagint as well or whether his work was subsequently assimilated to the Septuagint.[52] Even the Vulgate (= generally spread abroad), the Latin translation (A.D. 390–405) made by Jerome,[53] which quickly superseded the Vetus Itala, the old Latin translation of the second century, is less useful for tracing the pre-Masoretic text, because Jerome used the Septuagint and occasionally also the Jewish tradition in addition to the Hebrew original. This Jewish tradition is written down in the Targums (= translations), which, however, are interpretations rather than mere translations. Their dates vary greatly, but are mainly within the fifth century A.D.: one must, however, bear in mind that parts are very much older, dating back perhaps even to the lifetime of Jesus. Brief mention should also be made of the Armenian translation from the beginning of the fifth century, the Gothic one made by Bishop Ulfilas (*d.* 383), the Coptic in Zahidic dialect (Upper Egyptian) around A.D. 300, and the later one (? seventh century) in Bohairic dialect (Lower Egyptian). The Ethiopian translation is preserved only in late manuscripts (thirteenth century), and due to the extensive revision which it has undergone it is of as little value for textual criticism as the Arabic translation of the seventh century. The Polyglots,[54] which appeared on the scene in the sixteenth and seventeenth centuries, are more useful for practical purposes than for textual criticism.

[52] L. Haefeli, *Die Peschitta des Alten Testaments mit Rücksicht auf ihre textkritische Bearbeitung und Herausgabe*, Münster 1927.

[53] In arrangement and extent the Vulgate follows the Septuagint. In the fourth session of 8th April 1546, the Council of Trent declared the Vulgate text to be the standard for the Roman Catholic Church. Textual editions: M. Hetzenauer, *Biblia Sacra vulgatae editionis*, 2nd edn., Innsbrück 1922; cf. F. Stummer, *Einführung in die lateinische Bibel*, Paderborn 1928; F. Kaulen, *Geschichte der Vulgata*, Mainz 1938.

[54] The best-known polyglots are the Complutensian (1514–17), the Antwerp (1566–72), the Parisian (1629–45), the London (1653–7). Cf. H. S. Nyberg in *Z. alttest. W.*, LII (1934), pp. 241–54.

The Canon of the Old Testament

When we speak of the Old Testament we assume a firmly fixed entity complete in itself, such as we know it in our own Bible. And that it is; but that it has become. The growth and making of this great collection which, according to the evidence of the Septuagint, included far more than is now contained in the Hebrew Canon, shows both expansion and limitation. So the question arises, when, how, and according to what principles the selection was made which declared one scripture to be canonical and another unworthy to be considered as "Holy Scripture." The Old Testament itself gives us some clues, but these—assuming that the tradition is reliable, which is by no means always certain—relate only to part collections. When we read "Moses wrote this law and gave it to the priests" (Deut. XXXI. 9, 24), this cannot mean the whole Torah but only parts of Deuteronomy; just as the observation "Joshua wrote these words in the book of the Law of God" (Josh. XXIV. 26) very probably means that this is only a continuation, by means of supplements, of what had already been written. According to the scripture, Samuel described the rights and duties of the kingship for the people and then "wrote them in a book and laid it up before the Lord" (I Sam. X. 25); and of Hezekiah we read that he undertook a collection of the Songs of David and of Asaph (II Chron. XXIX. 30) and also of the proverbs of Solomon (Prov. XXV. 1).

Greater significance would attach to the finding of the book of the law (II Kings XXII. 8) in the year 622 B.C., but for the fact that here also only part of the Torah is concerned. That the whole extent of the Torah was not yet known at that time is evident from the reform programme which was introduced on the basis of this law, and from the fact that this book, which came to light during the restoration of the Temple, could be read aloud twice in one day (II Kings XXII. 8, 10). Nevertheless one must not deduce from this that nothing at all of the Torah was known at the time of Josiah. The event is significant as showing the great effect of a book of laws, and the authority which this particular book thus acquired. There is a valuable report from the post-exilic period telling how Ezra, who had been granted full authority by the Persian king, came to Jerusalem to bring some order into the chaos reigning there.

A vivid description is given (Nehem. VIII. 1 ff.) of how from morning till midday on New Year's Day before the assembled populace, both men and women, Ezra read aloud from "the book of the law of Moses which the Lord had given to Israel" (Nehem. VIII. 1) and which Ezra had no doubt brought back with him out of exile (Ezra VII. 14, 25–6). This reading, as one gathers from the expression used in Nehem. VIII. 8 in the Persian court language (Ezra IV. 18), was made in Aramaic translation so that everyone could understand. The description used here (as Ezra VII. 25) for the Law presupposes that it was a known Law and not one which Ezra had just manufactured. It is hardly likely, however, that it could have been the whole Torah handed down in the Old Testament: it must rather have been as much of the Torah as was available to the exiles. More, however, cannot be said on this point.

The fact that Ezra played a particularly important role in the production of the final Torah is the historical basis for the legend from the apocryphal II Esdras (*c.* A.D. 100) which was adopted by the Christians in the second century and prevailed throughout the Middle Ages. According to the legend Ezra, when the Law was burned (II Esdras IV. 23, XIV. 21 ff), obeyed a vision and dictated to five men for forty days, "in characters which they did not know," ninety-four books in all. The account goes on to say: "Make public the twenty-four books that you wrote first and let the worthy and the unworthy read them; but keep the seventy that were written last, in order to give them to the wise among your people." This statement is also valuable for its suggestion of a canon of twenty-four books; but it is worth noting that here, just as in the case of the grandson of Jesus ben Sirach two centuries earlier, there is still no one unifying, dominating conception for this limited collection such as Christianity provided in the term "Old Testament." In the apocryphal book II Maccabees (VIII. 23) the expression "Holy Book" does occur, but the very fact that Eleazer could read it before the battle shows that it could not have contained the whole twenty-four books. And when Josephus speaks of "Holy Scriptures," the expression (since the "Law" is expressly named) cannot have been a title for the whole Testament. That did not happen till later in the Talmud tradition; but the word "Law" is still used on occasion in quotations from the Prophets and the Psalms.

Throughout the traditions, starting from Jesus ben Sirach's grandson, the designation generally applied is the threefold one of Law, Prophets, and Writings. This suggests that the canon was not fixed all at once, but in stages, according to the varying importance and value attributed to the individual sections. On this basis there is no question that for the Jews the Torah must come first, since it surpasses all else in importance. In their eyes the Torah, and the Torah alone, is the foundation of life, of teaching, and of religious belief; it is of divine origin, a document of revelation given by God Himself to Moses. In addition it is a document which is binding as the basis of the covenant between Yahweh and His people,[55] and for this reason it is considered as "holy of holies." Even if this high esteem and binding significance might at first have applied to the contents of the Law, the Law itself was nevertheless set in a historical framework. What held good for the content was extended to the form: not only the content, but the form too was considered as given by God. Thus the transmitted collection of the Law assumed a more solid shape. In the reforms of Josiah we have something like the beginnings of canonisation: under Ezra further important steps were taken, though the work was not completed—contrary to the later tradition about Ezra. No exact dates are available for the completion and conclusion of the canon of the Law. But we have an important clue in the Samaritan Pentateuch, which the Samaritans, after the breach, adopted as one "Holy Book." It contains essentially the same text as we have in the Five Books of Moses, which presupposes that the Pentateuch must have been available to the Samaritans as a whole in its finished form. Unfortunately, however, we have no exact records of the development of the Samaritan community. According to the evidence of Josephus, which differs by a round 100 years from the reference in Nehemiah (xiii. 28), the Samaritans built their temple on Mount Gerizim about 330 B.C. with the permission of Alexander the Great. Thus the fixing of the contents of the Torah should be dated as somewhat earlier than the building of this temple. At all events comparison with the

[55] Deut. v. 2 and *passim;* Josh. xxiv. 25; ii Kings xxiii. 2–3: Neh. x. 1.

Septuagint translation, in which the description of the tabernacle (Ex. XXXV–XL) differs not inconsiderably from the Hebrew text, shows that even though the Law was thus now laid down, it had not yet reached a final form, rigid to the last detail.

The final words of the Torah: "And there has not arisen a prophet since in Israel like Moses" (Deut. XXXIV. 10) testify to the wide, intrinsic gulf that separates the Law and the Prophets. So even the writings of the prophets were not accorded the same overriding value as was attributed to the Law. This must be recognised even from the purely external evidence that the Samaritans adopted the Torah alone as their Holy Book, and that in the first instance the Septuagint was also restricted to a translation of the Torah. Great significance was, however, attached to the prophetic writings; for the prophets were indeed the bearers of the divine revelation, and what they had to say by way of warnings and promises, threats and consolation, was the word of God, with which they were entrusted by Yahweh and which they had to proclaim. The collection of actual prophetic writings (designated as Latter Prophets in the Hebrew tradition) comprises four rolls: Isaiah, Jeremiah, Ezekiel, and the Twelve Prophets, and is limited in time by the fact that there were no longer any prophets in the later period (Ps. LXXIV. 9). The post-exilic Zechariah (c. 519 B.C.) speaks these memorable words: "Your fathers, where are they? and the prophets, do they live for ever?" (Zech. I. 5). One should not understand by these words that just as the fathers, the objects of divine proclamation, are now to be considered as something finished and done with, so also the prophets, the subjects, or better, the bearers of Yahweh's proclamation, are similarly a thing of the past. One should rather take this statement to mean that prophecy was in the process of dying out. A quite late extract from the second century (Zech. XIII. 2 ff.), with a quiet hint at Am. VII. 14, certainly speaks of the end of prophecy. True, the writer clothes his words in a prophecy foretelling the last day, but one senses only too clearly in his bitter and sarcastic words that he is describing the present.

Closely linked with these Latter Prophets are the four rolls, again, of the Former Prophets: Joshua, Judges, Samuel, Kings.

The authority of these books does not lie in the fact that their subject-matter connects up with the Torah, of which they are thus the historical continuation. The more probable reason is that they deal to a large extent with prophets whose books have not been preserved. In addition to Samuel, Elijah, and Elisha, mention should be made of Gad (I Sam. XXII. 5) and Nathan (II Sam. VII. 2) in David's time; of Ahijah of Shiloh (I Kings XI. 29) and the anonymous prophet of Bethel (I Kings XIII. 11) in the period shortly after the separation of the kingdoms (c. 922 B.C.), and of Jehu (I Kings XVI. 7) some time later; also in the time of Jeroboam II (c. 750 B.C.) Jonah of Gath-hepher (II Kings XIV. 25), who, however, is not identical with the well-known minor prophet of the same name. According to the Talmud tradition the decisive—though incorrect—reason for giving these historical books the title Former Prophets was the belief that they had been written by Joshua and by the prophets Samuel and Jeremiah. If this tradition is of ancient date, it is understandable that these books were accorded the same prophetic authority as the Latter Prophets. What reasons can have determined the division into "former" and "latter" it is impossible to decide. Since the very late book of Daniel (c. 164 B.C.) is not included with the prophets in the Hebrew text, the second stage of the canonical collection, the Prophets, must be older than Daniel. The fact that the prophet Jeremiah (XXV. 11–12) is referred to by name in Dan. IX. 2 allows no further conclusions to be drawn. A better clue is the detailed reference in the original text of Ecclesiasticus (c. 190 B.C.) in the "Praise of the fathers of olden times" to Isaiah, Jeremiah, Ezekiel, and the Twelve Prophets. More important than the enumeration itself are the facts first, that the short description of Isaiah is of the book exactly as it is handed down in the Masoretic text; and secondly, that the grouping together of the Twelve Prophets as one unit presupposes once more that they were already available as a single book. Accordingly, it is fairly certain that the second stage of the Canon was completed by about 200 B.C.

We have no evidence at all about the coming into being of the third and last stage, the collection of the Writings. Attempts have been made to pick out of Ecclesiasticus references to particular books (like Job, Psalms, Proverbs, Nehemiah);

but these are not justified. Nor can one legitimately draw conclusions about the formation of the Canon from the fact that Ruth, Ecclesiastes, the Song of Solomon, and Ezra are not referred to in the New Testament. Anything that can be said about the establishment of this stage of the Canon is mere supposition; but it is probable that the Psalms and the great historical work of the Chronicler represent early stages in the collection of this section of the Canon. For its completion reference should be made to Josephus and II Esdras, both of whom, with their twenty-two and twenty-four scriptures, presuppose the Canon in its present compass. In addition it is fairly certain that the Pharisees finally defined the Canon of the Old Testament as we know it at the Council of Jamnia (c. A.D. 90).

Any canonisation entails selection, definition, rejection, limitation, for which definite basic principles and motives are necessary. Why was Esther accepted into the Canon but not Judith; why were the Proverbs of Solomon considered worthy, but not those of Ecclesiasticus; why are Chronicles held to be canonical, but not I Maccabees? For an answer to these questions we are indebted to Josephus, according to whom the following points were decisive. Canonical books must be inspired, and, since inspiration was restricted to the period between Moses and Artaxerxes, must originate within this time limit: moreover, they must be of holy character and the text unimpeachable. These principles determined the extent of the Canon and the content; hence also the authority of the text and the authority of the letter, and therefore the crystallisation of God's revelation.

The motives for the formation of the Canon are fairly clear. From the time of the Maccabees Judaism had been threatened by a very real danger, namely the rapid rise and spread of apocalyptic literature, some short samples of which are contained in the Old Testament (e.g. Is. XXIV–XXVII). Scriptures of this type appeared with the claim that they were just as inspired as the writings of the prophets. Since they went so far as to maintain that they were older than Moses, and since they appeared under the names of Adam and Eve, Enoch, Noah, and the twelve patriarchs, the all-surpassing importance of the Torah might only too easily have been shaken. So the

Jews, for reasons of self-preservation, were compelled to reject this type of religious writing (Pseudepigrapha) by strictly delimiting the books. One may perhaps go a step further and draw attention to the fact that in the development of the Jewish community from the Maccabean period onwards the tendency had been more and more towards secularisation. So it was an act, not only of self-preservation, but of self-examination and reconsideration of God's will, when with one sharp stroke they cut themselves off from the new and returned once more to the old sources of the revelation.

This Jewish conception of the Canon necessarily led to the Septuagint being discarded. The Hellenistic Jews in Alexandria, the most important representative of whom was Philo (d. A.D. 40), rejected any narrowing of the conception of revelation and any time limit on inspiration; they thus also rejected the strict differentiation between canonical and profane writings. Since they incorporated all writings which in their opinion served the purpose of edification, the Septuagint came in time to contain, in addition to the twenty-four canonical books, a whole series of others which are known generically by the name Apocrypha (= "hidden" books, i.e. excluded from circulation). The Christian Church did not use the Hebrew Canon, but the Septuagint collection and then later the Vulgate translation which covers the same ground as the Septuagint. The Canon was fixed by many Councils in the fourth century A.D., and at the Council of Trent (1546) the majority of these apocryphal writings were also recognised by the Church as canonical. The Protestant Churches did not agree to this recognition and went back to the limitation of the Old Testament in the Jewish Canon. Nevertheless Protestant editions of the Bible often include part or all of this Apocrypha as a supplement to the Old Testament, on the ground that, to use Luther's words, the books, though "not considered equal to the Holy Scriptures," are "nevertheless useful and good reading."[56]

---

[56] Cf. L. Diestel, *Geschichte des Alten Testaments in der christlichen Kirche*, Jena 1869; E. G. Kraeling, *The Old Testament since the Reformation*, London 1955; H. J. Kraus, *Geschichte der historischkritischen Erforschung des Alten Testaments von der Reformation bis zur Gegenwart*, Neukirchen 1956; H. F. Hahn, *The Old Testament in Modern Research*, London 1956.

The Literary Character of the Old Testament

Very appropriately a collection of essays on the Old Testament bore the title "The book that grew for a thousand years," expressing the fact that here we have a tradition with a long history of development. What is gathered together under this name is a great collection of the most diverse writings: nor are these entities in themselves, but in their turn they represent collections. The scriptures of the Old Testament span a wide period of time, both in their subject-matter and in their date of origin. It is our task to investigate how and when they came into being. Their content also is very diverse and by no means always deals only with religious matters; on the contrary, it comprises much that is secular, lists and registers of many kinds, political interpretations of the law, historical documents and annals, reports and memoirs; and in addition much that has been preserved from an earlier, pre-literary period. This material cannot be simply dismissed.[57]

It is astonishing how much has been preserved from olden times; and just as astonishing is the almost childlike impartiality with which it is presented. Let us think for a moment of Mazzebah and Asherah, these ancient Canaanite sanctuaries, worship at which was expressly forbidden (Ex. xxxiv. 13–14; Deut. xvi. 21–2) because "the Lord your God hates them." Yet Jacob, Joshua, and Samuel[58] erected such stone pillars and wooden posts; and centuries later Jeremiah was lamenting about the children of Israel who "say to a tree, 'you are my father,' and to a stone, 'You gave me birth'." (Jer. ii. 27). With the same impartiality we are told of the worship of "God of Bethel," of the "fear of Isaac," or the "mighty one of Jacob," descriptions of God which must still have been in use during the exile.[59]

On the other hand, much, too much, has been lost in the course of the centuries. So the story of the sons of God and daughters of men breaks off abruptly (Gen. vi. 1–4), never to be continued. As for two Egyptians, Jannes and Jambres, mentioned in the New Testament (ii Tim. iii. 8), the Old Testament

---

[57] For books on the development of the Old Testament, see Bibliography, and cf. p. 13, note 24.

[58] Jacob: Gen. xxviii. 18, 22, xxxi. 45, xxxiii. 20, xxxv. 20; Joshua: Josh. xxiv. 26; Samuel: i Sam. vii. 12.

[59] Gen. xxxi. 42, 53; xlix. 24; Is. xl. 26, lx. 16; Ps. cxxxii. 2, 5. Cf. also A. Alt, *Der Gott der Väter*, Stuttgart 1929.

does not even know their names. There are many song cycles which are expressly referred to but have not been transmitted, such as "the book of the wars of Yahweh" (Num. XXI. 14) or "the book of Jashar."[60] Not only must a special chronicle have been kept of Solomon's deeds (I Kings XI. 41), but there must have been complete annals of the kings of Israel and Judah, since they are repeatedly referred to.[61] On no account, however, must we confuse these with the transmitted historical work of our Chronicles, which itself constantly refers to them[62] and to similar sources, such as the "Chronicles of King David" (I Chron. XXVII. 24) or the "Acts of Uzziah" (II Chron. XXVI. 22), as well as to a whole series of prophetic writings, no longer preserved, of which we need mention here only those of Samuel, Nathan, and Gad (I Chron. XXIX. 29).

The intention here was quite evidently to supplement the available sources and documents concerning a certain period from personal knowledge. Moses puts down in writing for posterity a report on the great victory over the Amalekites "as a memorial" (Ex. XVII. 14); Jeremiah writes "all the words" (Jer. XXX. 2) in a little book of consolation, and "all the words that I have spoken to you against Israel and Judah and against all the nations . . . from the days of Josiah until today" (Jer. XXXVI. 2). When his roll is burned by the King he makes the scribe Baruch rewrite all that was in it (Jer. XXXVI. 28, 32). If in all these cases it is firmly stressed that God commanded these records, on the other hand the fact of a conscious literary interest must not be overlooked—an interest which in the preacher Solomon's day was particularly pronounced: "My son, beware of anything beyond these. Of making many books there is no end" (Eccles. XII. 12). If there is no specific mention of the literary activities of other prophets, with the exception of Isaiah (XXX. 8) and Habakkuk (II. 2), this may be due to the fragmentary way in which their writings have been handed down.

The art of writing is very old: Palestine formed the bridge

---

[60] Josh. X. 13; II Sam. I. 18; the same book is perhaps meant in I Kings VIII. 13 (Septuagint); but it is possible that instead of "jaschar" (the upright one) one should read "Jeschurun," a poetic name for Israel (Deut. XXXII. 15).

[61] For Judah I Kings XIV. 29, XV. 7, 23 and *passim*; for Israel I Kings XIV. 19, XV. 31 and *passim*.

[62] I Chron. IX. 1; II Chron. XVI. 11, XXVII, 7, XXXII. 32 and quite frequently.

between the two mighty civilisations Egypt and Assyria-Babylonia, where writing had long been practised. Even the small Canaanite city kings were carrying on a diplomatic correspondence as early as Amarna's time (*c.* 1400 B.C.). A report from Wen-Amon informs us that King Zekar-Baal of Byblos (*c.* 1100 B.C.) had "the diaries of his fathers" read to him, so he must have possessed something in the nature of court annals. That the city of Debir must have been a centre of learning and of the writer's art can be concluded from the fact that, before its conquest by Israel, it bore the name Kiriath-sepher (= city of writing or city of books; cf. Jos. xv. 15).[63] When Israel took possession of the country, it could not shun the culture it encountered: and so the art of writing would be introduced among the Israelites. But the tradition must certainly have been exaggerating somewhat when it recorded that Gideon selected one at random from among the young men of Succoth to prepare a list of the rulers of the place for him (Jg. VIII. 14).

We can also build up a fair picture of the content and compass of this writing activity. First and foremost it would be a case of setting down the laws concerning religion and the cult (Ex. XXIV. 4, 12; Deut. XVII. 18); of listing legal precepts, as when Samuel detailed "the rights and duties of the kingship" (1 Sam. X. 25); of recording purchase agreements (Jer. XXXII. 10), divorces (Deut. XXIV. 1), court decrees Is. X. 1), and even accusations (Job XIII. 26, XXXI. 35). On the Canaanite model, David created at his court the office of scribe (II Sam. VIII. 17) which persisted under Solomon (1 Kings IV. 3) and became very important in the ensuing period, being responsible for official correspondence, keeping the annals, recording government measures, and drawing up levy lists (II Kings XXV. 19). The importance of this office is made plain by the fact that the King of Babylon after the conquest of Jerusalem included "the principal scribe of the host" among those whom he slew at Riblah (II Kings XXV. 21). Chronicles tells of a special "family of scribes" (1 Chron. II. 55). Private correspondence is mentioned even in the older monarchical period (II Sam. XI. 14); we also hear that Jehu wrote letters to Samaria (II Kings X. 1, 6).

[63] Others interpret the name as "bronze city," corresponding to the Accadian "siparru-bronze."

It appears then that reading and writing are to be looked upon as general accomplishments, at least among the upper classes. This, of course, does not exclude the fact that the great mass of the people were illiterate (Is. XXIX. 12).

Even though great significance is ascribed to the written word, one must not overlook the fact that it did not come first and that it is not the original. For right at the beginning there was not the written, but the spoken word; not literature, but singing and reciting; not books, but oral transmission which was rooted deep in the life of the people and was passed on from mouth to mouth and from family to family with a faithfulness and reliability peculiar to those whose memories had not yet been spoiled by much writing. The reader of the Old Testament therefore will stumble repeatedly (especially in the historical books) on such songs, which in general are older than the text which surrounds them. Originally they were quite short and were sung, during dancing, to the accompaniment of musical instruments. They would often be sung in chorus (Ex. xv. 20–1; Num. xxi. 17; 1 Sam. xviii. 6–7), the solemnity of the occasion being increased by repetition of the same words, and often also antiphonally (1 Sam. xviii. 7), which was also a Canaanite custom (Jg. xvi. 23–4). Singing was very popular in Israel and was indulged in at every possible opportunity; for it is of the very nature of folk poetry[64] to accompany all the events of human life with its songs. The fact that only isolated examples of these songs have been preserved is explained by their purely secular character. In spite of this a whole collection of love and marriage songs has been handed down, and these we owe to the mere fact that their meaning

---

[64] Like Near Eastern poetry as a whole, Israelite poetry is characterised by *parallelismus membrorum*. The lines go in pairs; according to the nature of their relationship one differentiates between synonymous parallelism, where the second line is merely a variation on the thought in the first (e.g. Ps. I. 5), antithetic parallelism, where the second line expresses the opposite idea (e.g. Prov. x. 1), and synthetic parallelism, where the second line merely continues the thought of the first (e.g. Ps. II. 6). In addition to couplets triplets are also found. There are several theories as to the rhythm of these, but it seems to us that accentuating rhythm is the most probable. Here one marks off the stanzas according to the number of stresses. The Quina (=lament) stanza, consisting of 3+2 stresses, which was found by K. Budde, "Das hebräische Klagelied," in *Z. alttest. W.*, II (1882), pp. 1 ff. in particular, seems to be firmly established. Whether strophes were also formed can only be seen in songs where a refrain is indicated, such as Pss. XLII, LXXX, CVII, etc.

was now transferred to the relationship between God and His people. The people sang at their work, at the completion of a well (Num. XXI. 17–18), and also while harvesting and treading the grapes (Jer. XXV. 30, XLVIII. 33). At social gatherings and feasts (Am. VI. 4 ff.; Is. V. 11 f.) men rejoiced and forgot their cares (Is. XXII. 13), not always in moderation (Is. XXVIII. 8), or they would while away the time with riddles (Jg. XIV. 14, 18). Those setting out for distant parts were blessed (Gen. XXIV. 60) and seen off with music and song (Gen. XXXI. 27). Physical imperfections, such as bald heads (II Kings II. 23) or faded beauty (Is. XXIII. 15–16), were mocked in song.

Mention should be made in this connexion of the wide range of proverbs with their penetrating insight into life.[65] A development of these was the wisdom aphorism which blossomed under Solomon (I Kings V. 11–12) and later gave rise to the so-called "Proverbs of Solomon." The prophetic saying, the first stage of prophetic preaching, would also develop from the proverb. With a song Deborah (Jg. V. 12) inflamed the tribes of Israel to fight; songs of victory and triumph—on the boastful and ostentatious side for our liking today,[66] songs deriding the enemy (Num. XXI. 27), and laments for those fallen in battle (II Sam. I. 19, XVIII. 33) have been preserved. As the many references show, dirges and funeral laments occupy a great place in popular poetry. Many of the beginnings of such songs have been handed down, such as "Lamentation for an only son,"[67] "My father" (II Kings II. 12, XIII. 14), or "Ah my brother, Ah sister" and "Alas, Lord."[68] But there were also seditious political songs, like that of Sheba (II Sam XX. 1), which re-echoed strongly among the people (I Kings XII. 16) and helped to influence the defection of the Northern Kingdom from the royal house of David. But this purely temporal popular poetry is not the important thing in the Old Testament.

The national character of Israel was rooted not in a political act, but in a religious event—the making of the covenant with Yahweh, its God: the wars which were waged were Yahweh's wars and everything else that happened was considered from

---

[65] I Sam. XXIV. 14; I Kings XX. 11; Is. X. 15; Jer. XXXI. 29; Ezek. XVI. 44, etc.

[66] Gen. IV. 23–4; Jg. XV. 16; I Sam. XVIII. 7.

[67] Jer. VI. 26; Am. VIII. 10; Zech. XII. 10.

[68] Jer. XXII. 18, XXXIV. 5, which is probably to be equated with "The mourning for Hadadrimmon in the plain of Meggido," Zech. XII. 11.

the angle of Yahweh's behaviour among and towards His people. This special outlook naturally and necessarily resulted in the predominance of the religious theme in its songs. Indeed, this became the basic reason for all Israel's poetry, as is evident in the oldest examples, such as the Ark formula (Num. x. 35–6), the victory song of Miriam (Ex. xv. 21), and the song of Deborah (Jg. v), with its special ending "So perish all thine enemies, O Lord." The religious connexion is equally strong in the special group of curses and blessings,[69] which very probably developed from the proverb by way of the aphorism. But there is no need to go into details here on this point. Taken as a whole, the poetry of Israel was and remained religious and cultic poetry. The development of the monarchy did not alter the situation. It is true that we are expressly told that David was praised as the psalmist of Israel (ii Sam xxiii. i); and of the King's songs (like Pss. xx, xxi) it is the accession songs (Pss. ii, cx) and the king's wedding song (Ps. xlv) which stand out in particular. Nevertheless in Israel the person even of the king took second place to God, who, after all, had installed him in his office (i Sam. x. i).

The religious, cultic poetry, as handed down especially in the great song collection of the Psalter, presents prayers and songs from the most diverse situations in the life of the individual and in the life of the nation as a whole: but this will be discussed elsewhere.[70] Mention has still to be made of the oracles, which contain Yahweh's answers to questioners seeking advice and help. At all times, even in Israel, men questioned the deity[71] by means of the sacred lot.[72] The use of the Urim and Thummim[73] anticipates a short answer of "yes" or "no"; but more extensive oracular statements in poetic form do occur.[74] These, especially in the prophecies, have an eschatological character; that is, they are directed towards the final great "Day of Yahweh," the day on which, with might and majesty, to His own people and the heathen alike, He will reveal His kingdom on earth by judgment and by salvation.

[69] Like Gen. ix. 25 ff., xxvii. 27 ff., xxxix–xl, xlviii. 15–16, xlix. 3 ff.
[70] Cf. Chapter V, under Psalms.
[71] Jg. xviii. 5; i Sam. xiv. 41, xxiii. 9; Jer. iii. 16; Ezek. viii. 1.
[72] Prov. xvi. 33; Josh. vii. 14 ff.; i Sam. x. 20 ff.; Ezek. xxi. 26.
[73] Ex. xxviii. 30; Lev. viii. 8.
[74] Gen. xvi. 11–12, xxv. 22–3; Balaam prophecies: Num. xxiii–xxiv.

The prose of the Old Testament also contains many survivals of oral tradition incorporated into conscious literary compositions. It cannot be established beyond doubt that the Israelites had professional story-tellers of the type still found today in the East; but it may be assumed that in this, as in other respects, Israel would not differ from her neighbours. In connexion with the Feast of the Passover we read: "When your children say unto you, 'What do you mean by this service?' you shall say . . ." (Ex. xii. 26, xiii. 14), and then follows[75] an explanation of God's grace in choosing and leading His people. Such reports are not isolated, but occur, with slight variations, fairly frequently.[76] It is therefore reasonable to conclude that these are old oral tradition.

The material and form of such tradition are very varied in kind. The myth, the ancient tale of the gods, naturally takes up but little space, for Israel, in contrast with its neighbours, recognised and worshipped only one God, the God of the covenant at Sinai. Nevertheless foreign influences show up here and there, especially in the earliest history (Gen. i–xi), and in the prophets and Psalms in particular many allusions and references to such mythological material have been preserved. So we learn of Yahweh's fight with the dragon (Is. xxvii. 1, li. 9), the primeval creature Tehom (translated as "depths of the sea") which had to tremble in fear before Yahweh, and which He overcame;[77] of Sheol, the kingdom of the dead, that fearful monster, which, with wide-open jaws, swallows up men,[78] and from which Yahweh alone can save (Ps. xlix. 15, lxxxvi. 13). Or we read of the morning star which tried to set its throne above that of God and was hurled into the depths (Is. xiv. 12 ff.); another story tells of a primitive man, born even before the mountains, who listened in at a meeting held by God,[79] and limited wisdom to himself (Job xv. 7–8). The Old Testament is rich in such allusions. There was a time when in the light of such references research workers ended up by emphasising Israel's spiritual dependence on the surrounding world and pointing out its own spiritual inferiority.

---

[75] Ex. xiii. 14; Deut. vi. 20–1, xxxii. 7.
[76] Josh. xxiv. 2 ff.; 1 Sam. xii. 6 ff.; Ezek. xx. 5 ff.
[77] Ps. lxxvii. 16; Is. xiv. 9, xliv. 27, li. 10; Zech. x. 11.
[78] Is. v. 14; Prov. i. 12; Hab. ii. 5.
[79] 1 Kings xxii. 19 ff.; Jer. xxiii. 18; Zech. iii. 1 ff.; Job i. 6 ff.

But it is not so much a matter of what connects, as of what separates; not of what is held in common, but of what differentiates. Anyone approaching such a comparison without prejudice must in his heart be deeply convinced that the higher religion of Israel renovated this traditional material and gave it greater depth, but in so doing, also essentially triumphed over it.

In addition to this mythical material there is much in the Old Testament that smacks of the world of the *Märchen*,[80] particularly in the writings of the prophets. In no case, however, has a complete *Märchen* been transmitted; what we always find are merely allusions or single features, like the foundling who lay naked and bare but finally rose, through marriage, to a high position (Ezek. XVI. 4 ff.); or the unlucky man who escapes the danger of a lion only to meet a bear, or who is bitten by a serpent in the safety of his own house (Am. V. 19). We are told of the dreadful sword from whose constant fury there is no escape, and which God alone can bring to rest (Ezek. XXI); of the wonderful tree, so great and so beautiful that no tree in God's garden could equal it (Ezek. XXXI. 4 ff.); of all kinds of animals with the power of speech, like the serpent in Paradise (Gen. III. 1) and Balaam's ass (Num. XXII. 30), which fast and do penance with the citizens of Nineveh (Jon. III. 7–8), and which supply Elijah with bread and meat (I Kings XVII. 6). Further features are the sending of many messengers (I Sam XIX, 18 ff.; II Kings I. 9 ff.); the giving of a choice of wishes (I Kings III. 5; II Kings II. 9, IV. 2) or the granting of a child, long desired, to a childless couple.[81] Many more examples could be added to this list, but in every case we are dealing only with *Märchen* motifs, which have been woven into a story expressly to illustrate the power of Yahweh.

The fable too has no independent significance in the Old Testament, although it must have been very popular in Israel. This is evident from the story telling that Solomon "spoke of trees . . . also of beasts, and of birds, and of reptiles, and of fish" (I Kings IV. 33). Material of this kind is introduced in the quarrel between the axe and the arm (Is. X. 15) and between

[80] The term *Märchen* is here retained in German. The nearest English equivalent, "fairy-tale," is not always suitable, since the *Märchen* does not necessarily deal with fairies or with supernatural beings of any kind. It is simply a story, which does not aim at explaining or recording.—Tr.

[81] Gen. XVIII. 11, XXX. 22; Jg. XIII. 2; I Sam. I. 10–11.

D

the clay and the potter.[82] Perhaps a fable is to be assumed in
the dispute of the vineyard (Is. v. 1 ff.), just as there is still a
glimmer of an original fable in many of the poems of Ezekiel
(e.g. Ezek. xv, xvii, xix). The fable of Jotham (Jg. ix. 8–15)
is transmitted in detail, and that of Jehoash (ii Kings xiv. 9) in
more concise form. But it is quite plain that neither of these
fables is meant to be merely generally instructive: they have a
deeper purpose. The one, with its harsh criticism, is aimed at
discrediting the monarchy, while the other, telling of the
thistle's wooing and its trampling by a wild beast, is to warn
King Amaziah against his presumptuous challenge to fight.
The fact that the content does not altogether fit the story
which frames it will be a sign that it has been removed from
tradition's store and inserted here to make the account more
lively and vivid. In this it approaches the allegory and the
parable, forms of literary art whose object is to be vivid and
impressive,[83] and which blossomed especially in the wisdom of
the proverbs.[84]

A very important and extensive role is played by the legends[85]
which are transmitted in the Old Testament, and especially in
the first book of Moses. It would be wrong to shut one's eyes
to the presence of these legends and to try to find shelter
behind the earlier conception of the absolute historical reliability of the tradition to the last detail. But it would be an
even graver error to dismiss them simply as fiction and therefore untrue and of no value. They are a special form of
narrative occupying a place between the *Märchen* and history:
and for this reason they are on quite a different plane from a
purely historical view of a situation. They are the translation
of reality into the poetic: they are poetry, even when written
in prose, and are often masterly in construction and in artistic
form. The legends do not merely spring from "the desire to
invent stories"; their aim is to instruct and to explain, and that
in their own way. Not with learned discussion and profound
thoughts but smoothly and simply, naively and in popular
terms, they provide an answer to all manner of questions. And

[82] Is. xxix. 16, xlv. 9; Jer. xviii. 6.
[83] Am. iii. 8; ii Sam. xii. 1 ff.; ii Kings xviii. 21.
[84] Prov. x. 25, xi. 22, xix. 12.
[85] The term "legend" is here used to translate the German *Saga*, and "sacred
legend" the German *Legende*.—Tr.

there are so many questions! Why is the area round the Salt
Sea so dead and deserted? Was it always so? The legend knows
that once upon a time the vale of Siddim was here (Gen. xiv.
3), a garden of the Lord like the land of Egypt (Gen. xiii. 10);
but then the Lord sent down His punishment upon Sodom and
Gomorrah for their sins (Gen. xix. 24–5). And the high stone
pillar on the Jebel Usdum, a mountain ridge to the south-west
of the Dead Sea, is nothing but Lot's wife, whom God turned
into a pillar of salt on account of her disobedience (Gen. xix.
26). Why must the serpent crawl on its belly and (according to
popular opinion) eat dust? The popular explanation is given in
the story of the fall of Man and the cursing of the serpent by
God (Gen. iii. 14). The mutual attraction of the sexes is
interpreted by the legend as an act of God (Gen. ii. 22 ff.). In
Luz there was an old Canaanite place of worship with a
Mazzebah which was taken over without scruple by Israel;
but ought one to do such a thing? It was necessary to prove the
holiness of this place; and the legend is able to tell of Jacob's
experience there and how he made the Mazzebah into a
"Bethel," a house of God (Gen. xxviii. 22). The cultic custom
of not eating the thigh muscle is traced back to Jacob's struggle
with God at the Jabbok (Gen. xxxii. 32). The legend is particularly fond of explaining names which are not immediately
comprehensible to those unacquainted with Hebrew. The
name of the ancestor Abram should be Abraham (= father of a
crowd), because God means to make him father of many nations
(Gen. xvii. 5). Isaac, the name of the second patriarch
(literally "he laughed") is given three different explanations:
that Abraham (Gen. xvii. 17), or his wife Sarah (Gen. xviii. 12)
laughed at the promise; or else that others will laugh at her joy
in motherhood so late in life (Gen. xxi. 6). The name Beer-sheba
also has two explanations, according to the two different possible meanings "seven wells" or "well of the oath": in the first
instance the seven lambs were witnesses to Abraham's having
dug the well (Gen. xxi. 30), and in the second an oath was
taken by two partners at the well (Gen. xxi. 31, xxvi. 33). The
simplicity of the legend is shown by its treatment of the Sumerian name Babel (= gate of God), which it derives quite
simply from the Hebrew and explains that God "confused"
the languages there (Gen. xi. 9).

In these examples, which could be added to at will, it will not have escaped the reader that these etiological legends have one thing in common which fundamentally distinguishes them from others of their type, as for example the Germanic sagas. That common feature is their connexion with God; thus they become the reflected image of the religious belief of the people which sought for and found the rule of God everywhere. There is a special group of legends surrounding particular personages of days gone past—the figures of the three patriarchs; that powerful man of God, Moses; leaders of the people such as Joshua and Gideon; heroes like Samson; mighty prophets like Samuel, Elijah, and Elisha; famous kings like David and Solomon. Historical writing is not concerned with the person, but with the thing, with great political events. The legend, on the other hand, is not interested in historical cause and event; it loves anecdotes from the lives of great personalities, and tries to draw character sketches of them, moulding the pictures together with loving emphasis on particular features. Its concern is not with the broad lines, but with the private life of its hero. That it tends to stray in the process, not without distortions and exaggerations, is natural. The more popular a hero is, the more readily do folk tales gather round his name and age: in so doing it happens more than once that a legend "strays," that is, its material is borrowed from elsewhere and adapted to suit the new case. Finally, it does not stop at the single legend. Figures like Joseph, Samson, Elijah, and Elisha become the centre round which a whole cycle crystallises. Very often these cycles had already assumed so fixed a form in preliterary times that this was simply retained in the course of the literary revision.

Varieties of the legend are the short story (Ruth; Abigail 1 Sam. xxv), an individual legend further elaborated poetically, and the sacred legend (older prophetic sacred legends) which was a popular form of religious narrative, particularly in the later period (e.g. Daniel).

Since our present concern is predominantly with preliterary material, we need not go into historical writing in this connexion. Nevertheless mention must be made of the priestly Torah and of legal statutes. The priestly Torah, which later assumed a rhythmic form,[86] instructs by means of "you shall" and "you shall not" (Ex. xx; Deut. v): its aim is to teach, on the basis of the law of Yahweh (the Torah), His commandments and His prohibitions, to instruct the individual in matters of ritual and cultic usages, to explain the difference between clean and unclean, between what is holy and what is not (Ex. xxxiv. 14 ff.). Beside these religious instructions are found legal ordinances of a general nature, which embrace the various aspects of human life and are comparable to a penal code. They are constructed in the form "if anyone does such and such, then such and such is to take place" (Ex. xxi. 26, xxii 1 f., 5 f.), and in this, as in their content, they show their relationship to the ancient Babylonian Code of Hammurabi, from which they have taken over a great deal via Canaanite law as an intermediate stage. In the first instance the adoption took place orally.

Much, therefore, that is contained in this great collection we call the Old Testament was in oral circulation a long time before it was put down in writing. Much of it has gone into literature in a form which still carries the impress of its oral tradition and in some instances is immediately recognisable by its clumsy adaptation to the context. Other portions have undergone a centuries-long development and have been subjected in the process to the laws of selection. As a result much has not been preserved or has been transferred to another context, if it has not been completely altered under the influence of different national and priestly points of view. These hazards of oral transmission, and also the great interval of time which often separates the oral from the written tradition, are worthy of consideration if one wants to understand the growth of the Old Testament.

[86] Ezek. xviii. 5 ff., 16–17, 21; Pss. xv. 2 ff., xxiv. 4 ff.

CHAPTER II

THE LAW (PENTATEUCH)

TITLE AND CONTENTS

THE FIRST main section of the Old Testament consists of
the five books of Moses. Originally neither the section
nor the individual books it comprises had titles, but
from the earliest times it was known to Jews and Christians
alike (Lk. x. 26) by the name Torah, or Law. We have already
mentioned in the introduction the central position which this
Law occupied in the religion of Judah and Israel. One might
expect from the name that its contents consist exclusively (or
principally) of regulations and instructions relating to religion and
to the cult. This, however, is not so. The Torah, it is true, contains a multitude of laws and a number of law codes, especially
in the third book, but also in the fifth and in isolated but fairly
extensive parts of the second and fourth books. By far the
greater part, however, is pure narrative; the stories, some
closely, some loosely knit, relating events from the creation of
the world to the death of Moses and including the origin of the
world and of mankind in general and the fate of the patriarchs
and of Jacob in particular. From the time of Origen onwards,
the Greek fathers of the Christian Church, following the
Talmudic description "five fifths of the Law," which can be
cited as early as Josephus, gave it the title Pentateuch (book
consisting of five parts), a title which expresses the thought
that these five books are to be considered as together forming
one complete unit.

The names given by Jewish tradition to the individual books
do not describe their contents, but merely consist of the opening
words of each book: "In the beginning," "The names," "The
Lord called," "In the wilderness," and "The words." The
titles in the Septuagint, on the other hand, take into consideration at least part of the content, and it is these which have
been adopted in the Latin translation and in English. So the
first book, which contains the primeval history of mankind and

the stories of the patriarchs, is called Genesis (Origin); the second book, which tells the story of the people of Israel, their flight and sojourn in the wilderness of Sinai up to the building of the tabernacle, Exodus; the third, which contains the regulations governing religious practice in the wilderness, Leviticus (Book of priestly ordinances); the fourth, starting from the sojourn in the wilderness, is called Numeri (Numbers) after the census of the tribes which took place there; while the fifth, containing the great speech in which Moses summarises and repeats the law, is entitled Deuteronomium (Repetition of the Law). The separation of one book from another was dictated less by content than by the practical need to keep the book rolls as uniform in size as possible.

The title "Five Books of Moses" not only suggests that the books are mainly about Moses, but also that they are by him. And, indeed, this is the opinion of Jewish tradition from the time that Philo of Alexandria and Josephus, contemporaries of Jesus, expressly declared that the Pentateuch is undoubtedly the work of Moses.[1] The Talmud, it is true, makes the justified reservation that the last eight verses of the Pentateuch, which describe the death of Moses, were added by Joshua. It is strange, however, that the Talmud goes on to say in this connexion: "Moses wrote his book, the part concerning Balaam and Job"; for why should it specially mention the Balaam story (Num. XXIII f.), which is part of the Pentateuch in any case? In other respects, too, this tradition, which the Christian Church has also followed, is very insecurely founded.

Firstly, there is not one single instance of Moses himself stating that he is the author; and secondly, there is no suggestion in the Pentateuch itself that this is the case. Such information as there is on this point refers only to the authorship of individual sections, e.g. the Book of the Covenant (Ex. XXIV. 4, 7), the words of the Covenant (Ex. XXXIV. 27 f.), the report on the war with Amalek (Ex. XVII. 14), the list of encampments (Num. XXXIII. 2), the code of Deuteronomy (Deut. XXXI. 9). Observations that "Moses wrote this book of laws" (e.g. Deut. XXVIII. 61, XXXI. 24) also refer only to strictly limited sections but never to the Pentateuch as a whole. If these observations show

---

[1] Josephus, *Antiquitates judaicae*, IV. 8, 48; Philo, *Vita Mosis*, III; Baba bathra 14*b* = Goldschmidt, *Talmud*, VOL. VIII, p 56.

anything at all, it is, at the most, that their writer regarded
these sections as the work of Moses: more, however, cannot be
deduced. The witness of the New Testament[2] is of as little value
for evidence that Moses wrote the Pentateuch as are the few
passages in the Old Testament[3] where reference is made to the
Law of Moses. It is significant too that the Psalms often refer to
the Law of God or of Yahweh, but never to the Law of Moses.
The idea that Moses was the author of the Book of Laws is
first met in the historical writings of the Chronicler.[4]

On the other hand, a whole series of instances can be cited
as evidence for rejecting the Mosaic authorship of the Pentateuch. In the first place, it is striking that the author has no
desire to be regarded as synonymous with Moses, otherwise he
would not have written of him constantly in the third person;
neither would he have given descriptions which could hardly
have emanated from Moses himself, such as, for example, the
reference to his meekness (Num. XII. 3) and to his greatness "in
the sight of Pharaoh's servants and in the sight of the people"
(Ex. XI. 3). That the report of his death (Deut. XXXIV. 5 ff.)
could not have been made by Moses himself was already admitted by old Jewish tradition. But there are still other and
more important considerations; in particular certain geographical details which cannot possibly be fitted into Moses' lifetime,
since they presuppose that the writer was already living west of
the Jordan: for only from such a standpoint is it possible, as
regularly happens,[5] to describe eastern Jordan as "beyond the
Jordan." And only from Palestine—not from the Sinai
peninsula—could one understand such directions as "Negeb"
for the south (Ex.XXVI. 18) and "Jam" (= sea) for the west (Ex.
XXVI. 22). In addition there are chronological impossibilities.
One could not speak of the city of Dan (Gen. XIV. 14; Deut.
XXXIV. 1) or of the villages of Jair (Num. XXXII. 41; Deut. III.
14) in the time of Moses, since they were not founded until the
era of the Judges (Jg. X. 4, XVIII. 29). Nor can the renaming of
the city of Luz (Gen. XXVIII. 19) be reconciled with the story
told in Jg. I. 21 ff. The many references to the Canaanites

[2] Lk. II. 22, XXIV. 44; Jn. VII. 23, etc.
[3] Josh. I. 7–8; I Kings III. 2; II Kings XXI. 8; Mal. IV. 4.
[4] II Chron. XXIII. 18, XXV. 4; Ezra III. 2, VII. 6.
[5] Gen. L. 10–11; Num. XXII. 1, XXXII. 32, XXXV. 14; Deut. I. 1, 5, III. 8, IV. 46, etc.

being "then" in the land (Gen. xii. 6, xiii. 7) lead one to assume that they are "now"—that is, at the time of writing—no longer the rulers of the country, and that this position is occupied by the Israelites. In other parts of the Pentateuch, too,[6] the Israelites are assumed to be in possession of the Promised Land which as early as the story of Joseph was named, with remarkable thoughtlessness, the "Land of the Hebrews" (Gen. xl. 15). A statement like "before any king reigned over the Israelites" (Gen. xxxvi. 31; cf. also Num. xxiv. 7) can only have been made in the era of the kings of Israel, and therefore not before the time of Saul. Moreover, the frequent "to this day,"[7] and such a statement as "there has not arisen a prophet since in Israel like Moses," clearly indicate that there was a great interval of time between the author and the events he is describing.

And so the question arises: if not Moses, who is the author of the Pentateuch? Indeed, is there any literary unity at all? Is it the work of one author? If we take a broad view of the contents, it seems at first as if the answers to these questions should be in the affirmative, because the Pentateuch is quite evidently divided up according to a deliberate plan: (1) earliest history (Gen. i–xi); (2) patriarchs (Gen. xii–l); (3) lifetime of Moses (Ex. i–Deut. xxxiv.), which in turn can be divided into the sojourn in Egypt, the flight and the journey to Sinai (Ex. i–xix. 2), the events at Sinai (Ex. xix. 3–Num. x. 10) with the greater part of the laws, the journey to eastern Jordan (Num. x. 11–xxxvi. 13) and the last days of Moses (Deut. i–xxxiv).

But despite the evident organisation in the broad outlines, a number of considerations of detail lead one to question the unity of the material. For instance, the laws governing sacrifice (Lev. i–vii.) interrupt the general narrative (Ex. xxxv–xli and Lev. viii f.), as does the Law of Holiness (Lev. xvii–xxvi) with its supplement on vows and tithes (Lev. xxvii). Further doubt is cast by the inappropriate addition of the laws of cleanliness (Lev. xi–xv) and the inclusion of various individual laws (Num. v–vi), and also—to take an example from the

---

[6] Ex. xv. 15–17; Lev. xviii. 24–7; Deut. ii. 12.

[7] Gen. xxxv. 20, xlvii. 26, xlviii. 15; Ex. x. 6; Num. xxii. 30; Deut. ii. 22, x. 8, xi. 4.

narrative—by Judah's wronging of Tamar (Gen. xxxviii) which breaks the continuity of the Joseph story.

Moreover, it is remarkable how many reports are given of the same event. Thus there are two creation stories, two stories of the flood, of Hagar (Gen. xvi. 4–14 and xxi. 9–21), of the calling of Moses (Ex. iii and vi), and of many other events, especially in the stories of the patriarchs. These duplicated reports cannot be explained by the fact that the author, in his own peculiar expansive style of presentation, is repeating what has already been said. Neither can they be attributed to later additions and extensions to the existing material, for then either the old story would be enhanced by certain new features or else it would be replaced completely by the new version. In fact, however, it is the same stories which are told, in different clothing; and the interesting thing is that these parallels exhibit certain fundamental differences, just as different viewpoints govern the presentation of the material.[8] For instance, different interpretations are found in the explanations of such names as Beer-sheba (Gen. xxi. 31, xxvi. 33), Israel (Gen. xxxii. 29, xxxv. 10), Bethel (Gen. xxviii. 18 f., xxxv. 14 f.), and Isaac (see above p. 43). The one creation story has Man created last, the crowning glory of the creation, while in the other (Gen. ii. 4 ff.) Man was created first, then vegetation and then the animals. According to one report the flood was due to a rainstorm which lasted for forty days (Gen. vii. 12) and Noah took seven of each of the clean animals (i.e. those suitable for sacrifice) into the ark (vii. 2) and three times sent forth a dove (Gen. viii. 8, 10, 12). The other story reports that the waters of Heaven and under the earth broke loose (Gen. vii. 11) over a period of more than a year (vii. 11, viii. 14); Noah took two of every animal into the ark (vii. 9) and only once sent forth a bird, in this case a raven (viii. 7). The scene of Sarah's adventure is in one case Egypt (Gen. xii. 10–20) and in the other the court of the king at Gerar (Gen. xx. 1–18). Ishmael, son of Hagar, was born in Abraham's house according to one report (Gen. xxi. 9 f.), while in the other he was not born until after Hagar had been cast out, and then in the wilderness (Gen. xvi. 11). In one version of the story of Joseph, Judah is the spokesman on whose advice Joseph is sold by his brothers to

[8] Cf. O. Eissfeldt, *Hexateuchsynopse*, Leipzig 1922.

the Ishmaelites for twenty pieces of silver (Gen. xxxvii. 26–8). In the other Joseph is thrown by his brothers into a dry pit on the advice of Reuben (Gen. xxxvii. 21 f., 24): here he is found by the Midianite merchants, who take him away with them (vs. 28). In one place Reuel (Ex. ii. 18), in another Jethro (Ex. iii. 1) is named as the father-in-law of Moses. There are many similar examples, but these may suffice. The attentive reader of the Pentateuch will repeatedly come across duplicate reports differently presented, which will leave him in no doubt that they are the outcome of different traditions.

The same is true of the sections dealing with the laws. Thus for example the tabernacle, according to one reading, stands outside the camp (Ex. xxxiii. 7), while in another place it is reported as in the centre. At one time (Ex. xxiii. 14, xxxiv. 23) rules and regulations were set out for three great feasts, at another for five (Lev. xxiii; Num. xxviii f.). Deuteronomy speaks quite generally of Levite priests (e.g. Deut. xviii. 7), while other parts of the Pentateuch are at pains to differentiate between the priests, as the descendants of Aaron, and the other Levites who are allowed only to assist at the altar. This cannot be due to the same author writing at different times, for the differences, especially in the regulations for the cult, are too fundamental and too important. The only possible explanation is that they originate from different periods of time, different points of view, and different schools of thought.

Recognition of this fact is of paramount importance for the understanding of the Pentateuch as a whole. For it is here that severe criticism has always started, pointing out the variations and contradictions in the narrative as well as in the laws; and from this basis discredit has been thrown upon the whole of the Old Testament. It would be fundamentally wrong, as well as rendering the Church and the Faith a disservice, to ignore such criticism. Similarly it would be wrong to deny the contradictions or to try to eradicate them or paper over the cracks. The best approach to attacks of this nature is to recognise that contradictions and differences do exist and then to investigate the reason for their existence. This is to be found in the fact that in the Pentateuch we are dealing not with the work of a single author, but with a document which has been compiled from many sources from different periods of time. Even the Papal Biblical Commission, which upholds the theory of Mosaic authorship, maintains that written sources as well as oral traditions are used in the Pentateuch, the former being incorporated either word for word or in a condensed or expanded form. It also takes into consideration the fact that the Pentateuch has undergone many changes with the passage of time.[9]

Knowledge of the origins and composition of the Pentateuch is still relatively new. The foundations were laid over 200 years ago, when it was observed that in the Book of Genesis the name given to God varies, apparently quite arbitrarily, between Yahweh and Elohim. This was taken as evidence of two different sources, an assumption which was at least on the right lines, to judge by the statement in Ex. VI. 2 f. "I am the Lord. I appeared to Abraham, to Isaac, and to Jacob as God Almighty, but by my name Yahweh did I not make myself known to them." And yet we find stated quite simply in the primeval history (Gen. IV. 26): "At that time men began to call upon the name of Yahweh." It is impossible for these two sentences to have been written by the same author. The variation in the name applied to God was used as a yardstick for dividing up the material into two sources, which were then named, according to God's titles, Yahwist and Elohist.[10] Out

---

[9] Decision of the Papal Bible Commission *De Mosaica authentia Pentateuchi* of 27th June 1906; cf. the interpretation of E. Mangenot, *L'Authenticité mosaique du Pentateuque*, Paris 1907; A. Bea, *De Pentateucho*, 2nd edn., Rome 1933; id., "Der heutige Stand der Pentateuchfrage," in *Biblica*, henceforth cited as *Bibl.*, XVI (1935), pp. 175-200.

[10] More important for the development of Pentateuchal criticism than the question of Mosaic authorship, which was disputed by Karlstadt (1520), Masius (1547), and, above all, Thomas Hobbes in his *Leviathian* (1651), is the knowledge that different sources are present in the Pentateuch. The Calvinist Isaac de la Peyère in his anonymously published book *Praeadamitae* (1651) was already considering the sources which Moses might have used; but only parts of the Pentateuch stem from Moses. Baruch Spinoza, in his *Tractatus theologico-politicus* (1670), showed the multiplicity of strands involved in the tradition and declared that Ezra produced a final composition out of the many pieces. His opponent Richard Simon, *Histoire Critique du Vieux Testament* (1678), considered only the laws as Mosaic and ascribed the remainder to "inspired writers of annals." Jean Leclerc also, *Sentiments de quelques théologiens de Hollande sur l'historie critique du Vieux Testament par le P. Richard Simon* (1685), assumed a later author for many parts of the Pentateuch and dated the final editing of the whole in the period after the fall of the Northern Kingdom, considering it as the work of the priests mentioned in

of these beginnings there gradually developed that conception of the origin of the Pentateuch which, with only a few exceptions,[11] still prevails today. Naturally the name given to God could not be applied strictly as the only criterion in separating out the material. Many other considerations had also to be noted, e.g. content, variations in vocabulary, peculiarities of style and of grammar. It is not our intention here to give a detailed account of Pentateuchal criticism and its development

[11] A. Klostermann, *Der Pentateuch. Beiträge zu seinem Verständnis und seiner Entstehungsgeschichte*, Leipzig 1893; new series 1907, starts from the idea of a Mosaic basic law as a nucleus round which all manner of supplements and extensions have crystallised in the course of its being read aloud in public; the rules for the sanctuary and camp were added under Solomon, and Deuteronomy under Josiah. B. D. Eerdmans, *Alttestamentliche Studien*, VOLS. I–IV, Giessen 1908–12, assuming four stages of religious development, differentiates between four corresponding strata in the narrative material: a polytheistic, Palestinian book of Adam (Jacob recension) originating before 700 B.C., a polytheistic historical work from the period before 620 B.C. (Israel recension), a monotheistic revision of both documents around 620, and post-exilic components with a definitely monotheistic outlook. J. Dahse, *Textkritische Materialien zur Hexateuchfrage*, Giessen 1912, on the basis of the Septuagint tradition, refuses to differentiate according to the names applied to God and divides the whole up into old narrative material, a prophetic and a priestly revision. The theory of the four sources is even more sharply rejected by H. M. Wiener, *Pentateuchal Studies*, London 1912 (and other works); E. Naville, *La Haute Critique dans le Pentateuque*, Paris 1921; W. Moller, *Die Einheit und Echtheit der fünf Bücher Mose*, Zwickau 1930; A. Sanda, *Moses und der Pentateuch*, Münster 1924; W. J. Martin, *Stylistic Criteria and the Analysis of the Pentateuch*, London 1955; K. Rabast, *Die Genesis*, VOL. I, Berlin 1951; cf. also the great critical review in O. T. Allis, *The Five Books of Moses*, Philadelphia 1943. F. V. Winnet, *The Mosaic Tradition*, Toronto and London 1949, supports a connected tradition with occasional notes added by P. U. Cassuto, *La questione della Genesi*, Florence 1934, and D. B. Macdonald, *The Hebrew Literary Genius*, Princeton 1933, explain the Pentateuch as the uniform work of one author who, according to Cassuto, was dependent on oral tradition and according to Macdonald on E, J, P, and the remainder: this means, however, equating the author with the final redactor.

---

11 Kings XVII. 27 f. The first critical research work on the sources was done by the Hildesheim pastor B. Witter, *Jura Israelitorum in Palaestinam* (1711), who, on the basis of the different names applied to God, produced two different stories of the Creation. His work, which unfortunately did not cover the whole of Genesis, aroused just as little attention as did, at first, the *Conjectures* (appeared anonymously in Brussels, 1753) of the French doctor Jean Astruc, who, from the use of the various names for God, postulated two larger (A and B) and ten smaller sources for Genesis; cf. A. Lods, in *Z. alttest. W.* XLII (1925), pp. 134–5; id., *Jean Astruc et la critique biblique au XVIIIe siècle*, Paris 1924. It was Eichhorn in his *Einleitung in das Alte Testament* (1780–3) who rescued this theory from the oblivion into which it had sunk, thus opening the gates for a spate of research on the sources. Cf. further note 12.

but to restrict ourselves to its outcome.[12] As a result of protracted

[12] The development of Pentateuchal criticism took place in several phases, the first of which is generally designated as the older document hypothesis. Its main representatives are Eichhorn, who, influenced by Astruc's thinking, worked out two main sources (E and J) for Genesis—it is particularly important that he pointed out their literary character, and C. D. Ilgen, *Die Urkunden des Jerusalemer Tempelarchivs in ihrer Urgestalt* (1798), who assumed two Elohists and one Jehovist. As investigations were extended to cover the whole Pentateuch this was replaced by the fragment hypothesis. Since the threads of the narrative in Genesis cannot be determined in the law sections, the English priest Alexander Geddes in two investigations (1792 and 1800) assumed numerous fragments for the Pentateuch from the Solomon period, originating from two circles of authors and recognisable by the names for God, Yahweh and Elohim. In his three-volume commentary on the Pentateuch (1805) J. S. Vater accepted these ideas; failing to recognise the planned continuity in the structure and arrangement of the whole, he developed the theory that the Pentateuch consists of 39 independent parts brought together without having any intrinsic connexion one with the other; the nucleus is provided by Deuteronomy, to which, in the course of the pre-exilic period, historical and law sections were gradually added. Then in a book review in *Theologische Studien und Kritiken*, henceforth cited as *Theol. Stud. u. Krit.*, IV (1831), pp. 595–606, H. G. A. Ewald put forward the so-called supplement hypothesis: that a basic Elohistic scripture with some older sections like the Decalogue and Book of the Covenant had been supplemented by a parallel Yahwistic scripture. F. Bleek (1836) disputed the existence of this second source and equated the Jehovist with the final redactor who supplemented the Elohist with his own additions. This theory, supported particularly by F. Tuch (1838), W. Martin Leberecht De Wette (1840 and 1845), and F. Delitzsch (1852), was then given up by Ewald himself (1843–5) in favour of the assumption of two Elohistic threads of narrative with a Jehovist as supplementer and redactor. A similar view was held by E. Schrader (1869), who picked out an E annalist from David's time, a theocratic narrator soon after the separation of the kingdoms, and a prophetic Jehovist who worked the other two in together and supplemented them about the middle of the 8th century B.C. A new phase, the newer document hypothesis, began with H. Hupfeld (1853), who, in addition to the three sources indicated (first Elohist = P, second Elohist = E, and Jehovist = Yahwist = J), postulated a special redactor as a fourth. If this theory was developed solely on the basis of Genesis, A. Dillmann (1875 ff.) and F. Delitzsch (1880) applied it to the whole Hexateuch. Almost simultaneously with Hupfeld's works, E. Riem (1854) had recognised Deuteronomy as an independent scripture. Up to this point P, E, J, D had been the sequence in time of the sources, but in 1834 E. Reuss saw that P could not be the oldest written source. G. Graf (1866) pointed to its late origin, which was subsequently transferred to post-exilic times by A. Kuenen (1869 ff.). But it was not until Julius Wellhausen with his brilliant publications that this Graf-Wellhausen hypothesis, with its sequence J, E, D, P, first attained general recognition; in this connexion it does not make very much difference that some research workers look upon E as older than J, nor that there is a great deal of variation in the general dating from that put forward by the Wellhausen school. More recent works of literary criticism on the Pentateuch are characterised by their attempts to enlarge upon the knowledge which has been attained and to arrange the individual source documents in different, more or less independent strata; cf. below in the treatment of the individual sources. Research by literary historians, starting from H. Gunkel, has investigated the smallest literary units, laying more stress on the compilations than on the personalities of the

and ingenious study—sometimes indeed too ingenious—the extent of the two sources has been worked out in sentences, parts of sentences, and indeed parts of parts of sentences; and to these two sources another two have been added—the Deuteronomist, called after the fifth Book of Moses (Deuteronomy) and restricted in the Pentateuch, with very few exceptions, to the fifth Book; and the Priestly Code (originally given the unsuitable title "Elohist") which occurs in all five books and is named after the law sections found therein and after the special character of the books. This latter document, which is relatively easily distinguished from the remainder of the Pentateuch, was long held to be the oldest source—until it was discovered that it was in fact the youngest of all.

We must guard against going into too minute detail when discussing the content and development of the individual sources within the framework of this book. Nevertheless enough will be said to give the reader an impression of their extent and special character.

THE PRIESTLY CODE (P)

From the name Priestly Code[13] it might appear that this document is exclusively a collection of ordinances for priests and regulations governing the cult. Although, however, a large part of the material of the laws found in the Pentateuch is ascribed to this Code, it nevertheless belongs, just as much as the Yahwist and Elohist, to the ranks of the great narratives. The structure and composition of the document are particularly rigid. The subject-matter extends, if somewhat sketchily, from the creation of the world to the death of Moses. Attempts were made in the past to trace the narrative as a continuous thread through Joshua down to the end of II Kings, but these

---

[13] For literature on P, see the Bibliography.

authors. E. Sellin has concentrated on picking out the old folk material and has traced the religious trend of the sources. G. von Rad and M. Noth, recognising the four sources present in the Pentateuch, are intent upon indicating the growth of the individual traditions, while the Swedish school at Uppsala (Engnell, Widengren, Danell) ascribe much space—and time—to oral transmission. But how can one, on the basis of oral transmission, explain the growing together to form one whole of such a heterogeneous mass of material as is present in the Pentateuch? Cf. C. R. North, "Pentateuchal Criticism," in *The Old Testament and Modern Study*, ed. H. H. Rowley, Oxford 1951, p. 78; W. F. Albright, *From the Stone Age to Christianity*, 2nd edn., Baltimore 1957, Chapter IV, section B2.

have been gradually abandoned in more recent times. The Priestly Code is the basis of the Pentateuch into which the other sources have been worked, but we must not forget that here too, as in the majority of the books of the Old Testament, supplements, often of no mean length, were added even after the work as a whole had been completed.

It begins with the first page of the Bible, relating how God worked for six days to create the world (Gen. I. 1–II. 4) and completing the story with the words: "These are the generations of the heavens and the earth" (Gen. II. 4). These words are of particular significance for the Priestly Code, where they recur again and again when genealogies are being traced and lists of families given, as in the case of the sons of Noah (Gen. VI. 9 f.) and their descendants (Gen. X *),[14] the descendants of Shem (XI. 10–26), of Terah (XI. 27), of Ishmael (XXV. 12–17), of Isaac (XXV. 19 ff.), of Esau (XXXVI. 1–8, 9–14) with a later continuation (vss. 15–43), and of Jacob (XXXVII. 1 f.). The genealogy of Noah with its slightly different introduction: "This is the book of the generations" (Gen. V), and the list of the sons of Jacob: "These are the names of the sons of Israel" (Ex. I. 1–4) belong to the same category. But these family lists, all of which probably have a common source in the Book of Generations (Tholedoth, see below), are more than the expression of a certain pleasure found in their compilation. They have a deeper meaning and are the products of a well-considered plan: they lead from the general to the particular, from the human race to the children of Israel, becoming ever narrower until they finally culminate in Moses and Aaron (Num. III. 1 ff.), their goal and crowning glory. Of the earliest history, the story of the flood (Gen. VI. 9–22, VII, VIII), God's covenant with Noah (IX. 1–17), and Noah's death (IX. 28 f.) belong to the Priestly Code.

In the stories of the patriarchal period, the portion belonging to the Priestly Code is somewhat meagre. Of Abraham we learn only of his journey to Canaan (Gen. XII. 4 f.) and his parting from Lot (XIII. 6, 11 f.), the story of Ishmael and his mother Hagar (XVI *), the birth of Isaac (XXI. 1–5*), and the death of Abraham (XXV. 7–11). All this is very brief and to

[14] An asterisk indicates that the section or verse does not belong completely, but only partially, to the source work.

the point: only God's covenant (XVII. 1–27) and the burial of Sarah after the purchase of the cave of Machpelah at Hebron (XXIII. 1–20) are reported in detail and in story form. We have even less information about Isaac, who is completely in the background here, as in all the sources. We are told only of the birth of his sons (XXV. 19, 20, 26), of the grief caused him by Esau (XXVI. 34 f.), and of his death (XXXV. 27–9). Of Jacob, on the other hand, somewhat more is recorded—his mission to Mesopotamia (XXVII. 46–XXVIII. 9) and, after a brief mention of his relations with Laban (XXIX. 24, 28, 29), his sojourn in Bethel (XXXV. 6–15*). A list of his sons is provided (XXXV. 22–6), and a little is told of the days he spent in Egypt, but with no reference to the Joseph stories, very little of which belongs to the Priestly Code (XXXVII. 1 f., XLI. 46*). We hear of Jacob's removal to Egypt (XLVI. 6 f.) with subsequent expansion (XLVI. 8–27), his old age (XLVII. 27 f.), his blessing and final instructions (XLIX. 1, 29–33), his death and burial at Hebron (L. 12 f.). That is all. In vain do we search for any one complete story of any length from his life in Egypt.

Much more generous is the contribution of the Priestly Code to the history of Moses. After a description of the state of the Israelites in Egypt (Ex. I. 1–14*, II. 23–5) P tells of the calling of Moses (VI. 2–VII. 7), the miracle of his rod (VII. 8–13), and the various plagues which God sent down upon Egypt—the turning of water to blood (VII. 19–22), frogs (VIII. 1–3, 11*), flies (VIII. 21–4), boils (IX. 8–12). It records further the institution of the Passover (XII. 1–20, 28) and the departure from Egypt (XII. 37, 40–2), to which the law of the Passover (XII. 43–51) is appended. Later rules governing the first-born and unleavened bread (Mazzoth) were added to this ordinance (XIII. 1–16). The saving of the children of Israel by the Red Sea (Ex. XIV*, XV. 22*, 27) and the wonderful manna in the wilderness (Ex. XVI*) are reported in detail. With the arrival at Sinai (XIX. 2*, 1, XXIV. 15–18) there begins a broad description of the events which took place on this mountain. Here Moses receives from God instructions on the building of the tabernacle and its furnishing, on the priests and their clothing, on the sacrifices and the offerings to be made (XXV. 1–XXXI. 18). A brief summary of all the instructions is given (XXXI. 7–11), and then the section ends with a repetition of the commandment

E

to observe the Sabbath day. As Moses' restatement of the
commandment shows (xxxv. 2), the Priestly Code is continued
in Ex. xxxv, and from there on it records how God's instructions were carried out (xxxv. 1–xxxix. 43) until the tabernacle
was finally consecrated (Ex. xl). It goes on to describe the
consecration of the priests, the first sacrifice made by Aaron
and the death of his sons Nadab and Abihu, and issues
further orders for the priests (Lev. viii–x). Then follows the
survey of the number of men fit to go to war, in conjunction
with which lists of the tribes are given (Num. i–iv), and the
offerings which the princes of the tribes made at the dedication
of the altar (Num. vii) are detailed. With the consecration of
the Levites (Num. viii. 5 ff.), the celebration of the Passover
in the second year after the exodus from Egypt (Num. ix. 1–14),
the journeying and encamping by the sign of the cloud (Num.
ix. 15–23), and God's command concerning the silver trumpets
(Num. x. 1–10) we come to the end of this large and important
part recording the events at Sinai.

The last large section begins with the departure from Sinai
(Num. x. 11–28) and tells of the sending out of spies (Num.
xiii. 1–17, 21–6*), the murmuring of the people, and the
report made by the spies on their return (parts of Num. xiv).
We hear in detail of the rebellion of Korah (Num. xvi–xvii*);
then, after outlining the services of the priests and Levites
(xviii. 1–7) and the arrangements for the maintenance of the
priests (xviii. 8–32), the record gives an equally vivid description of the anger of the people towards Moses and Aaron when
there was no water and of the water flowing from the rock
(xx. 2–13*). This story is framed within brief announcements
of the deaths of Miriam (xx. 1) and Aaron (xx. 22–9*). In
the next two chapters only two references to the journeying of
the Israelites (xxi. 4a, and xxii. 1b) belong to the Priestly Code,
which now hastens towards its close with the announcement of
the death of Moses and the appointment of Joshua as his
successor (xxvii. 12–23). The end of the document, however, as
a comparison of Num. xxvii. 12 ff. with Deut. xxxii. 48 ff.
clearly indicates, does not come till the end of the whole
Pentateuch and takes the form of a brief report on the death of
Moses (Deut. xxxiv. 1, 7–9). It is possible that the report on
the war with the Midianites (Num. xxxi. 1–12) also belongs

to the Priestly Code, but the various supplements to this report (vss. 13–54) belong to a later period, possibly even after the completion of the Pentateuch.

Even this brief summary of the contents shows the special character and particular aim of the Priestly Code. There is no doubt that it concentrates on the lifetime of Moses, with particular emphasis on the events at Sinai, the tabernacle, the priests, and the offering of sacrifices. The constitution of the social and religious community at Sinai is the core and focal point of the whole work,[15] towards which all the rest leads. For this reason the document is in general concise, laconic, and essentially restrained, avoiding the details which alone lend life and colour to a description. In the places where somewhat more detail is found, a particular intention bound up with the cult is immediately evident. So the creation story ends in the consecration of the Sabbath as a day of rest, the covenant with Noah in the prohibition of blood and murder, the covenant with Abraham in the institution of circumcision, while Isaac's journey to Mesopotamia is directed against mixed marriages. All these stories have a very definite purpose. Their aim is less to tell a story than to instruct in and point the way to the correct behaviour demanded by the cult. For this reason, too, P is very detailed about matters of the cult, which are traced back to Moses and which Moses instituted on instructions from God. More than once it is expressly emphasised that these institutions are to be adhered to for all time. "Throughout your generations you shall observe it as an ordinance for ever" (Ex. XII. 14, XXIX. 9).

But the regulations governing the cult as described in the Priestly Code correspond not with the time of Moses, but with the author's day. They presuppose the Deuteronomic reforms, with the elimination of worship in "high places" and the centralisation of the cult. The Priestly Code therefore assiduously avoids anything which could be linked up with other customs. In contrast with the other Pentateuchal sources, the Yahwist and the Elohist, no mention is made in P of any sacrificial

---

[15] Cf. M. Noth, *Überlieferungsgeschichtliche Studien I*, henceforth cited as *Überlief. Stud.* Halle 1943, p. 208, and his argument with G. von Rad, *Die Priesterschrift im Hexateuch*, Stuttgart 1934, p. 175, who understands the account given by P as three concentric cycles (that of the universe, that of Noah, and that of Abraham).

offering or any place of worship in pre-Mosaic times. Even into the Ark only two of each animal were taken, which practically excluded the possibility of sacrifice. So the author portrays in the cult not the time of Moses, but his own. He describes what seemed to him appropriate and right, whether his portrayal was based on what was in existence in his own time or on an ideal to strive after in the future. To the modern way of thinking it is not history we are offered here, but interpretation. But it would be unjust to the author to conclude that all this is the product of his own invention. Much can be verified in older sources; and even where such evidence is lacking an old tradition should often be assumed. And where that is impossible, we have recourse to the author's religious outlook and his absolute conviction that since the cult, as it is today, is right, it must stem from the past, from Moses. And so these details, in the faith and because of the faith, are projected from the present back into the past, and have the further task of serving as a programme for the future.

The piety of the Priestly Code emanates wholly from this strong interest in the cult. When we compare the Code with the other sources of the Pentateuch, the difference is immediately evident. People appear not as men of flesh and blood, but as colourless shadows: the small personal details which make a portrait live are lacking. For the business of the author of the Priestly Code is not with men. His whole interest is directed towards God and in what comes from God—His statutes and ordinances. While in the other sources God appears quite naturally in human form, talking and acting—for example, He walks in the Garden of Eden in the cool of the evening (Gen. III. 8), He visits Abraham and is entertained by him (Gen. XVIII), men speak with Him as with an equal—it is quite otherwise in the Priestly Code. It tells, it is true, of God's human qualities (His anger, for example) and speaks of His resting on the seventh day of the creation. But throughout the whole document the great contrast between God and the world, and the enormous distance separating Man from God, are stressed. What a high conception of God is expressed right at the beginning in the creation story itself! Here the picture of the world is stripped of all mythical features and Man is allotted a particular position therein. And the creation itself? God does not refashion some already existing, primary matter, as in the creation stories of other religions: God creates from nothing, by His Word alone. And as God is perfect, so also is His work perfect. The great distance separating God and Man necessarily makes P reluctant to describe God's appearance: where He does appear, it is as a light covered in cloud (Ex. xxiv. 16 f.). Moreover, God does not speak directly to man, neither to individuals nor to the tribes as a whole, but uses Moses, who is characterised as the interpreter and conveyor of God's instructions. This meeting with God's presence affects Moses as a glow of light, and he has to cover his shining face with a veil before he can convey these instructions to the children of Israel (Ex. xxxiv. 33 f.). Conversely, no one can approach God directly: priests are necessary as mediators. How carelessly the Ark of the Covenant is handled in the older stories: it is taken along into battle and stored in a private house (ii Sam. vi. 1–3). How different, on the other hand, is the layout of the camp in the Priestly Code, where the distance between people and tabernacle is rigidly maintained. The tabernacle is the centre of the camp, around which the tribes are grouped but from which they are separated by the Levites, who "shall encamp around the tabernacle of the witness" (Num. i. 53). Like the cult of the Mosaic period, the moral behaviour of the patriarchal stories is also presented in the best possible light. The Priestly Code makes no mention of a quarrel between Abraham and Lot, or of Hagar being driven out: on the contrary, Isaac and Ishmael together pay their last respects to their father (Gen. xxv. 9). Neither do we hear of the imperilling of Sarah by Abraham's extraordinary conduct nor of Jacob's cheating his brother Esau. The greatest care is taken to avoid anything which might degrade the Fathers in the eyes of the reader.

The statistics in the Priestly Code, which aim at an impression of exactness and reliability but unfortunately do not stand the test of closer examination, form a special chapter. Particularly striking is the great age ascribed to the first generations of Man, for which we have no explanation. In this, however, the author is a true child of his time and is only following the old oriental custom of ascribing an exceptionally long life to one's earliest forebears. Nevertheless it is worthy of note that he grades the ages downwards—from Adam to Noah (except Enoch) a life-span is 700–1,000 years, from Noah to Abraham (except Nahor) 200–600 years, among the patriarchs 100–200 years, and in the present 70–80 years. Herein lies a definite intention. Since the author knows no special story of the Fall of Man, he establishes the fact, at least, of the deterioration of man's vital energy, but without seeing his sinfulness as the cause.

In the figures, in which there is some variation between the Hebrew text and the old translations, some definite system seems to be present. If we begin to calculate, we find that there are 1,656 years up to the flood, which is exactly four times the length of the period between the flood and Abraham's calling (414 years; Gen. XI. 24 should read 79). The period from the Creation to the exodus from Egypt covers 2,666 years, or in other words exactly two thirds of a world period of 4,000 years which ends 374 years after the return from the exile (538 B.C.), that is, in the year 164 B.C. This date is of great importance in Dan. IX. 24 ff. as the end of the seventieth week, with the antici-pated coming of the kingdom of God (Dan. VII. 25, XII. 1 ff.). Or the 215 years from Abraham until the removal into Egypt is exactly half of the time spent in Egypt. Thus these figures conceal some definite plan and intention which we no longer understand. Let us just consider the number of men capable of military service (Num. I. 46), which is estimated as 603,550. This can be explained if one reads the Hebraic characters of the words "all the congregation of the children of Israel" (Num. I. 2) as numerals, which give the figures 603 and 551.

In other respects, too, the Priestly Code impresses us with its systematic presentation. Repeated formulae such as "The Lord said to Moses, Speak to the people of Israel" (Ex. XXV. 1, XXXI. 12, etc.) or "you shall" (Ex. XXV. 11, 17, etc.), make it possible in large measure to separate this particular source from the great complex of the Pentateuch, and give it such a high degree of probability. The Priestly Code extends from the creation of the world to the death of Moses, and reaches its peak in the promise of God's presence: "I will dwell among the people of Israel and will be their God" (Ex. XXIX. 43–6). It further differs from the other sources in that it has no interest in the annexation of Palestine, which, for the others, is the fulfil-ment of God's promise to the Fathers.

The content of the document is certain proof that the author came from priestly circles. The great store he sets on the cult leads up to that paralysis of living piety and over-stressing of the formal which was so decisive for later Judaism. It is not easy to give an exact date to P. On the one hand one must take into consideration the fact that a series of extensions were added to the text, the most important we shall mention being the instructions for the altar of incense (Ex. xxx) and for the Feast of the Atonement (Lev. xvi), which was not added until quite late. As a result of the many additions, attempts have been made to indicate various strata within P,[16] but a simple, gradual growth of the individual parts into the final text would be more probable. On the other hand, the author has included and adapted much older material in his work. We can draw only a very imperfect picture of this, since it is not always complete in itself. Older traditions are found, especially in the tribal lists, and it is possible that a particularly old "Book of Generations" (Book of Tholedoth) should be taken as their source.[17] To this older material belongs, in particular, a whole series of law codes, especially the Law of Holiness (Lev. xvii–xxvi) with its supplements (Lev. xxvii) and a further appendix (Lev. xxx), probably also the laws of sacrifice (Lev. i–vii) with supplements (Num. v–vi), and the laws of cleanliness (Lev. xi–xv). A third difficulty lies in the absence of any allusion by the author of P (in common with the other sources) to contemporary events and conditions. As far as dates are concerned, therefore, we are completely dependent on internal

[16] Thus von Rad, *Die Priesterschrift im Hexateuch*, seeks to prove that P is composed of two, on the whole parallel narratives (P A and P B), after E. Sievers, *Metrische Studien, II. Die Genesis*, Leipzig 1904, on the basis of his sound analyses, had already postulated six sub-sources for P. Cf., however, P. Humbert, "Die literarische Zweiheit des Priester-Codex in der Genesis," in *Z. alttest, W.*, LVIII (1940–1), pp. 30–57.

[17] E.g. Gen. v. 1, vi. 9, x. 1, xi. 10, 27, xxv. 12, 19, xxxvi. 1, 9, xxxvii. 2, Num. iii. 1. According to von Rad, *Die Priesterschrift im Hexateuch*, pp. 33 ff., and *Das erste Buch Mose*, Das Alte Testament Deutsch, henceforth cited as A.T.D., edd. V. Herntrich and A. Weiser, Göttingen 1949, p. 55 f., this Book of Origins, consisting only of genealogies, lists, and at the most quite short theological remarks, formed "probably the oldest basic material of the Priestly Code, which grew up slowly therefrom, extending itself according to plan from the most varied sacral traditions." But no doubt we should consider the Book of Origins rather as a model used by P and made subservient to his complete work; cf. also M. Noth, *Überlieferungsgeschichte des Pentateuchs*, henceforth cited as *Überlieferungsgeschichte*, Stuttgart 1948, p. 10.

evidence. In this connexion the relationship to Deuteronomy (q.v.) is decisive: the demands of Deuteronomy, like the measures of Josiah's reforms, are already taken for granted in the Code. The Priestly Code must therefore be later than Deuteronomy. It is almost generally accepted that P originated in the time of the exile and can be identified with the "Book of the law of Moses, which the Lord had given to Israel," which Ezra brought with him from exile to Jerusalem and made the basis of his religious reforms (Neh. VIII. 1 ff.).

THE YAHWIST (J)

Although the Priestly Code has been detached, the doubts and objections to the unity of the Pentateuch are still not cleared up, particularly in the first Book of Moses of which P is only a small component. Nor are the different names given to God explained; but the variation connects up the remainder of the Pentateuch with two sources, which are so closely merged in parts that it is not always possible to separate them completely. In many cases one must be satisfied with merely establishing their presence.

The Yahwist (J)[18] also begins with primordial history. Like P, it starts with the Creation, but here the most highly prized and important achievement is the creation of Man (Gen. II. 4–25). The first men, however, show themselves unworthy of their high calling and become sinful and disobedient (Gen. III). It is uncertain whether the story of Cain and the list of his descendants (Gen. XXIV) also belonged originally to this version: at all events neither is essential to its continuity and both assume a larger population on the earth (IV. 14 f., 17) than can be reconciled with the rest of the story. After a fragmentary account of the generations of Seth (IV. 25 f., V. 29) there follows the story of the great flood (VI. 5–8, parts of chs. VII–VIII), Noah's cursing and blessing (IX. 18–27), parts of the generations of the peoples (X. 8–19, 25–30), and the story of the building of the tower of Babel (XI. 1–9) with a part of the generations of Terah (XI. 28–30).

The period of the patriarchs is reported here in very much

---

[18] Cf. S. Mowinckel, *The Two Sources of the pre-Deuteronomic primeval history (JE) in Gen. I–XI*, henceforth cited as *Two Sources*, Oslo 1937; H. Schmökel, "Zur Datierung der Pentateuchquelle J," in *Z. alttest. W.*, LXII (1950), pp. 319–21.

more detail than in P. We hear of Abraham's calling and God's promise (xii. 1–4), his journey to Canaan, Sichem, and Bethel with the appearance of God and the building of the altar, his continued journey into Egypt and the endangering of Sarah (xii. 6–20). On his return from Egypt to Canaan Abraham parts company with Lot (xiii. 1–5, 7–18*). God promises Abraham a posterity (xv. 1–6*) and makes a covenant with him (xv. 7–12, 17 f.). The record then tells of the flight of the pregnant Hagar (xvi. 1*–2, 4–8, 11–14) and of God's visit to Abraham and the latter's intercession for Sodom (Gen. xviii). But Sodom must perish for its wickedness: only Lot and his family are saved, but his wife is severely punished for her disobedience (xix. 1–18). Then we hear of the origin of Moabites and Ammonites in the story of Lot and his daughters (xix. 20–38) and the birth of Isaac is briefly mentioned (xxi. 1*, 7). The list of descendants of Nahor (xxii. 20–4) gives the cue (vs. 23) for the story of Isaac seeking Rebekah's hand (Gen. xxiv). Perhaps the list of Abraham's descendants by his second marriage (xxv. 1–4) also belongs to the Yahwist: the settlement with his other children in favour of Isaac certainly does (xxv. 5 f., 11*). Of the Isaac story itself the Yahwist includes relatively little: due to famine Isaac goes to Gerar, where (like Abraham in Egypt) he denies his wife (xxvi. 1–11*); quarrels take place about the wells, but finally agreement is reached in the form of a sworn contract (xxvi. 12–33*)—this story explains the name of the city Beer-sheba (well of the oath) "to this day." These few episodes from the life of Isaac are embedded in the Jacob story. This begins in detail with the birth of the twins and the selling of the birthright (xxv. 21–34), and tells how Jacob surreptitiously obtains his father's blessing but later has to flee from his brother to Laban in Haran (xxvii. 1–45): on his way there he receives the Lord's promise in a dream (xxviii. 10–19*). Concerning his twenty years' sojourn with Laban we learn of his love for Rachel (xxix. 1–31) and the birth of his sons (xxix. 32–xxx. 24, with later additions). Since his cunning brings him great prosperity in Haran (xxx. 25–43) he arouses the envy of Laban's sons and is ordered by God to return home (xxxi. 1, 3). Fear for his possessions makes him flee in secret with his family and all his goods, and he is pursued and overtaken by Laban: a peaceful conclusion is

reached, however, and Jacob and Laban make a covenant at
Gilead (parts of XXXI. 17–53). After this danger has been
averted, others threaten him—this time from his brother.
For this reason Jacob sends messengers to Esau and asks God's
assistance (XXXII. 4–14). In the night he wrestles at the ford
Jabbok with "a man," a divinity (very probably the river
spirit), and obtains the name Israel (XXXII. 23–32). Now
follow the meeting and reconciliation with his brother (XXXIII.
1–3, 6–7, 12–17). Jacob stays first in Succoth (v. 17) and
then goes on to Shechem. From then on his character retreats
into the background.

Instead we hear of a few episodes concerning his sons
Simeon and Levi, who avenge with the blood of the Sheche-
mites the defiling of their sister Dinah (Gen. XXXIV.*; cf. also
XLIX. 5–7); Reuben and his misconduct with Bilhah (XXXV.
21 f.); Joseph, his father's favourite, and hated for this and for
his dreams by his brothers, who throw him into a pit (XXXVII.
3–5*, 6–21) and sell him to a caravan of Ishmaelites (XXXVII.
25–7, 28*); Judah and Tamar's forced marriage (Gen.
XXXVIII)—until finally Joseph steps into the foreground. We
hear of his temptation and his imprisonment along with two
high officials of Pharaoh's court (XXIX–XL. 1). Here the Yahwist
breaks off and is combined with the other source (E), from
which (in contrast with what has gone before) the main part of
the narrative is taken from now on. The Yahwist tells us little
about subsequent events—only of Joseph's appointment to a
high official position to ensure food supplies (parts of XLI.
34–57), and nothing but fragments about his brothers' first
journey to Egypt (small parts of Gen. XLII). J takes up the lead
again with the report of the second journey of the brothers up
till the moment when Joseph reveals his identity to them
(XLIII. 1–XLV. 4, 5a). We learn that Jacob is to come to Egypt
(XLV. 16–28), but the journey itself is only very briefly mentioned (XLVI. 1*, 5*). We hear more about the reunion of
father and son (XLVI. 28–34) and the settlement in Goshen
(XLVII. 1–6*), that Joseph uses the famine to make the Egyptians Pharaoh's slaves (XLVII. 13–26) and that finally, in accordance with his promise (XLVII. 29–31), he buries his father in
Hebron (L. 1–10) and then returns to Egypt (L. 14).

These stories are closely followed by the next main section, dealing with the escape from Egypt. A long time has elapsed: a new Pharaoh "who knew not Joseph" has ascended the throne and is oppressing the Israelites (Ex. i. 8–12). He even goes so far as to order all newborn male infants of Israel to be drowned (Ex. i. 22). Moses, who is born soon after this decree, is hidden by his mother in the rushes: there he is found by Pharaoh's daughter, who brings him up (ii. 1–10*). One day when he is a grown man, he is so enraged by the harsh treatment of his countrymen that he kills an Egyptian overseer and then flees to Midian, where he marries and makes his home (ii. 11–23). Whether the detailed story of the calling of Moses (iii. 1–4, 16*) originally also belonged to the Yahwist is the more questionable, as God's order to return (iv. 19*) follows on well after the words "In the course of those many days" (ii. 23). Once back in Egypt, Moses—Aaron is no doubt a later addition—gathers the elders (iv. 24–30), and pleads with Pharaoh to free the Israelites—with the negative result that their oppression becomes even more severe (v. 1–21). The Lord encourages the downcast Moses (v. 22–vi. 1) and demonstrates his power to the Egyptians, sending all manner of plagues down upon them—water turned to blood (vii. 14–18, 20 f.*, 23–5), frogs (vii. 25b–viii. 3, 4–11), gnats and flies (viii. 16–28), murrain (ix. 1–7), hail (ix. 13–35), and locusts (x. 1–20). The darkness (x. 21–7), like God's message (xi. 1–3), was probably incorporated later. Finally, under the pressure of the last and worst plague, the death of all the firstborn (xi. 4–8, xii. 29–34), against which the children of Israel were instructed how to protect themselves (xii. 21–3), they gain their freedom. The Lord leads them on their journey as a pillar of cloud and a pillar of fire (xiii. 20–3). But Pharaoh regrets having freed them and sets out in pursuit (xiv. 5–10*). The terrified Israelites are comforted by Moses: "The Lord will fight for you" (xiv. 13 f.), and God saves them miraculously by means of the sea (xiv. 19–30*), spreading panic among the Egyptians, who drown. On the journey through the wilderness God feeds the Israelites with manna (xvi. 4 f.*), which they gather, but not on the Sabbath day, in accordance with the commandment (xvi. 29–31, 35 f.*). Also by a miracle they are supplied with badly needed drinking water (xvii. 1–7*) and get as far as Rephidim, where, under Joshua's leadership, they are victorious over the Amalekites (XVII. 8–16). They encamp at Sinai (XIX. 2*).

The next large section concerning events at Sinai has been so extended by additions and insertions that it is difficult to ascertain what is the original. There is much doubt about some passages. In the first place, the whole story of the golden calf and what is connected with it—for example the building of the altar (XXXII. 4–6*), Moses' first ascent of Mount Sinai (XXIV. 12–15), his breaking of the two tables of the Law and destruction of the image (XXXII. 15–20), with the probably even later extension regarding punishment for disobedience to God (XXXII. 25–9) and Moses' prayer for the sins of the people (XXXII. 30–5*)—seems to be supplementary to the original, and Ex. XXXIII is probably also to be looked upon as an addendum. The actual story of the events at Sinai is relatively short in J. It contains essentially the preparations for the theophany (XIX. 20–5*) and considerable portions of Ex. XXXIV: Moses is to make two tables, which he takes up on to the mountain with him and there worships God as He appears to him. The Lord gives him His commandments which, in part, tie up with the Ten Commandments, and Moses writes them down. He comes down from the mountain with his face shining, and all are afraid of him. He "gave them in commandment all that the Lord had spoken with him in Mount Sinai" (Ex. XXXIV. 32).

The last main section of J tells of the journey into the land east of the Jordan. It begins with the departure from Sinai (Num. x. 29–33) and Moses' invocation on this occasion (v. 35). The stages of the journey are pinpointed by the names Hazeroth (Num. XI. 35), the wilderness of Paran (XII. 16), thence again in the direction of the Red Sea (XIV. 25), Hormah, north of Kadesh (XIV. 45), the desert of Zin (XX. 1), Mount Hor (XX. 22), Shittim east of the Jordan (XXV. 1), and occupied land in that country (XXXII. 1). These places form the external framework into which the individual stories of this great journey are worked, as for example the fire in the camp (XI. 1–3), and the story of the Israelites' craving for meat XI.(4–15), which God satisfies in such excess that a serious plague results, killing many (XI. 16–35); also the story of Miriam's grumbling and leprosy, which has been so enlarged upon, however, that one can hardly define the original (Num. XII.*). From the region of

Kadesh Moses sends spies southwards into Canaan (XIII. 17–20*); they cross the Jordan as far as Hebron and the brook of Eshcol (XIII. 22–8*). But the news of the great walled cities and their mighty inhabitants, the sons of Anak, has such a demoralising effect on the people of Israel, in spite of Caleb's confident reassurance (XIII. 30 f.), that they weep and cry out against Moses (XIV. 1*, 4) and contemplate returning to Egypt. This behaviour is considered by Yahweh as a personal insult (XIV. 11). Therefore no one but Caleb is allowed to see the Promised Land: the others must return to the wilderness (in the direction of the Red Sea: XIV. 23–5*). In trying to move forward into Palestine in spite of the Lord they are attacked by the Amalekites and Canaanites and scattered as far as Hormah (XIV. 39–45). There Dathan and Abiram rebel against Moses (XVI. 1 f.*, 12–15), and as a punishment they and their followers are subsequently swallowed up by an earthquake (XVI. 25–34). The Israelites arrive in the wilderness of Zin, but the Edomites refuse them permission to proceed through their land (XX. 19 f.). If it indeed belongs to J, the short report on the battle with the Canaanites (XXI. 1–3) is certainly in the wrong place: it is difficult, however, to say where it should be. The story of the fiery serpents (XXI. 4–9*) also gives the impression of having been added, and the list of encampments is certainly a later addition, and, moreover, imperfectly transmitted. It is included here to bridge the gap to the subsequent stories of the Yahwist, which are centred in Transjordan (Moab), although no mention is made of how the Israelites arrived there. The Moabites view them with fear and trembling. Their King Balak sends messengers to a wizard Balaam,[19] asking him to curse the enemy (XXII. 3*–8). After many requests, Balaam finally sets out to meet the King (XXII. 13–19): on the way, warned by the words of his ass, he is instructed by the appearance of an angel as to what he must do (XXII. 21–38*). When he meets the King in Kirath-huzoth (XXII. 39 f.) and they

---

[19] Cf. S. Mowinckel, "Der Ursprung der Bileamsage," in *Z. alttest. W.*, XLVIII (1930), pp. 233–71; O. Eissfeldt, "Die Komposition der Bileam-Erzählung. Eine Nachprüfung von Rudolphs Beitrag zur Hexateuchkritik," in *Z. alttest. W.*, LVII (1939), pp. 212–41. It still remains to be considered whether, instead of "Balaam son of Beor," "Balaam, son of Peor" should not be read: this would define Balaam as the man from Peor, i.e. the settlement near the sanctuary; cf. Noth. *Überlief. Stud.*, p. 83.

go up to the mountain of Peor (XXIII. 28) he must speak the word that God puts in his mouth, and that is: Blessed be Israel. In spite of the King's wrath, he persists in this blessing (XXIV. 1–19). Finally he returns home (vs. 25). Through Moses God metes out harsh punishment on the Israelites who have deserted to the Baal of Peor (xxv. 1*–5). We then hear of something like the beginning of a land annexation policy by Reuben, Gad, and some of the tribe of Manasseh, who take possession of Jazer and Gilead, Nobah and "the villages of Jair" (XXXII. 1, 16, 39–42*).

Here the Yahwist source breaks off, without reaching any proper conclusion. One would expect at least a mention of the death of Moses or of the final occupation of the Promised Land, and it is very probable that these did exist at one time in J. However, they have not been handed down.[20] Attempts have been made to attribute some of what follows to J—especially in the Book of Joshua, which deals in detail with the taking over of the Promised Land, and also in the Books of Judges, Samuel, and Kings[21]—but the results are very uncertain. On the other hand, one must take account of the possibility that, since Moses is no longer mentioned in Numbers XXXII, the report of his death may have been lost in the process of combining the various Pentateuch sources into one whole: this may also explain the omission of further reports of land annexation.

In spite of uncertainty over the details, what we know for certain is that the Yahwist presents us with a picture of events from the creation to the flood, from God's promise to Abraham up to the final settlement east of Jordan. The whole forms a continuous, connected series of stories. Because the individual stories do not fit together well from a literary point of view, attempts have been made to divide J up into various subsidiary

[20] Cf. Beatrice L. Goff, "The lost Jahwistic account of the conquest of Canaan," in *Journal of Biblical Literature and Exegesis*, henceforth cited as *J. Bib. Lit.*, LIII (1934), pp. 241–9.

[21] Cf. especially G. Hölscher, "Die Anfänge der hebräischen Geschichtsausschreibung," in *Sitzungsberichte der Heidelberger Akademie der Wissenschaften*, 1942, who tries to indicate Yahwistic material from Joshua down to 1 Kings and looks upon J as the first author to write a history of Israel from the beginnings down to the separation of the kingdoms, basing himself on 1 Kings XII. 19: "So Israel rebelled against the House of David unto this day." Cf. O. Eissfeldt, *Geschichtsschreibung im Alten Testament*, Berlin 1948.

sources.[22] But the evident joins and unevenness are quite easily explained by the way the work as a whole developed. It is not an original creation: the Yahwist gathered together old traditional material, which was available to him not only orally but also very probably in written form. He left the individual stories or story cycles with their own special character and adopted them as far as possible unaltered. The fact that there are still gaps and slight discrepancies within the individual stories is due to the transmission of the completed work: more than once we find evidence of later extensions and amplifications to the text. For a time it was customary to regard the title "Yahwist" as a collective name for a group which was said to have edited the work. But the basic idea is so consistent throughout the document that a single author seems a more probable assumption than a group of editors.

The theme of his work lies in the promise "I will bless you and make your name great. . . . In you all the families of the earth will be blessed" (Gen. XII. 2 f.). These words express a

[22] After doubts had already been cast on the unity of J (Schrader, Reuss, Kuenen) K. Budde, *Die Urgeschichte*, Giessen 1883, divided the Yahwist into two threads of narrative (J^1 and J^2); cf. also C. Bruston, "Les deux Jéhovistes," in *Revue de theologie et de philosophie*, henceforth cited as *R. th. ph.*, 1885; R. Smend, *Die Erzählung des Hexateuchs*, Leipzig 1912; W. Eichrodt, *Die Quellen der Genesis*, Beihefte z. *Z. alttest. W.*, No. 31, Giessen 1916, p. 110–40. S. Mowinckel, *Two Sources*, equates J^1 with J and J^2 with E. Reference should be made in particular to the great new investigation of C. A. Simpson, *The Early Traditions of Israel*, Oxford 1948, with which O. Eissfeldt, *Die ältesten Traditionen Israels*, Beihefte z. *Z. alttest. W.*, No. 71, Berlin 1950, disagrees. Eissfeldt rejects Simpson's division and stands by his thesis of a lay source (L), to which he ascribes archaic and crude sections which cannot be grouped under J, E, and P, neither are they secondary ingredients, but he shows that they belong together in some way or other (Eissfeldt, *Einleitung in das Alte Testament;* henceforth cited as *Einleitung*, 2nd edn., Tübingen 1956, pp. 215–22). Robert H. Pfeiffer, "A non-Israelitic source of the Book of Genesis," in *Z. alttest. W.*, XLVIII, (1930), pp. 66–73 (cf. his *Introduction to the Old Testament*, henceforth cited as *Introduction*, New York 1941, pp. 159–67), also assumes a source of this nature which he labels, according to its supposed origin, S (= south or seir source); to it he ascribes the primeval history (in so far as it does not belong to P), legendary folk-tales, and the review of the history of Edom (parts of Gen. XIV–XXXV, XXXVIII, XXXVI). J. Morgenstern, "The oldest document of the Hexateuch," in *Hebrew Union College Annual*, henceforth cited as *H.U.C.A.*, IV, (1927), pp. 1–138, affirms in place of the above a Kenite source (K) which was written prior to 899 B.C. and inspired Asa's reforms (1 Kings XV. 9–15). It contains a biography of Moses, laying particular stress on his relations with the Kenites, and closes with the settlement of the Israelites and Kenites; the religious climax of the document is the revelation of the Kenite god, Yahweh, to Israel (Ex. XXXIII–XXXIV). Nevertheless we still consider it more probable that *one* author, using a single thread, strung the stories together as fixed component parts.

deeply religious thought which is illuminated, in particular, by the method of presenting primordial history. No doubt a great deal was adopted from other sources, Babylonian and Old Canaanite, but what is important is the way this material has been used and what the Yahwist has made of it. How different is the creation story from P! It is not nature, not the world, not the cosmos that stands in the forefront of this story: its main concern is with Man. Here in J for the first time we meet the idea of a unified history of the human race: but it is for him, at the same time, a story of human sinfulness. This man wants to be equal with God. And so his story is one great tragedy, a chain of sins both of omission and commission, from the first human being down to the building of the Tower of Babel, from the deceitfulness of Abraham (Gen. XII. 10 f.) to the murmurings of the children of Israel against God's guidance. On this basis it becomes clear how the Yahwist wanted his work understood, even if he does not carry out his intention very closely in the details of his story. Only once (Gen. XVIII. 22 ff.) does he interrupt his story to question, for the first time, the righteousness of God, "Far be it from thee to do such a thing, to slay the righteous with the wicked, so that the righteous fare as the wicked! Far be it from thee! Shall not the judge of all the earth do right?" (v. 25). At the same time these words raise his concept of God above all national boundaries and all racial limitations. The guilt of man is set up against the promise of God: and that promise prevails and proceeds to fulfilment in spite of all the obstructions which are constantly looming up in its path. So the Yahwist, with his basic conception of a divine plan for salvation, stands on a religious height which brings him very close to the great writing prophets.

It is not possible to be more exact regarding the Yahwist's date or identity. For lack of any chronological relationships we are dependent once more, as in P, on internal evidence and on supposition. The author's special preference for Judah and the Judaean area, especially Hebron, would suggest that the work originated in the Southern Kingdom. For the date of writing there is more latitude; but it is not advisable to place J later than the David–Solomon era.

THE ELOHIST (E) AND THE REDACTION

The last of the three great sources within the first four Books of Moses is known as the Elohist (E),[23] after the name Elohim which it applies to God. Broadly, it contains everything which does not belong to P or J; but it differs from these two works in that it contains no primordial history, but starts off at Genesis xv with Abraham. A further point to note is that in general it is preserved only in the form of short supplements and additions to the text of the Yahwist, and where it does contain whole narratives it presents them not (like J and P) in a continuous sequence but as independent, single stories.

Additions from the Elohist are found in the promise to Abraham, with that lovely simile of the countless stars in the heavens (Gen. xv. 1–5*, 13–16*); in the Jacob story in the vision of the ladder leading to heaven (Gen. xxviii. 11 f.), his vow at Bethel (xxviii. 13–22*), and the information about the sons of Rachel and Jacob (xxx. 1–3*, 6, 17–23*); in the Joseph story, in the motif of the many-coloured coat (xxxvii. 1*) and Reuben's plan to throw Joseph into a well (xxxvii. 23 f.) where the Midianites find him and take him away with them (vs. 28*), the stressing of Joseph's emotion when he reveals his identity to his brothers (xlv. 2 f.), and his grief at the death of his father with the explanation of the place-name Abel-Mizraim, "mourning of the Egyptians" (l. 10 f.). To the story of the departure from Egypt E contributes the tale of the Hebrew midwives (Ex. i. 15–20), the reasons for the Israelites avoiding the usual caravan routes (Ex. xiii. 17–19), and a few variants on the pursuit by Pharaoh and on the panic loosed by God among the Egyptian army (parts of Ex. xiv); the murmuring of the people (xvii. 3) is perhaps also to be considered as an Elohist variant of the foregoing. Apart from smaller additions to the theophany at Sinai (Ex. xix. 3, 13–19*, xx. 18–21*, xxiv. 1), mention must also be made here of the Moabites' fear of the Israelites (Num. xxii. 2 f.*).

Where the Elohist tells more comprehensive stories these are not simply parallels to the reports contained in J, but are

---

[23] Cf. O. Procksch, *Das nordhebräische Sagenbuch. Die Elohimquelle*, Leipzig 1906; H. Hellbardt, "Der Elohist als selbständige Geschichtsquelle," in *Theologische Blätter*, henceforth cited as *Th. Bl.*, xii (1933), cols. 241–3 (discussion with Volz and Rudolph).

F

rather variants. So the story of the adventure of Abraham and
Sarah is told once more (Gen. xx. 1–17), being regarded as a
separate story because of its different location (Gerar); or the
banishing of Ishmael and his mother Hagar (Gen. xxi. 6,
8–20), and Abraham's covenant with Abimelech with the
alternative explanation of the name Beer-sheba (Well of the
Seven—i.e. lambs; Gen. xxi. 21–33). The quarrel and final
reconciliation of Jacob and Laban (parts of Gen. xxxi. 19–54),
the installation of Joseph in his high office in Egypt (Gen. xli.
37–40), and the invitation to his father (Gen. xlv. 5*–15) who
comes to Egypt (Gen. xlvi. 1–5*), are all in a different form
from that found in J. The same may be said of the calling of
Moses (Ex. iii. 4*, 6, 9–14) and his return to Egypt (Ex. iv.
17 f., 20*). Further variants on the Yahwistic tradition found
in E are the story of the golden calf (Ex. xxxii. 1–4*, 21–4),
the refusal of passage through Edom (Num. xx. 14–18*, 21)
and the Balaam story (Num. xxii. 9–12, 20, 38*, 41, xxiii*).

In addition to these, there are stories which consist chiefly of
peculiarly Elohistic material; in particular the account of the
sacrifice of Isaac (Gen. xxii. 1–19) with a later extension promising future blessings (vss. 15–18), Jacob's conversation with
his wives before his flight (Gen. xxxi. 2, 4–16), and the strange
behaviour of Rachel in removing the teraphim from her father's
house (Gen. xxxi. 19–35*). This category would also include
the report on the vision of the angel as an explanation of the
place name Mahanaim (Gen. xxxii. 1–3), the present to Esau
(Gen. xxxii. 14*–22), the meeting of Esau and Jacob (Gen.
xxxiii. 4 f., 8–11), and the purchase of a piece of land in Shechem (Gen. xxxiii. 19 f.), Jacob in Bethel (Gen. xxxv. 1–8, 14,
omitting vs. 6), Benjamin's birth, and the death of Rachel
(Gen. xxxv. 16–20). In the Joseph stories the news of Joseph's
supposed death brought by his brothers (Gen. xxxvii. 28–36*)
also belongs to the Elohist. We have already seen that the
contribution of J to the Joseph stories is very incomplete,
especially in the first part of the narrative. E steps in to fill the
gaps and recounts in detail the imprisonment of Pharaoh's two
court officials (Gen. xl. 2–5*), their dreams and Joseph's
interpretation (Gen. xl. 6–23), Pharaoh's dreams (Gen. xli.
1–13), Joseph's explanation (Gen. xli. 14–36), and his work in
high office (Gen. xli. 47–54). The first journey of the brothers

into Egypt (Gen. XLII*) also goes back in the main to E (with the exception of small later extensions). Further material additional to the other sources is found in the accounts of Jacob's reception by Pharaoh (Gen. XLVII. 5–12*), his illness (Gen. XLVIII. 1 f.), his blessing of Joseph's sons Ephraim and Manasseh (Gen. XLVIII. 7–22*), Joseph's generosity towards his brothers, even after his father's death, and Joseph's own decease (Gen. L. 15–26). Peculiarly Elohistic material in the stories of Moses is found in the visit of Jethro, who takes Moses' wife and their two sons to him in Egypt (Ex. XVIII. 1–8, with later extensions in vss. 9–11), and in the appointment of judges to relieve Moses (Ex. XVIII. 12–27). With regard to the events at Sinai the Elohist alone of all the sources knows of the revelation of God to the elders (Ex. XXIV. 9–11), and in the last large section E alone tells of the victory over the Amorites (Num. XXI. 21–31), with a supplement reporting the victory over Og, King of Bashan (Num. XXI. 32–5).

This summary of the contents shows how scant is the flow of the sources where the Elohist is concerned. Not much in the Pentateuch is ascribed to it, and the little that has been handed down to us is but an accumulation of unrelated fragments. Because of its sparse and fragmentary nature, some have felt inclined to deny the writer the character of a narrator at all.[24] And one must admit that in the condition in which it has been transmitted E can never have existed as an independent source. That, however, does not mean that what is available to us is the whole Elohist as it was written. On the contrary, we should rather consider that it was originally one large and complete record as is indicated by the fairly long and coherent sections in the Joseph story.

If the Elohistic narrative exists today only as fragments, this can be laid to the account of the so-called Jehovist—the name applied to the compiler (redactor) or reviser of the older version of the Pentateuch, who fused the two works of J and E to form one unit (JE). The basis he employed for his work was J. He did use the account given by E, but not simply by adding the two sources (J and E) together or by dovetailing one into the

---

[24] P. Volz and W. Rudolph, *Der Elohist als Erzähler. Ein Irrweg der Pentateuch-kritik?*, Beihefte z. Z. alttest. W., No. 63, Giessen 1933; W. Rudolph, *Der Elohist von Exodus bis Josua*, Beihefte z. Z. alttest. W., No. 68, Berlin 1938.

other. He worked E into his Yahwistic basis only in so far as it presented something not contained in J's account. Anything that E related differently from or in addition to the Yahwist—and that alone—was inserted by the redactor into the Yahwistic work as a supplement, variant, or special item. A comparison from this point of view of the contents of E and J immediately confirms this working principle on the part of the redactor. But we must beware of drawing conclusions regarding the whole work from what has not been—or, more correctly, is no longer—handed down from E. Because the Elohistic material transmitted to us is so limited and incomplete, it is necessary to be very cautious in making generalisations: moreover, with the paucity of material available to us, we are in no position to obtain a correct picture of the Elohist.

Nevertheless here, as in the case of J and P, one would deprecate the opinion that this narrative is to be considered as the combined effort of a "school." Here, too, we assume that the author was a single individual, although the facts permit no more detailed statement about him. From the resources at our disposal, however, we can gather at least a little about his religious views. In contrast with the natural, direct, oral communication between God and Man in J, the Elohist emphasises the great gulf separating the two—God never makes His wishes known directly but reveals them to man by means of dreams, angels, or a voice from heaven. We are aware, moreover, of a definite antipathy towards strange gods (Gen. xxxv. 2), which, for example, are buried by Jacob at Shechem (Gen. xxxv. 4). Similarly the worship of a calf image is regarded as a grievous sin (Ex. xxxii. 21). At the same time E speaks quite openly and innocently of the erection of stone pillars (Mazzebah), the landmarks of the heathen cult, which have, however, lost their religious meaning here and serve as a monument at Bethel (Gen. xxviii. 22) and as a tombstone for Rachel (Gen. xxxv. 20). A further characteristic of E is his presentation of the patriarchs in as favourable a light as possible: he tries to justify Abraham's lie about Sarah (Gen. xx. 12) and particularly stresses Abraham's sympathy and kindness when Hagar is driven out (Gen. xxi. 11–14). Similarly, Jacob's behaviour towards his father-in-law is explained by the fact that Laban had deceived him (Gen. xxxi. 6 f.). Attempts have been made to trace one main line throughout the Elohistic version, and this has been sought in the words: "You meant evil against me; but God meant it for good" (Gen. L. 20). But there is not enough material to make this possible.

There is still much uncertainty about the Elohist: indeed, the questions are more numerous than the answers. Should J and E be traced back to a common source (G)?[25] Little can be deduced from the fact that their outlines run parallel, because the general dividing up of the material was dictated by the course of the story itself. What is the origin of the material peculiar to E? The common source G? But, if so, why did the Jehovist not use it too? What is known is that E reveals a special preference for Joseph and Ephraim, which may perhaps lead us to assume that his work originated in central Palestine. On the other hand, the material peculiar to E refers to the south of the country. Nor is it possible to date the document precisely. It is usually assumed—because of the more spiritual representation of God than that found in J—that the Elohistic account is more recent than the Yahwistic, being ascribed to the ninth century B.C., if not even later (c. 750 B.C.). However, from the point of view of the history of the traditions the Elohist is nearer to the older tradition than the Yahwist. This would indicate a greater age and would suggest that the Elohistic account originated not much later than the David–Solomon period. No details can be given about the personality and period of the Jehovist redactor, as no clues or hints whatever are available.

A further question which arises is how the complete work we know as the Pentateuch came into being out of the three great narratives (J, E, and P). So far we have not considered the fourth and last great source, Deuteronomy (D); but since this source represents an isolated and independent unit it can safely be disregarded for the present. Seen as a whole, the Pentateuch contains a large-scale and heterogeneous account of events from the creation of the world down to the death of Moses. It is no mere coincidence that the first and last parts of the Pentateuch (Gen. I. 1–2, 4 and Deut. XXXIV. 7–9)

[25] Thus Noth, *Überlieferungsgeschichte*, pp. 40–4, drawing attention to "the agreement between J and E in the elements of the tradition in which their course is parallel" (p. 41).

are from the same source—the Priestly Code. For this was the basis used for combining the individual units into one complete whole. The unknown writer or redactor who combined P with the earlier collation of J and E by the Jehovist was on the whole more systematic in his work than the latter. His work as redactor was easier. As P and J treat of quite different material for long stretches, he could make do for the most part with merely adding them together. But he did not accept the material in its entirety as he found it and simply string the sources together: his task was to supplement, at his own discretion, his main source P from the combination of older material.

It must indeed be recognised that he attempted to incorporate as much as possible from the older sources. That did not hinder him, however, since the Priestly Code was for him the most important, from selecting from the other sources or abbreviating them where necessary. An example which amply illustrates his method of working is found in P's narrative of Moses and the strife about water (Num. xx. 1–13*), which he elaborated with details from the older source, although he had already told the same story once before from the same source (Ex. xvii. 1*–7). His great interest in the Priestly Code is immediately evident. That it was for him paramount is also clear from the primordial history. The Yahwistic account of Man's creation and fall seems like an appendix to P's creation story; in the story of the flood the older sources are used merely as supplements and the redactor is not in the least concerned that the resulting picture contradicts itself; in the list of generations (Gen. x) the parts taken from the older traditions merely fill out the account of the Priestly Code, which also to a certain extent provides the cue (Gen. ix. 28, x. 32b) for the inclusion of the stories of Noah (Gen. ix. 18–27) and of the building of the Tower of Babel (Gen. xi. 1–9). The situation is naturally somewhat different in the stories of the patriarchs, where the Priestly Code apparently had little material at its disposal, so that the redactor had to make greater use of the older sources. But in this instance too there is evidence that the older tradition suffered in favour of the Priestly Code. Even more pronounced is the reappearance of P in the Moses narrative. Here the redactor succeeded in very skilfully incorporating the older

tradition almost in its entirety. In the events at Sinai, it is
mainly the theophany and the making of the covenant which
are worked in to supplement the priestly version, while for the
remainder of this large section (up to Num. x. 11) the latter
alone holds the field. This dominance is so striking that one
cannot overlook the possibility that parts of the older tradition
were suppressed. This probability finally becomes a certainty
in the last large section, where the many promises have led us
to expect the older traditions to contain reports of land annexation even after the death of Moses and particularly west of the
Jordan. These are completely overlooked by the redactor,
however, since the Priestly Code, due to its completely different
historical situation—exile, had no further interest in such hap-
penings and concluded with the death of Moses.

What this redactor achieved is not the welding of his originals
into an integrated and unified whole. Neither does he show any
all-sustaining, all-overruling fundamental principle, on the
basis of which he could have combined the individual offerings
of his sources to form a higher unity. We may certainly assume
that he intended to do more than merely collect and preserve:
he would also be guided in his work by certain theological considerations; but we can no longer recognise them. And so the
Pentateuch comes to us not as one homogeneous work, but as a
heterogeneous collection in which the different fundamental
religious ideas still stand unreconciled, side by side. In the
creation stories a great tension is evident between Man as the
image of God and Man who presumes to be equal with God:
similarly the conception of the history of mankind as the story
of human transgression and the divine promise of forgiveness
stands unrelenting and unreconciled beside the cultic theology
as expressed in the Priestly Code.

Of the redactor as a person we know nothing, although many
like to think of him as Ezra. We are more able to give details
about the date of this final redaction. The unification of the
individual sources to form the complete Pentateuch must have
taken place in the fourth century B.C., at the earliest in the time
of Ezra and Nehemiah or very soon thereafter, and at the latest
before the breaking away of the Samaritans, who took over the
Pentateuch in its present extent and final size.

While dealing with the literary prehistory and final form of the Pentateuch, we may briefly refer to the question of the origin of the material on which the sources are based. Less attention is paid today to the "authors," although it is to them that we owe the final formulation. The main concern is with the basic form of their various works, and today it is not considered that these developed out of the organisation and combination of individual traditions or complexes of tradition. It is believed that a few great themes most intimately connected with the cult can be recognised as the roots of the traditions. Outstanding among these are the exodus from Egypt and the entry into the civilised land of Palestine, the promise to the patriarchs, guidance through the wilderness, and the revelation on Sinai. The assumption is that individual stories about people and things accrued to these beliefs in the course of time.[26] In this way the basic matter may have been produced from which the individual sources or the model for them could develop.

DEUTERONOMY (D) AND THE DEUTERONOMIST (DTR)

In the year 622 B.C., while the Temple at Jerusalem was under repair, a "book of the law" was found and brought to King Josiah (II Kings XXII. 3–XXIII. 25). The impression made upon the King by the reading of this book was so strong that he immediately embarked upon a strict reform of the cult. The content of his programme is set out in detail in II Kings. The principal aim was to eliminate all the symbols of heathen worship and all the sacrificial altars in the country, and to concentrate the lawful worship of God in one place and one place only, the Temple at Jerusalem. Unfortunately, however, no further details are given about "the book of the law" which gave rise to this plan. But since the fifth Book of Moses is the only book of the law known to us in which everything which went to make up the subjects of the Josian Reformation is held up before us as a command—with the single exception of the ruling concerning the priests of the land (II Kings XXIII. 9; Deut. XVIII. 6–8); and since it is the only book in which the centralisation of worship—in "the place which the Lord has

---

[26] Cf. Noth, *Überlieferungsgeschichte*, pp. 48–67; similarly G. von Rad, *Das formgeschichtliche Problem des Hexateuchs*, Stuttgart 1938, who traces the rise of the Pentateuch back to definite religious beliefs rooted in the cult (cultic Credo).

chosen to cause his name to dwell there"—is plainly and formally laid down, it is assumed with good reason that the book of the law found in the Temple is to be equated with the fifth Book of Moses.[27] Not, of course, with the whole book of the size that we know, for one can hardly imagine this being read several times in a day (II Kings XXII. 8, 10, XXIII. 2). No doubt it was the central section (Deut. XII-XXVI), the so-called Code of Deuteronomy,[28] and perhaps also some of the threats of curses which follow it. It is only when we read these chapters that the deep impression left on King and people by the reading aloud of this book becomes fully comprehensible to us.

This book of law differs from the law sections in the other Books of Moses in that it is not only purely law-giving in character, but explains the laws which it contains and expands upon their moral significance. So the individual ordinances are often followed by more detailed instructions, delivered in an edifying and hortatory manner. Moreover the fifth Book of Moses, or the *Deuteronomium*, as the Septuagint calls it on the basis of Deut. XVII. 18, differs as a whole from the remainder of the Pentateuch. It contains little narrative—only in the introductory sentences and in the final chapters which tell of the last month of the forty years spent in the wilderness. Everything else is clothed in the form of farewell speeches made by Moses to the Israelites before his death. But apart from the fact that these speeches cannot be traced back to Moses, since they presuppose quite different conditions, and above all residence west of the Jordan, they differ from other Mosaic speeches scattered throughout the Pentateuch. There Moses speaks by God's command,[29] as mediator of the divine revelation: here, on his own initiative, he is speaking to the people of matters of special concern to them.

[27] Even G. E. Lessing held this view. The thesis of G. R. Berry, "The Code found in the Temple," in *J. Bib. Lit.*, XXXIX (1920), pp. 44–51, that the Law of Holiness was meant thereby (Lev. XVII–XXVI), has not proved successful. See also Bibliography.

[28] For commentaries on Deuteronomy and literature on D, see bibliography. C. Steuernagel, *Das Deuteronomium*, Göttingen 1923, p. 6, gives further references.

[29] The exceptions (VII. 4, XI. 13–15, XVII. 3, XXVIII. 20, XXIX. 4–5) which, according to G. von Rad, *Deuteronomium-Studien*, henceforth cited as *Deut.-Studien*, 2nd edn. Göttingen 1948, Eng. trans. *Studies in Deuteronomy*, tr. D. Stalker, London 1953, are to be "regarded as something like stylistic aberrations," do not belong to the actual Code.

If for the moment we leave aside the historical framework (Deut. I–IV, XXXI–XXXIV) we see that these speeches do not form a unity either. This is evident in the different beginnings and introductions (Deut. VI. 1, XII. 1, etc.); in the way the formulation of the laws varies from the absolute and unconditional "You shall" (apodictic legal maxim) to the generally accepted possibility "If anyone" (conditional legal maxim); and finally in the form of address, which is sometimes singular and sometimes plural. In this connexion it should be noted that the parts in the singular are probably the older.[30] Whether or not, as many now hold,[31] the words of the prophet Jeremiah (Jer. VIII. 8): "How can you say, 'We are wise, and the law of the Lord is with us'? But, behold, the false pen of the scribes has made it into a lie" are particularly and consciously aimed at Deuteronomy with its strong emphasis on the cult, the fact remains that because of its great importance the book of laws found in the time of Josiah has frequently been copied and even more frequently commented upon. This means, however, that the law sections of the book have been much added to and amplified, as is evident even in the introduction (Deut. VI. 1), which takes up again the end of Deut. IV (vs. 44). This, as well as the contents, shows that ch. V is an insertion, its purpose being to set out the Ten Commandments of Horeb (the Decalogue). The end of the introduction (Deut. XI. 16–32) must also have been added, in order to re-emphasise in detail a warning already given (Deut. VI. 6–9). Chapters IX and X also contain longish extensions (between IX. 7 and X. 10), all given in the plural. A review of this whole introduction (Deut. VI–XI) reveals religious exhortations of a general and basic nature, about whose meaning and significance there can be no doubt. These introductory chapters can be nothing other than paraenesis, homiletic introductions, which were read before the Law itself so that the minds of the listeners might be adequately prepared.[32]

[30] In addition to F. Horst, *Das Privilegrecht Jahwes*, Göttingen 1930, cf. also A. Alt, *Die Ursprünge des israelitischen Rechts*, henceforth cited as *Ursprünge*, Leipzig 1934; K. Rabast, *Das apodiktische Recht im Deuteronomium und im Heiligkeitsgesetz*, Berlin 1948.

[31] Thus W. Rudolph, *Jeremia*, Handbuch zum Alten Testament, ed. O. Eissfeldt, henceforth cited as Hb. A.T., 1st series, VOL. XII. Tübingen 1947, p. 53.

[32] On the homiletic character cf. Hempel, *Alt-hebräische Literatur*, p. 140; L. Kohler, *Die hebräische Rechtsgemeinde*, Zürich 1930, pp. 17–18. "It is Law preached" —von Rad, *Deut.-Studien*, p. 11, Eng. trans., p. 16.

The actual code (Deut. XII–XXVI) contains religious ordinances (XII. 1–XVI. 17) and civil laws (XVI. 18–XXVI. 15) and agrees in essence with the Book of the Covenant (q.v.). It omits rules regarding compensation and also a number of rulings about the cult, but these deviations from the older models can easily be understood against the background of Deuteronomy's special purpose. It is not a question of the most comprehensive possible collection of all the laws prescribed; here we are concerned with the fundamental basis, with the direction of the whole life of the people towards and according to the will of God. This explains the selection of suitable homiletic material from the old tradition, and also the fact that Deuteronomy contains a whole series of statements concerning spheres of life which have nothing at all to do with the Law as such. This is particularly true of the sections dealing with prophets (Deut. XIII. 1–6) and kings (Deut. XVII. 14–20); and some other instructions which are not attached to any laws, and which therefore cannot be looked upon as explanations or interpretations. Nevertheless these themes are discussed in detail and treated paraenetically, so they must have been matters of some importance at the time of Deuteronomy. The same may be said of the instructions concerning "holy war" (law of war, Deut. XX. 1–9; siege of cities, XX. 10–20; captive wives, XXI. 10–14; camp laws, XXIII. 10–14; exemption of newly married men, XXIV. 5; and the Amalekite law XXV. 17–19).[33] These without doubt belong to an older version but have been interpreted and brought up to date in the sense of Deuteronomy. In the sections on unsolved murder (Deut. XXI. 1–9) and on the offering of the firstfruits (Deut. XXVI. 1–11) we are again undoubtedly dealing with older material.

Like the introduction, the conclusion of the Code has been expanded and amplified far beyond its original content (Deut. XXVII. 9 f. XXVIII. 1–68, XXX. 15–20). This is evident from the new beginning (Deut. XXIX. 1), from the new idea of a holy covenant in the land of Moab (Deut. XXIX), and finally from the consolation speech (Deut. XXX. 1–4) with its reference to exilic conditions (v. 3). As in the introduction, the reason for expansion here will lie in the reading aloud of the Law. So Deuteronomy appears as the outcome of a long process of

[33] Cf. particularly von Rad, *Deut.-Studien*, p. 11, Eng. trans., p. 16.

development, in which all manner of regulations and sermon-like instructions have crystallised round one nucleus.

Opinions vary as to how it came into being. That it cannot have originated with Moses is immediately apparent from the contents, for the cultural and religious conditions do not correspond with the period when individual tribes were wandering in the wilderness, but presuppose a state ruled over by a king. If the whole thing is represented as a speech written and made by Moses, that is a favourite stylistic archaism adopted to give the book more dignity and weight. In addition, however, the theological intention must not be overlooked; namely a return to the old Yahweh religion which had existed before the settlement in Palestine. The opinion is widely held that this book is a piece of trickery; that it was composed by the circles surrounding the High Priest Hilkiah and skilfully manœuvred by them, when the opportunity presented, into the hands of King Josiah.[34] But since Deuteronomy also contains laws which are not directly applicable to that period but reflect older traditions, one must reject this theory and ascribe a greater age to the book. At all events it did not originate earlier than the eighth century B.C., for the prophets of the time condemned only the silver and golden images (Hos.; Is., xxx. 22, xxxi. 7), and were not yet inspired with Deuteronomy's radical attack on Mazzebah and Asherah. Similarly, it can hardly be dated before Hezekiah, in whose religious reform there was as yet no idea of centralising the cult in Jerusalem. The book, however, originated very shortly afterwards, that is at the beginning or in the middle of the seventh century B.C.[35]

[34] For this assumption of mystification, which was very widely held at one time, see H. Schmidt, *Die grossen Propheten*, 2nd edn., Göttingen 1923, p. 183. For the contrary view see Rudolph, *Jeremia*, p. 53; V. Maag, "Erwägungen zur deuterono-mischen Kultzentralisation," in *Vetus Testamentum*, henceforth cited as *Vet. test.*, VI. (1956), pp. 10–18; Walker, "The date of Deuteronomy," in *Vet. test.*, III (1953), pp. 413–14.

[35] For the date of writing cf. von Rad, *Deut.-Studien*, p. 47, Eng. trans., p. 66 f. G. R. Berry, "The date of Deuteronomy," in *J. Bib. Lit.*, LIX (1940), pp. 133–9; W. A. Irwin, "An objective criterion for the dating of Deuteronomy," in *American Journal of Semitic Languages and Literatures*, henceforth cited as *A.J.S.L.*, LVI (1939), pp. 337–49; J. N. Schofield, "The significance of the Prophets for dating Deutero-nomy," in *Studies in History and Religion presented to Dr H. Wheeler*, ed. E. A. Payne, London 1942, pp. 44–60; J. P. Hyatt, "Jeremiah and Deuteronomy," in *Journal of Near Eastern Studies*, henceforth cited as *J.N.E.S.*, I (1942), pp. 153–73; H. H.

The local priests are generally considered to have been the authors of the document. Here, however, it is important not to look only at the religious and cultic side of Deuteronomy: the fact that it is inspired to a great extent by a warlike spirit and supported by a national desire to make a new beginning must also be borne in mind. So in addition to the local Levites the local aristocracy will also have made a decisive contribution as supporters of a restoration movement. King Josiah made Deuteronomy a national law code and pledged himself and his people thereon to a new covenant with God—a pledge very soon forgotten by his successors.

This is not the end of Deuteronomy's importance. It provides a summary of the whole faith of the people, and the thoughts expressed in it had a decisive influence on the whole religious life and piety of the succeeding period. Deuteronomy has not incorrectly been called "the centre of the Old Testament." With it begins a new epoch in Old Testament religion. The turning point is recognisable superficially in the great emphasis laid on "this day"—a phrase which occurs more frequently here than in any other scripture of the Old Testament. With these words a new beginning is made between Yahweh and the people, and at the same time a centuries-long story of divine guidance and human disobedience to God is regarded as simply non-existent. Deuteronomy links up directly with the events on the mountain of God's revelation on the one hand, while the relationship with the celebration of the divine covenant at Shechem is outlined on the other. Deuteronomy, with its commandment to love God and one's neighbour, seems to relate in part to the older prophets, but here we have neither the heights of the old prophetic writings nor the profound fulfilment of the New Testament. Deuteronomy extends only to keeping the commandments and to worshipping Yahweh as opposed to other gods: it does make isolated references to loving one's neighbour, but this is not the deep-rooted principle which determines the whole mutual relationship between man and man. Deuteronomy, moreover, does more than purge the cult, which is not only reformed but even sanctified. And so

Rowley, "The Prophet Jeremiah and the Book of Deuteronomy," in *Studies in Old Testament Prophecy, presented to Professor Theodore H. Robinson*, ed. H. H. Rowley, Edinburgh 1950, pp. 157–74.

from this time onwards the cult is given a primary, indeed a decisive significance in the religious life of the people. This is the beginning of the movement which the prophet Jeremiah so bitterly opposed (Jer. VII. 4); the movement which led and was bound to lead in time to overestimation of the cult, and therefore to the destruction and alienation of individual piety.

This book of the law, this Deuteronomy together with its later additions and extensions (Deut. v–xxx), has been fitted as an established unit into a framework provided by chs. I–IV and XXXI–XXXIV.[36] Originally this framework had nothing at all to do with Deuteronomy, even although its introduction retains the speech form peculiar to the book of the law. Its character is different: here we are concerned not with laws, but with history. One gains the impression throughout that what is reported here is reported for the sake of the events themselves. So this framework turns out to be the beginning of the great traditional work commonly referred to as the Deuteronomic History. The great historical account covers the books from Joshua to II Kings. It begins with the departure from the mountain of God's revelation and ends with the decline of the kingdom of Judah. For its content it utilises the most varied source material: this—after any discrepancies have been sorted out—is taken over as intact and in as much detail as possible and fused into the whole.[37] One might make an objection of the fact that at the beginning of this historical work exactly the same speech form is maintained as in Deuteronomy. This may have been dictated not only by a special preference of the author for speeches in general, but above all by the intention to provide a smooth transition to Deuteronomy which he wanted to incorporate in his work exactly as he found it. The author begins with introductory geographical details, setting his work in Transjordan (Deut. I. 1–5), and then returns to the speech form for the departure from Mount Horeb (Deut. I. 6–8), the dividing up of the tribes, and the appointment of officials and judges (I. 9–18). He reports the journey through the wilderness and, in great detail, the

[36] Cf. Noth, *Überlief. Stud.* pp. 12 ff., 93 f.; I. Engnell, *Gamla Testamentet. En traditionshistorisk inledning*, Stockholm 1945, p. 246 f.

[37] According to Noth, *Überlief. Stud.* p. 99, the one instance of a conscious correction to the copy before him is his interpretation of the story of Saul's elevation to the throne.

sending out of spies and the sojourn in Kadesh (I. 19–46). There follow the journey into Transjordan through Edomite and Moabite territory (II. 1–25), and, after the victory over the Kings Sihon of Heshbon (II. 26–37) and Og of Bashan (III. 1–11), the distribution of the conquered land (III. 12–17) to two and a half tribes who are pledged to give support in war when the country west of the Jordan is occupied in the future (III. 18–22). This material reminds us forcibly of the accounts given in the other great sources of the Pentateuch, particularly the Elohist. But closer comparison, especially of the geographical data, leads one to conclude that the Deuteronomist had access to other traditional material. It is very questionable whether the warnings to obey the commandments (Deut. IV), which however do not form a unit in themselves, also belong to the original; the more so when the train of thought followed so far is later resumed (Deut. XXXI). Here Joshua is again appointed by Moses as his successor, the Law is put down in writing, and its public reading commanded (XXXI. 1–15*, 24–6*). The end is reached with the death of Moses (XXXIV. 1–6*).

In parts this final section is very much padded out and revised. The Blessing of Moses (Deut. XXXIII), standing as it does on its own, appears to be an interloper. It is framed within a hymn-like psalm fragment (XXXIII. 2–5, 26–9) from the post-exilic period. Very little that is definite can be said about the Blessing itself. The references to the individual tribes (vss. 1, 6–25) remind us of the Blessing of Jacob (Gen. XLIX); but comparison shows that the Blessing of Moses was made under different conditions. For example, Simeon is completely absent and Reuben is of only minor importance, while Levi appears as the tribe of priests. In its present form the statement about Levi (vss. 8–11) with its allusions to P[38] would seem to belong to post-exilic times. The other individual blessings will date from all periods, perhaps from the early monarchy or even earlier.

Parallel to the Blessing in certain respects is another great

[38] Thus Pfeiffer, *Introduction*, p. 279, taking into consideration the Urim and Thummin (Ex. XXVIII. 30; Lev. VIII. 8), to which Deut. XXXIII. 8 refers only vaguely, and the confused allusions to Num. XVI, while vs. 9 probably represents a reminiscence of Ex. XXXII. 27–9. Eissfeldt, *Einleitung*, p. 274, on the other hand, traces the differences with Gen. XLIX. 5–7 back to two different social strata.

interpolation, the "Song of Moses" (Deut. xxxii. 1–43), which to a certain extent is fitted into the body of the work[39] by some isolated references to it (Deut. xxxi. 19–22, 28–30, xxxii. 44). Here we are dealing with a psalm from the early post-exilic period which shows a certain relationship with Trito-Isaiah and proclaims the destruction of the hostile mixed population of the promised land and the glorification of Israel.

That traces of revision may be found elsewhere[40] need not surprise us. For the redaction of the Pentateuch by the priests included the beginning of the Deuteronomic history, but only in so far as it was of interest to their own account—that is, down to the death of Moses. The best place to insert it seemed to be towards the end with their own account of the death of Moses, which is now reported twice by the pen of the priest-redactor and embraces as it were the adopted Deuteronomic section; in so doing the second priestly account is worked in with that of the Deuteronomist on the same theme. On the other hand, a reciprocal effect could not be avoided, and so the Deuteronomic version has likewise, in parts,[41] influenced the remainder of the Pentateuch.

The complete historical work of the Deuteronomist must have originated in the middle of the sixth century B.C., that is at a time when Israel and Judah had already disappeared from the picture as states. The use of certain local traditions of Mizpah and Bethel lead us to suppose that the account was written in that neighbourhood.[42] It is to the special credit of the Deuteronomist that from his account, and his alone, we derive quite a detailed knowledge of the history of his people. His work is the more valuable as it has committed to writing, in some detail and with great faithfulness, large parts of the sources

---

[39] Cf. K. Budde, *Das Lied Moses Deut.* 32 *erläutert und übersetzt*, Tübingen 1920; E. Sellin, "Wann wurde das Moselied Dtn. 32 gedichtet?" in *Z. alttest. W.*, XLIII (1925), pp. 161–73; P. W. Skehan, "The structure of the Song of Moses in Deuteronomy (Deut. xxxii. 1–43)," in *Catholic Biblical Quarterly*, henceforth cited as *C.B.Q.*, XIII (1951), pp. 153–63, supposes good transmission of the text and an early date of origin; E. Baumann, "Das Lied Mosis (Dtn. xxxii, 1–43) auf seine gedankliche Geschlossenheit undersucht," in *Vet. test.*, VI (1956), pp. 414–24.

[40] Deut. xxxi. 14–15, 23, xxxii. 48–52, xxxiv. 1–12.

[41] Ex. xii. 24–7, xiii. 1–16, xxxii. 7–14; Num. xxi. 33–5 is a secondary excerpt from Deut. iii. 1–3.

[42] Cf. Noth, *Überlief. Stud.* pp. 97, 110.

at his disposal. But he was not only a collector or editor: he organised his material in the light of one uniform, fundamental idea. That he includes Deuteronomy in his historical work, and that he passes on the account of the finding of the laws (II Kings XXII. 3–XXIII. 3) and excerpts from the annals concerning Josiah's reform of the cult (II Kings XXIII. 4–15, 19, 20a), shows the enormous importance he ascribed to this "book of the law." On this basis he comes to terms with the great political catastrophe of his people; and from the basis of his religious beliefs he considers the history of Israel, which to him is synonymous with a progressive turning away from the will of God, which was bound to lead to the decline and final destruction of its people. So he demonstrates in the course of events the judgment of God, which to him is conclusive and final. Thoughts about the power of God in the future are but few (I Kings VIII. 41–3, 60, IX. 7–9); in this the Deuteronomist differs from the prophets of his day (Deutero-Isaiah and Ezekiel). His gaze is directed mainly from the present into the past.

VARIOUS FRAGMENTS

Although we have divided up the Pentateuch tradition according to the major sources, traced the redaction by the priests and the historical work of the Deuteronomist, and recognised the manifold later additions and supplements the question of the development of the Pentateuch is not yet exhausted. A few fragments remain, which are small in size and for whose date of origin no clues exist. Thus the Song of Lamech (Gen. IV. 23 f.), which is evidently not Israelite, may already have been adopted by the Bedouin of the wilderness before the time of Moses. The so-called Priestly Blessing (Num. VI. 24–6), with its peculiar diction, also has very archaic features. The individual short statements in Numbers XXI—the Song of the Well (vs. 17 f.), the Song of Sihon (vss. 27–9), and the citing of the camping places (vs. 14 f.)—leave an impression of archaism and are best placed in the period before the advance of Israel out of the wilderness towards Palestine. The Ark Formula (Num. X. 35 f.) is also often attributed to this period, but in the light of I Sam. IV–VI it would perhaps be more correctly placed in the age of the Judges or of David, just as the oath against

Amalek (Ex. XVII. 16) is best explained in the time of Saul or
David. The Blessing and Curse of Noah (Gen. IX. 25–7), in
which the Philistines[43] are surely to be understood by Japheth,
presuppose the subjection of the Canaanites and the rise of the
Philistines and so can hardly have originated before the
eleventh century B.C. (Judges era); perhaps, however, they did
not exist until David's day, when the Canaanite city-states
were done away with and the Philistines obtained certain
rights. It is probable that the statements about Esau (Gen.
XXV. 22 f., XXVII. 39 f.) and the blessing of Jacob (Gen. XXVII.
27–9) belong to the period of the Edomite subjection, while
the other oracular statements in Genesis about the founders of
the race[44] will originate from a somewhat earlier period
(Judges or I Kings).

In addition there are a few other more considerable fragments which stand out from their surroundings and cannot
possibly have belonged originally to any of the larger sources.
Foremost in this category is the blessing of Jacob (Gen. XLIX.
3–27),[45] a collection of oracles about each of his twelve sons,
who are synonymous with the tribes of Israel (vs. 28). The
poem, as far as content is concerned, is cleverly attached to the
E story of the blessing of Joseph's sons Ephraim and Manasseh,
but the new introduction (Gen. XLIX. 1 f.), and also the words
of the blessing of Joseph, show that this collection does not
belong in the context. Neither do the presupposed circumstances correspond with the content. For these words do not
look forward into the future as one would expect with a
blessing, but in many cases (vss. 9, 15, 23 f.) they point clearly
backwards, into the past. It is true that the first three statements, which however are more like curses than blessings,
refer to events in the time of Jacob; but the majority presuppose events which took place during the occupation of
Palestine. Because of the irregular form, and the fact that, for

---

[43] Thus von Rad, *Das erste Buch Mose*, VOL. II, p. 114 f., where he discusses other
views (E. Meyer, Procksch).

[44] Abraham oracles: Gen. XII. 2–3, 7, XIII. 14–17; Isaac: Gen. XXVI. 4; Jacob:
Gen. XXVIII. 13–14; Joseph: Gen. XLVIII. 21–2.

[45] J. Coppens, "La Bénédiction de Jacob. Son cadre historique à la lumière des
parallèles ougaritiques," in *Vet. test.*, Suppl. IV (1957), pp. 97–115; J. Lindblom,
"The political background of the Shiloh oracle," in *Vet. test.*, suppl. I (1953),
pp. 78–87.

example, several statements have been transmitted concerning Judah and Dan, one is forced to the conclusion that these are tribal oracles which originally circulated separately. The secretive, allusive rather than detailed nature of the statements gives few clues as to their date origin: Palestine, however, is already assumed as the place of residence. In addition, mention is made of Simeon and Benjamin and of Zebulon's home by the sea which is correct for the era of Judges, but not for that of the Kings (cf. Josh. xix. 10–16). Definite viewpoints have certainly influenced the collecting and grouping, because the sons of Leah are presented first, then the sons of the two maids, and then those of Rachel. The intention behind this grouping seems to be to emphasise and explain the leading role of Judah. Since the prophecy concerning Judah can only have obtained its present form in the time of David, it is probable that individual statements in the form in which we know them were first collected under Solomon.

A poem of quite different character is the Song of Moses and the people at the Red Sea (Ex. xv. 1–18).[46] According to the extant text, it was sung by Moses and the children of Israel after their miraculous escape from Egypt. Certainly God's great deed is praised here in the form of a hymn, telling how the Lord in His omnipotence destroyed the pursuing enemy with the sea. But the remainder of the contents shows how much time has passed since that event, because the song goes on to tell of God's gracious guidance through the wilderness, of the great terror which seized "the inhabitants of Philistia . . . the chiefs of Edom . . . the leaders of Moab . . . and all the inhabitants of Canaan" when they were confronted with the "great arm of the Lord," and of "thy own mountain, the place, O Lord, which thou hast made for thine abode, the sanctuary, O Lord, which thy hands have established," and concludes in jubilant praise of God's everlasting kingdom. The song, therefore, is aware not only of the beginning of the journey through the wilderness and the passage through the Red Sea, but also of its end, the occupation of land east and west of the

---

[46] Cf. A. Bender, "Das Lied Exodus xv," in Z. alttest. W., xxiii (1903), pp. 1–48; H. Schmidt, "Das Meerlied Ex. xv. 2–9," in Z. alttest. W., xlix (1931), pp. 59–66; M. Rozelaar, "The Song of the Sea," in Vet. test., ii (1952), pp. 221–8; F. M. Cross and D. N. Freedman, "The Song of Miriam," in J.N.E.S., xiv (1955), pp. 237–50.

Jordan; and it can also refer to the building of the Temple and the centralisation of the cult. The suggestion has been made that we are to understand by this the second Temple, which was built in the days of the prophets Haggai and Zechariah; but there are no grounds for placing the song in this post-exilic period.[47] A nearer estimate would be the later monarchy. As the song contains a festival cantata for the Passover, we may assume that it originates from the reign of Josiah, in which the Feast of the Passover obtained a new significance (cf. II Kings XXIII. 22). The song has been inserted here because of the ancient Victory Song of Miriam (vs. 21), whose theme it treats in greater detail. Its religious strength lies in the fact that it disregards all human action—even in the occupation of the promised land—and ascribes all the honour to God alone.

Of the historical material, the "Battle of the Kings" (Gen. XIV)[48] is a completely independent and isolated tale rather inadequately (vss. 13, 24) linked up with the preceding narrative. It concerns five kings of the region around the Dead Sea: according to the text, they served Chedorlaomer, King of Elam, for twelve years but are now willing to do so no longer. Accordingly Chedorlaomer, in company with three other kings from the east, undertakes a punitive expedition against them. Chedorlaomer conquers a number of the original tribes of the land, and his victory over the kings is decisive. We hear no more about three of them, but we do learn that the Kings of Sodom and Gomorrah were able to flee, but apparently perished in the bitumen pits. Lot, with all his possessions, falls

---

[47] Thus A. Bender, "Das Lied Ex. xv"; Pfeiffer follows him—*Introduction*, p. 281: "second half of the 5th century." The later monarchical period is supported by Eissfeldt, *Einleitung*, p. 238; E. Sellin, *Einleitung in das Alte Testament*, henceforth cited as *Einleitung*, 8th edn., ed. L. Rost, Heidelberg 1950, p. 36; G. Beer, *Exodus*, Tübingen 1939, p. 84.

[48] J. Meinhold, *I. Mose* 14. *Eine historisch-kritische Untersuchung*, Beihefte z. *Z. alttest. W.*, No. 22, Giessen 1911; F. M. T. Böhl, "Die Könige von Genesis XIV," in *Z. alttest, W.*, XXXVI (1916), pp. 65–73; id., "Tud'alia I, Zeitgenosse Abrahams um 1650 v. Chr.," in *Z. alttest. W.*, XLII (1924), pp. 148–53; id., *Das Zeitalter Abrahams*, Leipzig 1930; id., *King Hammurabi of Babylon in the Setting of his Time*, Amsterdam 1946, pp. 16–18; J. H. Kroeze, *Genesis veertin; een exegetisch-historische studie*, Hilversum 1937; H. Hellbardt, *Das Alte Testament und das Evangelium. Melchisedek*, Munich 1938; A. Vaccari, "Melchisedec, rex Salem, proferens panem et vinum (Gen. XIV. 18)," in *Verbum Domini*, XVIII (1938), pp. 208–14, 235–43; W. F. Albright, "A fixed date in early Hebrew history," in *Bulletin of the American Schools of Oriental Research*, henceforth cited as *B.A.S.O.R.*, LXXXVIII (1942), pp. 33–6.

into the hands of the Elamites. When Abraham hears this news from one who has escaped, he sets out with a small army of 318 of his servants and pursues the enemy as far as Dan. There he routs and scatters them far to the north of Damascus, and thus succeeds in freeing Lot. He is also able to restore part of his possessions to the King of Sodom, an action which specially exemplifies Abraham's noble and worthy disposition. A small episode (Gen. xiv. 18–20) is inserted into this story: a previously unknown king, Melchizedek, King of Salem, who, it is parti-cularly impressed upon us, was also a priest, comes to meet the victorious Abraham bearing bread and wine with which to bless him and "God Most High." In return Abraham gives him a tenth of everything (meaning, no doubt, of all his booty). Having discarded the once favoured but problematic equation Amraphel = Hammurabi, one can relate the names of the Kings of the east to some extent to Hittite and Mitanni names from the middle of the second millennium B.C. The absence of the name of the King of Bela is, however, striking. Another strange feature is that the names of the three men, Aner, Eshcol, and Mamre are the names of places, while place names like Dan instead of Laish, and En-mishpat (fountain of judgment), do not fit in with the times of Abraham but rather indicate Moses (Ex. xvii. 7), or indeed even the age of the Judges (Jg. xviii. 29). Many other questions and problems arise from this story. Why are four great rulers called to arms against the Kings of five small city-states? Why do they not make war immediately and directly against those who have been disloyal, instead of first attacking all the states round about them? Why do the victors withdraw as if in flight, at such a speed that they are far away to the north before Abraham can catch them up? Why does Abraham take so long to come to Lot's assistance? How is a great victory achieved without any mention of divine intervention in the battle? What is the origin of the strange number 318, which corre-sponds to the numerical value of the name Eliezer (Gen. xv. 2)? Why does Melchizedek come to meet Abraham, who is he, and where is this Salem for which some want to read Jerusalem? Why is Abraham described as "the Hebrew" (vs. 13)? From the original text it is not immediately clear who gives whom the tithe. Why do we learn nothing of the fate of the other three city-state kings? Why is the information about the fate of the King of Sodom so vague? Why is Abraham's behaviour towards him so noble, when Sodom in all other respects is an object of loathing? So much of the detail of this chapter still remains obscure. It is hardly doing the facts justice to regard the whole simply as late Jewish legend. Undoubtedly it is a case of individual fragments from a valuable old tradition being cemented together, but we have no information as to the age of the fragments and the date of their unification. The main difficulty in the way of understanding this chapter lies in determining what is the main point of the story. It is certainly not the kings from the east: indeed, it is highly questionable whether the sentences referring to them (vss. 1, 4–9, 15, 17) are not an elaboration of different material inserted in order to bring in Abraham, taking a hand in the course of the world's history. The meaning of the original text would suggest rather (vs. 2) that it began as a war between the Kings of Admah, Zeboiim, and Bela on the one hand and Sodom and Gomorrah on the other, and that Abraham appeared to the conquered as their saviour and liberator. That might bring many of the open questions nearer to solution. But the core and deeper meaning of the chapter lies in the meeting of Abraham and Melchizedek, when Melchizedek blesses Abraham and Abraham reciprocates by giving him the tithe. His descendants were to act similarly towards the priest-king of Jerusalem. In Ps. cx. 4 we read "You are a priest for ever after the order of Melchizedek"—a statement incomprehensible in itself, which has found its classical interpretation in the Epistle to the Hebrews. There the priesthood after the order of Melchizedek is valued far above that of the Levites (Heb. vii), and his counterpart in the New Testament is considered to be Jesus Christ (Heb. v. 6, vi. 20, vii. 17, 21). For the date of origin we must again have recourse to supposition. While the majority of scholars consider the chapter as a late Midrasch,[49]

[49] "A very late and unreliable product," S. Mowinckel, *Psalmenstudien, III, Kultprophetie und prophetische Psalmen*, Kristiania 1923, p. 92. Pfeiffer, *Introduction*, p. 162, on the other hand, ascribes Gen. xiv (with the exception of the Melchizedek episode) to his assumed S source; and Sellin, *Einleitung*, ed. Rost, p. 45, sees in Gen. xiv the translation of a Canaanite memoir from the period round 1500 B.C. which David found in the Jerusalem archives when he took over the city; Rost himself (p. 46) considers the assumption of an early midrash more probable.

opinion has recently tended to ascribe it to the time of David.[50]

In discussing the Priestly Code we mentioned that the Pentateuch, especially Leviticus, contains legal sections which belong to none of the larger sources. Foremost among these is the Law of Holiness (H, Lev. xvii–xxvi),[51] so called because of its preoccupation with the idea of holiness and because of its reverence towards God.[52] That it is a special section of the tradition and a self-contained entity is evident to the reader from its new beginning (Lev. xvii. 1) and particularly from the great final paraenesis (Lev. xxvi) with its summary, "These are the statutes and ordinances and laws which the Lord made between him and the people of Israel on Mount Sinai by Moses" (Lev. xxvi. 46). The structure of the Law of Holiness also indicates its separate nature: like the other great codes, Deuteronomy and the Book of the Covenant, it begins with details about the place for presenting sacrifices, and finishes with exhortations. The contents likewise point to an independent tradition, because the laws here deal, in part, with the same matters as the other sources. For the rest it is very varied, dealing with religious and cultic regulations and with penal laws. Taken as a whole, it is far from being a unity; indeed, it is a typical collection. This is shown by the change in person, or the parallelism between the prohibitions in ch. xviii and the penal laws in ch. xx, which can only be explained by the existence of different sources. The use of different endings[53]

[50] Cf. H. H. Rowley, "Melchizedek and Zadok," in *Festschrift für Alfred Bertholet zum 80. Geburtstag gewidmet*, edd. W. Baumgartner, O. Eissfeldt, K. Elliger, and L. Rost, henceforth cited as *Bertholet-Festschrift*, Tübingen 1950, pp. 461–72.

[51] Cf. S. Küchler, *Das Heiligkeitsgesetz*, Diss., Königsberg 1929; Alt, *Ursprunge;* M. Noth, *Die Gesetze im Pentateuch*, Halle 1940; von Rad, *Deut.-Studien;* J. M. P. Smith, *The Origin and History of Hebrew Law*, Chicago 1931; W. Kornfeld, *Studien zum Heiligkeitsgesetz*, Vienna 1952; L. E. Elliott-Binns, "Some Problems of the Holiness Code," in *Z. alttest. W.*, lxvii. (1955), pp. 26–40; J. Morgenstern, "The Decalogue of the Holiness Code," in *H.U.C.A.* xxvi (1955) pp. 1–27; K. Elliger, "Das Gesetz Leviticus 18," in *Z. alttest. W.*, lxvii (1955) pp. 1–25.

[52] The name "Law of Holiness" originates from A. Klostermann, "Beiträge zur Entstehungsgeschichte des Pentateuchs," in *Zeitschrift für die gesamte lütherische Theologie und Kirche* (1877), pp. 401 ff., having regard to the repeated demand of the Law: "You shall be holy; for I am holy" (Lev. xix. 2, xx. 7, 26, xxi. 6, xxi. 8, xxii. 2); cf. also xi. 44, 45.

[53] As a final formula we find in particular: "For I am Yahweh" (xviii. 5, 6, xix. 12, 14, 16, 18, 28, 32, 37, xxii. 2, 3, 8, 31, xxvi. 2), frequently with the addition of "your God" (xviii. 4, 30, xix. 3, 4, 10, 25, 31, 34, xx. 7, 24, xxiii. 22, 43, xxiv. 22, xxv. 38, 55, xxvi. 1, 13, 44) or with the addition of "who sanctify you"

points in the same direction. The complete absence of these in ch. xvii is striking: since this portion presupposes the centralisation of the cult, it cannot have originated before the time of the exile. The individual rulings about killing and wounding (Lev. xxiv. 17–21) have been inserted later into the story of the man who blasphemes the Lord; nevertheless the whole episode does not fit in here and is quite different in character from the remainder. Instructions about the Sabbath years (Lev. xxv) are now extended to include instructions for the year of jubilee—to such an extent that complete confusion reigns (cf. vss. 11, 20). The greatest impression of completeness and uniformity is given by what is said about priests and sacrifices (Lev. xxi f.), and the calendar of feasts (Lev. xxiii). So the Law of Holiness is revealed as a very complex creation which, as a "collection of smaller collections," has no planned or definite structure. Moreover, the original form has undergone many changes, due to additions made in order to assimilate it to the Priestly Code. As well as being connected with P, it is in some way related to the Book of the Covenant, and in particular to the legal parts of the Book of Ezekiel (Ezek. xl–xlviii). Consequently some have wished to ascribe Ezek. xl–xlviii and the Law of Holiness to the same author.[54] We are still uncertain about the date of origin, but scholars agree that, even though it has been much revised and extended, this is very old traditional material in loose homiletic form, stretching back far into the past and comprising primeval customs and cultic ordinances. It cannot have obtained its final form, however, until about 550 B.C.

What has been said about the Law of Holiness also applies to the Book of the Covenant (Ex. xx. 22–xxiii. 33),[55] which is similar in form and structure. Here too there is the distinction between singular and plural, between apodictic statements and general assumptions, between laws relating to persons and property and cultic directions. Here too the diversity of nature

[54] Pfeiffer, *Introduction*, pp. 241–6, refers in detail to the relationship between the Law of Holiness and Ezekiel.

[55] For literature on the Book of the Covenant, see Bibliography.

(xx. 8, xxi. 8, 15, 23, xxii. 9, 16, 32); cf. also xx. 24–6. Those addressed are the "people of Israel" (xvii 8, xviii. 2, xix. 2, xx. 2, xxiii. 2, 10, 24, 34, 44, xxiv. 2, xxv. 2), along with Aaron (xvii. 2), Aaron alone (xxi. 17) or together with his sons, the priests (xxi. 1, xxii. 2), and Israel (xvii. 2, xxii. 17).

and form points to the existence of several sources, so that it is not one complete, self-contained code of laws which we have before us, but a collection. The principles which governed the arrangement are no longer recognisable. All that can be said is that the beginning and the end consist of cultic regulations regarding images and altars (Ex. xx. 22–6), and contain instructions for feasts and sacrifices (Ex. xxiii. 10–19) which are very similar to the Decalogue of Ex. xxxiv. 14–19; while the middle is filled up on the one hand with mishpat (legal judgments) which have apparently been handed down fairly intact (Ex. xxi. 2–xxii. 16), and on the other with diverse cultic laws in the form of priestly Torah and moral prohibitions (Ex. xxii. 17–xxiii. 9). In addition to its affinity with the Law of Holiness, the Book of the Covenant is clearly linked with the great Old Babylonian legal document, the Codex Hammurabi, and also with Old Assyrian and Hittite laws. It is not, however, directly derived from these laws; the connexion may be traced through Canaanite culture which took over these general oriental laws and handed them on to Israel as the Canaanite Law Code. This supposition is strengthened by the fact that Canaanite city-states surrounded by individual Israelite tribes also belonged, at least in the later period, to the sacral tribal union (amphictyon) (cf. Num. xxvi).[56] But the Book of the Covenant has not simply adopted this Canaanite mishpat (Ex. xxi. 2–11, 18–22, xxi. 28–xxii. 16): it has adapted it[57] to suit its own requirements and ideas, with the inclusion here and there of Israelite mishpat (Ex. xxi. 12, 15–17, xxii. 18–20). The Book of the Covenant, which gets its name from Ex. xxiv. 7, is fitted on to an Elohistic frame, and thus comes under the dignity and authority of the revelation at Sinai. In itself it has nothing at all to do with the events at Sinai. For it presupposes residence in the promised land and also contains simple rules suited to the lives of peasants and shepherds. To judge by the very pronounced interest in the altar and the cult (Ex. xx. 25 ff., xxi. 13*b*, 14*b*, xxiii. 12 ff.) the author or, more correctly, the redactor is no doubt to be sought in the circles of the Israelite priesthood. The date of origin is variously estimated

---

[56] M. Noth, *Das System der zwölf Stämme Israels*, henceforth cited as *System der Stämme*, Stuttgart 1930, pp. 97–100.

[57] A. Jepsen, *Untersuchungen zum Bundesbuch*, Stuttgart 1927, p. 54.

between the time of Joshua and the seventh century B.C.[58] Since the Book of the Covenant says nothing about the centra-lisation of the cult, the final redaction must have been completed before the reforms of Josiah. As in other cases, this editorial work would include addition and revision, particularly on the part of the redactor responsible for uniting the original J and E. Are the prescriptions for altars of unhewn stone directed against Solomon? And do they allude to any definite precedent at all? We do not know. At all events, it can be said that the Book of the Covenant contains much old material. Since no king is named (cf. the tribal rulers in Ex. XXII. 28), no strict organisation is evident, and fixed taxes are not mentioned, the most probable time for the origin of this section is between Joshua and Samuel: the best time, indeed, is the period of the formation of the sacral union of the twelve tribes, that is, before Saul's formation of the states in the age of the Judges.[59]

Mention must also be made of the Ten Commandments (Decalogue; Ex. xx. 1–17)[60] which occur shortly before the above passage, and which many would like to attribute to an Elohist stratum. The lack of connexion with what follows, however (Ex. xx. 18 ff.), shows in itself that the Decalogue is a self-contained section. It deals not with actual laws, but with religious and moral instructions. Comparison with its repeti-tion in Deut. v. 6–18 shows differences of some magnitude, especially in the commandment relating to the Sabbath. Both versions, however, make it clear that the Decalogue has not been handed down in its original form. The original, as can still be seen in several places, would be restricted to quite short and lapidary sentences, while the present versions belong in part to the very detailed formulation of a later period. Some of these commandments are only comprehensible against the

---

[58] A. Jirku, *Das weltliche Recht im Alten Testament*, Gütersloh 1927, wants to trace the Book of the Covenant back to Moses but, at the most, the "wilderness period" could be the origin of the Israelite Mishpat and moral laws. Jirku's attempt comes to grief on the fact that the adoption of Canaanite Mishpat into the Book of the Covenant would not then be completely comprehensible: cf. also Jepsen, *Unter-suchungen zum Bundesbuch*, p. 98. A. Menes, *Die vorexilischen Gesetze Israels im Zusam-menhang seiner Kulturgeschichtlichen Entwicklung*, henceforth cited as *Die vorexilischen Gesetze*, Beihefte z. Z. alttest. W., No. 50, Giessen 1928, seeks to interpret the Book of the Covenant as the document of the Jehu revolution, while Eissfeldt, *Einleitung*, pp. 249 ff., stressing the primary position occupied by the altar laws, dates it around 700 B.C.

[59] For literature, see Bibliography.

background of a settled life. There are connexions with the Law of Holiness; in addition attempts have been made to find allusions to the Decalogue in Jeremiah (Jer. VII. 9) and Hosea (Hos. IV. 2, 6, VIII. 12). There is great divergence of opinion on the date of origin, varying from Moses to the exile. Some see the Decalogue as the product of the religious sterility of this late period.[60] However, it is widely admitted that old texts are present in these commandments. It is very probable that we have here the beginnings of an Israelite legal code, which appears as the absolute command of God and which, as one concludes from Deut. XXXI. 9–13, was read aloud as divine law in holy places at the Feast of Tabernacles, in order "that they may hear and may learn to fear the Lord your God, and be careful to do all the words of this law, and that their children, who have not known it, may hear and learn to fear the Lord your God." The origin and development of the Decalogue remains obscure. Is tradition right in tracing the Ten Commandments back to Moses? This question is not of fundamental importance. It is more important that purely legal demands are suppressed in these Ten Commandments and are replaced by religious and moral content. This is what has given the Decalogue its enormous value and its decisive importance, even in the Christian Church, in which the Ten Commandments are included among the most valuable possessions of the faithful—and not only through Luther's eventual formulation and interpretation of them in the spirit of Jesus.

[60] Thus G. Beer, *Exodus*, p. 103. C. Steuernagel, *Lehrbuch der Einleitung in das Alte Testament*, Tübingen 1912, p. 261, and J. Meinhold, *Der Dekalog*, Giessen 1927, p. 15, date the Decalogue in exilic or (like G. Hölscher, *Geschichte der israelitischen und jüdischen Religion*, Giessen 1922, p. 129) in post-exilic times. The usual dating is around 760 B.C. (cf. Menes, *Die vorexilischen Gesetze*, pp. 46 ff.; A. Lods, *Histoire de la littérature*, p. 342; J. Morgenstern in *Universal Jewish Encyclopaedia*, ed. I. Landman, VOL. III, New York 1941, p. 510); but present research is tending more towards considering the possibility of Mosaic authorship; cf. F. M. T. Bohl, *Exodus*, Groningen 1928, pp. 145 f.; L. Kohler, "Der Dekalog," in *Th. R.*, 1 (1929), pp. 161–84; A. Eberharter, *Der Dekalog;* W. Rudolph, *Der Aufbau von Exodus XIX-XXXIV*, Beihefte z. Z. alttest. W., No. 66, Berlin 1936, p. 43; A. C. Welch, *Deuteronomy: the Framework to the Code*, London 1932, p. 192; A. Weiser, *Einleitung in das Alte Testament*, henceforth cited as *Einleitung*, 2nd edn., Göttingen 1949, pp. 94 ff.; A. Bentzen, *Introduction to the Old Testament*, VOL. II, Copenhagen 1949, p. 55; S. Spiegel, "A prophetic attestation of the Decalogue; Hos. VI. 5, with some observations on Psalms XV and XXIV," in *Harvard Theological Review*, henceforth cited as *H.T.R.*, XXVII (1934), pp. 105–44, esp. pp. 140 ff.; M. Buber, *Moses*, Oxford 1947. H. H. Rowley, *Moses and the Decalogue*, Manchester 1951, now actively supports the Mosaic theory.

CHAPTER III

THE FORMER PROPHETS

The Book of Joshua

THE SECOND PART of the Canon of the Old Testament consists of the Books of Joshua, Judges, Samuel and Kings and records episodes in the history of Israel from the conquest of the land west of the Jordan down to the fall of the Southern Kingdom. Although it is predominantly historical, it bears the name "Former Prophets"; but this is less because it deals prominently with a number of prophetic figures than because, according to the Jewish tradition, the books are said to have been written by prophets.[1] The first of these books[2] is named after the man who on Moses' death succeeded him as leader of the Israelite tribes—Joshua,[3] son of Nun, servant of Moses. Although he appears in this book as a pious leader of the people, it is striking how little he is noticed elsewhere in the Bible. Apart from the allusion to his cursing of Jericho (1 Kings XVI. 34) and a general time reference "from the days of Joshua" (Neh. VIII. 17), the only mention is that he brought the tabernacle into the land (Acts VII. 45); likewise the contents of the book are only occasionally referred to (Acts VII. 16; Heb. XIII. 5). Nowhere in the book itself do we read that Joshua is the author: indeed, the laudatory statement (VI. 27) that throughout his life all Israel feared him as it had feared Moses (IV. 14), and the description of his death (XXIV. 29 f.), rather militate against such an assumption. The observation: "Joshua wrote these words in the book of the law of God" (XXIV. 26) can only refer to the statutes of the assembly at Shechem and not to the book as a whole.

The Book of Joshua appears to be part of a larger corpus,

---

[1] According to the Talmud Baba bathra, fol. 14–15, the Book of Joshua stems from Joshua, Judges and the Books of Samuel from Samuel, and the Books of Kings from Jeremiah; cf. Goldschmidt, *Talmud*, VOL. VIII, p. 56.

[2] For commentaries and literature see Bibliography, also notes 6 and 7 below.

[3] In the Septuagint the name Jehoshuah appears in the shortened form Jeshua, as in Neh. VIII. 17 (=Jesus; cf. Mt. I. 16).

because its end (xxiv. 28 ff.) is taken up again in Judges (II. 6 ff.) and its beginning links up with the end of the fifth Book of Moses (Deut. xxxiv. 5, 9). Its whole content too is closely bound up with what has gone before; for what was given to the Fathers in the Pentateuch as a hope and a promise here achieves reality and fulfilment—the possession of the Promised Land. And indeed one of the first sections (chs. II–XII) reports on individual events during the struggle for possession. After an introduction (ch. I) which aims at establishing a connexion with Deuteronomy (Deut. v. 28 f., xxxi. 7) and deals with the calling of Joshua (cf. Num. xxviii. 17 ff.) and his assumption of office, the actual story of the conquest begins with the sending out of spies across the Jordan into the area around Jericho. They get into the town itself, and escape imminent capture only through the help of Rahab, in return for which they pro- mise that the occupants of her house will be spared in the coming battle (ch. II). After their return the tribes strike camp: from Shittim (cf. Num. xxv. 1, xxxiii. 49) they cross the Jordan to the west bank, where at Gilgal (as if in the Jordan itself) they set up twelve stones (chs. III–IV) as a memorial and cele- brate the Passover (v. 10–12). Starting with the words "at that time" (v. 2), an account concerning circumcision is loosely inserted: it does not fit into the context and aims at explaining the name Gilgal (v. 2–9). Another insertion is the disconnected account of a visionary experience of Joshua's (v. 13 f.), which is only a fragment, for the main point, the content of the revelation, is missing and a sentence taken from Moses' vision of the burning bush (Ex. III. 5) has been added in vs. 15. The tribes march round the city of Jericho in complete and terrifying silence for six days: on the seventh day it is overcome and burned down. Everything is destroyed, men and animals alike. Only the family of Rahab is spared and still lives there "to this day" (vi. 25). But before the story (vi. 1–27) concludes with the observation "So the Lord was with Joshua, and his fame was in all the land" (vi. 27), a curse on Jericho is inserted (vi. 26).

The course of events, however, is by no means as simple and as clear as would at first appear. Obscure and questionable parts abound. Thus the "three days" in the introduction (I. 11) do not agree with what follows. From the sign in the window (II. 18) one must conclude that the town was taken by treachery; but no more is said of this afterwards, just as there is no essential connexion between the story of the spies and the capture of Jericho. What was the meaning of the trumpets (VI. 8) in a silent circuit of the town? It is also not clear where the stones were actually erected—in the Jordan, at Gilgal, or both. Why was circumcision undertaken at a time so unsuitable from a military point of view? The hill Gibeath-haareloth (hill of the foreskins, v. 3) alludes to a sanctuary about which we learn absolutely nothing.

Thus many questions arise which indicate that we are dealing here not with an independent historical report but with a complexity of ætiological tradition. These stories attach to definite places and names. Where did the stone pillars come from? "When your children ask in time to come . . . you shall tell them" (IV. 6, 21). Why is the place called Gilgal? In the legend this strange name is derived from the verb "galal," to roll off, and in connexion with the hill Haraloth it indicates the rolling away of the humiliation of Egypt. Why in the destruction of Jericho did one Canaanite house remain intact? The answer is found in the story of the two spies. What is the origin of the ruins of a great wall at Jericho? The legend knows about God's miraculous intervention. So everything is given a religious interpretation as signs of the might and strength of Yahweh, who stands behind and above all things.

In the long-winded story of the conquest of Ai (chs. VII–VIII) we are also dealing with legendary tradition, relating to a definite place and name and with the aim of "explaining" what still remains "to this day," such as the heap of ruins (VIII. 28), the heap of stones at the gate of the city (VIII. 29), and the heap of stones in the valley of Achor, whose name the story derives from the verb "to confuse, trouble." The same may be said of the voluntary servitude of the Gibeonites: the aim here is to explain why they are "hewers of wood and drawers of water for the . . . altar of the Lord, to continue to this day" (IX. 3–27). Introduced by "then," the building of the altar at Shechem and the public reading of the law are inserted between these two legends (VIII. 30–5). The context and also the fact that Joshua kept his base at Gilgal (X. 6, 15, 43) near Jericho show that this portion must belong to a later

period. The story which follows (x. 1–27), of Joshua's expedition (x. 7, 15) to Gibeon to help the city against five Amorite
kings, reports a great victory and the pursuit of the enemy. The
kings were imprisoned in a cave at Makkedah sealed off with
great stones, which lie there "to this very day" (x. 27). This
legend is bound up with another story, but so closely that the
latter is no longer recognisable in the context. This much is
evident: it is a case of five kings of cities of the south, among
them Jerusalem which at that time was called Jebus (xv. 63).
No more is said about the conquest of Jerusalem as distinct from
the other cities, and the Septuagint, taking offence at this,
has assumed the name of the king, Adoni-zedek, to be synonymous with Adoni-Bezek of Bezek (Jg. 1. 5). Woven into the tale
are a quotation from the Book of Jashar (cf. 11 Sam. 1. 18),
which, however, is handed down only as a fragment out of a
larger context (x. 12 f.), and a short description of Yahweh's
miraculous intervention during the battle and in the flight of
the enemy (vs. 10 f.). There follows a systematic report (x.
28 ff.) in stereotyped phrases reminiscent of Assyrian royal
inscriptions which tells of the further individual successes of
Joshua over the cities of the south, finishing with the words
"Because the Lord God of Israel fought for Israel. Then
Joshua returned, and all Israel with him, to the camp at
Gilgal" (vs. 42 f. = vs. 14 f.). Similar in structure and style is the
succeeding episode from the conquest of Galilee, in which the
use of horses and chariots is particularly emphasised. A
meaningless "at that time" introduces an account of the burning
down of Hazor (xi. 10–15), the importance of which is rightly
judged, and a very succinct report on the conquest of other
Galilean cities. Now a line is drawn below the story and a
summary is given from the Jewish standpoint (xi. 16–20) of
what, to the narrator, amounts to the total conquest of the
land west of the Jordan. As a postscript, linked by the words
"and at that time," we hear of the annihilation of the Anakim
(xi. 21–2): the contents of this version, however, hardly tie up
with the subsequent story of Caleb (xv. 13–19). A long list of
the conquered kings (xii. 7–24)[4] is based initially (vss. 9–13) on
the report of events made in the Book of Joshua up to this point:

---

[4] Cf. M. Noth, *Das Buch Josua*, henceforth cited as *Josua*, Hb. A. T., VOL. VII,
p. 45. 2nd edn., Tübingen 1953.

for the rest, however, it appears to go back to some old list unknown to us. Quite out of place among the achievements of Joshua is the beginning of the list (XII. 1–6), which tells of the conquest of the country east of the Jordan under Moses.

As is evident from the frequent repetitions (XIII. 14, 33, XIV. 3, XVIII. 7), the second part of the book (XIII. 1–XXI. 42), telling of the apportionment of the land among the tribes, is a very composite structure. It is loosely connected with the preceding chapters by its general time reference "Now Joshua was old and advanced in years" (XIII. 1), and, in contrast with their closing remarks (XI. 23), it stresses several times (XIII. 1, XVII. 12) and by name (XV. 63, XVI. 10) the areas which remain in foreign hands "to this day." Standing out as particular episodes from among all the geographical data are the story of Joseph's dissatisfaction with the portion assigned to him (XVII. 16–18, XVII. 14–15) and the business of Caleb's inheritance (XIV. 6–15), to whom Hebron belongs "to this day," with the story of his wedding gift to his daughter (XV. 13–19 = Jg. I. 10–15), local lore which explains why two springs of water belong to the city of Debir rather than to Hebron. The remainder of this part consists of lists and geographical details, which are enormously important for our knowledge of the ancient geography of Palestine.[5] These data are based on two sources: firstly, a system of tribal boundaries[6] which contains a complete partitioning of the whole territory west of the Jordan over and above what is actually possessed by the tribes. This originates from an early period, even before the formation of the Israelite state. The other is a district list of the time of King Josiah,[7] in which the kingdom of Judah is divided up into

---

[5] Cf. M. Noth, "Studien zu den historisch-geographischen Dokumenten des Josuabuches," in *Zeitchrift des deutschen Palästina Vereins*, henceforth cited as *Z.D.P.V.*, LVIII (1938), pp. 185–255. On the basis of results of previous research Noth, *Josua*, pp. 113–22, gives a list of the place names with their modern Arabic identification.

[6] A. Alt, "Das System der Stammesgrenzen im Buche Josua," in *Beiträge zur Religionsgeschichte und Archäologie Palästinas. Ernst Sellin zum 60. Geburtstage darge-bracht*, Leipzig 1927, pp. 13–24; id., "Die Landnahme der Israeliten in Palästina. Territorialgeschichtliche Studien," in *Reformationsprogramm der Universität Leipzig*, 1925, pp. 1–35; cf. M. Noth in *Z.D.P.V.*, LVIII (1935) pp. 185 ff.

[7] A. Alt, "Judas Gaue unter Josia," in *Palästina-Jahrbuch*, henceforth cited as *P. Jb.*, XXI (1925), pp. 108–17; id., "Israels Gaue unter Salomo," in *Alttestamentliche Studien, Rudolf Kittel zum 60. Geburtstag dargebracht*, 1913, pp. 1–19; id., "Bemerkungen zu einigen judäischen Ortslisten des Alten Testaments," in *Z.D.P.V.*, LXVIII (1951),

twelve districts. The merging of these two documents resulted in the ideal apportionment of land of which we read in the Book of Joshua. There follow, like an appendix, two chapters dealing with cities of refuge and Levite cities (xx. 1–xxi. 42).[8]

The material in the third part of the book (xxi. 43–xxiv. 33) is likewise not presented in corrected form. It is linked with the end of the first part, where the Promised Land has been occupied and apportioned and peace reigns (xi. 23), by the assertion that Yahweh has granted peace on all sides and has delivered all their enemies into Israel's hand (xxi. 44). In logical sequence there follows the sending to their homes of the tribes from the other side of the Jordan (xxii. 1–8): this report originates from the same source as the news of their co-operation in the conquest of the land west of the river (i. 11–18). The following verses (xxii. 9–34) recount in detail an episode which explains the name (now no longer there in the very much revised text) of the altar on the Jordan. This altar has the same significance as the stone erected by Joshua (xxiv. 27): it is a witness for Yahweh. Now that Joshua has grown old, his work comes to an end with the assembling of the people at Shechem (xxiv. 1–28). This passage is certainly based on valuable old tradition about the importance of the sanctuary at Shechem. From the historical point of view the Sinai covenant is here extended to all the tribes of Israel and the foundations are solemnly laid for their merging into a sacral union of twelve tribes.[9] To this tradition, to which a shorter parallel has been added by a later hand (xxiii. 2–16), no doubt originally belonged also the mention of Joshua's death and burial (xxiv. 29 f.), and of Eleazar's burial in Gibea of Phinehas (xxiv. 33); but, as the name of the place indicates, the document was probably originally concerned not with Eleazar but with Phinehas. On the other hand, the details about Joseph's grave (xxiv. 32), which are supported by the Pentateuch (Gen. xxxiii. 19; Ex. xiii. 19), give the impression of being a later addition.

[8] Cf. in this connexion Noth, *Josua*, pp. 95–101; M. Lohr, *Das Asylwesen im Alten Testament*, Halle 1930; N. Nicolsky, "Das Asylrecht in Israel," in *Z. alttest. W.*, XLVIII (1930), pp. 146–75.

[9] Cf. Noth, *System der Stämme*; id., *Die Geschichte Israels*, Göttingen 1950, pp. 74–95. pp. 193–210; id., "Festungen und Levitenorte im Lande Juda," in *Kleine Schriften zur Geschichte des Volkes Israel*, VOL. II, Munich 1953, pp. 306–15.

H

To consider now the development of this book, it is evident from what has already been said that we are confronted with a very involved and difficult story of tradition and revision. Because of its intimate connexion with the Pentateuch—for which reason indeed some include the Book of Joshua and speak of a Hexateuch—some scholars apply the sources and individual threads of narrative established for the Pentateuch to the Book of Joshua also. Against this, however, this book contains traditions parallel to the Pentateuch to only a slight extent. Moreover, it is possible to trace material, but not literary relationships with the narrative portions of the Pentateuch, as a comparison of the references (II. 10, IV. 23) to the miracle of the Red Sea with the account in Ex. XIV immediately shows.[10] The whole book is founded on a logical sequence of ideas: crossing the Jordan, headquarters at Gilgal, conquest of Canaan from the Jordan by way of Jericho up into the western mountain region (Ai, Gibeon), from there southwards (chs. II–X), and then to the north (ch. XI); then apportionment of the land (chs. XIII ff.,) and renewal of God's covenant at the assembly at Shechem. A proper picture of the conquest of the whole country, however, is denied us, due to the fragmentary nature of the presentation. Jerusalem, for example, is mentioned but no more is said about it, and the information given us about the taking of Bethel, which was much more important than that of Ai, is more than scant (VIII. 17). There are many indications, however, that we are dealing, especially in the first part of the book, not with historical accounts but with stories which at first circulated independently but were later collected and combined. That is the first stage in the growth

---

[10] Here too Eissfeldt sees the sources J and E and for Josh. I–VII and probably also Josh. XXIV an additional source L. An older Book of Joshua (L+J+E) was the subject of two Deuteronomic redactions one, of which retained the E and L contributions to Josh. XXIV while the other replaced Joshua's farewell speech (XXIV. 1–27) with one of its own (Josh. XXIII); cf. *Einleitung*, pp. 282–6. Lods, *Histoire de la littérature*, p. 118, also suspects several redactions of the book by a Deuteronomistic school. G. Hölscher, "Die Anfänge der hebräischen Geschichtsschreibung," in *Sitzungsberichte der Heidelberger Akademie der Wissenschaften*, 1942, deals only with J, but what he makes out to be J material in the Book of Joshua is very little indeed (parts of Josh. II, VIII, XI, two and a half verses and two part verses from Josh. III–VI), and comes very close (in Josh. II, VI, and VIII) to Simpson's source E. That the separation of the sources is particularly difficult in the case of the Book of Joshua (cf. Pfeiffer, *Introduction*, p. 296) is shown by Simpson's J[1] source to which he ascribes only Josh. IX. 6–7, 14–15.

of the Book of Joshua. The date of the actual work of compilation can be established with relative accuracy. The compiler did not know that Ai was occupied by Israel until the tenth century B.C. (VIII. 28); on the other hand, the usual "to this day" is omitted in the destruction of Hazor (XI. 13), because it had meanwhile been rebuilt by Solomon (1 Kings IX, 15). This collection therefore originated around 900 B.C., and in Judah, because the individually collected legends are almost exclusively concerned with places in the south. The initially independent tradition concerning the assembly at Shechem (basis of Josh. XXIV) was very probably also available to this collector and included by him. Nothing more exact is known, because the text, even in ancient times, underwent much glossing and extension.

This collection, then, was the model for the Deuteronomist, whose task it was to incorporate and assimilate the transmitted material into his great narrative work. To him we owe the portions of the first part which we attributed to "a later hand" (above all Josh. I, VIII. 30–5, XII); and in the third part the concluding remarks, the sending home of the men of the Transjordanian tribes (XXI. 43–XXII. 6) and Joshua's exhortation of the assembled people (ch. XXIII); and particularly the fitting in of the second part (chs. XIII ff.), which had developed separately.

Revision from the priestly standpoint followed at a later date, but so far as we can ascertain this was accompanied by little decisive interference with the text. Apart from certain extensions in ch. XX and the addition of the list of Levite cities (XXI. 1–42), it was restricted to fairly small corrections and additions, in the course of which, above all, the priest Eleazar[11] was brought into the foreground beside Joshua.

It is very doubtful whether Joshua[12] was the great leader from the tribe of Ephraim which the book makes him out to be. It was not in a tremendous warlike enterprise with a general levy from all the tribes, not in a great victorious march from east to west and south to north that the whole area, "all the land," was conquered. The historical truth is quite different. Bit by

[11] Josh. XIV. 1, XVII. 4, XIX. 51, XXI. 1, XXIV. 33.
[12] Cf. A. Alt, *Josua*, Beihefte z. *Z. alttest. W.*, No. 66, Berlin 1936, pp. 13–29, especially pp. 25 f.

bit, in several waves and over the course of centuries, even before Moses and Joshua, individual Israelite tribes had infiltrated into Canaan from the south[13] and settled wherever they could find room between the city-states; that is, in the sparsely populated or even unpopulated mountain regions, where they cleared the forest to make room for themselves (cf. Josh. xvii. 15 f.). The extent to which they permeated the country depended on the strength of the individual city-states. Depending on how far these states were able to resist, Israelite annexation progressed either peacefully (ix. 15) or by warlike action, limited in extent and area, which the Israelites avoided where possible. The memory of the battles still percolates through in a few places.[14] The report of land annexation in Judges 1 is much more sensible and in keeping with the facts. To what extent a last immigrant wave of Israelite tribes under Joshua conquered parts of the land of Canaan by force is difficult to judge from the insufficient source material. The possibility is, however, not to be rejected out of hand, even if the scale of such battles, and especially the success attributed to them, is grossly exaggerated in the report. Here we find ourselves on very insecure ground. The making of the Covenant at Shechem, on the other hand, will be based on a good and reliable tradition, even if it is a long way from amalgamation to a sacral union of tribes and on to the growth of a nation. The beginnings of national history are always—not only in Israel—enveloped in darkness: only legend can tell of them. The pious mind here looks back into the distant past of his people and sees its history filled with the wonderful works of God: indeed, the whole course of that history is one great testimony of His gracious guidance. What God once promised to the forefathers has now been miraculously fulfilled, "Now therefore fear the Lord and serve him in sincerity and faithfulness." That is the covenant with God; seen from the angle of the man and the people, the solemn vow: "As for me and my house, we will serve the Lord" (xxiv. 15).

[13] Especially Caleb and Othniel: cf. Num. xiv. 24 and 1 Sam. xv. 6. Y. Kaufmann, *The Biblical Account of the Conquest of Palestine*, tr. M. Dagut, Jerusalem 1953; O. Eissfeldt, "Die Eroberung Palästinas durch Alt-Israel," in *Welt des Orients*, ii, pt. ii (1955), pp 158–71. Cf. also Noth, *Geschichte Israels*, pp. 65–6.

[14] Josh. xiv. 12, xvi. 10, xvii. 16.

THE BOOK OF JUDGES

After the death of Joshua the Israelite tribes were without any unified leadership until the beginning of the monarchy under Saul. It is of this interim period that the Book of Judges tells.[15] Its title (Ecclesiasticus XLVI. 11) refers only to the main part (II. 6–XVI. 31), which contains the actual history of these judges and is not completely apt; for the book deals not only with judges in the usual sense of the word—about whom we learn very little indeed—but also, and primarily, with warriors and heroes, with charismatic leaders, who appeared as deliverers of their tribe in times of need and oppression.[16] We must bear in mind that the orbit is restricted. The concern is always only with the individual tribe, which suffered greatly at the hands of the original inhabitants and of plundering bands of nomads (cf. the description VI. 2–6). Only occasionally do several tribes join together to wage common war: the Song of Deborah (V. 16 f.) gives only too clear a picture of the disunion and strife in Israel. Since the period of "office" is quoted in the case of some of the judges, the impression might easily be given that their sway extended over Israel as a whole, as if they represent a kind of forerunner of the monarchy. This, however, is not so; not even in the case of Gideon and Abimelech, who had only a closely delimited tribal kingship. Also, the long intervals between the appearance of the individual charismata show that it was not a case of single rulers following one after the other in uninterrupted succession. The Book of Judges offers us not a complete connected account but rather individual pictures, the chronological sequence of which is not absolutely assured. Nevertheless the 480 years which, according to 1 Kings VI. 1, elapsed between the exodus from Egypt and the building of the Temple in the fourth year of Solomon's reign, can be fairly well reconciled with the data of the Book of Judges;[17] although too much value should not be put on these data in view of the repeatedly recurring round figure of forty years' peace.

The introduction of the book (I. 1–II. 5) is intended to link up with the Book of Joshua with its reference to Joshua's death

[15] For commentaries and literature, see Bibliography.
[16] Cf. O. Grether, "Die Bezeichnung "Richter" für die charismatischen Helden der vorstaatlichen Zeit," in *Z. alttest. W.*, LVII (1939), pp. 110–21.
[17] Proof in Noth, *Überlief. Stud.*, pp. 18–27.

(I. 1). Since, however, the end of the Book of Joshua (Josh. xxiv. 28–31) is repeated word for word in Jg. II. 6–9—a strange occurrence which is met with also in Ezra and II Chronicles, for example—it is certain that this point (II. 6) is where the continuation starts. The content of the intervening portion (I. 1–II. 5) reveals that it is not about the period after Joshua's death: the circumstances correspond rather with his lifetime. Contact with some older sections from Joshua is very evident, and the well-known story of the wells of Debir (Josh. xv. 13 ff.) is repeated almost word for word (I. 10–15). The starting point here too seems to be in the vicinity of Gilgal (II. 1) or near "the city of palm trees" (I. 16), by which one generally understands Jericho. This section does not, however, consider events common to all the tribes, but restricts its account to Judah alone (I. 1–4, 8 f., 18–20). Even the mention of Simeon's part in the conquest of Canaan (I. 3, 17) is quite incidental. The report on an episode from the history of the house of Joseph, the taking of Bethel by treachery (I. 21–6), is included less because of the event itself than because the episode belongs to the corpus of popular tradition, which attempts to explain here why, in addition to the well-known Luz which is identical with Bethel, there is a second Luz "to this day" (I. 26). Other material relates to particular names like Adoni-bezek (I. 5 ff.),[18] Hormah (I. 17), and Bochim (II. 1–5). Inserted between these is a fairly long list, apparently imperfectly preserved, of places which have remained in the hands of the original inhabitants (I. 21, 27–35). With its stereotyped repetition "did not drive out" it gives the impression of being a list in which undoubtedly good historical tradition has been preserved. The whole section originates from ancient times.[19] Whether it should be ascribed to one of the Pentateuch sources or to an otherwise unknown tradition of its own cannot be decided with any certainty. At all events, this is old and historically valuable material which breaks into the continuity like a foreign body.

The history proper of the judges (II. 6–XVI. 31) begins with an introduction (II. 6–III. 6), which contains ideas fundamental

[18] This should probably be read instead of "Adoni-Besek."

[19] According to A. Alt, *Die Staatenbildung der Israeliten in Palästina*, henceforth cited as *Staatenbildung*, Leipzig 1930, pp. 11 ff., this list of cities that did not become dependent on Israel till later presupposes the position created by David which, however, Solomon did not maintain.

to the account. A thoughtful and pious mind has taken exception to the fact that Yahweh did not annihilate the heathen and
thus present His people with unrestricted possession of the
Promised Land. But Yahweh acts in this way specifically in
order that Israel shall give proof of its religious loyalty. The
practical aspect of Yahweh's behaviour, viz. that Israel in this
way gains experience in war (III. 2), is mentioned quite by the
way. But the proximity of the heathen and, above all, intermarriage with the native population (III. 6) constitute a standing
temptation to Israel to succumb to the heathen cult and break
faith with Yahweh (II. 22, III. 4). And so the times are not only
troubled politically but full of religious tension. "The people of
Israel did what was evil in the sight of the Lord . . . they
forsook the Lord and served the Baals and the Ashtaroth. So
the anger of the Lord was kindled against Israel, and he gave
them over . . . into the power" of their enemies, who pressed
them sorely (II. 11–15). But "the Lord was moved to pity by
their groaning," and He raised them up judges and "saved
them from the hand of their enemies" (II. 16–18). So they
had a period of peace. But when the judge died, they returned
to their "other gods," thus arousing Yahweh's anger anew
(II. 19–20). Periods of defection from Yahweh are periods of
oppression and want, return to Yahweh is rest and peace.
From this special religious angle the history of the period of the
judges is presented as a faithful mirror of Israel's behaviour
towards Yahweh. So the history of Israel seesaws in constant
alternation between defection and conversion, between oppression and peace.

The following pages summarise the contents of the stories of
the judges and reveal the historical pattern.

> The people of Israel forget Yahweh and serve
> Canaanite gods. This enrages Yahweh and
> he causes them to serve under King Cushan-
> rishathaim for eight years (III. 7 f.).

> Because the Israelites cry out to Yahweh,
> He raises up a deliverer for them in Othniel of
> Judah, into whose hand He gives King
> Chushan-rishathaim of Mesopotamia. The
> land has forty years' peace (III. 9–11).

After Othniel's death the people of Israel again do evil in the sight of the Lord. He gives them into the hand of King Eglon of Moab, whom they serve, after their defeat, for eighteen years (III. 12–14).

When the Israelites call on Yahweh He gives them a deliverer in Ehud, a Benjamite (III. 15), who murders Eglon (III. 16–26) and decisively defeats the Moabites. The land has eighty years' peace (III. 27–30). Shamgar (no tribe is given) slays six hundred Philistines and delivers Israel (III. 31).

After Ehud's death the people of Israel do evil in the sight of Yahweh, who makes them servants of King Jabin of Hazor for twenty years (IV. 1–3).

Because Israel calls out to Yahweh (IV. 3) the prophetess Deborah calls on Barak of Naphtali to wage war against Sisera's army. Yahweh spreads panic among the enemy; they are overcome (IV. 4–16) and Sisera is killed in flight (IV. 17–24). The victory is recounted in poetic language in Deborah's song of thanks to Yahweh (ch. V). The land has forty years' peace (V. 31).

When the people of Israel do evil before Yahweh, He gives them into the hands of the Midianites for seven years (VI. 1). This period of oppression is vividly described (VI. 2–6).

Israel calls upon Yahweh (VI. 6 f.), who sends a prophet to reproach them with their disloyalty. Gideon of Manasseh, filled with the spirit of Yahweh (VI. 33 f.), attacks the enemy camp and puts them to flight (VII. 19–22), pursuing them across the Jordan (VII. 23–5). The land has forty years' peace (VIII. 28–32).

After Gideon's death the people of Israel again turn to the heathen gods (VIII. 33 f.). The consequences are not related.

Abimelech rules over Israel for three years (IX. 22). After his death Tola of Issachar is judge for twenty-three years (X. 1 f.), and after him Jair, a Gileadite, for twenty-two years (X. 3-5).

Because the people of Israel turn again to the heathen gods (X. 6 f.), Yahweh gives them into the hands of the Ammonites (and Philistines) for eighteen years (X. 6-8).

When the Israelites cry out to Yahweh (X. 10) He reprimands them for their faithlessness (X. 11-14). They repent, confess their sins and put away the strange gods (X. 15 ff.). The elders of Gilead appoint Jephthah as leader (X. 18, XI. 5-11). He defeats the Ammonites (XI. 29, 32 f.) and judges Israel for six years (XII. 7). After him Ibzan of Bethlehem is judge for seven years (XII. 8-10); after him Elon of Zebulon for ten years (XII. 11-12); after him Abdon of Ephraim for eight years (XII. 13-15).

The people of Israel do evil in the sight of Yahweh, who delivers them into the hands of the Philistines for forty years (XIII. 1).

Samson of Dan defeats the Philistines at Lehi (XV. 9) and is judge over Israel for twenty years (XV. 20-XVI. 31).

This survey brings to light the scheme to which the Deuteronomist harnessed his traditional material. Individual deviations from the pattern reveal that a considerable amount of folk-lore has been worked in; on the other hand, they indicate a second scheme which is found in X. 1-5 and XII. 7-15. These two sections deal not with warriors and heroes who act as deliverers

in times of need, but—and this is expressly stated—with
judges. The information about them, it is true, is brief and
formulary, so that one might question whether this is indeed
historical tradition or merely constructive padding in order to
arrive at the number of twelve judges to correspond with the
number of the tribes. But these few details, which report only
the lineage, the duration of office, the possessions, and the burial
place of the lesser judges, create by their very restraint and
objectivity the impression of extreme reliability. The formula
"after him . . . judged"[20] leads us to assume an office giving
authority over the whole union of the twelve tribes.[21] So here
we shall be dealing with old authentic and consecutive lists of
the official custodians of the law in the amphictyon.[22]

This provides certain information about the development
of the book. The list was used by the Deuteronomist as the
essential framework, which he then proceeded to fill out with
legends about his heroes. Even Jephthah belonged originally
to the list, as is evident from XII. 7, but the information there is
now replaced by legend. Shamgar from Beth-Anath (III. 31)[23]
gives rise to certain doubts: he is not described as a judge, and
the little that is said about him is strongly reminiscent of the
Samson legend (XV. 15); moreover, he appears in the Song of
Deborah (V. 6) as a sort of ruler over Israel. At all events he is
not in the right place in this grouping, because the twenty
years' dependence expressly follows on after Ehud's death
(IV. 1). On the other hand, the reference to Shamgar seems to
have been available to the Deuteronomist, for he quotes the
period of rest enjoyed by the land as twice forty years (III. 30).
In the case of Othniel too we may ask whether he is indeed a
great historical character. His existence has been doubted, and
it has been pointed out that this section is derived from the
story of the wells (Josh. XV. 16 f.) in order that Judah too may
be represented by a judge. The formulation of the story
(III. 1–11) seems to be the work of the Deuteronomist. In the

[20] Cf. XII. 8, 11, 13; in X. 1 and 3 the verb has been changed to conform with the
heroic sagas (cf. VII. 1).
[21] Cf. M. Noth, "Das Amt des 'Richters Israel'," in *Bertholet-Festschrift*, pp. 404–
17; H. W. Hertzberg, "Die kleinen Richter," in *Theologische Literaturzeitung*,
henceforth cited as *Th. Lz.*, LXXIX (1954), cols. 285–90; cf. also note 16 below.
[22] Cf. Noth, *Überlief. Stud.*, p. 48.
[23] Cf. Alt, *Staatenbildung*, p. 12.

Gideon story (VI. 11–VIII. 32) he has intentionally interrupted his scheme with a long introduction (VI. 2–10): the different ending (VIII. 33–5) is also intentional—it provides a link-up with the Abimelech story.

If we ask what kind of literary material was employed, the answer would be primarily traditional historical tales like that of the murder of Eglon (III. 16 ff.), the battle with Sisera of Harosheth (ch. IV), who has already been wrongly connected in the Deuteronomist's scheme with Jabin of Hazor (Josh. XI. 10 ff.). A valuable parallel to this is contained in the old highly poetic tradition, the song of the prophetess (and judge) Deborah (ch. V), which has fortunately been included in the Book of Judges and thus handed down to us.[24] There are further reports of Gideon's battle against Zebah and Zalmunna (VIII. 4 ff.), and of Jephthah's march against the Ammonites (XI. 1–11, 29, 32 f.) or more correctly the Moabites, since the god mentioned, Chemosh (XI. 24), is Moabite. Here long diplomatic transactions with the unnamed King of the Ammonites are a later insertion into the text (XI. 12–28), just as Gideon's reign over all Israel (VII. 2–8) is also a later extension; for his power, in reality, was confined to the Abiezrites, or at the most to the tribe of Manasseh. The Abimelech episode (ch. IX) with its very apt fable about the plants (vss. 8–15) will likewise present historical material, even if it is coloured by religion and shows legendary characteristics in places.

In addition we have the well-known aetiological stories or explanations of names: how Gideon destroyed the altar of Baal in Ophrah and "on that day" was called Jerubbaal (= Baal fights); "Let Baal contend against him, because he pulled down his altar" (VI. 32), or the origin of the altar Yahweh-shalom (= the Lord is peace) which stands "to this day" at Ophrah (VI. 24). Legend can tell also of such remarkable names as "winepress of the wolf" and "rock of the raven" (VII. 25), the memory of which remained alive for a long time (cf. Is. X. 26). Bound up with

[24] E. Sellin, "Das Deboralied," in *Festschrift Otto Procksch zum 60. Geburtstag überreicht*, Leipzig 1934, pp. 149–66; I. W. Slotki, "The Song of Deborah," in *Journal of Theological Studies*, XXXIII (1932), pp. 341–54; O. Grether, *Das Deboralied. Eine metrische Rekonstruktion*, Gutersloh 1941; G. Gerleman, "The Song of Deborah in the light of stylistics," in *Vet. test.*, I (1951), pp. 168–80; cf. also P. R. Ackroyd, "The composition of the Song of Deborah," in *Vet. test.*, II (1952), pp. 160–2.

legend, too, are "the spring of him who called" (xv. 19) at Lehi, which is so called "to this day," "the hill of the jawbone" xv. 17), as well as "the gate of Gaza" (xvi. 2), which it can explain more fully.

Besides these there are the cultic legends of the founding of a sanctuary in Ophrah and the sacrifices offered there (vi. 11–21), of the making of the ephod (viii. 27), and of Manoah's sacrifice at Zorah (xiii. 19 f.). The story of Jephthah's daughter also belongs to this category, with its mythical touch in the bewailing of her virginity "upon the mountains" (xi. 38), which is to explain an old custom according to which the daughters of Israel lamented Jephthah's daughter for four days in the year. Among other traditions we should mention also the jealousy and the imperious nature of Ephraim, which emerge on several occasions (viii. 1 ff., xii. 1 ff.), and "the camp of Dan" between Zorah and Eshtaol, with its old burying place (xvi. 31) which is so called "to this day."

Some of these stories circulated singly and independently; some, however, had already been gathered together into groups (Gideon, Samson) before they came into the hands of the Deuteronomist.[25] This is particularly evident in the case of Samson, where there is much old material in the series of single stories, occasionally reminiscent of the legends of Hercules, which describe, if somewhat crudely, the strength of this great child of nature from Dan in his struggle against his Philistine enemies. There have been accretions to this legend-cycle in the course of time, for example the story of the promise of his coming (ch. xiii) which, for all its many differences, still contains much that reminds us of Gideon's calling. The Delilah story (ch. xvi) is a later addition, as is shown by the repetition of the closing observation of xv. 20 in xvi. 31. Particularly worthy of note is the fact that none of the Samson stories show, or even hint, that Samson was a judge. It was only at a later period that he was given this office and included in the Deuteronomistic arrangement.

Since they originally derived from old folk traditions these

[25] H. Gunkel, "Simson," in Reden und Aufsätze, Göttingen 1913, pp. 38–64; P. Humbert, "Les Métamorphoses de Samson, ou l'empreinte israélite sur la légende de Samson," in Revue de l'histoire des religions, LXXX (1919), pp. 154–70; A. Lods, "Quelques remarques sur l'histoire de Samson," in Actes du Congrès international d'Histoire des Religions, Paris 1923, pp. 504–16.

tribal and heroic legends will be very old. Attempts have been made to attribute them individually to the various narrative sources of the Pentateuch, and many parallel traditions have been pointed out.[26] But one or more continuous threads of narrative would have to be traced throughout the whole book, which hardly seems possible in view of the special nature of the material. The variations and partial parallels in the train of thought are more easily explained on the basis of oral tradition, which altered such legends in the course of frequent repetition and combined them with related material.

From the historical point of view, the Book of Judges tells us about the disunity of the Israelite tribes, who were fully occupied pursuing their own interests; of their hardships and their subjection to the native population of the individual city-states. But it also tells of the Israelites' ever-increasing success, first in gaining a foothold in Canaan and subsequently in spreading out over the greater part of the land.

The Book of Judges proper (II. 6–XVI. 31) concludes with the burial of Samson in the old burying place between Zorah and Eshtaol, in the vicinity of "the camp of Dan" (cf. XIII. 25). Appended to this, and probably also influenced by this recurring phrase "camp of Dan," is a special tradition (Jg. XVII–XVIII) about a tribe's change of settlement. The small tribe of Dan, which is settled north-west of Jerusalem in the region of Kiriath-jearim, has difficulty in holding its own against the Philistines and moves out of "the camp of Dan" (XVIII. 11) in search of a new dwelling-place. It finds one in the north of Galilee, after sending out scouts to search out the land. There in Laish a certain Micah had his own house of gods with ephod and teraphim (XVII. 5) and a silver image which the Danites take away from him together with his priest, a wandering Levite, to use as their own. The peaceful city of Laish, "a people quiet and unsuspecting" (XVIII. 27) cannot defend

---

[26] Eissfeldt, *Einleitung*, p. 299, assumes three parallel story complexes as the preliminary stage of the added L, J and E narratives. Pfeiffer, *Introduction*, p. 328, divides the material between J and E but has to admit that, in stylistic and historical value, the E stories are inferior to the J accounts. Lods, *Histoire de la littérature*, p. 119, also speaks of J and E (without a detailed division) but stresses that these are not the same writers as were at work in the Hexateuch: only the milieu is the same. K. Wiese, *Zur Literarkritik des Buches der Richter*, Stuttgart 1926, is at pains to point out that dividing the Book of Judges up between J and E is a mistake.

herself against them without outside help. The Danites attack and destroy the city, rebuilding it as their own property under the name of Dan. This story in itself has nothing to do with the Book of Judges and would fit better into the land annexation period, that is into the Book of Joshua. In the list Jg. I. 34–5 it is the old seats of the tribe of Dan that are mentioned, while the Song of Deborah assumes that the change of settlement has already taken place (v. 17). In spite of many legendary features, there is a reliable tradition here. It is concerned with the "hieros logos" of the sanctuary of Dan.[27] The story itself has been extended and glossed, for the cult in Dan must have aroused misgivings. For this reason it is repeatedly stressed that there was at that time no king in Israel (XVII. 6, XVIII. 1). The removal of the image was also objectionable, so it was added that Micah had stolen the silver for it from his mother (XVII. 2–4). In conclusion there are two vague references: that Jonathan, the grandson of Moses (Ex. XVIII. 3), whose name has of course been changed for religious reasons to Manasseh, and his descendants staffed the sanctuary there until the time of the captivity (Jg. XVIII. 30), very probably by Tiglath-pileser III about 732 B.C. (II Kings XV. 29). This reference is difficult to reconcile with the second: that this image was worshipped in Dan as long as the house of God—no doubt the Ark of the Covenant is meant here (I Sam. IV. 3)—remained in Shiloh (XVIII. 31), that is until it was removed by the Philistines (I Sam. IV. 11). This independent and isolated story has very probably only been preserved because in its present form it clearly disparages the sanctuary at Dan, for which (and similarly for the one in Bethel) King Jeroboam I had a golden calf made (I Kings XII. 28 f.).

A further story from the same period, when "there was no king in Israel" (XIX. 1, XXI. 25), is appended to the Book of Judges (chs. XIX–XXI). It tells of the outraging of the wife of a Levite by the inhabitants of Gibeah, for which "all the people of Israel" take vengeance on Benjamin, who would not deliver up the guilty men. Despite their mighty army they are twice heavily defeated with severe loss. Only after they have set an ambush do they succeed in achieving victory. They exact stern

---

[27] Cf. Noth, *System der Stämme*, pp. 168 ff.; cf. also W. R. Arnold, *Ephod and Ark*, Cambridge (Mass.) 1917, pp. 95–122.

retribution (xx. 43 ff.), but subsequently make peace with the remaining six hundred men. In future, however, the *ius conubii* regarding intermarriage with the tribe of Benjamin reads: "no one of us shall give his daughter in marriage to Benjamin" (xxi. 1), and this is confirmed by a solemn oath on the altar at Bethel. Later they regret this measure, but they are bound: once an oath, always an oath. So they suggest to the Benjamites that they steal the wives they lack at the feast of Yahweh in Shiloh, and this is done without opposition.

In its details this story is drawn-out and verbose. Particularly striking are the enormous numbers of left-handed men, of levies, and of casualties, and the interplay of religious motives in prayer and oracles. The taking of Gibeah reminds us only too strongly of the conquest of Ai (Josh. VIII. 12 ff.). The dividing up of the corpse in order to raise the armies is parallelled in the action of Saul (1 Sam. XI. 7). The outrage reminds us of the Sodom story (Gen. XIX. 1 ff.); the expedition against Jabesh cites the same number of troops as the march against Midian (Num. XXXI. 5). Rape is a favourite subject of legend —compare the rape of the Sabine women in Roman history. We must never forget that stories which have circulated for a long time orally have acquired all sorts of extensions and additions in the process. So the whole of ch. XXI with its various aetiological legends should be looked upon as secondary.

The basis of the tradition is and remains the most important thing; and this, in its historical essence, is reliable. Even Hosea makes several references to it (Hos. IX. 9, X. 9). It deals with the fact that the union of the twelve tribes of Israel undertake a punitive expedition against one of their members because the latter has trespassed against the law of the amphictyon.[28] But perhaps we may go a step further and see, as elsewhere,[29] this alleged outrage of Gibeah more as a pretext for intervention, while the real cause lies deeper and is political in nature. Benjamin, as a tribe, appears in the Song of Deborah (v. 14), it is true, but is not mentioned in the old list in ch. 1. There is no lack of indication that Benjamin first became a

---

[28] Cf. Noth, *System der Stämme*, p. 170; A. Bruno, *Gibeon*, Leipzig 1923, pp. 88–142.

[29] Examples in O. Eissfeldt, "Der geschichtliche Hintergrund der Erzählung von Gibeas Schandtat (Richter XIX–XXI)," in *Festschrift Georg Beer*, Stuttgart 1935, pp. 28–30.

distinct tribe in Canaan. So we should not reject the possibility that our story deals with Benjamin's assertion of its independence and its separation from Ephraim, whose southern district it had formed up to that time.[30] The story names the priest Phinehas, son of Eleazar (xx. 28): it will therefore originate from the early judges period (Josh. xxiv. 33), some one generation after Joshua. The fact that Bethel plays a part in the story (like Dan in the first appendix) is no mere accident, when one considers that in the period of the monarchy sanctuaries of the northern kingdom of Israel were found in both places. Neither of the two additions are connected with the Deuteronomist: they were very likely not added until later.

THE BOOKS OF SAMUEL

In the Hebrew manuscripts the Books of Samuel[31] follow directly after the Book of Judges, whereas in the Septuagint the Book of Ruth comes between them. In the Septuagint the Books of Samuel and of Kings are called the four books of "Kingdoms," unlike the Hebrew arrangement which divides the whole into one Book of Samuel and one Book of Kings—an arrangement which is not particularly suitable, since the beginning of the Book of Kings, which deals with David's last wishes and death (I Kings I. 1–II. 11), still belongs naturally to what goes before. But this division of the material may have been conditioned by the fact that the end of Samuel (II Sam. xxi–xxiv), like the end of Judges, contains appendixes to the books proper. The name Samuel is based less on the content, which deals only in part with Samuel, than on the Talmudic tradition which regards Samuel as the author.[32] This assumption, however, is untenable, because Samuel's death is already reported in I Sam. xxv; in addition, the Books of Samuel are not uniform but are based on a number of sources.

The contents of the Books of Samuel can best be grouped under four main headings: (1) Stories of the priests and of the Ark (I Sam. I. 1–VII. 1); (2) Stories of Samuel and Saul (I Sam. VII. 2–XV. 35); (3) Stories of the rise of David (I Sam. XVI–II Sam. VIII); and (4) Stories about the succession to the

[30] Cf. *op. cit.*, pp. 19–40.
[31] For commentaries and literature, see Bibliography.
[32] Baba bathra fol. 14–15; cf. Goldschmidt, *Talmud*, VOL. VIII, p. 56.

throne of David (II Sam. IX–XX and I Kings I–II). The first
section begins with the story of the birth of Samuel (= granted
by God, or one over whom the name of God was spoken),
whose name is explained "Because I have asked him of the
Lord" (I. 20).[33] The prayer of the childless Hannah is answered
and she gives birth to a son (I. 1–20), whom she takes to Eli in
the house of God at Shiloh that he may be dedicated to
Yahweh (I. 21–8). After the Song of Hannah (II. 1–10), the
content of which is hardly appropriate, there is a description
(II. 12–17) of the godless activities of Eli's sons Hophni and
Phinehas (I. 3, II. 34), for which a prophet threatens them with
the judgment of Yahweh (II. 27–36): a few scattered remarks in
these passages refer to Samuel's growth and development
(II. 11, 18 f.) and to his parents (II. 20 f.). Yahweh reveals
Himself to Samuel (III. 1–18) who shows himself as a true
prophet (III. 19–21). After this follows the account of the fate
of the Ark—how it falls into the hands of the Philistines during a
battle in which the sons of Eli are slain, as the prophet warned
(IV. 1–11). At the news of the loss of the Ark Eli collapses and
dies—"he had judged Israel forty years" (IV. 12–18): his
daughter-in-law bears a son whom she names Ichabod[34]—"the
glory has departed from Israel" (IV. 19–22). The Philistines
take the Ark into the temple of their god Dagon at Ashdod,
where it proves more powerful than Dagon and overturns his
statue, which lies broken on the threshold: for this reason the
priests and followers of Dagon will not tread on the threshold
"to this day" (V. 1–5). The Ark is moved several times, to
Gath, to Ekron. Everywhere it causes plague and panic (V.
6–12). Finally after seven months it is taken with a gold guilt
offering to the border at Bethshemesh (VI. 1–12), where the
inhabitants joyfully make a sacrifice to Yahweh. Evidence of
this is the great stone in the field of Joshua "to this day"
(VI. 13–18). Because the irreverent, who try to inspect the
Ark, are smitten by Yahweh, a message is sent to the people of
Kirjath-jearim to come and collect it. They do so, and set it up
in the house of Abinadab (VI. 19–VII. 1). Here the story of the

---

[33] Ša'alti (I have prayed for) fits quite well as an explanation of the name Saul,
but not of Samuel; cf. Hempel, *Alt-hebräische Literatur*, p. 91.

[34] Wrongly interpreted by the writer of this part as "without glory"; it probably
means exactly the opposite, viz. "man of glory."

I

Ark suddenly breaks off, not to be finally concluded until II Sam. VI with its transfer to Jerusalem.

The second main section, the stories of Samuel and Saul (VII. 1–XV. 35), begins with Samuel's struggle against the Philistines. In accordance with the Deuteronomistic arrangement, with which we are familiar from the Book of Judges, we have accounts of twenty years' oppression by the Philistines, of the people's conversion to Yahweh with fasting and sacrifices, and of their deliverance by Yahweh, who spreads panic among the enemy so that they are easily defeated and Israel has peace from them as long as Samuel is alive. At Mizpeh Samuel erects a memorial "Ebenezer" (Stone of help) and moves his house to Ramah, where he builds an altar (VII. 2–17). He appoints his sons as judges, but since they are avaricious and corrupt all the elders of Israel ask for a king. At first Samuel disagrees with them, but later at Yahweh's command he accedes to their request (VIII. 1–9 [=22]). Inserted here is a list of the king's privileges (VIII. 10–18), but this is far in advance of events (cf. X. 25). One would expect the choice of the king (X. 17) to follow here, but first of all we hear the well-known and instructive tale of Saul who goes with a servant in search of his father's lost asses. When they cannot find the animals anywhere they make enquiries, on the servant's suggestion, from the famous "man of God" (IX. 1–14). On the revelation of Yahweh, Saul is invited to eat with Samuel, stays overnight, and is anointed king the following morning (IX. 15–X. 1). As signs that God is with Saul, Samuel tells him of some encounters he will have on the way back: these prophecies are fulfilled. One of these signs is the origin of the proverb "Is Saul also among the prophets?" On his return home he says nothing of his secret anointing (X. 2–16). Another report recounts that Samuel calls the people to Mizpeh to choose their king: the lot falls on Saul, who has to be brought out from a hiding place. All pay homage to him, and after Samuel has proclaimed and written down the rights of the king, everyone, including the newly chosen king, returns home (X. 17–27). There follows yet another account of the institution of the monarchy: here it is not the story of a young man a head taller than anyone else (X. 23), nor of one chosen by lot, but of a man of action and energy. Here it is not the world of wonders that speaks, but history. The inhabitants of Jabesh east of the Jordan, hard pressed by the Ammonites, send messengers seeking help "through all the territory of Israel." While others weep and wail, Saul, returning from the field, immediately takes the initiative and resolutely summons "all the territory of Israel" to joint action. He sets out on forced marches and conquers the Ammonites. Thereupon the people proceed to Gilgal, where Saul is made king (xi. 1–15). Following on x. 24, Samuel gives account of himself before all Israel, draws attention to the actions of Yahweh in the past, illustrates Yahweh's power with a miraculous rainstorm, and exhorts the people to fear Yahweh and serve Him truly (xii. 1–25).

Saul's struggle against the Philistines begins with a time reference which has unfortunately been mutilated in the text. The initial phase consists of the destruction of an enemy garrison by Saul's son Jonathan (xiii. 1–4). The Philistines do not take this lying down, and indeed retaliate so fiercely that the Israelites have to flee and hide in caves in the rocks (xiii. 5–7); enemy columns roam over the whole country, while Saul remains in Gibeah with a small band of men (xiii. 15–18). An episode from this time, Jonathan's surprise attack on an enemy outpost (xiv. 1–14), could have led to victory (xiv. 15–23, 31). But the great achievement of the day is not exploited, because the oracle consulted gives no answer (xiv. 36–7). The innocent-guilty cause of this is Jonathan, who knew nothing of the oath that had been taken (xiv. 24–30), but is saved from the death penalty (xiv. 38–45). For the time being hostilities with the Philistines are suspended (xiv. 46), but no decision is reached (xiv. 52). Many insertions interrupt the continuity of this war report, which, in spite of much touching up, still contains many truly historical features. For example (referring back to x. 8), Saul's waiting for Samuel in Gilgal until he finally offers the sacrifice himself, destroying his descendants' chances of ever becoming king (xiii. 8–15); also the observation about the smiths (xiii. 19–22), and the description of the sin of the people, the punishment for which is averted by Saul building an altar (xiv. 32–5). The summary of Saul's deeds (xiv. 47 f.), which should really be ascribed to David, and a family tree based on good sources (xiv. 49–51) give the impression that the story of Saul is at an end: one expects a report of his death to follow (cf. 1 Sam. xxxi).

But what follows, completely unconnected and giving the
effect of a supplement, is a self-contained report of an expedition against the Amalekites, the Bedouin in the south of the
country. Saul decisively defeats the enemy and takes their
king prisoner (xv. 1–9). But these events, which certainly
contain valuable traditions, are not the crux of the narrative:
they only give the reason for Saul's rejection (xv. 10–35). For
the last time Saul and Samuel confront one another; but in all
personal and human matters the two are separated by Saul's
disobedience to Yahweh in not completely carrying out the ban
on the Amalekites. If we survey the whole period of Saul's
reign, this account seems meagre and stinted indeed.

The rest of our information about Saul, apart from the
questioning of the dead (ch. xxviii) and the report of his death
(ch. xxxi), is intended merely to provide a background for
David, whose rise forms the subject-matter of the third main
section (1 Sam. xvi–ii Sam. viii). The introduction to this is a
story in which David is secretly anointed king by Samuel
(xvi. 1–13); but we cannot draw conclusions from this any
more than from the anointing of Saul in Ramah. As an adult,
"a man of valour, a man of war, prudent in speech," he enters
the court as a harpist, wins the favour of the King and becomes
his armour-bearer (xvi. 14–23). In the struggle against the
Philistines he covers himself with glory (xviii. 7), so that all the
people love him and the King's jealousy is aroused. Nevertheless Saul gives him command over a section of the army, and
promises him his eldest daughter as a reward for his outstanding
bravery. The King does not keep his word, but after another
spectacular feat of arms David receives his second daughter in
marriage (xviii. 6–30). Popular tradition, however, tells a
different story: it transfers Elhanan's victory over the giant
(ii Sam. xxi. 19) to its favourite. With many features from
Märchen the legend tells of the shepherd boy who comes to
visit his brothers in camp and overcomes the powerful giant
who for forty days has challenged the Israelites without
anyone daring to try his strength. For this the boy is to receive
the hand of the king's daughter. He comes to the court,
becomes the trusted friend of the heir to the throne, and is
given command of all the military forces (xvii–xviii. 5). The
vigour of this tradition is evident from the repeated references

to the exploit.[35] When Saul plots against David's life—not only in the hour of depression, when the evil spirit comes upon him—Jonathan's intercession (XIX. 1–7) is of no avail. The king is resolved on David's death: the only solution is for him to flee, which he does with the help of his wife Michal (XIX. 8–17). He sets off for Ramah and Samuel (XXIX. 18–24—here there is a somewhat different explanation of the proverb from that in x. 10 ff.). Once more Jonathan acts as go-between, but without success (ch. XX).

So David flees to the priest Ahimelech in the priestly city of Nob (XXI. 1–10); then to the Philistine King Achish of Gath, where he is recognised and saves himself only by a ruse (XXI. 11–16); then to the King of Moab, under whose protection he places his parents while he himself, on the advice of the prophet Gad, returns to the mountains of Judah (XXII. 1–15). Saul meanwhile has taken terrible vengeance on the whole priesthood and on the city of Nob; only Abiathar, a son of Ahimelech the priest, is able to escape and join David (XXII. 20–3). The following chapters (XXIII–XXVI) are taken up with stories of the wandering and outlawed David, dodging with his followers among the mountains of Judah and along their western slopes ever further towards the south, nowhere safe from betrayal. He saves the harvested grain from the Philistines for the inhabitants of Keilah, but the oracle of Yahweh tells him that he cannot rely on their friendship (XXIII. 1–13). He is denounced by the Ziphites and finds himself in great danger. The two parties are on different sides of the same mountain—an explanation of the name "Sela-hammahlekoth" (rock of escape). David is finally encircled and only escapes because the Philistines have attacked and Saul has to go off to confront them (XXIII. 14–28). Next Saul is told that David is in the wilderness of Engedi. David lies hidden in a cave, which the King chances to enter in passing, without noticing the fugitive. When he leaves, David calls after him and shows him the corner that he secretly cut from his coat as evidence that Saul's life was in his hand. There follows a reconciliation (ch. XXIV). A

[35] Cf. I Sam. XIX. 5, XXI, 9, XXII. 10, 14. But cf. also J. N. Schofield, "Mari and the Old Testament," in *Expository Times*, henceforth cited as *Ex. Times*, LXVI (1954–5), pp. 250–2; L. M. von Pákozdy, "'Elhanan—der frühere Name Davids?" in *Z. alttest. W.*, LXVIII (1956), pp. 157–9.

variant of this story is preserved in ch. XXVI, the beginning of which agrees almost word for word with the story of the rock of escape and which ends with the same final effect. Here, however, David—even braver—penetrates by night right into the camp and takes the King's spear and jar of water which are lying at the end of his bed. That David did not follow the life of a robber is shown by the intervening story of Nabal of Maon, whose herds he and his men protect against attacks without demanding any recompense: the clever Abigail becomes David's wife after Nabal's death (ch. XXVI). In the end, however, David feels that, in spite of repeated reconciliations, he is nowhere safe from Saul's pursuit and he flees with his men, now 600 in number, to the protection of the Philistine King Achis at Gath. The latter grants his request for the city of Ziklag (XXVII. 1–6). For this reason Ziklag belongs to the kings of Judah "to this day" (vs. 6). There David fights many battles with the nomadic tribes (XXVII. 7–12). When the Philistines once again call up their troops against Israel, David and his men have to turn out as vassals of Achis (XXVIII. 1 f.); at the review of the troops, however, they are sent back to Ziklag as unreliable (ch. XXIX). Meanwhile the Amalekites have been raiding and have attacked the area round Ziklag, destroyed the city and carried off prisoners. With the help of a captured Egyptian David gets on their trail and mercilessly slaughters the nomads as, joyful and carefree, they celebrate their victory: only 400 young men are able to escape on camels (XXX. 1–17). The prisoners are freed and the loot divided up among them all, including even the 200 who had fallen out on the march and therefore had taken no part in the battle. "From that day forward he made it a statute and an ordinance for Israel to this day" (XXX. 18–25).

In order to win over the cities of the south of Judah, which are named individually, David prudently and with great political foresight sends them a portion of the booty: "Here is a present for you from the spoil of the enemies of the Lord" (XXX. 26–31).

Here a twice-told reference to Samuel's death has been inserted (XXV. 1, XXVIII. 3), followed by the story of Saul's secret visit to the witch at Endor, when Samuel's spirit appears and prophesies that both Saul and his sons shall die in battle the following day (XXVIII. 4–25). And so it turns out: the Israelites

flee, the King's three sons are slain, and Saul himself is mor-
tally wounded (xxxi. 1–6). The Philistines occupy the abandoned cities and violate Saul's dead body (xxxi. 7–10).
However, the grateful inhabitants of Jabesh (cf. xi. 4 ff.) come
to take away the corpse and bury it with due solemnity "under
the tamarisk tree at Jabesh" (xxxi. 11–13), from where, as we
learn from an appendix to the Books of Samuel (ii Sam. xxi.
11–14), David has the bones removed to the family burial place
at Zelah. A man who is trying to ingratiate himself with David
brings him news of the battle and hands over the royal insignia
he has taken from Saul. His report of the King's death does not
agree with the previous version (ii Sam. i. 1–10). Perhaps he is
hoping for a large reward when he claims that he personally
killed the King, but he has miscalculated. David believes his
story, but has him slain for killing Yahweh's anointed (i. 11–16).
A moving lament follows (i. 17–27), taken from the famous Book
of Jashar (cf. Josh. x. 13).

Circumstances have now basically changed. The right to act
is now in David's hands: the way is open for him. Thanks to
his clever foresight (cf. i Sam. xxx. 26), he can count on the
cities of the south. He therefore leaves the remote city of
Ziklag, after consulting the oracle of Yahweh, and proceeds to
Hebron, which is centrally situated and where he is anointed
by the men of Judah as "king over the house of Judah" (ii Sam.
ii. 1–4). One of his first acts as King is to thank the Jabeshites
officially for their reverent treatment of Saul's mortal remains
(ii. 5–7). But this is more than a noble gesture; it is at the same
time a cautious political feeler put out to explore the attitude of
the northern tribes to his kingship. About this, however, there is
soon very little doubt. So far we have only heard of three sons
of Saul (i Sam. xiv. 49, xxxi. 6) who fell together in battle, but
here now we learn of the existence of a fourth called Esh-baal.[36]
His great-uncle, the Commander-in-Chief Abner, took him to
safety east of the Jordan to the vicinity of Jabesh, which was
friendly to Saul, and there made him king over Israel (ii. Sam.
ii. 8 f.). From this point onwards in the subsequent history of
the monarchy we must always differentiate quite clearly
between the kingdom of Judah, by which is meant the smaller

---

[36] Deliberately misrepresented here as Ish-bosheth (= man of shame); cf. i
Chron. viii. 33, ix. 39.

southern kingdom, and the kingdom of Israel, by which the
Bible means the great northern kingdom of ten tribes. The
chronological statement (II Sam. II. 10 f.), immediately suspect
with its typical forty years, is a later addition.

Dissension between the Northern and Southern Kingdoms
is not long delayed. Abner wants control of Judah also. It
comes to an armed clash at Gibeon (II. 12 f.), of which two
episodes are reported: a legendary battle between twelve of
each side, which explains the name Helkath-hazzurim (II.
13–16), and the death of Asahel, brother of Joab, at the hand of
Abner (II. 17–24). After a temporary truce (II. 24–31) the
struggle proceeds—"There was a long war between the house
of Saul and the house of David" (III. 1)—until Abner abandons
Esh-baal after an episode involving a woman (III. 6–10), joins
David (III. 11–13), and canvasses on his behalf in the Northern
Kingdom (III. 17–19). At David's request he brings Michal (III.
14–16) back to Hebron, where he is well received (III. 20).
When Joab hears that Abner is on his way back to the Northern
Kingdom with a special mission (III. 21) he reproaches the King,
makes a pretext to bring Abner back, and avenges the death of
Asahel (III. 22–7). David naturally takes no part in this act, as
he makes abundantly and publicly clear by giving Abner an
impressive state funeral (III. 28–39), part of the lament from
which has been handed down (III. 33–4). The last obstacle in
David's way is removed by the murder of Esh-baal by two men
from Beeroth, whose inhabitants live as guests in Gittaim "to
this day" (IV. 3). The murderers in turn are slain (ch. IV)—
they valued the deed but not the doers. Allying himself with all
the tribes of Israel, David is anointed king over Israel also at
Hebron (V. 1–3) and, having captured the stronghold of the
Jebusites, moves his residence to Jerusalem (V. 6–10).

This is the climax and conclusion of the third main section of
the Books of Samuel. It uses older material and also material
from folk tradition like the legends attached to heroes and places
(I Sam. XVII, XXIII, XXVIII; II Sam. II. 16, IV. 4), and explanations
of proverbs (I Sam. XIX. 24; II Sam. V. 8), customs, (I Sam. XXX.
25), and traditional rights (I Sam. XXVII. 6). In general,
however, it is based on the solid historical foundation of a connected account, the theme of which is David, always noble
and irreproachable in spite of the hostility surrounding him.

Characteristic of this source "of the rise of David," as it is usually called, is the consulting of the oracle of Yahweh before making important decisions,[37] and the way one idea is steadily pursued in the development. The account tells of the rise of David from harpist and armour-bearer, from fugitive and refugee, to absolute monarch of Judah and Israel and conqueror of the new capital, Jerusalem. What follows this section are merely fragments and supplements, such as appear elsewhere at the end of the longer narratives. So we find a reference to David's palace (II Sam. v. 11 f.) and a list of his children (v. 13–16), although a shorter one (III. 2–5) had already been inserted earlier at an unsuitable place, where it completely destroys the continuity. Another list enumerates David's campaigns (VIII. 1–14) and his dignitaries (VIII. 15–18). The report of the Philistine war (v. 17–25) now forms an isolated and independent section.

Appended also is the conclusion (II Sam. VI) of the story of the Ark (I Sam. IV–VII. 1), which has no proper connexion with the foregoing. It too contains much legendary material (I Sam. VI. 18), and popular explanations of names (I Sam. IV. 21; II Sam. VI. 8) and customs (I Sam. V. 5) in use "to this day." But more important than these or political matters in this present section is the fate of the Ark, which is traced from its removal from the sanctuary at Shiloh until it is finally set up in Jerusalem. The author would be a priest of the Ark, who wrote his account at the beginning of Solomon's reign even before the building of the Temple,[38] or towards the end of David's reign.

There still remains the prophecy of Nathan (II Sam. VII), which also forms an independent unit outside the continuity and which deals with Yahweh's favouring of individuals. This chapter is a very composite piece of work, but it does contain valuable old traditions, particularly in parts of Nathan's prophecy (VII. 8–17) and in the words of David (VII. 18–27), which—spoken as a prayer in the manner of the older monarchical period—may perhaps be traced back to David himself—except, of course, for the addition from exilic times (VII. 23–4), when, after the annihilation of the House of David, the promise

[37] Cf. I Sam. XXIII. 2, 4, 9 ff.; II Sam. II, 1, v. 19, 23.
[38] The building of the Temple (II Sam. VI. 17) is not yet mentioned here.

was interpreted as referring collectively to the people as a whole.

If there are undeniable traces of a particular aim in the third main section of the Books of Samuel, it becomes even more evident in the last section (II Sam. IX–XX; I Kings I–II). Here on epic scale is the story of the succession to the throne of David. "My lord, you swore to your maidservant by the Lord your God, saying, Solomon your son shall reign after me, and he shall sit upon my throne" (I Kings I. 17). This is Bathsheba's reminder (cf. also vs. 13), and the whole detailed account is designed to eliminate any rival powers or personalities so that Solomon is the one, undisputed monarch. This history of the succession is linked up with the preceding narrative through part of Nathan's prophecy (II Sam. VII. 11, 16) and through an episode (VI. 16, 20–3) which organically certainly has no connexion with the story of the Ark but is nevertheless significant because it establishes that Michal was childless (VI. 23).

The actual story of the succession begins with David's apparent generosity towards Jonathan's lame son Merib-baal,[39] whom he takes into his closest circle after the usual oriental custom, in order to keep him under surveillance. Then the future queen mother takes the stage: the adultery (XI. 1–13), Nathan's warning (XII. 1–12), David's penitence (XII. 13–14), the death of the child conceived in sin (XII. 15–23) and the birth of Solomon, to whom his teacher, the prophet Nathan, gives the significant name Jedidah (=favourite of Yahweh) (XII. 24 f.). This story is inserted into an old military report of the Ammonite war (X. 17–19, XII. 26–31), which must serve to give the reason for Uriah's death (XI. 14–27). The importance of the story about Amnon's offence against his half-sister Tamar (XIII. 1–20) lies only in the motive it provides for his murder by Absalom (XIII. 21–33). The latter flees before David's wrath to Geshur far up in the north-east (XIII. 34–9) and remains there for three years, until Joab arranges a reconciliation (ch. XIV). Absalom knows how to win popular favour and in the space of four years—"forty" in XV. 7 is certainly an error—has acquired such a following that he can dare to have himself proclaimed king in Hebron (XV. 1–12). David has to flee (XV. 13–23) but leaves the Ark behind in Jerusalem (XV. 24–9), as well as

[39] Misrepresented here as Mephibosheth; cf. note 36.

devoted and reliable servants like Hushai (xv. 30–7). Merib-baal also remains behind, even if the statement that he considers that the great hour is come when he will become king is very probably only a calumny of Ziba's (xvi. 1–4). While David continues his flight eastwards over the Jordan, jeered at by Shimei and grossly insulted (xvi. 5–14), Absalom settles in Jerusalem (xvi. 15–23); but he disregards the prudent advice of Ahithophel and follows the plan of Hushai (xvii. 1–14), which allows David to gain time. Hushai secretly sends messengers to David who barely escape Absalom's guards (xvii. 15–23). David gathers an army (xvii. 24–9) east of the Jordan at Mahanaim, once the refuge of Saul's son Esh-baal (cf. ii. 8). A battle is fought (xviii. 1–8) in which Joab takes matters into his own hands and against David's express instructions kills the usurper Absalom (xviii. 9–18). When David receives the news (xviii. 19–32) his grief is great (xix. 1–5). He regains his kingdom (xix. 6–16) and shows grace to Shimei (xix. 17–24) and Merib-baal (xix. 25–31), takes leave of Barzillai (xix. 32–40) and returns to Jerusalem, but during the journey petty jealousy comes to light between men of Judah and Israel (xix. 41–4).

Meanwhile fresh trouble breaks out: "Sheba will do us more harm than Absalom" (xx. 6). This Sheba, probably a close relative of Saul, rouses Israel to revolt against David. "We have no portion in David, and we have no inheritance in the son of Jesse; every man to his tents, O Israel"—everywhere can be heard his song, which later, on Israel's final rejection of David's dynasty, was to become the "Israelite Marseillaise"[40] (1 Kings xii. 16). David commissions Amasa, the leader of his armies and successor of Joab who has fallen into disfavour (ii Sam. xix. 13), to pursue Sheba (xxi. 1–4). But Joab is quicker than the dilatory Amasa, whom he stabs to death at Gibeon (xx. 5–12), and personally pursues the fleeing Sheba with all his troops throughout the land until he finally overtakes and encircles him in the far north at Abel of Beth-Maacah. There is no battle, however, for Sheba is murdered in the city (xx. 13–22). David's attitude towards the victorious Joab, to whose speedy intervention he owes so much, is not recorded.

---

[40] Thus H. Gressmann, *Die älteste Geschichtsschreibung und Prophetie Israels*, 2nd edn., Göttingen 1921, p. 180.

This cannot be the end of the story, for many questions remain unsolved. In the last chapters of the Books of Samuel we search in vain for a continuation: this is delayed until the First Book of Kings, which takes up the old thread again after a short episode involving the aged David (1 Kings 1. 1–4). Joab cannot forget David's insult nor the undoubtedly bad treatment he received after the rising of Sheba. So he goes over to the side of the king's son, Adonijah, who invites all his brothers and half-brothers except Solomon and has himself proclaimed king after offering up a sacrifice (1 Kings 1. 5–10). But the court prophet Nathan immediately gets wind of the affair and, in league with Bathsheba, manages to make David keep his promise. So Solomon is solemnly proclaimed David's successor (1 Kings 1. 11–31) and anointed king to the great satisfaction of the people (1 Kings 1. 32–40). When Adonijah hears of this (1 Kings 1. 41–8) he gives up everything for lost and flees in terror to seek shelter on the altar of burnt offerings. Solomon spares him on condition that he abstains from wickedness (1 Kings 1. 49–53). When, however, he asks, through the queen mother, for the hand of Abishag the Shunammite (cf. 1. 3) Solomon takes this as an excuse to have him murdered forthwith as a rebel (1 Kings 11. 13–25). And now the great clearance commences: Abiathar is deprived of his priesthood and banished to Anathoth (1 Kings 11. 26 f.); Joab, bereft of further hope, seeks sanctuary at the altar, but in vain: at Solomon's command he is slain (1 Kings 11. 28–35). Shimei is confined to Jerusalem, but after three years he is caught outside his restricted area and is killed by the same Benaiah who had already acted as the executioner of Adonijah and Joab (1 Kings 11. 36–46). With the assertion that Solomon was sitting on the throne of his father David and that his kingdom was well established (1 Kings 11. 46) this great account of David's succession closes.

In contrast to the other sources used in the Books of Samuel the history of the succession is written in a broad and easy style: its reports are vivid, with many comparisons, and display a particular delight in detail. Messengers play a particularly important role.[41] David comes off very badly. Although

---

[41] Cf. the excellent and detailed study of this source work by L. Rost, *Die Überlieferung von der Thronnachfolge Davids*, Stuttgart 1926, pp. 111–27. Another

almost the whole history of the succession is played out in his reign, nothing special or praiseworthy is reported about David himself. In the wars he remains as a secondary figure in the background; and what is said about him elsewhere is restricted to less pleasant matters like Michal's scorn, his adultery, his flight, his intelligence service (Hushai), his attitude towards Joab, his advancing age, and his weakness in the face of the court camarilla embodied in Nathan and Bathsheba. There is not a single report of his death. True, it is mentioned (1 Kings II. 1–12), but this section is a later addition to give the story of the succession the necessary historical framework. All kinds of suggestions have been made as to the authorship of this source. It must have been a contemporary who could describe the events from his own knowledge; that is, one who came and went in the court. Many have tried to identify him with Abiathar, but he stands a little too much in the background of the picture for this.

Into the context of this history of the succession have been inserted a few portions with supplementary information about David's time. It must have been difficult to find the right place for them. They would have fitted in best after the synopsis of David's wars (II Sam. VIII). But the Deuteronomist, whose work here consisted more in arranging than in revising his sources, has used "Joab" as the cue for joining on his appendixes (II Sam. XX, XXII). First there is a list of dignitaries under David (II Sam. XX. 23–6), then a list of victories over the Philistines, with emphasis on the heroic deeds of individuals (II Sam. XXI. 15–22), and further lists of heroes and their deeds (II Sam. XXIII. 8–23, 24–39). From what period these portions originate one cannot say: but just because they are so restrained we must reckon that this is old and reliable material, in spite of the amount of over-painting that has taken place.

Other special episodes of the David period are the revenge of the Gibeonites on Saul's descendants (II Sam. XXI. 1–11), with an appended reference to the transfer and reburial of Saul's and Jonathan's remains (II Sam. XXI. 12–14); and the story,

---

viewpoint is represented by J. Schildenberger, "Zur Einleitung in die Samuelis-bücher," in *Studia Anselmiana*, XXVII–XXVIII (1951), pp. 130–68, who, on the basis of the concluding observations (1 Sam. VII. 15–17, XIV. 47–52; II Sam. VIII. 15–18, XX. 23–6), assumes one uniform, complete account.

which from the literary standpoint belongs with the foregoing, of the numbering of the people and the plague (II Sam. XXIV. 1–15), and of the purchase of the place for the Temple and the building of the altar on the threshing floor of Araunah (II Sam. XXIV. 16–25).

When we look at the whole work we see that while the Books of Samuel tell of the rise of Saul and David in fair detail, they do not present a clear and exact picture of their actual rule. Moreover, it is clear that this is not one single piece of work but a series of juxtaposed individual tales and legends, lists and reports, some of them quite incompatible, indeed completely contradictory. Because of this parallelism some scholars have tried to trace two different threads of narrative here also, a Yahwistic (K) and an Elohistic (K₁), which have been combined on the model of the Pentateuch and revised by the Deuteronomist. From the similarity of the lists (II Sam. VIII. 16–18, XX. 23–6) it has been considered that the Deuteronomist left out II Sam. IX–XX and a post-exilic redactor reintroduced it. But II Sam. IX–XX is only part of a larger work; and the undeniable parallels (especially in the institution of the monarchy and in the stories of David) are not extensive enough for one to produce two threads of narrative from them.[42] The stories of the Books of Samuel are not transmitted individually but are combined to form individual cycles with a special literary aim. The most important of these are the cycles dealing with the rise of Saul and the rise of David, both of which have absorbed much parallel tradition; and then the story of the Ark, the prophecy of Nathan, the report of the Ammonite war and, the most extensive cycle of all, the history of the succession to David. These individual cycles were the model from which the Deuteronomist compiled his historical work. In so doing he strung his sources somewhat loosely together and revised them, often only slightly. He was more drastic only in the case of the beginning of the Ammonite

[42] Lods, *Histoire de la littérature*, p. 122, claims three cycles: two royalist (J and E₁) and one anti-monarchical (E₂) corresponding with Eissfeldt's (*Einleitung*, p. 311) description of his sources (L and J on the one hand and E on the other). Even Eissfeldt, however, is of the opinion that in II Sam. "perhaps single parts of the E stratum can be discerned, but not connected portions." Pfeiffer divides into two sources, an earlier with the theme Samuel and a later concerning Saul and David. Naturally, a Deuteronomic stratum and revision are also generally accepted.

war report (II Sam. x. 1–6), and also in the motives for the institution of the monarchy. In contrast with the original conception, he regards the monarchy from his own particular viewpoint, and, after many bitter experiences with the avaricious kings, sees it as something hostile to Yahweh and anti-godly, as defection from and rejection of Yahweh (I Sam. VIII. 2–8, 22, x. 17–27, XII. 1–25). A further source to be assumed for the older period is a didactic history of the prophets, from which the early story of Samuel, in particular, is taken (I Sam. I–III). The Deuteronomist was able to make this serve his own particular purpose and extended his "judges scheme" to make Samuel a judge also (I Sam. VIII. 2 ff.).

Of later, post-Deuteronomic date is the Song of Hannah (I Sam. II. 1–10) in particular, besides individual shorter additions. On the other hand, David's Hymn of Praise (II Sam. XXII), which is identical with Psalm XVIII, and the Testament of David (II Sam. XXIII. 1–7),[43] which contains the image of a ruler, probably originated in the later period of the monarchy and were not assimilated into the Books of Samuel until after the Deuteronomist.

THE BOOKS OF KINGS

The two Books of Kings[44] connect up, both in time and content, with the succession to the throne of David (II Sam. IX–XX; I Kings I–II). The first part, as is evident from the typical formulae (I Kings XI. 41–3), extends to I Kings XI and deals with the reign of Solomon. This is not a single large coherent account, but merely a collection of larger or smaller individual units of varying literary character which have been put together in a loose and desultory fashion. The central point here is undoubtedly the description of Solomon's buildings (v. 1–IX. 14). This begins with the contract for supplies between Hiram of Tyre and Solomon (I Kings v. 1–12), the work of a later hand, and with the secondary references to the preparations for the building of the Temple (I Kings v. 13–18), which is reported in detail in I Kings VI framed within typical chronological data (I Kings VI. 1, 37–8). There follows the description of the

---

[43] Cf. S. Mowinckel, "Die letzten Worte Davids II Sam. XXIII. 1–7," in *Z. alttest. W.*, XLV (1927), pp. 30–58.

[44] For commentaries and literature, see Bibliography.

building of the palace (I Kings VII. 1–5) and then short extracts
from the sources in use (I Kings VII. 6–8) on the subject of
further building. After this we are given technical details about
the preparation of the stones and the metalwork (VII. 9 ff.) and
an old, probably official, list of the furnishings of the Temple
(VII. 40–6), to which a later writer has appended a brief
summary (VII. 47–51). After the Ark has been solemnly
brought up (VIII. 1–11) from its temporary shelter (cf. II Sam.
VI. 17) the actual dedication of the Temple takes place with the
poetic dedication formula (VIII. 12–13) spoken by Solomon.
His words, however, as comparison with the Septuagint shows,
have been mutilated in transmission in the Masoretic text and
originate, as the Septuagint also confirms, from the Book of the
Song.[45] A longer dedication prayer follows (VIII. 14–61), the
introduction to which (VIII. 14–21) originates from a later
period. A second subsection begins, like the first (III. 11–15),
with a theophany (IX. 1–9) with promises and threats, in which
a later hand traces the principles for the religious interpretation
of the whole subsequent period of the monarchy. Of similar
origin is the framework (IX. 10, 14) of the reference to the
cities ceded by Solomon, which were not to Hiram's satisfaction
and which are called "the land of Cabul" "to this day"
(IX. 11–13). Both subsections are framed by individual smaller
parts. Thus the story of Solomon begins with a reference to his
marriage to a daughter of Pharaoh (III. 1) without any indication of the political significance of this union (otherwise in IX.
16). Then follows Solomon's sacrifice on the height at Gibeon
(III. 2, 4); his dream with the request for a wise and understanding heart (III. 5–15), an episode which with its "judgment
of Solomon" is specially suited for putting Solomon's wisdom
in its proper light (III. 16–28); lists of his officers of state (IV. 1–6)
and his twelve stewards (IV. 7–19); and finally a description of
his power and of his expenditure on his household (IV. 20–8)
which considerably interrupts the continuity, as does the section
dealing with Solomon's wisdom (IV. 29–34).

The third subsection (IX. 15–XI. 43) shows certain similarities
to these fragments. It is concerned with the most diverse
matters: the strongholds and store cities established by Solomon

[45] Probably the well-known "Book of the Upright" is meant; cf. Josh. x. 13;
II Sam. I. 18.

(IX. 15–19), military and bond service "to this day," task-masters (IX. 20–3), and the official sacrifices (IX. 25). Information about foreign trade and the wealth derived from it (IX. 26 ff.) is now interrupted by a popular story of the Queen of Sheba's visit (X. 1–13). For the rest the whole exuberant description of Solomon's wealth, display of magnificence, and wisdom (X. 14–29) gives a distinct impression of having been pieced together. The details of Solomon's large harem, the idolatry associated with it, and Yahweh's threat to ruin his kingdom as a punishment (XI. 1–13) come from a later writer who took his material from II Kings XXIII. 13. For in the following verses the decline of Edom (XI. 14–22), with its parallel the loss of Damascus (XI. 23–5), are attributed not to Solomon's idolatry but to the battles of David (cf. vss. 15, 24). Finally comes a report of the rebellious taskmaster Jeroboam of Ephraim (XI. 26–40), who has to take refuge in Egypt and remain there until Solomon's death. Inserted into this narrative is a story concerning the prophet Ahijah of Shiloh (XI. 29–39), the spirit of which is similar to the addition in XI. 13, namely that Yahweh will take the greater part of the kingdom out of Solomon's hand (vs. 31 f.). With definite, clear statements regarding Solomon's reign, death, and successor (XI. 41–3) the first main section of the Books of Kings draws to a close.

It is expedient to consider at this point the development of this particular section. In contrast with the Books of Samuel, the Deuteronomist was not here in the pleasant position of working with large original documents complete in themselves: he had to build up his account from various individual traditions. It is questionable whether he had access to a special book of the prophet Ahijah, for this source is supposedly of a later date and was worked into the present context later. On the other hand, the author expressly acknowledges one of his sources —the book of the Acts of Solomon (I Kings XI. 41). But the very nature of the quotation shows that he is merely summarising it. From the summary of the chronological data (VI. 37–VII. 1) it seems probable that this "Book of Solomon" was not annals, arranged chronologically, but a document arranged systematically according to subject.[46] In addition the Deuteronomist had at his disposal a few more stories about Solomon

[46] Cf. Noth, *Überlief. Stud.*, pp. 66 ff.

K

and various individual scraps of material. All this he attempted to combine, as far as possible, into one coherent, continuous document; and added from his own pen, in addition to his corrections to the Gibeon story, everything that we have attributed to a later hand.[47] It was no easy task, and the present text of this section shows how far he succeeded.

If we look at the picture of Solomon presented to us, we see a ruler with a great and difficult inheritance to administer. His task was to consolidate the achievements of David and to expand the great power he had inherited. Much that is praiseworthy is told us about his trading enterprises, including those with foreign countries, and the prosperity they brought in their train: also how his marriages with foreigners brought his kingdom into the ranks of the greater powers. An agreement was even reached with Pharaoh, to whom he was indebted for the important Canaanite town of Geser as a dowry. Solomon built strong fortresses to defend his kingdom and attended to war supplies and manpower. But this did not prevent the secession of Edom and Damascus; and the surrender of twenty cities of Galilee to pay for timber from Tyre meant further loss of territory. Internally Solomon had an efficient administration, organised taxation, and a well-ordered legal system. His costly buildings and the heavy burden they placed on the population, however, caused much dissatisfaction—indeed, an open revolt, which Solomon immediately crushed with great vigour. But the accomplishment of his greatest task, namely, to weld the tribes together into one unit and to remove the ancient breach between north and south, between Israel and Judah, was denied him. After his death the kingdoms bound together in personal union again split apart. In the Biblical tradition, however, these events recede more and more into the background before the might and majesty of Solomon, who is first and foremost the embodiment of wisdom and the builder of the Temple, and whose piety is reflected in the prayers offered up at its dedication.

The second main section of the Books of Kings (I Kings XII–II Kings XVII) deals with the history of the two separate kingdoms, Israel and Judah, and embraces the period from Solomon's death down to the fall of Israel, i.e. from about 922 B.C. to

[47] Particularly V, VI. 1, VIII. 14–21, IX. 1–9, XI. 1–13, 41–3.

about 722 B.C. Since at that time there was no way of reckoning time as we know it today, the accession of the king of one kingdom is dated by the year of the reign of the king of the other kingdom (synchronism); individual dates can be calculated from this mutual relationship. This seems very simple at first sight, but unfortunately the resulting totals cannot be made to agree. From Jeroboam I to Joram is 98 years, but the data given for Judah for this same period total only 95 years. In the period from Jehu to Hosea the variations are even greater, and in addition the two series are respectively more than 20 and 40 years longer than the more reliable Assyrian dates for this period. However, these discrepancies can be explained partly as slips of the pen and also partly by the use of different counting systems, which it is difficult to reconcile.[48] For this reason the dates given below—even if fairly certain—may only be taken as guides, with no claim to complete exactitude.

In describing the individual reigns the author uses a scheme which is quite clearly recognised from the introductory formulae. It consists of synchronism and data regarding length of reign, age at accession, and name of mother: the two last, however, are usually omitted in the case of the kings of Israel. The framework is completed by the concluding formulae, which, with slight variations, are generally similar and give details of the king's death, reference to additional historical sources, and the name of his successor. Reports on individual kings are usually very brief and concise, even in the case of such important kings as Jeroboam II and Azariah. There are, however, some longer continuous stories, mostly relating to the influence of a prophet. For the Deuteronomist the crucial point is the assessment of the individual, the yardstick employed being his attitude to the cult outside the Temple at Jerusalem. It goes without saying, then, that the kings of Israel are unfavourably judged. But even of the kings of Judah only a few (Asa, Jehoshaphat, Joash, Azarjah, and Jotham) are granted at least conditional approval. Only Hezekiah and Josiah correspond to the ideal king, because they took determined action against "high place" worship. The formula is always the same: "He did good (or evil) in the sight of Yahweh."

[48] See Bibliography. The dates used here conform to W. F. Albright, "The chronology of the divided monarchy of Israel," in *B.A.S.O.R.*, c (1945), pp. 16–22.

In the interests of a better synopsis, we give below the contents of the second main section, omitting the stories of the individual prophets and treating Israel and Judah side by side.[49]

Northern Kingdom (Israel)

Jeroboam I (922–901 B.C.) returns from Egypt after Solomon's death and is made king over Israel (1 Kings XII. 2 f., 20, XIV. 19 f.). He erects two golden images at Dan and Bethel, builds sanctuaries there and installs priests (XII. 25–33).

His son Nadab (901–900 B.C.) is murdered during a campaign against the Philistines (XV. 25 ff.) by **Baasha** (900–877 B.C.) of the house of Issachar, who annihilates the whole house of Jeroboam (XV. 27–34). The treachery of his ally Damascus, who attack his land and conquer several cities, compels him to give up the struggle against Judah (XV. 16, 20 f.). His son Elah (877–876 B.C.), while his army is fighting the Philistines, is murdered in his residence in Tirzah (XVI. 8–14) by **Zimri** (876 B.C.), who commits suicide (XVI. 15–22) when

Southern Kingdom (Judah)

Rehoboam (922–915 B.C.), son and successor of Solomon. His severity causes the final break with the Northern Kingdom: "So Israel has been in rebellion against the house of David to this day" (1 Kings XII. 1–19). He tolerates idolatry in the land and all his life wages war against the Northern Kingdom (XIV. 29–31). His resulting military weakness is exploited by Pharaoh Shishak, who makes a raid on Judah and plunders the Temple (XIV. 25–8). His son Abijam (915–913 B.C.) continues the wars against Israel (XV. 1–8), as does his son Asa (913–873 B.C.), who by paying money makes a treaty with the Syrians of Damascus, who now turn against their old allies. Judah is thus freed from the oppression of the Northern Kingdom (XV. 16–23)

---

[49] Bold type for a name denotes the beginning of a new dynasty.

Omri (876–869 B.C.), the commander chosen by the army, besieges Tirzah. The rival king Tibni dies after four years (XVI. 21 f.). Omri shifts his residence to Samaria, which was naturally defensible. The report on him in the Book of Kings does not do justice to his actual importance. He did lose a few cities in a war against the Syrians (XX. 34), but on the other hand he defeated and made tributaries of the Moabites (cf. Mesa inscription). He is the first king of Israel to be mentioned in Assyrian records.

His son Ahab (869–850 B.C.), through his marriage with the Phoenician princess Jezebel, is assured of support in face of the Syrian threat. Against Moab he builds Jericho (XVI. 29–34). The Syrians besiege Samaria, which Ahab is willing to surrender. Their surrender terms, however, are so harsh that Ahab renews the war and completely routs the Syrians (XX. 1–21). After the victory at Aphek (XX. 27–30) he makes a treaty with them, securing for himself trading establishments in Damsacus

Jehoshaphat (873–849 B.C.) is the first to accept the *fait accompli* of the separate kingdoms, and ends the quarrel with Israel (XXII. 41–51). He makes a marriage alliance with Ahab (II Kings VIII. 18) and helps Israel against the Syrians (XXII. 2 ff.) and against Moab (II Kings III. 7 ff.). He uses his overlordship over Edom and the access to the Red Sea which it assures to reopen the overseas trade of Solomon's age: this, however, stops after one unfortunate attempt. Chronicles (II Chron. XVII) gives a more detailed account of him.

and the return of the cities taken from Omri (xx. 31–4). Ramoth-Gilead is not handed back, and so Ahab launches a new campaign in which he is helped by Jehoshaphat of Judah (xxɪɪ. 1–6). Ahab is killed in the battle (xxɪɪ. 29–40), whose outcome is thereby decided, together with the fate of Ramoth.

On the accession of his son Ahaziah (850–849 B.C.) Moab rebels against Israel (ɪɪ Kings ɪ. 1, ɪɪɪ. 5). As the result of an unfortunate fall the king dies, childless (ɪ Kings xxɪɪ. 51–3; ɪɪ Kings ɪ. 2, 17 f.). His younger brother Jehoram (849–842 B.C.) fights as the ally of Jehoshaphat and the Edomites (ɪɪ Kings ɪɪɪ. 1–3, 6 ff.) against the Moabites. At first they are successful but are later forced to retreat (ɪɪɪ. 21–7). Wounded in battle against the Syrians (vɪɪɪ. 28–9), he becomes the victim of a revolt headed by Jehu (ɪx. 14–26) in which the prophet Elisha is also involved (ɪx. 1–13).

Under his son Jehoram (Joram, 849–842 B.C.), the son-in-law of Ahab of Israel, the Edomites revolt against Judah. They are beaten but "revolted from the rule of Judah to this day." The city of Libnah (cf. Josh. xɪɪ. 15) also revolts (ɪɪ Kings vɪɪɪ. 16–24).

The rebel **Jehu** (842–815 B.C.) makes a clean sweep, ɪx. 27–9 and has the King of Judah (vɪɪɪ. 29) and his kinsmen (x. 12–14) killed, as well

His son Ahaziah (842 B.C.) aids Joram against the Syrians (vɪɪɪ. 25–8). He dies, while visiting the wounded Joram (vɪɪɪ. 29), as a result of an

as the queen mother, Jezebel (IX. 30–7), and Ahab's numerous sons (X. 1–11). With similar bloodshed he suppresses worship of Baal in Israel (X. 15–31). He was unsuccessful in foreign policy. Even his payment of tribute to the rising great power Assyria (which we know from a monument of Shalmaneser III) makes no difference, for Assyria is not yet powerful enough to oppose the mighty Syrian Hazael of Damascus, who plunders the whole country and annexes eastern Jordan as far as the Arnon (X. 32–6). Under Jehu's son Jehoahaz (815–801 B.C.) Syrian oppression (XIII. 1–9, 22) reduces Israel to military insignificance (XIII. 7).

His son Jehoash (801–786 B.C.) wins back the lost territory in three expeditions (XIII. 22–5) when Damascus is hardest hit by the wars with Adadnirari III of Assyria. Challenged to battle by Amaziah, he conquers Judah at Beth-shemesh, overcomes Jerusalem, plunders the Temple and palace, and takes away hostages (XIV. 8–14).

Still more favoured by fortune is his son Jeroboam II (786–746 B.C.), who succeeds in restoring Israel's frontiers from the entrance to Hamath

attack by Jehu (IX. 27–9). His kinsmen are also slain (X. 12–14).

His tyrannical mother Athaliah (842–837 B.C.) assumes power but is murdered by the priestly faction under Jehoiada (XI. 13–16, 20) which puts her rescued son Joash (837–800 B.C.), still a minor, on the throne (XI. 17–19). Joash remains a tool in the hands of the priestly faction and provides for the maintenance of the Temple by taxation and voluntary donations (XII. 1–17). When the Syrians threaten Jerusalem itself, he submits to them by paying tribute (XII. 18 f.). He is murdered by his servants, who are executed in their turn by his son Amaziah (XII. 20–2).

Amaziah, son of Joash (800–783 B.C.), is successful against Edom (XIV. 1–7) but lets himself be misled into picking a quarrel with Israel. In the ensuing war he is severely defeated (XIV. 8–14). Like his father, he is the victim of a conspiracy (XIV. 19 f.).

as far as the Dead Sea (xiv. 23–9), thus making the extent of the kingdom almost the same as in David's time. He also gains control over Damascus, greatly weakened by many Assyrian attacks. Since Assyria does not interfere with him, Israel, externally, presents a strong appearance once more. Internally, the kingdom experiences a period of prosperity and well-being, for the assessment of which the Book of Amos provides valuable material.

Jeroboam's son Zachariah (746–745 B.C.) falls victim of a conspiracy (xv. 8–12). His murderer **Shallum** (745 B.C.) is in turn murdered (xv. 13–15) by his rival for the throne, Menahem.

Once the bulwark of Damascus is shaken, Assyria penetrates into Israel for the first time.

Menahem (745–738 B.C.) surrenders voluntarily and pays tribute to Tiglath-Pileser III (Pul), exacting the money from his people (xv. 17–22).

His son Pekahiah (738–737 B.C.) is murdered as the result of a conspiracy (xv. 23–6), the instigator of which is one of his captains **Pekah** (737–732 B.C.). He is one of the agitators for a coalition

His son Azariah (Uzziah, 783–742 B.C.) is successful against Edom and wins back the Red Sea port of Elath. Chronicles (II Chron. xxvi. 1–15, 16–23) reports his other successes. He falls sick with leprosy and has to abdicate in favour of his son Jotham (as regent 750–742 B.C.) (xv. 1–7).

Jotham (as king, 742–735 B.C.) deserves praise for his work on the Temple and sees the beginning of the Syro-Ephraimitic war (xv. 32–8). In the face of the increasing threat from Assyria, the old enemies Damascus and Israel try to achieve a coalition of all the Syrian states. When Jotham refuses his support they try to compel him to join. At the beginning of this war his son Ahaz (735–715 B.C.) loses the important port of Elath "to this day." When

against Assyria, which, in order to help Judah, is now attacking Damascus and Israel. Pekah loses considerable areas of land in the north and east, the inhabitants being deported. He himself is slain by an opposing political party (xv. 27–31).

His murderer,**Hoshea**(732–724 B.C.), utilises a change of king in Assyria to cease tribute payment and to make an alliance with Egypt. But he has underestimated Assyrian power; his policy fails. The Assyrians take Hoshea prisoner, conquer the capital Samaria after a three years' siege (722 B.C.), and deport the inhabitants (XVII. 1–6 = XVIII. 9–11).

Thus the kingdom of Israel, after two hundred years of existence, disappears from the ranks of the states, even vassal states.

Jerusalem is threatened, Ahaz sees no other way out than to submit to the Assyrians, to whom he becomes tributary (XVI. 1–9). By his short-term policy, which is strongly opposed by the prophet Isaiah, he manages to avert the threat to Judah for some time. As an Assyrian vassal he has to establish Assyrian worship in Jerusalem (XVI. 10–20).

In a final meditation the Deuteronomist considers the question of how a people to whom Yahweh had made His promises could decline (XVII. 7–23). He looks for an answer neither in political complications nor in the great train of historical events. From his religious standpoint the sole reason is Israel's unfaithfulness to Yahweh: because they broke away from the house of David and continued in the sins of Jeroboam, Yahweh rejected them and afflicted them and gave them into the hand of spoilers. Appended are final observations on the rise of the Samaritans: the Assyrians settled people from Babylon and the most diverse Syrian lands in Israelite territory which was but sparsely populated after the deportations; and these people, in addition to the worship of Yahweh, remained true to their own gods "to this day" (XVII. 24–41). So a population, mixed both in race and in religion, developed with whom the later post-exilic Jews would have no dealings of any kind: even Jesus subscribed to the general view when he called the Samaritan a foreigner (Lk. XVII. 18).

The third main section (II Kings XVIII–XXV) deals with the history of the Southern Kingdom down to the destruction of Jerusalem in 587 B.C. The loyal vassal of Assyria, King Ahaz, is succeeded by his son Hezekiah (715–687 B.C.), who follows in the footsteps of David and reforms the cult; he builds an aqueduct to ensure the city's water supply in case of a siege. He is very successful in his war against the Philistines (XVIII. 1–8, XX. 20 f.). In all the states of Palestine feeling is growing against Assyria, a trend which is fomented by the rising power of Babylon (XX. 12–13). The report in the Second Book of Kings on political affairs under Hezekiah is very brief; more details are given by Isaiah, who opposed the general conspiracy against Assyria and friendship towards Egypt. Assyrian punishment for Hezekiah's open revolt is not delayed. Sennacherib attacks and overcomes all the fortified places in Judah: Hezekiah has to surrender, paying a large tribute (XVIII. 13–16). Jerusalem itself is besieged (701 B.C.), but Sennacherib has to withdraw without having conquered the city.

Manasseh, Hezekiah's son (687–642 B.C.), proves himself a loyal vassal of Assyria and as such reintroduces foreign, par-ticularly Assyrian, worship. He suppresses religious and political opposition with ruthless severity (XXI. 1–9, 16–18.) Amon (642–640 B.C.), his son, follows the same policy and is murdered by a court clique. The extent of his popularity among his people is evident from the reprisals taken on his murderers (XXI. 19–26).

Josiah (640–609 B.C.), his son, is for the Deuteronomist the other ideal king, who carries out the great reform of the Temple and renews the covenant with Yahweh (XXII. 3–XXIII. 27): "he walked in all the way of David his father, and he did not turn aside to the right hand or to the left" (XXII. 2). The destruction of the Asherah images immediately acquires politi-cal significance, for such action is synonymous with revolt against the crumbling power of Assyria. Babylon has liberated herself and is becoming a dangerous opponent. Pharaoh Neco goes to the aid of Assyria, with the secondary intention, it is true, of gaining the support of Palestine. Nothing is known of the attitude of the other Palestinian states. Josiah at all events meets Neco in battle and falls at Megiddo (XXII. 1-2, XXIII. 29-30).

His son Jehoahaz (609 B.C.) is taken prisoner by Pharaoh and carried off to Egypt. Neco imposes a heavy tribute on the land (XXIII. 31-4) and installs as king Jehoahaz's brother, Eliakim, under the name Jehoiakim (609-598 B.C.). As a loyal vassal of Pharaoh he maintains the tribute payments to Egypt. He submits to the advance of Nebuchadnezzar of Babylon, but after three years he turns again to Egypt, deaf to all the warnings of the prophet Jeremiah. The land becomes a prey to bands of raiders (XXIII. 34-7, XXIV. 1-6).

His son, Jehoiachin (598 B.C.), called Coniah in Jeremiah, has to pay for his father's policy. When Jerusalem is besieged he voluntarily gives himself up, with his court, and goes into captivity. The Babylonians plunder the city and the Temple, and deport the upper class of the population and the artisans to Babylon (XXIV. 8-16). Nebuchadnezzar puts Jehoiachin's uncle Mattaniah on the throne, giving him the name of Zedekiah (598-587 B.C.). When he becomes disloyal the great punishment begins. After more than a year of siege Nebuchadnezzar takes the city (XXV. 1-4). The fleeing King is captured and inhumanly punished: his children are slaughtered before his eyes, he himself is blinded and put in chains (XXV. 4-7), the Temple is destroyed and a large part of the population deported (XXV. 8 ff.). Over those who remain Nebuchadnezzar installs a governor, Gedaliah, but he is murdered by members of a nationalist movement (XXV. 22-6).

With the assertion that Jehoiachin is shown mercy in 561 B.C. by Evil-merodach and sits in the royal court at Babylon (XXV. 27-30) the Second Book of Kings comes to its close.

The account of the separate kingdoms presented by the Books of Kings leaves a very disconnected and incomplete impression. More than once we have to depend on other sources, on the writings of the prophets or non-Israelite evidence, if we wish to understand the historical connexions to even a slight extent.

The Deuteronomist is not primarily concerned with the historical course of events; rather he assumes that these are already known. For this reason he generally presents only very short and concise extracts from the source works at his disposal, to which he refers his reader with the following stereotyped statement "Now the rest of the acts of So-and-so, and all that he did, they are written in the Book of the Chronicles of the Kings of Judah [or Israel]" (I Kings XIV. 19, 29 and *passim*). Unfortunately these valuable court annals of the Southern and Northern Kingdoms (which must not, however, be confused with the Books of Chronicles we know) are not preserved, so that for large sections of the history of Israel and Judah we are dependent solely on the two Books of Kings and their insufficient data. The very nature of extracts such as these leads to the transmitted material being generally very objectively and very dryly presented.

If the reigns of some kings have been infused with light and colour, we owe this to the fact that the author used a series of other sources for his account. Compared with the Books of Judges and Samuel, popular explanations of names and customs are not prominent. Instead the author has inserted into his work some historical reports of Ahab's war with the Ammonites (I Kings XX); the account from the Temple chronicles of the discovery of the Book of the Law (II Kings XXII. 3–XXIII. 3); excerpts concerning Josiah's reform of the cult (II Kings XXIII. 4–20a); and a detailed history of Jehu (II Kings IX. 14–X. 31). Moreover there are a number of didactic stories concerning prophets: indeed, the Deuteronomist shows such a preference for these that the continuity of the narrative is often lost. This is particularly clear in his use of a whole cycle of stories concerning Elijah and Elisha. These were originally single stories, circulating independently, which were transmitted orally at first and then gathered together by the pupils of the prophets.

In the Elijah cycle[50] (I Kings XVII–XIX, XXI; II Kings I–II) two

---

[50] H. Gunkel, *Elias*, Tübingen 1906; id., *Die Geschichten von Elisa*, Berlin 1932, A. Alt, "Das Gottesurteil auf dem Karmel," *Festschrift Georg Beer*, Stuttgart 1935, pp. 1–18; H. Rust, "Elia am Horeb, I Kön. XIX," in *Evangelische Theologie*, V (1938), pp. 443–51; R. de Vaux, "Les Prophètes de Baal sur le Mont Carmel," in *Bulletin du Musée de Beyrouth*, V (1941), pp. 7–20; M. Avi-Yonah, "Mount Carmel and the god of Baalbek," in *Israel Exploration Journal*, II (1952), pp. 118–24; K.

different types of story can be distinguished. In the first place, stories related to historical events and to the person of the king, like Elijah's flight from Ahab (I Kings XVII. 1–3), his meeting with the royal official Obadiah (XVIII. 1–6), and with Ahab (XVIII. 17–20), the miraculous rainstorm in the King's presence (XVIII. 41–6), the flight from Jezebel (XIX. 1–8), the judgment on Ahab and Jezebel for the judicial murder of Naboth (XXI), and the announcement of the impending death of Ahaziah (II Kings I. 1–9). The anointing of Hazael as King of Damascus (I Kings XIX. 15–18) also belongs in this category. In addition there are numerous folk-tales of miracles, like the wonderful feeding in the wilderness (XVII. 4–7), the inexhaustible supply of oil in the cruse of the widow of Zarephath and the raising of her son from the dead (XVII. 8–24) to which we find obvious parallels in the Elisha stories (II Kings IV. 1–37), the judgment of God on Mount Carmel (XVIII. 21–40), the theophany at Horeb (XIX. 9–18), the miracle before Ahaziah's messengers (II Kings I. 10–16), and Elijah's ascension into heaven (II Kings II. 1–14).

The Books of Kings contain even more extensive stories of Elisha (II Kings II–IX, XIII. 14–21), whose calling as a prophet is expressly described (I Kings XIX. 16, 19–21). In content, this too is a heterogeneous collection of stories and legends. Here, however, in contrast with the Elijah tradition, the religious and ethical motive is rather subordinated to the legendary substance, which is much more strongly emphasised. Particularly connected with historical events are the promises to Hazael (II Kings VIII. 7–15) and the anointing of Jehu (IX. 1–13), both of which conflict with the Elijah tradition (I Kings XIX. 15–16)—proof of the independence of this tradition; and the promises to Joash (II Kings XIII. 14–19). The intervention of the prophet during the campaign against Moab (III. 4–27) should also be mentioned here. Between the historical tales and the legends there stands another group of Elisha stories, recognisable by the fact that its historical details are generalised, telling of the "King" or the "King of Israel" but without mentioning his

---

Galling, "Der Gott Karmel und die Ächtung der fremden Götter," in *Geschichte und Altes Testament (Alt-Festschrift)*, Tübingen 1953, pp. 105–25; id., "Der Ehrenname Elisas und die Entrückung Elias," in *Zeitschrift für Theologie und Kirche*, henceforth cited as *Z.Th.K.*, LIII (1956), pp. 129–48.

name: such are the famine and the period of plenty, the flight
of the Syrians and the death of the captain (II Kings VI. 24–VII.
20), the blindness of the Syrians (VI, 8–23), and the help of the
prophet in the time of scarcity (VIII. 1–6). The rest of what has
been transmitted concerning Elisha belongs to the category of
miracle stories. These begin with Elijah's ascension (II. 13–18),
the water at Jericho (II. 19–22), and the punishment of the
street urchins of Bethel who mock the bald-headed prophet
(II. 23–5); and they end with Elisha's death (XIII. 20–1). II Kings
IV–VI presents in a somewhat compressed form a series of
similar stories: the widow's cruse (IV. 1–7), the raising of the
Shunammite's son from the dead (IV. 8–37), the death in the
pot (IV. 38–41), the miraculous feeding of the hundred (IV.
42–4), the cure of the leprous Syrian commander Naaman
(V. 1–27), and the swimming iron (VI. 1–7).

Both cycles are undoubtedly very old, originating soon after
the death of the prophets. Thus the Elijah cycle dates back
perhaps to about 800 B.C., while the cycle of Elisha stories will
be about fifty years later.

The collection of various Isaiah stories stands out as a further
prophetic source (II Kings XVIII. 13, 17–XX. 19). These are
included in the account of the reign of Hezekiah and also
form a supplement to the Book of Isaiah (Is. XXXVI–XXXIX).
In all probability the cycle can be traced back to the circle of
Isaiah's pupils and would originate in the seventh century B.C.
Mention must be made of the visionary words of a Micaiah
(I Kings XXII. 5–28), who is not identical with the writing
prophet of similar name, and also of a few scattered episodes
from the lives of unknown prophets in the days of Ahab (I
Kings XX) and Manasseh (II Kings XXI. 7–15), unless these
fragments are later supplements.[51]

Remaining material of this nature in the Books of Kings
gives the impression of having been added in the post-exilic
period. For example, the words ascribed to Shemaiah, the
man of God (I Kings XII. 21–4), do not fit in with the actual
conditions prevailing in Rehoboam's day. Jehu's threat
against Baasha (I Kings XVI. 1 ff.) will also date from a later
period like the prophet legends of Bethel (I Kings XII. 33–XIII.
32), in which Josiah is already being mentioned by name. The

[51] Cf. Eissfeldt, *Einleitung*, p. 339 with reference to I Kings XX. 1–34.

same is very probably true of the words and symbolic action of Ahijah of Shiloh[52] (I Kings XI. 29–39, XIV. 1–18); at least the Deuteronomist has greatly revised both sections. If the Book of Kings was interspersed at all with stories of prophets, we must nevertheless bear in mind the probability that further material of this nature was assimilated at a later date.

In dealing above with the contents and their arrangment, we have already indicated the lines of development of the two Books of Kings. We have here a compilation, whose compiler had at his disposal a mass of official historical records, individual reports, and biographies of prophets. As already in the books from Joshua to Samuel, the Deuteronomist was more concerned with the selection and arrangement of this material than with creative writing of his own. With his own particular purpose in view, he has taken relatively little from his sources. The frame in which he has set the history of the individual kings and the formula-like assessment he makes are characteristic of his work. Along the same lines is a series of smaller appendixes in which the same intellectual attitude can be traced.

Of the larger additions from the Deuteronomist's pen in the second and third parts of the Books of Kings mention must be made of the following in particular: the threats against the house of Ahab (I Kings XXI. 24–6), the detailed description of religion under Manasseh (II Kings XXI. 4–15), the epilogue on the fall of the Northern Kingdom (II Kings XVII. 7–33) and the concluding report of the conquest of Jerusalem, Gedaliah's murder and the showing of favour to Jehoiachin (II Kings XXV), for which he probably had access to a report of Baruch (Jer. XXXIX–XLI).

The nature of the presentation of the material in the Books of Kings is easily recognisable. The Deuteronomist is not writing a history but is pursuing a specific religious purpose. This is shown by the standards he applies in evaluating the kings, but is even more evident in his great reflection on the decline of the Northern Kingdom. The Deuteronomist's aim is to show that idolatry brings misfortune to the state, while the suppression of

---

[52] Eissfeldt, *Einleitung*, p. 49; Noth, *Überlief. Stud.*, p. 79; but cf. von Rad, *Deut.-Studien*, p. 57, Eng. trans., p. 81, n. 1, who considers it very doubtful whether one may rank the stories of Ahijah the Shilonite with the Elijah, Elisha, and Isaiah stories.

"high place" worship brings happiness and prosperity. He tries to illustrate his conception of divine reward and punishment in the history of the kings and of the people. But—and herein lies the difference between him and the author of the Chronicles—in order to achieve this aim he neither twists individual events to suit his own purpose nor (like the Chronicler) alters or over-corrects the tradition: his peculiarity lies in his own distinctive view of cause and effect. It was because Solomon turned his heart from Yahweh and followed other gods that his kingdom was reduced by the revolt of the Northern Kingdom (1 Kings XI. 9–13).

The Deuteronomist tries to come to terms with the great catastrophe to the two kingdoms and to find its cause in his own beliefs. The righteousness of Yahweh is beyond question so far as he is concerned: it is now and for all time an unshakable certainty. But the history of his people is a story of disobedience, of defection and unfaithfulness towards Yahweh. For the Northern Kingdom the decisive sin was that of Jeroboam; every subsequent king is described as walking in the sins of Jeroboam. With Jeroboam's defection, Yahweh's judgment over Israel is already pronounced. If it is not carried out immediately, if the kingdom of Israel persists for another two centuries, this can be explained by the fact that individual kings like Ahab (1 Kings XXI. 29), Jehu (II Kings X. 30), and Jeroboam II (II Kings XIV. 26 f.) were pleasing to God in many respects. The history of the Southern Kingdom also is evidence of disobedience to Yahweh. Why was Yahweh so long-suffering and patient with it? There is only one answer, and it rings throughout the whole history of the Southern Kingdom as the Deuteronomist presents it: "for the sake of David my servant."[53] This may seem strange at first, since David is by no means over-favourably judged in this account, especially in the history of the succession. But that is not the Deuteronomist's own verdict: it is the judgment of his sources which he used in their original state in the Books of Samuel.

The picture of David drawn by the Deuteronomist is quite different: it is the ideal picture of a God-fearing, God-serving ruler: "my servant David, who kept my commandments and

[53] Thus 1 Kings XI. 13; II Kings VIII. 19, XIX. 34, XX. 6; "for the sake of David your father" 1 Kings XI. 12; "for David's sake" 1 Kings XV. 4, 5.

followed me with all his heart, doing only that which was right in my eyes."[54] As Jeroboam is the example and prototype of the godless king of the Northern Kingdom, so David, on the other hand, is the standard by which the author measures the behaviour of the kings of the Southern Kingdom: "and he did that which was right in the eyes of the Lord, as David his father had done."[55] For us, however, a certain difficulty arises here. The words "Yea, thou didst speak with thy mouth, and with thy hand hast fulfilled it" (1 Kings VIII. 24) characterise the close connexion between Yahweh's word and history; and the Deuteronomist emphasises strongly more than once how the word of Yahweh has been fulfilled in the life of an individual king.[56] This is the word, the judgment of God, inexorable and severe. But what about the fulfilment of the promise given in Nathan's prophecy (II Sam. 7) which is mentioned frequently in the Books of Kings (1 Kings II. 4, VIII. 25, IX. 5)? This question remains open for us. For the factual description of the favour shown to Jehoiachin cannot in this sense be taken as an answer.

It has been supposed that the account originally concluded with the period of the pious Josiah and that the remainder was added by another (later) Deuteronomist. The fact that the usual reference to the sources is lacking in the framework pattern for the last kings (cf. the last source reference II Kings XXIV. 5) would support this assumption;[57] but no more definite decision can be reached.

---

[54] 1 Kings XI. 33, 38, XIV. 8; cf. also 1 Kings IX. 4, XI. 4, 6, XV. 3, 5.

[55] 1 Kings XV. 11; II Kings XIV. 3, XVI. 2, XVIII. 3, XXII. 2.

[56] II Sam. VII. 13; cf. 1 Kings VIII. 20, 1 Kings XI. 29 ff.; cf. XII. 15. 1 Kings XIII; cf. II Kings XXIII. 16–18. 1 Kings XIV. 6 ff.; cf. XV. 29. 1 Kings XVI. 1 ff.; cf. XVI. 12. Josh. VI. 26; cf. 1 Kings XVI. 34. 1 Kings XXII. 17; cf. XXII. 35 f. 1 Kings XXI. 21 f.; cf. XXI. 27–9. II Kings I. 6; cf. I. 17. II Kings XXI. 10 ff.; cf. XXIV. 2. II Kings XXII. 15 ff.; cf. XXIII. 30. See also the survey in von Rad, *Deut.-Studien*, pp. 55–7, Eng. trans., pp. 78–81.

[57] For Pfeiffer, *Introduction*, pp. 409 ff., the second Deuteronomist is synonymous with our Deuteronomist who wrote the complete historical work around 550 B.C., while his First Deuteronomist is a sort of pre-Deuteronomist who composed a document around 600 B.C. using as his sources a history of Solomon, a history of the kings of Judah and one of the kings of Israel, and a Temple chronicle. Sellin, *Einleitung*, ed. Rost, p. 93 f., on the basis of the last source reference (II Kings XXIV. 5, Jehoiakim), dates the First Deuteronomist in the period immediately after 596 B.C. and the Second (=redactor of the Books of Kings) in the Babylonian exile after 561 (cf. II Kings XXV); this redactor is the source particularly of the references to future exile (1 Kings VIII. 44–51, IX. 1–9; II Kings XXI. 7–15, XXII. 15-20,

The Books of Kings do not stand alone but belong to the preceding books in the Canon. They form the conclusion of the great Deuteronomistic history (Deut. i–ii; Kings xxv) which originated about the middle of the sixth century B.C. It starts with a rebellion against Yahweh (Deut. i. 24–6) and finishes with the period of the kings who, instead of being custodians of the law of Yahweh, have shown themselves to be godless and disobedient to Him. The aim of this work is to furnish proof of the righteousness of Yahweh and the disobedience of man.

XXIII. 26 f., XXIV. 1–4 etc.). For G. Hölscher's quite different view cf. his essay "Das Buch der Könige; seine Quellen und seine Redaktion," in *Eucharisterion, Festschrift für Hermann Gunkel*, ed. H. Schmidt, Göttingen 1923, and also his *Geschichte der israelitischen und jüdischen Religion*.

CHAPTER IV

THE LATTER PROPHETS

PROPHETS IN ISRAEL

THE EVIDENCE of the Old Testament shows that prophets[1] existed in all periods of the history of Judah and Israel, but the idea associated with them did not always remain the same. So the name prophet (nabi) is generously applied to Abraham (Gen. xx. 7), to Aaron, who is described as the prophet of Moses (Ex. vii. 1), to Moses, and throughout the whole series of the Old Testament books. Women like Miriam (Ex. xv. 20), Deborah (Jg. iv. 4), Huldah (ii. Kings xxii. 14), and Noadiah (Nehem. vi. 14) are likewise named as prophetesses. From i Sam. ix. 9 one may conclude that the concept of the nabi did not replace the original "seer" until later in the early period. According to what the Old Testament tells us, they are to be imagined as men in simple clothing (ii Kings i. 8), comparable to the dervishes of the Orient, who joined together in small conventicles accompanied by supporters, disciples, or—their own description—"sons of the prophets" (ii Kings ii. 3, iv. 1). As with the Canaanite prophets, ecstasy is characteristic of the Israelite prophets:[2] with music (ii Kings iii. 15) and dancing (i Kings xviii. 26) they work themselves up into a state of excitement, of divine possession. They gash their skin (i Kings xviii. 28; Zech. xiii. 6), tear off their clothes, and rant and rave as they become possessed by God, whose spirit comes upon them and endows them with a secret strength—so much so that Samson can tear a lion apart with his bare hands (Jg. xiv. 6) and Saul cuts his oxen in pieces (i Sam. xi. 6) when he wants to summon Israel to battle. Anyone chancing upon these prophet gatherings is only too easily drawn not only into their circle, but also into their condition, and himself falls victim with them to this

---

[1] For literature on prophecy, see Bibliography.
[2] F. M. T. Böhl, "Het profetisme," in *Nieuwe Theologische Studien*, xvi (1933), pp. 133–45.

ecstasy, like Saul's messengers to Ramah (1 Sam. xix. 20 ff.).
Saul himself, on meeting a company of prophets from "the
hill of God," raves ecstatically with them (1 Sam. x. 10 ff.).
"Is Saul also among the prophets?" is not a compliment, not a
piece of flattery as is frequently thought, but a derogatory
observation referring to how he came to be associated with such
company.

1 Sam. ix. 9 (cf. also II Sam. xxiv. 11) seems to deny that
there were special *seers* (diviners) in addition to the prophets.
But the repeated juxtaposition of the two concepts (Deut. xiii.
3, 5; Is. xxix. 10), plus the fact that the seer is also mentioned
alone (II Sam. xv. 27; Is. xxx. 10; II Chron. xvi. 7), shows that
the two are to be differentiated, and that the seer occupied a
special position[3] even though the designations are not always
kept strictly apart (cf. Am. vii. 12 f.).

It is not possible to trace the details of the development of the
prophet's position. That there was such a development,
however, is evident from the fact that the prophet does not just
remain an ecstatic who babbles inarticulately in his excitement,
but becomes the messenger of Yahweh; indeed, it is Yahweh
himself who speaks through the mouth of the prophet (Is. xxxiv.
16).[4] So the prophet's words acquire a significance which cannot be sufficiently highly estimated. For these words are the
power of Yahweh (Jer. xxiii. 29), and so are able to influence
the shaping of the future (Is. lv. 11). In addition, the impart-
ing of oracles also apparently became solely the province of the
prophets (1 Sam. xiv. 37; II Kings i. 15, vii. 1). With this, the
prophet grows in power and in status. He is no longer merely
the helper in problems of daily life: he becomes the counsellor
and confidant of the royal house (II Kings iii. 13). Even the
state turns to him for advice on important decisions (1 Sam.
xxviii. 6; 1 Kings xxii. 6 ff.). So he commands great respect,
and it is not only the prophets of Asherah who enjoy hospitality

---

[3] Cf. W. Eichrodt, *Theologie des Alten Testaments*, 3rd., edn. Berlin 1948, vol. i,
pp. 146–50.

[4] M. Noth, *Geschichte und Gotteswort im Alten Testament*, Bonner Akademische
Reden No. 3, Krefeld 1950, Eng. trans., *History and the Word of God in the Old
Testament*, Manchester 1950, refers, p. 21 (Eng. trans., pp. 197–8), to three of the
newly found texts of Mari in which prophets know themselves to be messengers of
God and formulate their utterances accordingly. For all the difference in the intellectual levels of the oracles a historical connexion with later Israel is apparently
evident here. N. H. Ridderbos, *Israëls Profetie en "Profetie" buiten Israël*, Delft 1955.

at the king's table (1 Kings XVIII. 19). If the priest's function is primarily to make sacrifice, the nabi's is that of prayer; his, then, was a dual role: spokesman for Yahweh and interceder for the people.

More recent studies have shown that there were undoubtedly special cultic prophets who held an official position in the cult in addition to the priests.[5] This is supported not only by the fact that by King David's command the prophet Nathan officiated at Solomon's anointing as king in addition to the priest Zadok (1 Kings I. 34), but also by the fact that in quite a number of places[6] priests and prophets are named in one breath. The extent of these circles still requires clarification, and also whether they included all prophets or only a certain section, so that "free prophets" still existed alongside the cultic prophets.

At all events an established profession of prophets seems to have developed in the course of time. If these prophets were in any way officially appointed they would be bound up with the interests of the state, which would lead to certain conflicts of conscience. For the interests of the state did not always coincide with what the prophets, with all the earnestness at their command, had to proclaim as the will of Yahweh. The additional fact that it was an accepted custom to present gifts to the prophet for services rendered (1 Sam. IX. 7 f.; 1 Kings I. 34) could only further restrict their freedom of action. Very little of their preaching has been handed down to us, but we do have a sample of it in the words of Hananiah, who preaches salvation and freedom from the yoke of Babylon (Jer. XXVIII. 1 ff.). It may be over-subtle to see in Jer. XXIX. 27 an act by Jeremiah as a cultic prophet, or to differentiate, in the case of

---

[5] This was already being put forward by G. Hölscher, *Die Propheten*, Leipzig 1914; cf. A. C. Johnson, *The Cultic Prophet in Ancient Israel*, Cardiff 1944; A. Haldar, *Associations of Cult Prophets among the Ancient Semites*, henceforth cited as *Cult Prophets*, Uppsala 1945; K. Roubos, *Profetie en Cultus in Israël*, Wageningen 1956; R. Rendtorff, "Priesterliche Kulttheologie und prophetische Kultpolemik," in *Th. Lz.*, LXXXI (1956), cols. 339–342; G. Quell, "Der Kultprophet," in *Th, Lz.*, LXXXI (1956), cols. 401–4; R. Henschke, *Die Stellung der vorexilischen Schriftpropheten zum Kultus*, Beihefte z. Z. alttest. W., No. 75, Berlin 1957; S. Mowinckel, *Psalmenstudien III*, pp. 9–22, points out that the cultic prophets resolved themselves later into the Temple singers (1 Chron. XV. 22, 27; II Chron. XX. 14).

[6] For example, II Kings XXIII. 2; Is. XXVIII. 7; Lam. II. 20; above all in Jer. XXIII and XXIX. 26.

Amos, between his "nabi" period and his activity as a prophet of Yahweh; but it should very probably be assumed that Nahum and Habakkuk, and perhaps also Haggai, Zechariah, and Obadiah, belonged to the professional prophets. We should also take it that the collections of threat-oracles against foreign nations which, in the books of the great prophets, are completely alien in effect and are even differently arranged,[7] also originated from these circles: for they speak only of Yahweh's judgment on foreign peoples without drawing any practical application for their own people.

By "false prophets"[8] one should no doubt understand such cultic prophets as answered the people's enquiries about their fate with expectations of national and religious salvation. They are the barometer of the people's mood (Is. xxx. 10 f.) and not, as they should have been, the public conscience. In their spiritual struggles with these men the "classical" prophets constantly emphasise that the false prophets, for their own ends, tell the people what they want to be told. They speak of peace and there is no peace (Jer. vi. 13; Ezek. xiii. 10, 16), they claim to be preaching the word of Yahweh when in fact it is their own words (Ezek. xiii. 6), and these they adopt and steal from each other at every turn (Jer. xxiii. 30 f.). In addition they deceive men with their dreams (Jer. xxiii. 32). With unambiguous outspokenness Micah censured their actions:

> Its priests teach for hire,
> Its prophets divine for money;
> Yet they lean upon the Lord and say,
> "Is not the Lord in the midst of us?
> No evil shall come upon us." . . .
> Who cry "Peace" when they have something to eat,
> But declare war against him who puts nothing into
>   their mouths.   (Mic. iii. 11, 5)

What is the distinction between these and the "classical" prophets? On the basis of the episode recounted in Am. vii. 10–17 it has been believed that we ought to envisage a wide

---

[7] The oracles against foreign tribes appear in the Septuagint as the middle section of the great prophetic books.

[8] Cf. G. v. Rad, "Die falschen Propheten" in *Z. alttest. W.*, LI (1933), pp. 109–20; G. Quell, *Wahre und falsche Propheten, Versuch einer Interpretation*, Gütersloh 1952.

gulf separating the two. More recent investigations[9] have suggested a less harsh interpretation of these words and have shown that the differences are of degree rather than of kind. The distinction is best seen in the fact that the one "proclaims peace" and flatters the people, while the other threatens with judgment; the one acts as an appointed official, while the other derives his authority from the fact that he is under the special orders of Yahweh.[10]

The customary division of the writing prophets into major and minor has nothing to do with their importance but is a purely external standard denoting only the amount of their writings that has been handed down to us. These men, particularly in the pre-exilic period, are almost without exception great; they have something heroic about them. In all respects they are solitary figures. What they have to say is spoken from the depths of an inner loneliness, and they meet with no understanding from an impenitent people,[11] who in times of peace and freedom from care (Jer. VII. 4; Ezek. XII. 22) have no ears for talk of disasters and destruction (Jer. VI. 10, I. 10; Ezek. II. 10). God has to comfort and strengthen His prophets (Jer. I. 8; Ezek. II. 6, III. 8 f.) when they lose confidence in their calling (Jer. XX. 7 f.) and are inclined to despair of their people (Jer. IX. 1; Ezek. XXI. 6). So they are victims of a tremendous inner tension between their love for their people and the message which they have to deliver (Jer. XX. 18, XXXVIII. 15).

But this message does not come from within themselves; it is

---

[9] Cf. especially Haldar, *Cult Prophets* and E. Würthwein, "Amos-Studien," in *Z. alttest. W.*, LXII (1950), pp. 10–52, where further literature is quoted.

[10] More recently it has again been more firmly stressed that classical as well as other prophets were ecstatics: vide S. Mowinckel in several papers in *J. Bib. Lit.*, LIII (1934), pp. 199–227, LVI (1937) pp. 261–5; *Acta Orientalia*, henceforth cited as *Act. Or.*, XIII (1935), pp. 264–91; *Norsk Theologisk Tidskrift*, XLII (1941), XLIX (1948), pp. 129–221; and H. Knight, *The Hebrew Prophetic Consciousness*, London 1947. Purely superficially, the difference seems to us to be indicated by the fact that, in the professional prophets, the word of God is labelled as "Massa" (= burden): cf. Is. XIII. 1, XIV. 28, XV. 1, XVII. 1, XIX. 1, XXI. 1, 11, 13, XXII. 1, XXIII. 1, XXX. 6; Nah. I. 1; Zech. IX. 1, XII. 1; Mal. I. 1; Hab. I.1; Ezek. XII. 10; and in connexion with the prophet or priests (Jer. XXIII. 33, 34, 36, 38). The Yahweh oracle of the classical prophets is usually introduced by "Thus saith Yahweh" and concluded with "Oracle of Yahweh."

[11] For a characterisation of the people cf. Is. VI. 9; Jer. VII. 12, VIII. 4–5, XVII. 23; Ezek. II. 3–7, III. 11; Hos. IX. 7–9.

not the word of man but the powerful word of Yahweh, which
in many kinds of revelation, by inner hearing (audition) or
inner seeing (vision), has been conveyed to them from God
(Jer. I. 9; Ezek. III. 2 f.) by the hand of Yahweh which comes
over them and weighs heavily upon them (Is. VIII. 11; Ezek.
III. 22). This word, which beats down like a mighty hammer
(Jer. XXIII. 29), must be spread abroad whether they will or
not: they are only the tools of Yahweh.

"The lion has roared; who will not fear?
The Lord God has spoken; who can but prophesy?"

(Am. III. 8)

This is a mysterious driving force which compels them; a
sacred imperative which they cannot escape. For this reason
they know no personal considerations or hesitations, but set
about their task with all the passionate ardour of their souls.
They themselves are nothing; Yahweh and His word are all.

Swimming against the stream of public opinion in this way
was not always without danger. "Cords will be placed upon
you, and you shall be bound with them"—this is the lot which
Yahweh sketches for Ezekiel (Ezek. III. 25). Little is in fact
known of what became of the prophets. Jeremiah was thrown
into prison for his activities (Jer. XI. 19, XXXVII f.), and the
prophet Uriah was even slain by King Jehoiakim (Jer. XXVI.
20 ff.; cf. Jer. II. 30; Neh. IX. 26). Perhaps Hos. IX. 7 f. also
belongs in this context, just as a legend from the early Christian days reports the martyrdom of Isaiah. That is the fate of
those who proclaim the message of Yahweh: they stand alone
against a whole nation.

The prophets were first and foremost orators, not writers.
Occasionally they would act in private, like Jeremiah, to whom
King Zedekiah repeatedly sent seeking his intercession (Jer.
XXXVII. 3) and advice (Jer. XXI. 2, XXXVIII. 14), on one occasion
even in secret (Jer. XXXVII. 17, XXXVIII. 24). But their concern
was not with personalities, even if they did sometimes speak out
against individuals, as for example against the King (Jer. XXII.
18 f.; Ezek. XVII. 16 ff.), against various ranks and classes
(Ezek. XI. 5 ff.; Am. IV. 6; Mic. II), or against individual
personal opponents (Is. XXII. 15 ff.; Jer. XI. 20, XXVIII. 15 f.).
The faithfulness of Yahweh and the disobedience of the
people is their theme; the fate of State and people is meat for

their discussion. What they have to say as servants of Yahweh concerns everyone in general, the whole nation. And so their appearances are as public as possible, in front of the Temple (Am. VII. 10 ff.; Jer. XXVI. 2), in the streets of Jerusalem (Jer. XI. 6), and before the gates (Jer. XVII. 19); only thus can they reach the masses. They are popular speakers, and their speeches and language are of the people. Anyone who wants to influence the crowd must make them listen, must conquer their minds and bring them under his spell; must touch them emotionally with words both vivid and graphic, original and timely, otherwise the speech goes straight over their heads with no effect.

The prophets were aware of this psychological preconditioning and made abundant use of it. For this reason they attached their message to something well known, particularly to proverbs (Jer. XXXI. 29; Ezek. XVIII. 2) and catch-phrases current among the people (Ezek. XII. 22, XVI. 44). This method may be rather alien to our modern way of thinking, for it is easy to see in it an element of charlatanism; but we must not try to measure the Orient by a European standard. Their language is terse and precise, providing compact statements, flexible formulations, which readily imprint themselves on the memory, like: "For they sow the wind, and they shall reap the whirlwind" (Hos. VIII. 7). Their manner of speaking is lively and vigorous, full of short imperative statements.[12] They use rhetorical questions[13] to establish contact with their listeners: "Can the Ethiopian change his skin or the leopard his spots?" (Jer. XIII. 23), and play upon words[14] (in the manner of the famous Abraham and Santa Clara) to maintain the audience's attention. Thus the lament of the prophet Micah (I. 8 ff.) is like one long sequence of such consonant phrases. Nor did they always make long speeches. What they said was often quite short:

"Are you not like the Ethiopians to me,
    O children of Israel?" says the Lord.
"Did I not bring up Israel from the land of Egypt,
    and the Philistines from Caphtor and the Syrians
    from Kir?"   (Am. IX. 7)

---

[12] Is. XIII. 2; Jer. VI. 16 ff.; Joel II. 1; III. 13.
[13] Is. LXIII. 1 f.; Am. III. 3 f.; Zeph. II. 15.
[14] Hos. XIII. 12; Joel II. 23; Am. V. 5 ff. and *passim*.

Amos in particular is rich in short, rhythmic verses of this kind, which are not quickly forgotten and are passed from mouth to mouth, or else were noted down by the disciples of the prophets and distributed as leaflets.

Unfortunately our understanding has often been made considerably more difficult by the fact that the individual sayings (units) are not marked off from each other in the text, so that it is not always easy to see their original extent. This difficulty is further increased by the fact that the prophets naturally also wrote longer songs in poetic form and recited them publicly. Here too they knew how to affect the masses. They either added to songs already known or wrote new ones which make the audience listen expectantly. Thus Isaiah begins: "Let me sing for my beloved a love song concerning his vineyard" (Is. v. 1–7) and goes on to describe in a song, which involves the audience too from time to time, the dispute with the bad vineyard, ending effectively with: "The vineyard of the Lord of hosts is the house of Israel, and the men of Judah are his pleasant planting." Or the prophet may sing a dirge, which does not, however, contain any of the eulogies customary in such songs but depicts the fate of Israel (Am. v. 2); in other cases such a lamentation in the mouth of the prophet may be feigned and change later to ridicule of the enemy (Ezek. XXXII. 2 ff.). So they utilise many of the features of popular poetry. Ezekiel, in particular, shows a great preference for linking up with well-known songs and poems, which he then skilfully re-shapes to suit his own particular purpose. Amos also uses a joyful song of Yahweh's judgment upon the enemy (1, 3 ff.) which was surely widely known; and even if it was not, its verses are so similar in form that it is very easy to remember and would immediately be picked up by the audience. So it goes on from verse to verse, but then comes the great turning point (II. 6) and the song changes to a threat against Israel, whom the prophet reproaches with great earnestness for their sins.

Even more impressive than these songs, however, is the effect on the eye. The proclamations of the prophets are all underlined by a strange and surprising deed, the symbolic act. Not only do Isaiah (VII. 3, VIII. 1 ff.) and Hosea (I. 4, 6, 9) give their children symbolic names; Hosea represents his own

marriage (I. 3) as an image of the relationship between Yahweh
and his unfaithful people. In addition, there are a considerable
number of symbolic actions whose meaning is sufficiently
obvious. When Isaiah runs around naked and barefoot and
people ask him why—as indeed they are bound to do—the
explanation is: thus will the Egyptians be led into captivity
(Is. xx. 2 ff.). Jeremiah buries his girdle, which naturally can
no longer be used: "Even so will I spoil the pride of Judah and
the great pride of Jerusalem. This evil people . . . shall be like
this waistcloth, which is good for nothing" (Jer. xiii. 1 ff.).
Ezekiel digs a hole through the wall of his house and escapes
through this opening with his few possessions: "As I have done,
so shall it be done to them; they shall go into exile, into
captivity" (Ezek. xii. 11); or he paints on a tile the city of
Jerusalem and plays, like a child, at besieging it (Ezek. iv.
1 ff.): "a sign for the house of Israel." The most profound
effect, however, next to that of the broken vessel which cannot
be made whole again (Jer. xix. 1 ff.), is achieved by the episode
of the prophet going about with a wooden yoke round his neck
as a sign of approaching slavery. The prophet Hananiah
removes the yoke and breaks it: "Thus says the Lord: Even so
will I break the yoke of Nebuchadnezzar king of Babylon from
the neck of all the nations within two years." Apparently
defeated, Jeremiah departs: but later he returns and speaks, as
Yahweh has commanded him, his fearful threat of the breaking
of the wooden yoke and laying on of an iron one (Jer. xxviii.
14). What was said of the prophetic preaching applies equally
to these symbolic actions, strange as they may seem (e.g. Ezek.
iv. 12). In the last resort they do not come from the prophet
himself, nor do they have their origin in human thinking:
at bottom they are rooted in Yahweh, whose commands to the
prophets remain here too the deciding factor and the sole
authority.

In this connexion attention must be drawn to the prophetic
visions,[15] which are found in a whole series of prophetic books.

---

[15] Cf. in particular the works of J. Lindblom, *Profetismen i Israel*, Stockholm
1934; "Die Geschichte der Propheten," in *Studia theologica . . . Scandinavicorum*,
henceforth cited as *St. th.*, I (1935), pp. 7–28; "Die Religion der Propheten und die
Mystik," in *Z. alttest. W.*, lvii (1939), pp. 65–74; F. Häussermann, *Wortempfang
und Symbol in der alttestamentlichen Prophetie*, Beihefte z. *Z. alttest. W.*, No. 58, Giessen
1932.

In form they are all alike, but in the later books (Zechariah) the angel of Yahweh becomes an intermediary in the dialogue between God and man. In extent, however, they vary greatly, ranging from brief descriptions (Jer. I. 11 ff.), through longer ones (Ezek. xxxvii. Zech.) which include primarily the visions of the prophet's calling (Is. vi; Jer. I; Ezek. II f.), to the very extensive accounts of Ezekiel (1 f., viii ff.), which, as in the projected constitutional reform (Ezek. xl ff.), threaten to obscure the true character of the vision. The visions are written in prose and are enveloped in a peculiar, mysterious twilight. They provide a penetrating insight into the soul of the prophet; for they mirror his inner life in his contact with his God. Visions are almost symbolic actions performed by God with the prophet as the sole spectator and listener. But the most important thing even here is not what is seen (the vision), but the accompanying word of Yahweh (the audition) which Yahweh speaks to the prophet during the visionary experience. So the vision becomes an announcement from Yahweh destined only for the soul of the prophet. It is not to be assumed that the prophet repeated this in public before the assembled people; perhaps he spoke of it to the small circle of his special followers, and it will thus be to them that we owe its recording. At all events it is highly probable that the vision of the two fig baskets (Jer. xxiv) represents a prophetic announcement wrapped in visionary clothing, while in Ezek. xl–xlviii one cannot deny the efforts of a literary dresser-up even though these were not consistently applied. The transition to a conscious, intentional, literary form is clearly felt here.

In addition to the visions, other accounts written in the first person are essentially concerned with the work of the prophet. Their whole style suggests that they go back in the main to the individual prophet himself and are recorded by him or by his adherents. But there are also longer portions which (like the Book of Ezekiel) are almost completely written in the first person and so would appear to be autobiography.

Isolated prose sections are also encountered here and there giving information of some kind or other about the life of the prophet. These only occur occasionally and in the main only where a literary interest in the words of the prophet has assumed a more solid form and has been committed in writing.

At one time the prophet was generally considered as a writer, the Book of Ezekiel being cited as the example *par excellence*. It is true that this book has a pronounced literary character; as early as Isaiah (Is. xxx. 8), and even more clearly in Jeremiah (Jer. xxx. 2; xxxvi), we find definite traces also of the awakening of a literary sense. But can one generalise for all the prophetic books on this basis alone? Even a Jeremiah did not compile the first partial collection of his utterances until he had been working for two decades—at least according to the available evidence.

Progressive scholarship today takes a different line, and one which is more probable as regards the essence and development of the prophetic books. It is hardly to be supposed that the prophets made a point of personally writing down and collecting their utterances and oracles, for there is a fairly long period of prophetic activity from which only comparatively little has been transmitted: and this little is often very imperfectly arranged. So one will have to differentiate between the actual words of the prophet and the writing down of these words. What was communicated orally by the prophet would at first also circulate orally,[16] or perhaps it would be written down and preserved as a broadsheet. In any event the individual prophetic utterance, if it was not to be lost to posterity, would necessarily be recorded at some time or other, and by someone in the circles nearest the prophet (Is. viii. 16): it would then be copied by those who were specially interested. That this was not always done with the care and exactitude one would have wished is evident from the statement about Judah (Jer. vi. 22 ff.) which turns up in

---

[16] H. Birkeland, *Zum hebräischen Traditionswesen. Die Komposition der prophetischen Bücher des Alten Testaments*, Oslo 1938, assumes complexes of oral traditions which were passed on from generation to generation and were finally fixed as the common property of the Jewish community in the 4th cent. B.C., the traditional material being subjected to "the law of selection" as far as additions and omissions were concerned. These thoughts, inaugurated by H. S. Nyberg in his *Studien zum Hoseabuche*, Uppsala 1935, were continued to their ultimate conclusion by I. Engnell, *Gamla Testamentet: en traditionshistorisk inledning*, VOL. I, Stockholm 1945, and modified by S. Mowinckel, *Prophecy and Tradition*, Oslo 1946; cf. the critical attitude adopted in this connexion by O. Eissfeldt, "Zur Überlieferungsgeschichte der Prophetenbücher des Alten Testaments," in *Th. Lz.*, LXXIII (1948), cols. 529–34. In opposition to Engnell, G. Widengren, *Literary and Psychological Aspects of the Hebrew Prophets*, Uppsala and Leipzig 1948, represents the age of the fixation in writing as reversed and thus considers that the three great prophets and also Hosea and Amos themselves wrote or dictated a part of their works.

another place as an oracle against Babylon (Jer. L. 41 ff.), and also from the variants and doublets which occur, particularly in Ezekiel.

A second stage in the process of development is the compilation of small collections containing everything available about the prophet in question. These collections were often governed by considerations of material or of content; more frequently, however, the process was merely mechanical, heterogeneous statements being gathered together on the basis of purely superficial considerations, such as similar beginnings or recurring words. Moreover, there were no scruples about accepting current utterances from unknown sources. This explains the appearance of the same oracle in Micah (IV. 1 ff.) and Isaiah (II. 2 ff.). Prophecies directed against foreign peoples must have enjoyed particular popularity in this connexion: in them the Jews could give expression to their xenophobia. These also circulated singly in the first instance, as is clear from the words directed against Egypt (Is. XXXI. 3), which appear in another place directed against Tyre (Ezek. XXVIII. 2), or from the presence of the same statements about Edom (Ob.; Jer. XLIX. 7 ff.) and Moab (Is. XV f.; Jer. XLVIII. 29 ff.) in different collections. These individual oracles against foreign nations were then joined together to form their own smaller collections, and they now appear as special complexes in Isaiah (XIII–XXIII), Jeremiah (XLVI–LI), and Ezekiel (XXV–XXXII). Words of hope and salvation are generally added on at the end to soften to some extent the impression left by the threats, but these have no connexion with the prophet either in content or in time.

A third stage led to the unification of the small into larger collections. They were not always simply joined together, but were extended and supplemented here and there from the prose sections containing details from the life of the prophet, as already mentioned above. Here it may be observed that the nearer in time this stage of collecting (book forming) lay to the actual period of the prophet's activity, the richer are the sources; and the greater the interval the less interest is shown in his personal life. Apart from all kinds of contemporary additions (glosses), it was considered useful for the better understanding of the whole to put headings above the collections here and there or to add on historical reports taken from elsewhere (cf. Is. xxxvi–xxxix; Jer. lii). Finally one must also bear in mind that the writings of the prophets were handed down in four book rolls and that the prescribed distance between one set of writings and the next was not always adhered to in the course of repeated copying. So it happens that on the Isaiah roll there are several independent writings one after the other, giving the impression in the transmitted text that they belong together: also, in the Book of the Twelve Prophets, the transition from one book to the other is not always clearly recognisable.

One can see, then, that it is a long way and a complicated process from the utterance of the individual prophet to the compilation and transmission of the prophetic books, and many factors must be considered if one wishes to obtain a correct understanding of the prophetic writings and their coming into being. The old question of authenticity is now out of date. It is not a matter of the authority of the prophet, but of the authority of his word; and this word is the word of God and remains so, independent of whether it dates from this time or that and of whether it can be traced back to this or that prophet.

THE BOOK OF ISAIAH

The first Isaiah (Proto-Isaiah) and his Book (chs. 1–xxxix)

The Book of Isaiah[17] stands in the Masoretic text at the head of the Latter Prophets: this is different from the Septuagint, which puts the Book of the Twelve Prophets before the three major prophets, and different from the Jewish tradition, which puts Isaiah between Ezekiel and the Twelve, so that "destruction is arranged with destruction and promise of comfort with promise of comfort."[18] In both cases Isaiah therefore comes next to the Book of the Twelve, doubtless to give expression to the fact that neither book is an individual composition, but both represent collections. The individual headings (such as I. 1, II. 1, etc.), as well as the different forms of the component parts, provide some help towards understanding this collective work: apart from these, however, we are dependent on internal evidence.

Regarding Isaiah (= Yahweh is salvation) himself and his

---

[17] For commentaries and literature, see Bibliography.
[18] Baba bathra 14b; Goldschmidt, *Talmud*, vol. viii, p. 55.

day we gather from the book that he, the son of an unknown Amoz (I. 1, II. 1), whom a later age wrongly confused with the prophet Amos, was called by Yahweh to become a prophet (VI. 1 ff.) in the year that King Uzziah died (*c.* 742 B.C.), and that he was active into the reign of Hezekiah (I. 1), that is until after 701 B.C. Considering what a long and fateful period this was, all that has been handed down to posterity concerning his activity are very modest fragments indeed. Not much is told about his personal circumstances; nevertheless it is supposed that he probably lived in Jerusalem (VII. 3) and was perhaps a teacher of wisdom (XXVIII. 9),[19] gathering a circle of disciples around him (VIII. 16). Some have wished, without sufficient reason, to conclude from Is. XXXVIII. 21 and II Chron. XXVI. 22 that he was a physician or a royal court annalist. That he was a Temple official, as has recently been maintained, still requires proof. He went about dressed like a prophet (XX. 2) and described his wife as a prophetess (VIII. 3); also he had several sons, to whom he gave symbolic names (VII. 3, VIII. 3; perhaps also VII. 14).

Of his public activities, which took place in politically very troublous times, more is known than about his personal affairs. His lifetime is marked by the rise of Assyria as a great power; by names like Tiglath-pileser, Sargon, and Sennacherib; by the Syro-Ephraimite war, which aimed at winning Judah for the coalition against Assyria; by the much disputed policy of King Ahaz, who by voluntary submission to Assyria was able to protect his kingdom for a time from the fate of the northern kingdom Israel (722 B.C.); by unsuccessful risings and subsequent plundering, destruction, and territorial losses down to the siege of Jerusalem by Sennacherib (701 B.C.). These great events provide the background and the motive for Isaiah's activity; at the same time they provide certain possibilities for pin-pointing in time the individual collections of prophetic utterances, the first of which comprises chapters I–XII.

This structure (Is. I–XII) is not one unit but consists in turn of several smaller collections. At the beginning,[20] like a programme of work, there stands a short collection (I. 2–31) from

[19] Cf. J. Fichtner, "Jesaja unter den Weisen," in *Th. Lz.*, LXXIV (1949), cols. 75–80.

[20] K. Budde, "Zu Jesaja I–V," in *Z. alttest. W.*, XLIX (1931), pp. 16–40, 182–211.

quite a late period in the life of the prophet, in which the distress of the Sennacherib era is made only too clear: the land laid waste, cities burned down, Jerusalem only just escaping the same fate (I. 7 ff.). The spiritual attitude of the population corresponds to this external decline. If there is no internal renewal, says Isaiah, all their pretty piety, their sacrifices and prayers are of no avail. Yahweh is sick of this, and wants nothing to do with the strange combination: "I cannot endure iniquity and solemn assembly" (I. 13 f.). There is only one way to salvation, the way of conversion and repentance, of obedience to Yahweh (I. 19); otherwise judgment is inevitable.

A further collection (II. 1–IV. 6) which was originally independent, as the introduction itself shows (II. 1), and into which has been fitted an anonymous prophecy concerning the great joy of the last days (II. 2 ff. = Micah IV. 1 ff.), contains three longer poems of Isaiah, all in the same tone of Yahweh's judgment on His people. In the first (II. 5–21) the prophet brands the life of luxury, the idolatry, the riches, and the pride with which the people have made themselves worthy of judgment. "Thou hast rejected thy people . . . because they . . . strike hands with foreigners" (II. 6). The greatness of man is nothing; in reality there is only one greatness, the majesty of Yahweh. Inserted into this impressive prophecy, which sees the coming judgment as already present, is an oracle based on the popular idea of the Day of Yahweh (II. 12–17), designed to make the fearful compass of this judgment of Yahweh's even more vivid. The second poem (III. 1–15), against the men of distinction and the leaders of the people, carries the same message in violent terms: because they oppose the majesty of Yahweh, they incur divine punishment (III. 8, 13). Whether the third poem originally formed one unit or whether it comprises several single prophecies can be left undecided. The important thing is that here too judgment is given, this time because of the fashionable goings-on and coquettish vanity of the distinguished ladies of Jerusalem. Everything that is dear to their hearts—that is the inexorable message—will be taken from them: what is left to them is shame and disgrace (IV. 1), the mark of slavery branded upon them instead of their former beauty (III. 24). The whole thing (probably in imitation of Amos v. 2) is then re-interpreted from the *daughters* of Zion to *the daughter* of Zion, Jerusalem (III.

M

25 f.). This collection will date from the earlier days of the prophet, even before the Syro-Ephraimite war, when there was sure prosperity, a golden age, and no danger on the horizon threatened the carefree life of pleasure. As happens frequently with these smaller collections, it is brought to a close with a consoling utterance of salvation (IV. 2–6) concerning "that day," the great and fearful day of Yahweh. But this day of judgment is at the same time always a day of salvation, of divine grace and mercy. Following this we have Isaiah's song of the vineyard (v. 1–7), which starts off merrily like a love song, only to end with such a grave play upon words: "good rule —blood rule; law-giving—lawbreaking." It has probably been put in here by the compiler even though it has no connexion with what precedes it, just because of these concluding words.

Yet another small collection of Isaianic oracles is the "Seven Woes" (v. 8–24) concerning the rich and the wicked "who draw iniquity with cords of falsehood, who draw sin as it were with cart ropes" (v. 18). Whether the warning to the unrighteous judges (X. 1–4) also belonged to the above or whether one "woe" has been omitted (v. 14) remains questionable. Originally these would be threats spoken singly by the prophet or put into circulation separately, as the irregular structure of the cries of woe shows; nevertheless, the question remains whether the text has always been transmitted complete and intact, for in several places (v. 19, 20, 21) the actual threat is lacking. In content this group is closely connected with the preceding collection, from which (II. 11) it has adopted an amplification (v. 15 f.). Here we have the same reproach of unrighteousness, selfishness, and extravagance, which is manifested there among the women in coquetry and love of finery, and here among the men in feasting and revelling. Chronologically also this collection and the preceding one belong together.

Against all this there is the great vision (ch. VI.)[21] at the very beginning of Isaiah's career, which affords a deep insight into the decisive hour of his calling by Yahweh. In it he

---

[21] K. Budde, *Jesajas Erleben*, Gotha 1928; I. Engnell, *The Call of Isaiah*, Uppsala and Leipzig 1949; L. J. Leibreich, "The position of Chapter Six in the Book of Isaiah," in *H.U.C.A.*, XXV (1954), pp. 37–40; F. F. Hvidberg, "The Masseba and the Holy Seed," in *Norsk Theologisk Tidskrift*, LVI (1955), pp. 97–9.

experiences the holiness and the majesty of Yahweh. These become the two basic ideas in his preaching. Yahweh's holiness reveals the great gulf separating God from men, who must fear Him: "Woe is me, for I am lost; for I am a man of unclean lips" (VI. 5); but at the same time Yahweh's majesty is the power which forcefully reveals His plans and His desires in judgment and in mercy.

This vision, recounted in the first person, stands along with other autobiographical reports. This small collection (VI. 1–IX. 6) will therefore go back to the prophet himself or else will have been written down, based on his words, by his disciples. Even chapter VII, with its impressive "If you will not believe, surely you shall not be established," was probably also one of these autobiographical passages. The individual portions, with their oracles of comfort for Judah and judgment for Israel, deal with the dangerous period of the Syro-Ephraimite war; but they also include much that is personal and so would be destined for his small circle of disciples (VIII. 16). Of particular importance here are the promises of Immanuel[22] and of the birth of the child, the great Prince of Peace on the throne of David (IX. 5 f.)—Messianic prophecies which only attained their full significance and fulfilment in the New Testament.

This small collection has been inserted into another, (V. 24–30, IX. 8–21), recognisable by the last verse: "For all this his anger is not turned away and his hand is stretched out still." It contains single threat-oracles against Israel. In their thoughtless arrogance—"The bricks have fallen, but we will build with dressed stones; the sycamores have been cut down, but we will put cedars in their place" (IX. 10)—they misunderstand the extent and the fearful gravity of this judgment from God. In His wrath Yahweh will blind them and it will become a struggle of all against all, every man eating his neighbour's flesh (IX. 18–20). The historical references (IX. 10 f.) are too indefinite, however, to allow of conclusions regarding the time of origin of the individual oracles.

The last small collection (X. 5–XI. 10) finally contains a poem threatening Assyria (X. 5–15, 24–30) whose king in his arrogance has overstepped the limit set by Yahweh, namely that he should be His instrument. This divine judgment on the

[22] See Bibliography.

Assyrians is at the same time the beginning of a period of peace for the "remnant of Israel." Yahweh reveals Himself as the mighty One who will establish the kingdom of peace, the Messianic kingdom, the goal towards which all His paths lead, a new paradise. This is the content of several oracles, all of which begin with "in that day." Inserted into this poem is a poetic fragment (x. 16–23) threatening catastrophe for Jerusalem, which probably belongs to Isaiah's early days. An oracle of peace built up round the same image (a tree) is added at the end of the whole (xi. 1–10) and probably dates from later, post-exilic days.

Another post-exilic oracle (xi. 11–16) assumes the dispersal of the Jews in captivity, and has no doubt found its way in here because of its reference to Judah and Ephraim (xi. 13) and the catchword "in that day." The same words provide the link for another addition, a song of thanksgiving and praise (ch. xii) which does not belong to Isaiah but has been put here by the compiler to provide a proper conclusion for the summing up of all these smaller collections: "He has done gloriously . . .: for great in your midst is the Holy One of Israel." Thus the conclusion is reached, with due solemnity and with true Isaianic thoughts.

A further group of Isaianic oracles is contained in the Assyrian collection (chs. xxviii–xxxii), so called because these prophetic utterances are concerned with Judah's anti-Assyrian alliance with Egypt. They originate from the period 713–701 B.C.: only the first (xxviii, 1 ff.), referring to the decline of the Northern Kingdom, is older and was probably put at the beginning of this collection as a kind of programme. The individual oracles, short or longer, are all concerned with the same theme, the alliance with Egypt, and the prophet's impressive warnings do not flag. The people have bound themselves to death and Sheol and seek refuge in lies and falsehood (xxviii. 15): the Egyptians are mere men and not gods (xxxi. 3) and cannot help them. In their blindness they will not recognise this: the prophets must agree with them, they do not want to listen to anything else (xxx. 10). The word of Yahweh is to them like a sealed book which they cannot read (xxix. 11) and have no wish to understand; therefore they mock Isaiah's threats and warnings (xxviii. 9).

But Yahweh will remove their false security (xxviii. 17 f.) and will humble Judah (xxix. 8), acting like a ploughman following out his prearranged plan and design (xxviii. 23 ff.). There is only one way to happiness and salvation: to give up this policy of falsehood, turn back and seek refuge in Yahweh—"in quietness and in trust shall be your strength" (xxx. 15). Justice is his measuring tape and righteousness the plummet, but the foundation is: "He who believes will not be in haste" (xxviii. 16 f.).

This whole collection is interspersed with oracles of comfort and salvation, a few of which (xxviii. 5 f., xxx. 19 ff., xxxii) were not inserted here until the post-exilic period. The judgments against Assyria, on the other hand (xxx. 27 ff., xxxi. 4 ff.), will originate from the latter part of Isaiah's career; they are in the line of salvation oracles which were greatly favoured as conclusions to smaller collections. In addition there is a whole series of Isaianic utterances which have been included (neither by Isaiah nor by any of his pupils) in the Massah collection (see below): the impression they give is much too disconnected. For a few of them we possess exact dates, thanks to the headings; thus the oracle concerning the Philistines (xiv. 28 ff.) and the threat against Egypt (xx. 1 ff.) can be dated 711 B.C.: in other cases the situation described can be identified. The small collection of threats against Damascus and the Northern Kingdom (xvii. 1 ff.) dates from the time of the Syro-Ephraimite war (c. 735 B.C.); the warning against the ambassadors from Ethiopia (xviii. 1 ff.) can be understood against the background of the general conspiracy against Assyria (713 or 705 B.C.), while the great poem threatening Jerusalem (xxii. 1 ff.) refers to events during Sennacherib's siege (701 B.C.). The threat against the minister Shebna (xxii. 15 ff.), with the two supplements concerning his successor Eliakim, one full of promise (xxii. 20 ff.) the other menacing (xxii. 25), will likewise belong to the last period of the prophet's activity. No more certain knowledge can be obtained. In other words, we can only feel our way with the aid of scholarship. Nevertheless we must reckon that parts of the great oracle concerning Moab (ch. xv f.) and the lament about the Assyrian general levy (xvii. 12 ff.) are also of Isaianic origin. Why these utterances were inserted into the collection of oracles

concerning foreign nations—or was it the other way round?—
we can no more explain than the other phenomenon, that
foreign oracles should be included at all in the Book of
Isaiah.

Foremost among the collections of oracles concerning foreign
nations which have nothing to do with Isaiah or with his age is
the Massah collection (chs. XIII–XXIII), the oracles in which
almost all begin with the word "Massah" (= burden, doom-
oracle). They belong to the threats so popular in Israel against
foreign peoples, and originate in the most diverse periods. The
historical allusions in the oracles concerning Moab are too
indefinite to allow us to draw conclusions as to their origin.
Nevertheless they must be fairly old (in part probably Isaianic),
as is evident from the interval between them and their accompanying supplement (XVI. 13 f.). The middle of the seventh
century B.C. is taken as the date of origin of the oracle concerning Egypt, which was later extended (ch. XIX). The prophecies
against Babylon (chs. XIII–XIV), which are painted with the
many colours of the expectation of the Day of Judgment (eschatology) and include a highly poetic mockery of the King of
Babylon (XIV. 4 ff.), date from the exilic period: indeed, they
must be earlier than 539 B.C., for they announce the conquest
of the city by the Medes and not by Cyrus, and in addition
they allude to the coming return from exile (XIV. 1 ff.). The
additional oracle (XIV. 24–7), however, will perhaps date from
the late Isaianic period.[23] The utterances concerning "the
desert," Edom, and Arabia (ch. XXI) presuppose the fall of
Babylon (XXI. 9) and are exilic in time. Other oracles are even
later, particularly the burden of Tyre (ch. XXIII), probably
originally a poem on the fall of Sidon (348 B.C.) but ultimately
transferred to Tyre, which is here threatened with conquest by
Alexander (332 B.C.), while the supplement (XXIII. 15 ff.)
points to the time of Ptolemy II (274 B.C.). This provides us
with information of importance for understanding the development and growth of the individual scriptures, namely that even
collections such as these were not firmly fixed entities but remained in an indeterminate state, attracting to themselves
material of a similar nature, until quite late on.

Connected to the oracles of judgment and hope for Tyre

---

[23] Cf. Eissfeldt, *Einleitung*, p. 350.

an apocalypse (chs. XXIV–XXVII)[24] has been inserted into the Isaianic collection by the compiler; a fragment of literature which belongs in the vicinity of the books of Daniel and Enoch. These apocalypses comprise ideas of the last days and contrast the present with the world to come. They vibrate with the great and devout hope that out of all the distress of the present a new salvation will emerge under the rule of God. The generally imprecise description is fantastic and grandiose, and they paint with glowing colours the terror, but also the blessings of the judgment which God will pronounce on the last day. "On that day" (XXIV. 21, XXV. 9 and elsewhere), the day of fear (XXIV. 18), the day of Yahweh, Yahweh will come out of His place (XXVI. 21) to judge men, because they have broken the everlasting covenant (XXIV. 5); nature too will be included in the judgment because of her own transgressions (XXIV. 19 ff.); even the mythical monsters of the primeval world (XXVII. 1) are not excepted. Yahweh's judgment is the great catastrophe of the world, and yet it is the cause of exultation and rejoicing (XXIV. 14). For then Yahweh shall reign on Mount Zion in His glory which will cause even the sun and the moon to grow pale (XXIV. 23). And now comes the blessed salvation of the last day: Israel is gathered together again from all sides out of captivity (XXVII. 12 f.) and Yahweh holds His coronation feast on Zion, a feast of joy for all people. "And he will destroy on this mountain the covering that is cast over all peoples, the veil that is spread over all nations. He will swallow up death for ever, and the Lord God will wipe away tears from all faces, and the reproach of his people he will take away from all the earth" (XXV. 7–8). This apocalypse is interspersed with cultic and religious songs (such as XXV. 1 ff., 9 ff., XXVI. 3 ff., 7 ff.); indeed one particular, apparently familiar song is expressly cited (XXVII. 2 ff.), as a later period always delights in inserting pious songs in apparently suitable places. There is also a threat against Moab (XXV. 10 ff.), but this has been completely transformed in an eschatological mould. Attention has been drawn to certain contradictions, especially in the salvation for

[24] W. Rudolph, *Jesaja XXIV–XXVII*, Stuttgart 1933; J. Lindblom, *Die Jesaja-Apokalypse Jes. XXIV–XXVII*, Lund and Leipzig 1938; M. A. Beek, "Ein Erdbeben wird zum prophetischen Erleben (Jesaja XXIV–XXVII)," in *Archiv. Orientalni*, XVII (1949), pp. 31–40; E. S. Mulder, *Die Teologie van die Jesaja-Apokalipse*, Groningen 1954.

Israel (xxvii. 12) and for all people (xxv. 6), and some have attempted to explain these by the existence of several strata or of different individual portions. To this literary genre, however, one cannot apply modern standards of strict logic. It is true that this apocalypse stands out from other similar sections by virtue of its many concrete features (xxiv. 10 f., xxv. 2, xxvii. 10 f.). Some have therefore taken it to be a liturgy (xxvi. 2 f.), a sort of festival cantata on the fall of the "great city." But on closer examination these "concrete features" melt away again into indeterminate and uncertain expressions, which make application to a definite city and a definite historical event impossible. So the old conception will have to persist. An exact date—opinions vary from the exile down to the end of the second century b.c.—is as impossible here as in the other, probably somewhat older, apocalypse in chapters xxxiv–xxxv;[25] we date both in the early post-exilic period.

The second apocalypse (ch. xxxiv f.) also speaks of the Day of Yahweh (xxxiv. 8) as a general judgment over the whole cosmos (xxxiv. 1 ff.). But the redeemed shall return home from being scattered abroad and will come to everlasting joy along the holy way to Zion (xxxv. 8 ff.). The judgment itself is depicted here in a longish description of the fate of Edom (xxxiv. 5 ff.): some of the features are so concrete that one may assume that this is an older, tribal oracle eschatologically remodelled.

An appendix to the great compilation of the Isaianic collections is the Prophetic Liturgy (ch. xxxiii),[26] which will also date from post-exilic times. Such liturgies have their *Sitz im Leben* in the cult, in the prayers of the congregation and the divine answer: thus in the alternation between priests, choir, and congregation we see combined the prayers of the people (xxxiii. 2 f., 7 ff.), the priestly Torah (doctrine of the priests, xxxiii. 15 f.), and the divine promise (xxxiii. 5 f., 10 ff., 17 ff.).

---

[25] W. Caspari, "Jesaja xxxiv und xxxv," in *Z. alttest. W.*, xliv (1931), pp. 67–86; J. Muilenburg, "The literary character of Isaiah xxxiv," in *J. Bib. Lit.*, lix (1940), pp. 339–65; M. H. Pope, "Isaiah xxxiv in relation to Isaiah xxxv. 40–66," in *J. Bib. Lit.*, lxxi (1952), pp. 235–43. C. C. Torrey, *The Second Isaiah*, New York 1928, wants to attribute the poem to Deutero-Isaiah, as R. B. Y. Scott, in *A.J.S.L.*, lii (1936), pp. 178–91 and A. T. Olmstead, in *A.J.S.L.* liii (1937), p. 251–3 would do with ch. xxxv.

[26] H. Gunkel, "Jesaja xxxiii, eine prophetische Liturgie," in *Z. alttest. W.*, xlii (1924), pp. 177–208.

A last supplement (chs. XXXVI–XXXIX) finally treats of Sennacherib's siege of Jerusalem, but not because of the historical events, which are reported in almost the same words as in II Kings (XVIII. 13, 17–XX. 19). The concern here is with the prophet and the actual sources for this section are prophetic traditions which probably go back to the prophet himself or his disciples. The text is enlarged by the so-called Psalm of Hezekiah (XXXVIII. 9–20),[27] which in itself has no connexion with King Hezekiah but has been inserted here from the rich store of "songs of individual thanksgiving." Since in Chronicles (II Chron. XXXII. 32) the appendix is cited as merely a component part of the "book of the Kings of Judah and Israel" it is possible that it did not get into the Isaiah collection until late, the third century B.C. at the earliest.

The development of the Book of Isaiah shows that we are dealing not with one book, but with a whole library, which has grown up from the most varied origins and has a special character of its own. But all the parts are equally testimonies of God, and from them the pious man learns to recognise and comprehend His holiness and His majesty.

Anonymous Prophets (Isaiah XL–LXVI)

The anonymous prophecy (chs. XL–LV) which comes after Isaiah and now appears in the text with him as a unit is usually referred to as Deutero-Isaiah (second Isaiah).[28] Centuries separate it from the actual Isaiah. We encounter here quite a different world and another era. It is no longer a question of Assyria, which has long since receded into the past (LII. 4). A new power is on the increase, that of Cyrus, King of Persia (559–530 B.C.), who has started on his victorious march (XLI. 2 f., XLV. 1) and is now threatening Babylon (XLI. 25, XLIII. 14), an event with which the prophet has linked the greatest of hopes for his people: "He shall build my city and set my exiles free" (XLV. 13). For the present the people are in a state of utter despair. Judah is laid waste (XLIX. 19), Jerusalem is depopulated and deserted (XLIV. 26, LII. 9), the Temple is destroyed (XLIV. 28), and the people of Israel themselves are carried off into exile (XL. 2, 27) into Babylonian captivity

---

[27] J. Begrich, *Der Psalm des Hiskia*, Göttingen 1926.
[28] For commentaries and literature, see Bibliography.

(XLII. 7), which weighs heavily upon them like a yoke (XLVII. 6).

But now, and the whole prophecy is tuned to this confident and happy note, there is hope: slavery will soon come to an end (XL. 2 f., XLIX. 25). Yahweh has called upon an eagle from a far country (XLVI. 11) to be His instrument (XLI. 4). And so Cyrus is called by great names: "My shepherd" (XLIV. 28), even "My anointed" (XLV. 1); "The Lord loves him; he shall perform his purpose on Babylon, and his arm shall be against the Chaldeans" (XLVIII. 14). The prophet never tires of conveying, with ever new phrases and thoughts, his great and joyous message: "Comfort, comfort, my people" (XL. 1); there is no more need for fear and anxiety (XLI. 10, 14 and *passim*). The reproach-oracles are no longer bound up with threats, as was formerly the practice, but with promises. Israel called down this terrible fate upon herself (L. 1), for she was blind and deaf (XLIII. 8) and paid no heed to Yahweh's commandments (XLII. 20, XLVIII. 4, 18). And so Yahweh kept silence for a time (XLII. 14) and forsook the Israelites for a brief moment (LIV. 7) in order to refine and test them in the furnace of affliction (XLVIII. 10). He let them drink out of the cup of staggering; but now He is going to take it away from them and "put it into the hand of your tormentors" (LI. 17 ff.). For Yahweh loves His people (XLIII. 4) as a mother cherishes her children (XLIX. 15), and will have mercy on His chosen servant (XLI. 8, XLIV. 1 and *passim*) to the extent of an everlasting salvation (XLV. 17). For His own sake (XLVIII. 11) Yahweh has revealed Himself (XLIV. 23) before all the world (LII. 10), and "I will put salvation in Zion, for Israel my glory" (XLVI. 13). Yahweh is the first and the last (XLIV. 6, XLVIII. 12), the Almighty (XLIII. 11). This is specially stressed in a whole series of hymns on nature and the creation of the world by Yahweh.[29] Here the idea of universalism arises: there is no God except Yahweh and all other gods are idols, made by human hands and therefore nothing. All the ends of the earth must therefore turn to Yahweh (XLV. 22). This is the new idea of the mission to all nations. Although no doubt is left that Yahweh is the God of Israel in particular, His judgment is nevertheless described as "a light to the peoples."

[29] Cf. Is. XL. 22–4, 25–6, 28, XLII. 5, XLIII. 16–17, XLIV. 24–5; XLV. 5–8, 11–13, 18–19, XLVIII. 12–16, LI. 9–10, 13, 15–16.

For the heavens will vanish like smoke,
    the earth shall wear out like a garment . . .
but my salvation will be for ever,
    and my deliverance will never be ended.

                        (LI. 4 ff.)

For all its relationship to contemporary history this proclamation has a strong eschatological flavour.

Read as a connected whole this section may easily seem
monotonous, but one must bear in mind that it is not one
complete piece of work but a combination of single prophetic
utterances. Only when one takes each separately and allows it
to exert its individual influence does one feel something of the
strength and greatness of these oracles. The vividness and
simplicity of the images, such as the representation of Zion as
daughter (LII. 1 f.), bride (XLIX. 18), wife (LIV. 1), mother
(XLIX. 22), and widow (LIV. 4), the abundance of rhetorical
questions, the many demands, the large number of hymns
introduced, in general the whole liveliness and flexibility of the
style are obvious signs that these individual oracles were
recited orally, probably among small circles of devout exiles.
Forty-nine of these individual utterances have been distinguished, all standing quite disconnectedly side by side. It
would therefore appear to be a waste of time to look for any sort
of formal arrangement. Nevertheless it is worth noting that the
first nine chapters (XL–XLVIII) deal with Cyrus and the fall of
Babylon (Hymns of Yahweh and Israel), while the remainder
of the oracles (XLIX–LV, Hymns of Zion and Jerusalem)
contain nothing on this subject.

The date of the first collection is clearly indicated: these
oracles all belong to the period from Cyrus's first attack on
Babylonia (June 546 B.C.) down to before the fall of Babylon
(539 B.C.). Since, however—so the explanation continues—the
great hope for the captives which the prophet connected with
this event was not fulfilled, he said no more about it in the
later period. And so the second group, in so far as it is not
ascribed to a later hand altogether, is dated as falling in the
period from after the conquest of Babylon down to the decree of
Cyrus (538 B.C.; Ezra VI. 3 ff.). But it can hardly be assumed
that all these seven chapters originated within the short span of

only one year, so it is more probable that a portion of these oracles also belongs to the first period. They were later arranged, according to their content, into a "more historical" and a "more eschatological" collection. That the prophet (or the compiler in his immediate circle) was not entirely without a literary interest of this nature is evident from the conclusion of the work (LV. 11) which has a certain intrinsic connexion with the beginning (XL. 8).

The fact that the prophet does not go into particular details about conditions peculiar to Babylonia has led some to fix his sphere of activity as in Palestine, the Lebanon area, and even indeed in Egypt: it is and remains most probable, however, that he was active in Babylonia, where the exiles did not need an explicit account of conditions. And if he was at work during the exile, this explains the anonymity of this document so bitterly directed against Babylon, and the absence of all personal information.

An important group within the Deutero-Isaiah collection comprises the four (or, with a different method of counting, six) 'Ebed-Yahweh songs (XLII. 1–8, XLIX. 1–6, L. 1–9, LII. 13–LIII. 12, or divided, XLII. 1–4, XLII. 5–7, and in addition L. 10–11), which sing of "the servant of the Lord" ('Ebed-Yahweh).[30] In speech and in style, as well as in the thoughts expressed, they are to a large extent reminiscent of the second Isaiah. It is pointed out that they can be removed without

[30] It is almost impossible to survey the literature on these songs; cf. the references in G. Fohrer, in *Th. R.*, XIX (1951), pp. 298–304 and *Th. R.*, XX (1952), pp. 228–9. For the period up to 1952 we restrict ourselves to mentioning only H. H. Rowley, *The Servant of the Lord*, London 1952. Among the more important works which have appeared since are: V. de Leeuw, "De koninklijke verklaring van de Ebed-Jahweh-Zangen," in *Ephemerides Theologicae Lovanienses*, XXVIII (1952), pp. 449–71; id., "Le serviteur de Jahve, figure royale ou prophétique?" in *L'Attente du Messie*, Bruges 1954, pp. 51–6; H. L. Ginsberg, "The oldest interpretation of the Suffering Servant," in *Vet. test.*, III (1953), pp. 400–4; F. M. T. Böhl, "Prophetentum und stellvertretendes Leiden in Assyrien und Israel," in *Opera Minora*, Groningen 1953, pp. 63–80; H. G. May, "The righteous servant in Second Isaiah's Songs," in *Z. alttest. W.*, LXVI (1954), pp. 236–44; H. Cazelles, "Les poèmes du serviteur," in *Recherches de science religieuse*, XLIII (1955), pp. 5–55; R. Press, "Der Gottesknecht im Alten Testament," in *Z. alttest. W.*, LXVII (1955), pp. 67–99; H. W. Robinson, *The Cross in the Old Testament*, London 1955; C. Lindhagen, "The Servant of the Lord," in *Ex. Times*, LXVII (1955–56), pp. 279–88. 300–2; P. A. H. de Boer, "Second Isaiah's message," in *Oudtestamentische Studien*, henceforth cited as *Oudtest. St.*, XI (1956); V. de Leeuw, *De Ebed-Jahwe Profetieën*, Assen 1956; W. Zimmerli and J. Jeremias, *The Servant of God*, London 1957.

interrupting the continuity of the whole, but that does not mean very much with a loose collection of prophetic utterances such as we have here. Nevertheless it is possible that these songs, which belong closely together, originally circulated independently during the exile and were then included in the Deutero-Isaianic collection by the prophet himself (or by a later hand).

Their theme is the servant whom Yahweh chose even in his mother's womb and called (XLII. 6, XLIX. 1, 5) to glorify His name (XLIX. 3) and carry out His great plan of salvation. The servant, specially equipped for his task by Yahweh (XLII. 1. 4, XLIX. 2, L. 4 f.), is commissioned by Him to bring Israel back to be a light to the heathen (XLII. 6, XLIX. 6, LII. 15). His way is not through the streets (XLII. 2) but in silence, and leads him through suffering and death (L. 6 f., LIII). Above all, the idea of the vicarious suffering of this servant of God (ch. LIII) who has endured death to save men (LIII. 4–5) became of fundamental importance when related to the suffering and death of Jesus.[31]

The question here, however, is who was originally meant by the servant of God. As always, opinions on this subject differ greatly. The term "servant" has been taken collectively as referring to the people of Israel, who are quite often described in Deutero-Isaiah as the servant of God—indeed, this interpretation appears in one of these very songs (XLIX, 3); or an ideal nucleus of "spiritual" Israelites who suffer as the servant of God under their materialistic fellow countrymen. But the description has far too many personal characteristics to be understood as collective. Those who have postulated an individual have discussed all sorts of possibilities—Moses, Isaiah, Jeremiah, Jehoiachin, Zerubbabel; past, present, and Messianic future. Some have suspected this servant of God of being an unknown exilic prophet and martyr,[32] whose songs were adopted by Deutero-Isaiah who transferred their meaning to Israel and then finally included them in his collection. It is more probable, however, that what we should see in these songs is confessions of Deutero-Isaiah to a small circle of his followers.

[31] Cf. H. W. Wolff, *Jesaja 53 im Urchristentum*, 2nd edn. Berlin 1950.

[32] S. Smith, *Isaiah Chapters xl–lv: Literary criticism and history*, London 1944, examines the historical events from 547 to 538 B.C. and relates these to Isaiah, whom he suspects to be the leader of an underground movement against Babylon who sees in Cyrus the ruler promised by Yahweh and who is killed by his fellow countrymen.

This would bring his activities out of the previous darkness of the impersonal. But since LII. 13–LIII. 12 cannot very well come from himself, this song will have been written by a follower of Deutero-Isaiah. However, we cannot get beyond supposition, and we might well ask ourselves the question of the Ethiopian eunuch: "About whom, pray, does the prophet say this, about himself or about someone else?" (Acts VIII. 34). Because of these 'Ebed-Yahweh songs the second Isaiah has been labelled as "the evangelist of the Old Testament" and as "the precursor of Jesus."

The remainder of the present Book of Isaiah consists of later appendixes (chs. LVI–LXVI), which presuppose a different period from Deutero-Isaiah. The stage is no longer set in exile but in Jerusalem, where the Temple appears to have been rebuilt (LVI. 7, LXVI. 6). The return home has become a reality (LVI. 8), and more returned exiles are awaited (LVII. 14, 19). But this is no longer the central experience, as in the hope of Deutero-Isaiah. Quite different questions now stand in the forefront of interest, questions concerned with the structure of the community (LVI. 1 ff., 9 ff., LXV. 1 ff.) and with social evils (ch. LIX.). In addition cultic matters in particular occupy much space, such as proper fasting (LVIII. 2 ff.), keeping the Sabbath (LVI. 2, LVIII. 13), and the struggle against idol worship.

These appendixes are grouped together under the title Trito-Isaiah (third Isaiah). But this description is misleading in that it could easily give the impression that in these chapters, as in Deutero-Isaiah, we are dealing with one prophetic personality alone. In actual fact, what we have before us is a variegated collection from many centuries, and we cannot state with any certainty whether the component parts were incorporated individually into the Book of Isaiah or whether the whole was added to Isaiah as a complete collection.[33] Great difficulties arise in dating the individual parts, and in view of the limited space at our disposal here we will confine ourselves to giving dates for only a few of them. The most closely connected to Deutero-Isaiah in time and in content is a small collection (chs. LX–LXII), which also reveals strong contacts with the 'Ebed-Yahweh songs (LX. 1 ff.) and even contains in

---

[33] For literature, see Bibliography. Like B. Duhm at an earlier period, K. Elliger now—although he quotes a different starting time—supports the uniformity of Trito-Isaiah, whom he considers as a contemporary of Zechariah.

parts word for word citations from the latter (LX. 4, LXI. 8); it comes from the early post-exilic period and will include LVII. 14 ff. It is more difficult to date the great repentance liturgy (LXIII. 7–LXV. 25), the first part of which seems to date from the exile, even before Deutero-Isaiah, for it makes express mention of the destruction of the city and the Temple (LXIV. 9 f.); on the other hand, the polemic against the Samaritans in the second part (LXV. 1 ff.), and especially against the worship of the god of fortune, Gad, and the goddess of fate, Meni (LXV. 11) point to a much later exilic period. The great threat-oracle (LVI. 9–LVII. 21*), with its description of the godless, is best set in the period before 445 B.C. (Ezra IV. 7–23), while the oracle condemning the building of the temple (LXVI. 1–4) probably refers to the Samaritan temple on Mount Gerizim and would therefore originate about 330 B.C. Thus Trito-Isaiah is a very complicated structure; its special significance lies in the fact that it gives us some insight into the life of the post-exilic Jews on which the sources yield but little fruit.

THE BOOK OF JEREMIAH

For no other of the writing prophets are so many details of life and fate known as in the case of Jeremiah (= Yahweh exalts), who was born in Jerusalem about 650 B.C., the son of a priest Hilkiah of Anathoth (I. 1).[34] He had much in common with his great predecessor Isaiah. He too was chosen by God as a youth (I. 7) about 628 B.C. (I. 2; XXV. 3) and specially called to be a prophet (I. 5 ff.); he too worked in the Southern Kingdom under several kings; his life was also lived in politically important and troublous times. But what Isaiah was spared, he had to experience twice (598 and 587 B.C.), namely the conquest of Jerusalem and even more terrible, the collapse of his native land. Whether he is identical with the anonymous prophet of the contemporary Lachish Letters still requires clarification.[35] In the vision of his calling Yahweh sketched out the path he was to take and the task before him: to preach doom and repentance, "to pluck up and to break down" kingdoms (I. 10).

[34] For commentaries and literature, see Bibliography.
[35] The question is answered in the affirmative by R. Dussaud in *Syria*, XIX (1938), pp. 256–71 and by H. Michaud in *Revue des études sémitiques et babyloniens*, 1941, pp. 42–60, but in the negative by H. Torczyner, *The Lachish Letters*, London 1938, and D. W. Thomas, *"The Prophet" in the Lachish Ostraca*, London 1946.

How heavily this calling weighed upon him, to stand like
a "fortified wall of bronze" (xv. 20) against the people whom
he loves and for whom he prays (vii. 16; xi. 14), his confessions
bear moving witness. They provide us with a glimpse into the
life of the soul and the inner conflicts of this lonely man (xvi.
1 ff.). More than once he almost breaks down under the burden of being Yahweh's mouthpiece (xv. 19) and yet condemned
to have no success in his work. Because of this inner tension he is
overcome from time to time with the deepest depression and
despondency: in these moods his heart does not only overflow
with prayers of vengeance on his enemies (e.g. xi. 20, xviii. 21)
and, like Job, bitter curses upon himself (xv. 10, xx. 14 ff.);
more than once he is moved to remonstrate with God (xv. 18,
xx. 7), and yet he cannot escape from Yahweh. His obligation
to the service of Yahweh repeatedly reveals itself as stronger
than his own will: that is the true character of a prophet.

> If I say, "I will not mention him,
>   or speak any more in his name,"
> there is in my heart as it were a burning fire
>   shut up in my bones,
> and I am weary with holding it in
>   and I cannot.   (Jer. xx. 9)

His work began in his birthplace (xi. 18, xii. 6): we do not
know when he went from there to Jerusalem, nor whether the
trouble in Anathoth which threatened his life (xi. 21) belongs
at the beginning of his career or to the later period (under
Jehoiakim). Of the reasons which drove him to the capital he
himself writes:

> Then I said, "These are only the poor,
>   they have no sense;
> for they do not know the way of the Lord,
>   the law of their God.
> I will go to the great,
>   and will speak to them;
> for they know the way of the Lord,
>   the law of their God.
> But they all alike had broken the yoke,
>   they had burst the bonds."   (Jer. v. 4–5)

The first period of his activity (628–609 B.C.), during the reign of Josiah, is essentially recorded in the beginning of his book. After the call-vision (ch. I), with the two small visions of Yahweh's vigilance over the doing of His word (I. 11 f.) and of the pot as the symbol of approaching disaster from the north (I. 13 ff.), there follow individual prophetic utterances which are here combined to form a whole (II. 1–IV. 4). Dealing with the relationship between Yahweh and His people, they are modelled on well-known prophetic ideas (Hos. II. 17). The people followed Yahweh at first: He led them faithfully through the wilderness into a fertile land. But they rewarded their God with evil and by their idolatry broke the marriage: "For your gods have become as many as your cities, O Judah; and as many as the streets of Jerusalem are the altars you have set up to shame, altars to burn incense to Baal" (II. 28, XI. 13). Legally, therefore, there is no longer any possibility of Israel being taken back again by Yahweh (II. 1–III. 5). Yet there is one possibility; if the people repent and turn again to Yahweh: "If you return, O Israel . . . and do not waver . . . then nations shall bless themselves in him" (III. 14–IV. 4).

The next section from this period (IV. 5–VI. 30) is a new compilation. It has been suggested that what it contains are poems written by Jeremiah and not spoken words at all; however, it is all so lively and vivid that we may assume prophetic utterances and oracles here also. They have been arranged according to their subject-matter but reveal no one uniform train of thought. Their theme is judgment, its causes and its coming. Israel is going to be involved in war, and Yahweh (IV. 12) has brought about this evil (VI. 19); it will come from the north. These portions have been entitled Scythian songs, because they perhaps refer to the Scythian danger. With the well-known colours of popular tradition about the eschatological "enemy from the north," Jeremiah paints his pictures of a forthcoming catastrophe which is synonymous with "disaster on disaster" (IV. 20). From a far country (IV. 16), from the uttermost ends of the earth (VI. 22), the enemy approaches like a cloud (IV. 13) with horses and horsemen (VI. 22 f.), inexorable (VI. 4) and invincible (V. 15). There is no escape. Its coming brings chaos to the earth, so that the mountains tremble and the sun is eclipsed (IV. 23). This is the

N

punishment for the unfaithfulness of Israel; for they have broken Yahweh's covenant (IV. 18) and renounced it (V. 12) in their disobedience (VI. 16 ff.); there is not a man among them who does right (V. 1). In single images the prophet depicts the morally corrupt life and actions of Israel (V. 3 f., 23 ff., VI. 13 ff.). And yet: "Be warned, O Jerusalem, lest I be alienated from you; lest I make you a desolation, an uninhabited land" (VI. 8)—so there is a slight note of hope in this proclamation of doom, but it is very slight, for when Jeremiah assesses his effectiveness (VI. 27 ff.) all he can say of his people is that they are all bad in the same way (VI. 28); "Refuse silver they are called, for the Lord has rejected them" (VI. 30).

The sources of Jeremiah are not copious in the later Josianic period (622–609 B.C.). The explanation has been put forward that the reform of the cult brought about such decisive changes that Jeremiah, inwardly satisfied with this situation, would have had no more cause for preaching repentance. But it is more probable that much from this period has been lost in transmission; moreover it is noteworthy that the prophet describes the sinful conditions of this period also (III. 6–10)[36]. Assyria at that time was in a state of decay; the Medes and Babylonians had achieved independence and in 614 B.C. rose to strike the decisive blow which was crowned by the conquest of Nineveh (612 B.C.). From then on the great power of Assyria was no more, although the remnant of the state carried on a shadow existence for a further few years. So Judah's vassalage also was greatly lightened, and the account (II Kings XXIII. 15; II Chron. XXXIV. 6) will be reliable when it states that Josiah brought the erstwhile Northern Kingdom more and more under his influence politically—not only in religious and cultic matters. Suited to this period are the prophetic oracles dealing with the return of those deported from the Northern Kingdom, and in the first of these (3, 6–13) it is expressly emphasised that it dates from the days of Josiah. The majority of these utterances is found in the so-called "Book of Consolation" of Jeremiah (chs. XXX–XXXI). Psychologically, it is easy to understand

---

[36] Sellin, *Einleitung*, ed. Rost, p. 114 considers III. 6–18, with the exception of vss. 12b–13 (Lods, *Histoire de la littérature*, p. 425: vss. 11–13) as secondary, and establishes a certain dependence on Ezekiel; cf. on the other hand Eissfeldt, *Einleitung*, p. 394 and Rudolph, *Jeremia*, p. 21.

why they do not always exist in their original form but have been expanded by later writers and extended to include Judah (III. 14 ff. and above all XXXI. 23 ff.): the same applies to the later addition of the threat (XXX. 23 f.) and the Messianic prophecy (XXX. 8 f.), which is made up from other oracles.

For the second period of Jeremiah's career, during the reign of Jehoiakim (608–598 B.C.) the protégé of the King of Egypt, the material transmitted is much more extensive (chs. VII–XX), but it does not give the same impression of completeness as the prophecies of Josiah's reign. Here, too, we find numerous oracles in rhythmic form, on the great theme of Judah's sin and punishment (XIII. 15 ff., XVII. 1 ff., XVIII. 13 ff.) and particularly directed against the religious lapses of the people (VIII. 4 ff., 13 ff.). Because the people have renounced Yahweh, He will sling them out (X. 17 ff.) or consume them with fire (XI. 15 f.): the losses will be so severe (XV. 5 ff.), and the land so desolated, that a general great weeping and wailing will go up from the people (IX. 9 ff.), and the prophet (VIII. 18 ff.) and indeed Yahweh Himself will be forced to join in this lament over His wasted heritage (XII. 7 ff.). In addition to the invective against Shallum (XXII. 13 ff.) and the threat against Jehoiakim (XXII. 18 f.), some other rhythmic portions certainly would not be spoken in public. These include above all the passionate laments about the uselessness of Jeremiah's endeavours (IX. 1 ff.) and the difficulty of his task (XX. 7 ff.): besides his prayers for vengeance on his enemies (XVII. 14–18, XVIII. 19 ff.) there is that great dialogue in which his soul wrestles with Yahweh on behalf of the people (XIV. 7 ff., XV. 10 ff.). Moreover there are the wisdom oracles (XVII. 5 ff.), culminating in the assertion that Yahweh is the one true glory of man (IX. 22 f.); and for the first time in the religious history of the Old Testament the question is raised of the prosperity of the godless (XII. 1 ff.).

In addition to these poetic sections the prose material is quite extensive. Outstanding in this connexion are the prophet's two autobiographical reports, in which he tells of the danger which threatened his life in his birthplace (XI. 18–23, XII. 3–6), and of his visionary experience with the hidden and spoiled girdle (XIII. 1 ff.), which is symbolic of Judah's corruption.

Another part which stands out is a biographical prose account (parts of XIX, XX. I ff.) dealing with the symbolic action of the broken jug, and the prophet's clash with Pashur, as a result of which he was flogged, pilloried and forbidden to speak. These mostly give the exact circumstances of the prophetic utterances which are imparted only in prose, and reveal a particularly obvious interest in the life history of Jeremiah. The same source from the same period provides us with the remarkable account of the fate of Jeremiah's records and their rewriting by Baruch (ch. XXXVI). Similarly we have the report of his arrest and the threat to his life by the priests and prophets (ch. XXVI); only the facts that Micah had also spoken words of this nature and that the minister Ahikam protects him saves Jeremiah's life and spares him the fate of the prophet Uriah. These records are generally ascribed to Baruch. Nowhere, it is true, does the text directly support Baruch's authorship, but the assumption is justified. For these accounts are so rich in small personal features and so well versed in the trivial details of Jeremiah's life (e.g. XXXVIII. 11, XL. 12) that they could only have been written by an eye-witness and trusted friend.

The other source, which brings us the longer prose speeches (VII. 1–15, 20–8, XI. 1–14; XVI, XVII. 19–27, XVIII. 1–12), is quite different. The distinguishing feature of these speeches is that they present a number of utterances by Jeremiah with which we are already familiar in another context.[37] A comparison of the version of the Temple speech (ch. XXVI) with the account given here (VII. 1 ff.) shows the particular interest in cultic matters (VII. 16 ff.) which is frequently expressed. This does not mean that these portions had nothing to do with Jeremiah: they will be derived to a considerable extent from the prophet himself, perhaps from autobiographical reports which are not otherwise preserved. But this prophetic nucleus has been revised—very probably, as the close stylistic connexion with the Deuteronomist suggests, by his circle or, if one prefers, by disciples of Jeremiah who were at least very close to that circle. The story of the remarkable house of the Rechabites (ch. XXXV) has also been transmitted in this revision work.

The third period comprises the remainder of Jeremiah's

[37] As VIII. 10 ff. = VI. 13 ff.; XVI. 9 = VII. 34; XVI. 14 f. = XXIII. 7 f.

active life. This was a very troubled time for Judah, a period full of painful events. About the death of Jehoiakim and the first conquest of Jerusalem (598 B.C.) we learn very little; only in a few prophetic oracles is there any reference to the first captivity and the fate of the new king Jehoiakim (x. 17–21, XIII. 15 ff. xv. 5–9, XXII. 20 ff.). All the rest that has been preserved of Jeremiah's utterances is contained in two smaller collections concerning King Zedekiah and the ruling house (XXI. 11 ff.), and the professional prophets (XXIII. 9 ff.). The oracles are almost all delivered in rhythmic form. The short threat-poem against shepherds and masters (xxv. 34 ff.) also belongs here.

The prose sources are much more copious. Again there are a few autobiographical passages going back to the prophet himself, like the visions of the two fig baskets (ch. XXIV) and Yahweh's wine cup (xxv. 15 ff.) which the prophet is to offer to all people, the symbolic act with the wooden yoke (ch. XXVII) as a warning against the anti-Babylonian plot, and the prophet's purchase of a field (XXXII. 6 ff.), which also has symbolic significance.

The Baruch source reports in more detail, at least from 594 B.C. onwards. First of all, in two widely separated portions, we have a personal word of reproof and comfort (XLV. 1 ff.) and the pronouncement of threats against Babylon (LI. 59 ff.) which foresees that Yahweh's plan of salvation will include a settlement with this great power too. Then there is a series of descriptions of Jeremiah's fate; these present a very faithful picture of the spiritual life and political conditions at that time. The professional prophets regarded Nebuchadnezzar merely as a transitory figure, whose days were strictly numbered; hence they toyed with the idea of rebelling against Babylon. This necessarily led to a clash between them and Jeremiah, as is so vividly recounted in the story of the wooden and iron yokes (ch. XXVIII), a continuation of and supplement to Jeremiah's own personal account (ch. XXVII). Since Hananiah, as Jeremiah had foretold, did actually die shortly afterwards, the impression of Jeremiah's words may for a while have influenced political conduct. The next episode dates from the time when the King sent envoys to Babylon and Jeremiah gave them a letter addressed to the exiles. We owe

Baruch's report solely to the fact that this letter caused difficulties for Jeremiah (ch. XXIX). The next account leads straight into the beginning of the siege of Jerusalem (XXXIV. 1 ff.), where the prophet admonishes King Zedekiah that he should obey the will of Yahweh—which means in this instance that he must voluntarily surrender to Babylon. However, all the words of the prophet fell on deaf ears; in their deluded optimism the rulers and leaders completely failed to appreciate the true situation. Especially when the Egyptian advance temporarily reduced Babylonian pressure on the capital the people rejoiced, blind to all the warnings of the prophet, and only too readily anticipated the raising of the siege as an accomplished fact. When, in this uncomfortable situation, Jeremiah tries to leave the town on private business, he is arrested and imprisoned in a cistern; from here, at his request, he is transferred by the King to another prison (ch. XXXVII). A parallel to this (ch. XXXVIII), somewhat different in its details, admirably characterises the impotence of the weak King in the face of his princes. With the fall of Jerusalem (587 B.C.) Jeremiah's hour of liberation is at hand (ch. XXXIX). A variation on this story is contained in a second account (ch. XL). Jeremiah stays with the governor Gedaliah in Mizpah. When Gedaliah's murderer Ishmael flees to the Ammonites, Johanan is afraid of Nebuchadnezzar's wrath and decides, during the first uprising, to take refuge in Egypt; first of all he requests Jeremiah to consult the oracle of Yahweh. When the answer turns out to be unfavourable they accuse Jeremiah of lying and go ahead with their plan: Jeremiah is taken along with them as far as Tahpanhes (ch. XLI ff.). With oracles threatening a forthcoming invasion of Egypt by Nebuchadnezzar (XLIII. 8 ff.) and vowing vengeance on the fugitives for their idolatry (ch. XLIV), the records of Baruch come to an end. No exact information is available concerning the death of Jeremiah: legend tells that he was martyred in Egypt.

After the abundant fertility of the Baruch source we cannot be surprised that the last of the three prose sources, the Deuteronomistic, is so meagre. Its essential contribution is the oracles threatening Zedekiah and the people (XXI. 1 ff.), the threat in XXV. 1 ff., and the section which describes the despicable behaviour of the people when slavery was to be abolished (XXXIV. 8 ff.).

In spite of its relatively close-knit construction the Book of Jeremiah is not, from the beginning, one literary whole. The account of the life of the prophet, which we have just divided up among the different large sources, brings us a good deal nearer to understanding the development of the book. It is clear from the Baruch report (ch. xxxvi), as well as from the existence of the special Book of Consolation (chs. xxx–xxxi), to what extent Jeremiah and his circle were influenced by literary yearnings and a desire to collect in writing what had been said and done. The question as to the extent of the original roll, the collection of prophetic utterances which was burned by the King and then rewritten and extended by Baruch (xxxvi. 32), is difficult to answer. However, it would contain neither the Baruch memoirs, nor the Deuteronomistic sections, nor the autobiographical passages by the prophet: presumably it would contain only those parts relating to the whole nation or its leaders, such as the kings and professional prophets. What we have now is the final formulation, the result of various compilers' efforts. The work of redaction was largely guided by practical considerations, so that the oracles and prophecies were arranged either by subject-matter, like the oracles relating to kings and prophets, or chronologically, as indicated by the grouping of the first part (chs. i–xxv). The basis for this was provided by Baruch's extended original roll and what had been preserved of the prophet's auto-biographical writings, with the addition of the Baruch stories of Jeremiah's life and suffering. This material was grouped together in Deuteronomistic fashion and supplemented from personal knowledge of the prophet's work. The prophet was thereby naturally assimilated into the new outlook and the particularly cultic piety. The process of development, however, did not end with this fairly firmly established form in the exilic period. Since the idea of copyright was foreign to the ancients it is our quite general experience that compilations of this nature always represent only a relative conclusion.

In olden times it is a rule that like attracts like or similar material when a literary work is being created. So in this case a later addition still was the historical appendix on the fall of Jerusalem and the fate of the inhabitants: this is taken from the

Book of Kings (II Kings XXIV. 18–XXV. 21). But in contrast with the Isaiah appendix (Is. XXXVI–XXXIX) the concern here is not with the prophet, as is made abundantly clear in the final statement (LI. 64): "Thus far are the words of Jeremiah." Perhaps the intention was to emphasise in conclusion the extent to which the threatening words of the prophet had been fulfilled.

A further addition is the collection of oracles against foreign nations (chs. XLVI–LI). As in the case of Isaiah, at least a basic stock of these can be traced back to Jeremiah.[38] On the basis of the prophecy and the vision of the wine cup (ch. XXV) the Septuagint has arranged all of these after chapter XXV. In addition, besides smaller or larger glosses (like XXII. 8 f., 25 ff., XXV. 30 ff.), extra material from exilic (such as X. 1–16, XVI. 19–21) and post-exilic times (such as IX. 11–15, XXIII. 34–40) has been included. The fact that the Septuagint text in the Book of Jeremiah is approximately 2700 words (i.e. almost one-eighth of the whole book) shorter than the Masoretic Text cannot be attributed solely to attempts at simplification and abbreviation (as in ch. XXVIII f.), or to intentional omissions. We must consider the possibility that even in the period after the evolution of the Septuagint Jeremiah, a few additions (e.g. XXIX. 16 ff., XXXIII. 14 ff., XXXIX. 4 ff.) were made to the Hebrew text. Though from a different and later period, these too are evidence of religious devotion. They are also, however, a sign of the great importance and popularity attaching to the Book of Jeremiah in the religious worship and the life of the community. For the picture presented of the prophet is one of the greatest preacher of repentance among his people, a man filled with love and with passion; full of frustrated hopes, but always strictly obedient to his God. In this obedience, and never diverted by human considerations, he preached the word and the will of Yahweh and followed the path which his God had sketched out for him. In his prophecy of the New Covenant of grace and forgiveness of sins (XXXI. 31 ff.) he surpasses by far the other Old Testament prophets.

[38] H. Bardtke, "Jeremia, der Fremdvölkerprophet," in *Z. alttest. W.*, LIII (1935), pp. 209–39 and LIV (1936), pp. 240–62 (in contrast to Volz) supports their genuineness, as does Rudolph, *Jeremia*, p. 228.

THE BOOK OF EZEKIEL

The third and last of the great prophetic books deals with
Ezekiel (= God is strong, or perhaps also God makes strong).[39]
According to the text he was the son of a priest, Buzi (i. 3), of
whom nothing more is known, and lived in Babylon by the river
of Chebar at Tel-abib (iii. 15)—that is, among the exiles, the
Golah. Like his great predecessors Isaiah and Jeremiah, he was
called to be a prophet in a special vision, which is transmitted
to us in two versions (ii. 3 ff., iii. 4 ff.). From the evidence of
the text he worked among the exiles. Although it was long
assumed that Ezekiel was primarily an author, and that the
book which bears his name was written and put into its present
form by him, there is not the slightest reference to this in the
book itself. Nor is there any indication of particular literary
inclinations, or that the oracles were written down by Ezekiel
or his followers: neither xxiv. 2 nor xxxvii. 16, 20 can be taken
as evidence of this.

It must indeed be admitted that from beginning to end the
book gives the impression of a planned layout and represents to
a large extent a complete literary unit, in which the material is
logically arranged and fairly strictly grouped together. What
one may call a "destructive" or negative section contains
threats and symbolic actions directed against Jerusalem and
Judah (chs. iv–xxiv) and threat-oracles against foreign
nations (chs. xxv–xxxii), while a "constructive" or positive
part is devoted to symbolic actions and promises of comfort and
salvation for his people (chs. xxxiii–xxxix) with a vision of the
new Temple and a project of constitutional reform as its
crowning conclusion (chs. xl–xlviii). The hinge between the
two sections is the factual statement about the fall of Jerusalem
(xxxiii. 21).

The individual prophetic utterances, standing disconnectedly
side by side, are separated from each other, more than in the
case of other prophets, by circumstantial and detailed introductory (e.g. vi. 1 ff., vii. 1 ff.) and final formulae.[40] The
visions (such as i. 3, iii. 22) and symbolic acts (like iv. 1, 3,

[39] For commentaries and literature, see Bibliography.
[40] The concluding formula runs either "that they shall know that I am Yahweh"
(e.g. v. 13, vi. 7, vii. 4, 9, xi. 12, xii. 15, xiii. 9, xiv. 8 etc.) or "I, Yahweh, have
spoken" (as v. 15, 17, xvii. 21, xxi. 32, xxiv. 14 etc.) or "says Yahweh" (as
xi. 8, 21, xii. 25, 28, xv. 63, xx. 3, xxi. 13 etc.).

XII. 3) are also introduced by formulae. Moreover the whole book is clothed in the form of an autobiography, and throughout its contents is scattered a number of exact dates; but these only refer to the immediately succeeding passage and are generally arranged in proper sequence; only the latest date of all—571 B.C. (XXIX. 17)—if it has been correctly transmitted, has been set considerably too early.

But on closer inspection this apparently carefully planned literary structure turns out to have quite a few breaks. So the prophecies of calamity are occasionally (as V. 3, XI. 17 ff.) interspersed with words of comfort and in the prophecies of good things, on the other hand, we here and there find threats (e.g. XXXIII. 25 ff., XXXIV. 2 ff.). According to the various headings of the book, which are different from those used elsewhere, Ezekiel's career began "in the thirtieth year" (I. 1), but this year is not more closely defined. Probably the thirtieth year of his life is meant, as it was not customary to appear in public at an earlier age (cf. Num. IV. 20; Lk. III. 23). Since the text goes on to say (I. 2) that it was the fifth year of Jehoiachim's captivity, Ezekiel must have been born about 623 B.C. He is therefore to be regarded as a younger contemporary of Jeremiah, and must have been deported with him in 598 B.C. But that means that at the early age of twenty-five he was numbered among "the princes and the mighty men" in the land (II Kings XXIV. 14 ff.) or else belonged among the experts: both are equally improbable. The prophecy concerning the Ammonites (XXI. 28 ff.) is as incongruous in this context as the exile-symbolism (IV. 4 ff.). The interval of silence (III. 22 ff., XXIV. 27, XXXIII. 22) is filled up in the text with prophetic utterances. There are also many portions which contain parallels, just as many sections are word for word repetitions (III. 17 ff., XXXIII. 7 ff).

The vision of the holy waters (XLVII. 1 ff.) certainly has the characteristics of desk work. Yet Ezekiel was not primarily an author, but, as the book itself makes perfectly clear, just as much a prophet as his predecessors; a man of public action, who at the special command of Yahweh proclaims His word and has physical contact with his listeners whether in good or in evil. Among the prophets this book is the last link in the long development from the individually spoken oracle to the written and transmitted collection, after whatever fashion it may have been compiled. In many cases Ezekiel has been quite wrongly judged by those who, suffering from the after-effects of the old doctrine of verbal inspiration, would not take a flexible view but fitted everything into a uniform pattern. The threats against Jerusalem and Judah, in particular, presented difficulties. So there grew up a picture of the prophet which to a large extent seems bizarre and morbid, verging on the abnormal; indeed, with the assumption of cataleptic states and tele-kinesis, it more than once strays into the pathological.[41] Josephus, unacquainted with these modern explanations, seeks to explain the absurdity of a prophet among the Golah aiming threats at the inhabitants of Jerusalem quite simply by saying that Ezekiel wrote his prophecy in Babylonia and sent it to Jerusalem. This attempt to get out of a difficulty can if necessary be given some colour of probability as far as the threat-oracles are concerned, but it will never fit the symbolic actions, which assume the presence of spectators asking the prophet questions. For this reason some have argued that Ezekiel returned to Jerusalem from the Golah and then later went back. But such freedom of movement would hardly have been allowed to a prisoner. Thus, in more recent times, a double ministry by Ezekiel has been increasingly assumed, first in Jerusalem and Judah, and later in exile among the Golah. "Jeremiah was not the only one to prophesy this to the people: the prophet Ezekiel wrote two books on the subject and left them to us," says Josephus.[42] These words seem to reflect an established tradition that our Book of Ezekiel originally consisted of two books, whose limits are determined by the different settings of the action.

Ezekiel's Jerusalem Book (chs. iv–xxiv), to which the call-vision also belongs (ii. 3 ff.), contains a collection of independent portions of varying extent, from the short prophetic utterance to the long poetic recitation, from the symbolic action to the vision. The theme for his preaching was given to the prophet in his visionary experience with the written scroll:

---

[41] Cf. E. C. Broome, "Ezekiel's abnormal personality," in *J. Bib. Lit.*, LXV (1946), pp. 277–92; K. Jaspers, "Der Prophet Ezechiel. Eine pathographische Studie," in *Festschrift für Kurt Schneider*, ed. H. Kranz, Heidelberg 1947, pp. 77–85.

[42] Josephus, *Antiquitates judaicae*, x. 5. 1.

"lamentation and mourning and woe" (II. 10). And so the subject-matter is always the same, the impending fall of Jeru-salem as the punishment and judgment of Yahweh, who will send His plagues down upon the inhabitants "fire, plague, famine and the sword." There is no sign here of the pastoral concern of Jeremiah, who never tires of exhorting the people, urgently and passionately, to repentance and conversion. Here we find only grave pictures of catastrophe without a glimmer of hope. And anything that is said about deliverance and the good times which are to come (like v. 3, XVII. 22 f.) is a later addition, as the context occasionally (e.g. XX. 33 ff.) makes quite clear. That the prophet should find malicious satisfaction in the fate threatening his people (VI. 11) is indica-tive of the great difference between Ezekiel and them. Their desertion of and disobedience towards Yahweh (II. 3, 7), their self-delusion, obstinacy (II. 4 ff.), and thoughtlessness blind them to the coming disaster and its severity. Thus a great inner gulf separates the prophet from his listeners: and it is not to be wondered at that they do not understand him (cf. XII. 9, XX. 49), although his symbolic actions are clear and plain and his threats are penetrating and impossible to misunderstand for those who have ears to hear. This whole prophecy has about it something restrained and to the point, strict and inexorable. And yet there is no lack of warmer tones (as in ch. XVIII), as in the vision of God's judgment, when Ezekiel's whole heart and his love for his people break through in the anguished cry "Ah, Lord God! wilt thou destroy all that remains of Israel in the outpouring of thy wrath upon Jerusalem?" (IX. 8 = XI. 13). Sometimes he introduces a popular phrase into his preaching (as in XII. 22, XVI. 44), and he favours poems from the popular repertoire like love songs (chs. XVI, XXIII) or the fable of the eagle and the cedar shoot (ch. XVII). These he reshaped and revised to suit his own purpose. The fact that he raised these purely secular songs to the higher plane of thoughts bound up with God and endowed them with a religious content is evidence of his own piety and his prophetic gift.

Concerning his personal circumstances and fate during this period only very slight indications have been transmitted (III. 25). All that is said is that he speaks to the people (XXIV. 18) and that the elders seek him out to question Yahweh (VIII. 1,

xiv. 1, xx. 1). Otherwise there are only two short references to deaths (xi. 13, xxiv. 18), which, however, cannot take us any further in view of the very corrupt and, above all, incomplete state of the text. For, as is generally recognised, the Book of Ezekiel is particularly full of textual gaps (as iii. 24, vii. 23) and contains sections which have been broken up (xx. 20, 49) or incorrectly transmitted (as xiii. 5, xxi. 6 f.). On the other hand, there are a considerable number of later extensions of the text[43] which are not always immediately recognisable as such. It is extremely difficult therefore, to erase these attempts at touching up without damaging the original picture in the process. "Thus shall Ezekiel be to you a sign . . . you will know that I am the Lord God" (xxiv. 24 = xxiv. 27)—this observation seems finally to draw the line under this whole Jerusalem collection, the content of which embraces the activities of the prophet in the capital and its environs before the destruction of the city.

But when did Ezekiel come to Babylon?[44] Activities such as his in Jerusalem cannot have gone unopposed: so much is obvious, even if no details are given. Just as Uriah, the prophet of Yahweh, fled before Jehoiakim into Egypt, which as it turned out handed him back again (Jer. xxvi. 21-3), it is possible that Ezekiel fled to the Golah. A trace of evidence of this is found in Ezek. iii. 15, where the words "I came" rule out the possibility that he was complying with a vision, in which case it would read "the Spirit brought me." The date of this event seems to be indicated by "the fifth year of the exile of King Jehoiachin" (i. 2)—that is 593 B.C. When he arrived among the Golah he kept himself very quiet to begin with until he experienced another calling in a second vision (iii. 4 ff.). This makes the otherwise obscure reference to his "bitterness in the heat of my spirit" (iii. 14b) understandable. Similarly it helps to elucidate the statements about shutting himself up (iii. 24) and the long period of silence (iii. 26), which was only brought to an end when the news of the fall of Jerusalem was delivered by the refugee (xxxiii. 22).

After 587 B.C. Ezekiel embarked upon a second period of

---

[43] Cf. Fohrer, "Ezechielglossen."

[44] Cf. C. Kuhl, "Der Schauplatz der Wirksamkeit Hesekiels", in *Theologische Zeitschrift*, henceforth cited as *Th. Z.*, viii (1952), pp. 401-18.

activity, but this is set in a new key in keeping with the entirely different circumstances. We are told about it chiefly in the small Golah Book (chs. I–III*, XXXIII–XXXVII), but unfortunately this text, too, is full of gaps (like III. 16, XXXIV. 17, XXXVI. 17). What has been preserved gives only a very ineffectual picture of Ezekiel's work, which seems to have evoked little response among the Golah. They listen to the prophet, it is true, but they are not guided by his words and only later do they come to understand that a prophet has been among them (XXXIII. 30 ff.). This suggests that he spoke to them words of exhortation and repentance (XXXIII. 32) which, however, are not handed down here. Of particular significance is his vision of the valley of bones (XXXVII. 1 ff.) and the symbolic act of reuniting the two kingdoms of Israel and Judah (XXXVII. 15 ff.). In so far as his preaching has been preserved, it is wholly concerned with the promise of future salvation: "I will vindicate the holiness of my great name . . . for I will take you from the nations and gather you from all the countries" (XXXVI. 23–4); "I myself will be the shepherd of my sheep" (XXXIV. 15). The desolate land as a garden of Eden, the ruined cities rebuilt, and the people as a holy flock of Yahweh: thus will Yahweh display His power before the nations (XXXVI. 34 ff.). This proclamation of salvation does not attain the same heights as in Deutero-Isaiah: but some of its language belongs among the most beautiful and most precious, from the religious point of view, of all the prophecy contained in the Old Testament.

All these utterances, from the period of decline and from the Golah period alike, would have circulated orally to begin with before they were put down in writing. This gave rise to many different versions of Ezekiel's words and explains the many parallel texts,[45] which can hardly go back to the prophet himself. The second stage which followed saw the gathering together of these utterances according to certain points of view: hence the combination of the two call-visions, the symbolic acts in chs. IV–V, or the threats to the professional prophets (ch. XIII), or the sections united under the catchword "sword" in ch. XXI. This stage was also responsible for arranging the exile-symbolism (IV. 4 ff.) among the acts threatening Jerusalem,

[45] Shown in detail by A. Bertholet, *Hesekiel*, Hb. A. T., 1st ser., VOL. XIII, Tübingen 1936.

and for placing the oracle of salvation (XI. 20) and the threat to bad shepherds (ch. XXXIV) in their present position. Whether the extension of the Temple vision (ch. VIII) by approximation to the vision in ch. I took place at this stage or later, cannot be decided. At all events, a long and complicated process of development can be reckoned on.

A collection of oracles against foreign nations (chs. XXV–XXXII), the development of which is still recognisable to some extent, has been inserted into these prophecies of Ezekiel's more or less as a bridge between his prophecies of doom on the one hand and his prophecies of salvation on the other. The basis of these is one of the well-loved poems concerning foreign peoples.[46] In geographical sequence, starting from the Northeast, it contains uniformly constructed threats against the Ammonites, Moab, Edom, and the Philistines (ch. XXV), Tyre (XXVI. 2 ff.), and Sidon (XXVIII. 20 ff.): no doubt it originated in the period of the national revolts against Babylon (Jer. XXVII. 3 ff.). This song was later expanded to some extent by the inclusion of several threats and poems against Tyre (chs. XXVI. ff.). When this took place and why Tyre should have been singled out for such special enmity can no longer be made out. This first collection of oracles against foreign nations (chs. XXV–XXVIII) was not placed after the disaster prophecies until later, as is clearly shown by the conclusion (XXVIII. 25–6) which joins up with the train of thought of the ensuing prophecies of salvation: free from all her enemies and reunited after her dispersion, Israel will live in the promised land in peace and security.

The oracles against Egypt (chs. XXIX–XXXII) originally formed a completely independent collection and were not added to the book until later. They reflect the anti-Egyptian feelings which Jeremiah had also represented under Jehoiakim. This period produced the lament about Egypt the great sea monster (XXIX. 3 ff., XXXII. 2 ff.). The development of this collection in particular was a very complicated process, since according to the dates given its latest portion (XXIX. 20 ff.) dates back to 571 B.C. It has been fitted in here for different reasons: firstly, for the sake of completeness, since Egypt was omitted from the

---

[46] Cf. Am. I f.; Zeph. II. 4 ff.; Zech. IX. I ff. and the larger collections in Isaiah and Jeremiah.

great song against foreign nations, and secondly, as a reflexion and document of the period of the decline and exile.

Another insertion is the Gog prophecy (chs. XXXVIII–XXXIX), an eschatological painting of the great mythical enemy from the north, who has been brought down by Yahweh Himself and who will direct the powerful might and all the forces of foreign nations against the land of Israel. But then Yahweh will destroy him on the mountains of Israel, thus revealing His majesty to the nations, and causing Israel to rejoice in the certainty that "I am the Lord their God" (XXXIX. 22). Attempts have been made to trace definite historical references here, and to interpret the unknown Gog from the land of Magog as Babylon or Gyges of Lydia: but this can hardly be correct.[47] Of the origin and development of this prophecy we know absolutely nothing. That it was a later addition to the Book of Ezekiel, however, is shown by the fact that the thoughts on which Ezekiel's prophecy of salvation ends are taken up here again in conclusion (XXXIX. 25 ff.).

Clothed in the literary form of a vision and linked quite superficially with what precedes it by means of the usual introductory formula, there follows a literary product of a special type, the project of a constitutional reform (chs. XL–XLVIII). To judge by the date (XL. 1) it was written in 572 B.C., which will be correct inasmuch as this section, which is not uniform in itself, certainly dates from not too late in the exilic period. Its content is the testimony of a pious man sketching out a picture of the future (for him of the present)— a new Temple to which Yahweh returns and where His presence will dwell for ever (XLIII. 7, XLVIII. 35). So in a vision very reminiscent of that in chs. VIII–IX, he is taken by the hand of Yahweh and conducted through the new Temple which he describes, giving exact measurements (XL. 1–XLIII. 17).[48] In terms very similar to the Law of Holiness he gives

[47] J. G. Aalders, *Gog en Magog in Ezechiël*, Kampen 1951; A. van den Born, "Etude sur quelques toponymes bibliques. I. Le pays du Magog," in *Oudtest. St.*, x (1954), pp. 197–201, suspects that Magog is a mutilation of "hammeqedon" and explains this by the fact that the lands of Rosh, Meshach, and Tubal formed a part of the Kingdom of Alexander.

[48] There are, however, no heights given, and in other respects also one finds evidence of wilfulness and omissions which can be explained, according to K. Galling (G. Fohrer and K. Galling, *Ezechiel*, VOL. 1, Hb. A.T., 1st ser. VOL. XIII, Tübingen 1955, p. 222), by the assumption of definite proportions.

instructions, down to the last detail, as to how this Temple can be protected against desecration (chs. XLIV ff.), and adds stipulations regarding the distribution of the land which he sees as once more in the possession of his people (ch. XLVII f.). The focal point of the whole country is the Temple and Jerusalem is to be given a new name: "the Lord is there" (XLVIII. 35). This at the same time realistic and fantastic constitutional project which was never realised, is basically a piece of prophecy also. For in a period of servitude and absolute hopelessness he, in his faith, sees as already achieved the acts of Yahweh which are to become a reality at some future date.

Jewish tradition states that the Book of Ezekiel was written "by the men of the great synod": this recollection will be historically true in so far as the Book of Ezekiel did not attain its final form—that is, complete with oracles against foreign nations, Gog pericope and Temple vision—until after Ezra's time. But this does not exclude the possibility that the text was touched up even in a later period. The Book of Ezekiel is among the most difficult of the whole Old Testament, and opinions regarding the activities of Ezekiel and the development of this book are widely divergent. According to Talmudic tradition Rabbi Hanania (about the beginning of the Christian era) ordered 300 jars of oil for his lamp so that he might explain the words of Ezekiel which contradicted the Torah. But a lot more oil will still have to be used to penetrate more deeply into the understanding of this unique book. For on the tree of scholarship the fruits ripen but slowly.

THE BOOK OF THE TWELVE PROPHETS

Under the name "Twelve Prophets" (Ecclesiasticus XLIX. 10), in Greek *dodekapropheton*, from the time of St Augustine also called the minor prophets,[49] are assembled, as the fourth and last part of the Latter Prophets, twelve less extensive collections of prophetic utterances, one of which (Nah. I. 1) is expressly described as "the book." They date from many different centuries, from the days of Jeroboam II down to the late postexilic period. The fact that there are twelve, at least in the grouping that we know, is not a mere coincidence with the number of the tribes of Israel. Different points of view seem

[49] For commentaries and literature on the Minor Prophets, see Bibliography.

O

to have determined their arrangement. On the one hand is their assumed age, Jewish tradition considering Hosea as the oldest because of the word "first" (Hos. I. 2), and Jonah as synonymous with the prophet working under Jeroboam II (II Kings XIV. 25). In addition, it is possible to recognise a certain arrangement on the basis of recurring phrases, as in Joel (IV. 16) and Amos (I. 2), or by affinity of content, for Obadiah with his heralding of the Day of Yahweh is placed after Amos; while the grouping of the last, post-exilic prophets was determined by chronological considerations. The lack of a common principle, even in the form of heading the individual books, leads us to assume that the whole evolved gradually and in stages. Moreover, the different arrangement of the first six books in the Septuagint suggests that these originally formed an independent smaller collection. The Septuagint apparently classified according to length: Hosea, Amos, Micah, Joel, Obadiah. The placing of the longer book of Jonah after the very much smaller Obadiah is no doubt governed by the fact that Jonah contains only a story concerning a prophet and no prophetic oracles. We can glean no more about smaller collections and their development than about the evolution of the whole; but the grouping together of the pre-exilic prophets no doubt dates back to exilic times. According to the evidence of ben Sirach the latest date for the final completion of the collection is the end of the third century B.C. That such heterogeneous writings have been united at all in one book, is doubtless based on practical considerations—to facilitate their reading during worship. Nor are the individual books themselves by any means always uniform. For this reason each must be dealt with separately, and in so doing we will use the sequence of the Masoretic Text, which Luther also adopted.

Hosea

According to the heading, Hosea—his name is an abbreviated form of Hoshaiah (=saved by God; cf. Jer. XLII. 1)[50]—was the son of an otherwise unknown Beeri. He was active in the time of Jeroboam II and, as the content of the book makes plain, his successors. He is the only writing prophet to hail from the Northern Kingdom. He lived through the golden age

[50] For commentaries and literature, see Bibliography.

of the kingdom but also saw the fall of the dynasty of Jehu (I. 4), the bloody disturbances of one kind or another round the throne (VII. 3 ff., VIII. 4), the Syro-Ephraimite war (V. 10 ff.), the political fluctuations between Assyria and Egypt (V. 13, VII. 11): apparently, however, he did not witness the fall of the kingdom (XIII. 15, XIV. 1).

With regard to his personal circumstances we know only that he was married to a certain Gomer (I. 3) and had three children, each of whom bore a symbolic name (I. 4 ff.). His experience of marriage, an account of which is given in an autobiographical passage (ch. III) was so decisive for his whole life and way of thinking that it became for him the image of the relationship between Yahweh and His people. In warm-hearted tones he describes God's undying love for His ungrateful and unfaithful people (VI. 4, XI. 3 f.); like a father (XI. 1), indeed like a faithful husband (II. 2 ff.), He has drawn them with bands of love (XI. 4). But Israel has forgotten her covenant with God and worshipped Yahweh in the manner of the Canaanite fertility cults. Her concern is with the harvest, with the corn and the wine; her heart does not cry out to Yahweh (VII. 14). And so He must reject her, and all her worship of images and her sacrifices (V. 9, VIII. 5 f., 13, X. 5 f.) "For I desire steadfast love and not sacrifice, the knowledge of God, rather than burnt offerings" (VI. 6). With their idolatrous and immoral cultic practices the people are in the grip of a spiritual and mental inflation, and their normal social conduct has been seriously impaired (IV. 2, VII. 1, X. 4). Their kingdom too is a revolt against Yahweh (IX. 15, X. 3, XIII. 11) and their treacherous foreign policy cannot fail to bring ruin upon Israel (V. 8 ff., VIII. 1 ff., IX. 3). As the whole course of events shows (VI. 7 ff.), the root of all the evil lies in their unfaithfulness and forgetfulness of God (VIII. 14). Now they are charged with their misdeeds before Yahweh (VII. 2); they have ploughed iniquity, they must reap injustice (X. 13). Judgment is inevitable (XIII. 8–9); for the sins of Ephraim only destruction remains (V. 9, VII. 13). But above all this hopelessness of approaching judgment there gleams a new dawn: the mercy of Yahweh is greater (XI. 9). If they turn back and repent (VI. 1, XIV. 2) Yahweh will lead them into the wilderness (II. 14) and start again at the point where they defected from Him. And it will be again as formerly (XIV. 5) in the days of their first love: "I will betroth you to me for ever; I will betroth you to me in righteousness and in justice, in steadfast love, and in mercy. I will betroth you to me in faithfulness; and you shall know the Lord" (II. 19–20).

Although the date of Hosea's activity can be fairly accurately established (between 750 and 725 B.C.) the development of his book is more difficult to trace. The autobiographical passage (ch. III), which is very probably closely linked with the story of his marriage (ch. I), certainly goes back to the prophet himself. But since the whole book consists of short oracles, the divisions between which are often very vague, it is difficult to deduce any more exact information. Individual sections (like chs. II, XI) look as if they were originally independent smaller collections; similarly chs. I–III and IV ff. appear to be larger collections. Many of the oracles (like IV. 16 ff., X. 4 ff.) served Jeremiah as models, but this does not tell us whether the Book of Hosea was available to him as a whole. The complete collection could hardly have been finished before the sixth century B.C. The wording of the text is the worst preserved of the whole of the Old Testament, along with Ezekiel and the Books of Samuel. Many oracles are transmitted merely as mutilated fragments. Moreover, the whole prophecy of Hosea has been transmitted through southern circles alone, and quite often (if not always) Judah is included in Hosea's oracles only as an afterthought. The possibility of post-exilic supplements must also be reckoned with. In spite of all this, however, the preaching of Hosea shines forth as the message of the infinite love of God.

Joel

About the prophet Joel (=Yahweh is God) we have no more details than that he was the son of Pethuel.[51] The heading does not even indicate the period of his activity. The first two chapters are concerned with a great plague of locusts, the swarms of which are likened to a powerful enemy army (I. 6, II. 2 ff.), combined with a drought (I. 19 f.) which threatens the yield of the harvest (I. 10 f., 17 f.). The consequence is general famine for men and animals alike (I. 18, 20); but the

[51] For commentaries and literature, see Bibliography.

most tragic result is that the prescribed sacrifices can no longer be offered up to Yahweh (i. 9, 13). There is only one way out: "Return to me with all your heart, with fasting, with weeping, and with mourning: and rend your hearts and not your garments. Return to the Lord, your God" (ii. 12 ff.) trusting in his compassion; then He will perform the miracle of His mercy and will give to His people in plenty (ii. 19, 24 ff.). Chapters ii and iii present, out of all context, a prophecy of the outpouring of God's spirit and describe the signs by which men shall know that the Day of Yahweh is at hand (ii. 28–31): but from all the dangers of the day of judgment the pious will be saved (ii. 32). Then follow two poems on the Day of Yahweh, the first of which (iii. 1 ff.) is handed down only as a fragment and is filled out with a prose oracle against foreign nations (iii. 4–8). The judgment which Yahweh will execute on that day over all nations in the valley of Jehoshaphat (= Yahweh holds judgment) is described in the well-known and graphic picture of this assembly (iii. 2, 12). Yahweh Himself will dwell again in His holy mountain of Zion (iii. 17; cf. ii. 32, iii. 21) and reveal Himself there with might, gathering His people together again out of their dispersion (iii. 1, 16): Jerusalem will again be holy and no stranger shall dwell within her gates (iii. 17). Starting with "in that day" there is appended in conclusion a differently constructed prophecy of Israel's salvation (iii. 18 ff.); her greatness is illustrated by contrast with the desolation of Egypt and Edom.

Some have tried to divide the Book of Joel into two independent collections (i. 1–ii. 27, ii. 28–iii), each finishing with a promise (ii. 18 ff., iii. 18 ff.). It is true that the prophetic liturgy (i. 1–ii. 27) differs from the rest in that it deals with the quite definite and very concrete distress of the present, even although it weaves features of the idea of the Day of Yahweh into the picture it presents (i. 6, 15, ii. 1 f., 10 f.); moreover, like Rev. ix. 3–11, it raises locusts into the realm of the gigantic and mythical (ii. 4–7). There is no serious reason why the author of the liturgy should be denied the two poems (iii. 1–3, 9–20). The prose section (iii. 4–8) and the final promise are secondary, and in the latter, as in the supplement at the end of ch. ii, the catchword "Zion" provides the link. Despite the placing of the Joel collection among the eighth-century prophets its contents—

the destruction of Jerusalem and the exile are assumed, but the city and Temple have been rebuilt (I. 14, II. 7 ff., 16 f.) and sacrifice is specially emphasised (I. 9, 13, II. 14)—point to a later period, indeed to post-exilic times, perhaps at the beginning or even in the middle of the fourth century B.C. Although in its thoughts the prophecy of Joel belongs to the same school as such other prophets as Amos and Deutero-Isaiah, its preaching does not reach the same spiritual heights. With its consciously cultic and statutory piety, it has a certain rigidity and stiffness. Its particular importance lies in the fact that it affords us an insight into that mysterious strength which upheld the post-exilic Jews despite all their misery and suffering: the unshakeable hope of that Last Day when Yahweh would bestow upon His children blessings in plenty. For the Christian the special value of the book lies in the connexion between the promise of the spirit of God (II. 28 ff.) and its fulfilment on the day of Pentecost (Acts II. 16 ff.).

Amos

The oldest writing prophet of the Old Testament is Amos (= bearer) of Tekoa near Jerusalem, whose dates are somewhat earlier than Hosea's.[52] As is evident from the very informative account in the third person contained in ch. VII (10–17), he was no nabi and no prophet's disciple; he described himself as a herdsman, a dresser of sycamore trees. Inwardly equipped through his visionary encounters with God (VII. I ff.), and specially called by Yahweh to be a prophet, he saw himself as the servant of Yahweh and subject to a holy, inner compulsion (III. 8). He was active in the reign of Jeroboam II (I. 1, VII. 9 f.) about 760 B.C., in the Northern Kingdom, especially in the capital Samaria (III. 9, IV. 1, VI. 1) and in Bethel, until he was expelled from Israel by the royal High Priest Amaziah. Nothing is known of his fate thereafter. Only on one occasion (III. 8) does he attempt to prove his legitimacy to his audience, to whose attitude towards prophetic preaching he refers briefly elsewhere (V. 10).

This was a golden age, a period of economic prosperity. Jeroboam's victory over Damascus and Moab had resulted in great territorial acquisitions and in the restoration of the old

---

[52] For commentaries and literature, see Bibliography.

boundaries of the kingdom in the east (II Kings XIV. 25).
Amos hints at this when he mentions the villages of Lodabar
and Karnaim (VI. 13). But external success does not always
bring internal blessing for a nation: the preaching of Amos
and the contents of his sermon on God's judgment prove this
abundantly. The people enjoyed the fruits of their success and
surrendered themselves to luxury and voluptuousness (III. 12,
VI. 4 ff.); they built houses of ivory (III. 15) and caroused (VI. 6)
on costly beds and couches (III. 12, VI. 4). That riches bring
obligations no one would acknowledge. On the contrary in
their greed for profits they knew no restraint and feared no
offence against the law; they increased prices and falsified
weights, sold the poor for a pair of shoes and the innocent to
slavery for money (VIII. 4 ff.), stored up violence and robbery
in their palaces (III. 10) "turned justice into poison and the
fruit of righteousness into wormwood" (v. 7, 12, VI. 12). And
all the time they thought they were still being pious. They had
been successful in battle and so they boasted of the help of
Yahweh, from whom they hoped for even greater things (v. 18).
Indeed, they felt themselves to be something quite special
(VI. 1 f., 13) and imagined that with their sacrifices and visits to
sanctuaries (IV. 4 f., v. 21 ff.), indeed even in the immorality of
the cult (II. 7), they were honouring Yahweh; while in the long
run they were only serving their own interests. But Yahweh
would destroy these places of worship (IX. 1). Shrill and
piercing ring out the words of the prophet:

> I hate, I despise your feasts,
>   and I take no delight in your solemn assemblies.
> Even though you offer me your burnt offerings and
>   cereal offerings,
>   I will not accept them,
> and the peace offerings of your fatted beasts
>   I will not look upon.
> Take away from me the noise of your songs;
>   to the melody of your harps I will not listen.
>
> (v. 21–3)

All are ripe for judgment (IV. 2, VI. 11), in his description of
which Amos uses the old eschatological conceptions—earth-
quakes (IX. 1), famine (VIII. 11), the sun setting by day (VIII. 9),

plague (v. 16–17). He sees, too, an enemy ready to strike (vi. 14); but there are no comprehensible political allusions. Behind and above the enemy stands Yahweh Himself, who will exercise judgment with His sword (vii. 9, ix. 4): He sets His eyes upon Israel, "for evil and not for good" (ix. 4). For Yahweh is a God of righteousness (vii. 8); in His sight all nations are equal. There is no question of preferential treatment for His own people. True, He led them out of Egypt, but He also led the Philistines out of Caphtor and the Syrians from Kir (ix. 7). These ideas make Amos the pioneer of a new conception in the history of religion, which lifts God up above the limitations of national and tribal attachment and thus lays the foundation of universalism: Yahweh, in His righteousness, holds sway over all the nations.

The composition of the book, which is made up of a number of shorter oracles, shows clear evidence of an organising and formative hand at work. The great poem against foreign nations (chs. i–ii), which begins so pleasantly for the listeners and then takes such a serious personal turn, is followed by a collection of threats (chs. iii–vi) with a threefold "Hear!" (iii. 1, iv. 1, v. 1) and a twofold "Woe!" (v. 7, 18, vi. 1). Perhaps several smaller collections may be combined here, for the hymn-like fragments (iv. 13, v. 8) give the impression that they ought to constitute the end of a collection. But this conclusion is not decisive. The fact that there is another similar fragment (ix. 5 f.) may just as well be merely a sign that the Book of Amos was used liturgically.[53] Presumably the oracles concerning Samaria come before those spoken in Bethel, but it is not possible to be more definite. Particularly difficult is the construction of the last part, the collection of visions (chs. vii–ix) which, however, are now interrupted by single oracles (viii. 4 ff., ix. 16 ff.) and especially by the Bethel narrative (vii. 10 ff.).[54] The reports on the visions, if not the work of the prophet himself, can very probably be traced back, along with

---

[53] Cf. L. Horst, "Die Doxologien im Amosbuch," in *Z. alttest. W.*, XLVII (1929), pp. 45–54; T. H. Gaster, "An ancient hymn in the prophecies of Amos," in *Journal of the Manchester University Egyptian and Oriental Society*, XIX (1935), pp. 23–6.

[54] Not J. Morgenstern, "Amos studies," in *H.U.C.A.*, XI (1936), 19–140; XII (1937–38), pp. 1–53; XV (1940), pp. 59–304, who looks upon the whole as one unit comprising two collections: (*a*) VII. 10–17, III. 3–8, 14–15 and the visions, and (*b*) the speeches.

the narrative, to his followers, who would also see to the writing down and compiling of his threat-oracles. The whole then passed into the tradition of Judah, and after the fall of the Northern Kingdom additions concerning the Southern Kingdom were made, just as "Uzziah, King of Judah" was inserted into the heading. When finally the present conclusion (IX. 8 ff.) was added, assuming the exile from the Southern Kingdom (IX. 11, 14) and promising happiness in the post-exilic period, the narrative was displaced from the end of the book, which was very probably its original position, and inserted where it is now.

Obadiah

This book, which contains only twenty-one verses,[55] is headed "The vision of Obadiah" (= servant of God)—which raises the question whether it is the name of a person at all (cf. Deutero-Isaiah). The book in fact presents no vision but only threats against Edom in conjunction with conceptions of the Day of Yahweh. It is not particularly rich in ideas. Its development is even more difficult to trace; though not because vss. 1–9 are also contained in Jeremiah (Jer. XLIX. 7 ff.), for, as comparison of the texts shows, both portions are probably based on an older original from the repertoire of oracles against foreign nations. The prophet, one of the prophets of salvation or professional prophets left behind in Jerusalem, used it as a base to which he might link his own threat (vss. 10–14, 15b). This dates from the period after 587 B.C. and is caused by the particularly malicious joy with which Edom took advantage of the fall of Judah to appropriate the southern regions of the country (cf. Ezek. XXXV. 10, 12, XXXVI. 5). Edom will be paid back in her own coin. Since there is no sound reason for a later dating, this oracle should be dated around 500 B.C. or even somewhat earlier. Appended, probably influenced by another curse on Edom (Lam. IV. 21 f.), is a Day of Yahweh-oracle, dealing with Yahweh's cup from which Edom must drink (vss. 15a, 16-18). But more important than the threats against Edom is the positive idea of approaching salvation for the house of Jacob, its deliverance on the holy mountain of Zion. Since it goes back to later additions to the

[55] For commentaries and literature, see Bibliography.

Book of Joel (cf. Joel II. 32) this appendix will be later in date. From a later period still is the prose section (vss. 19–21) concerning the future possessions of the children of Israel which, despite its inherent modesty, nevertheless concludes with a confession that this is the kingdom of Yahweh.

Jonah

The Book of Jonah[56] has been described, and not incorrectly, as a pearl among the writings of the prophets, although its content is not prophecy but a story about a prophet. Jonah (= dove) tries to escape Yahweh's commission to go and preach against Nineveh: he flees from Joppa (the modern Jaffa) to Tarshish (Tartessus in Spain) by boat (I. 1–3). But Yahweh sends down a great storm and the boat gets into difficulties. It is established that Jonah is to blame, and so, at his own request, he is thrown overboard into the sea, which thereupon becomes calm (I. 4–16). A great fish prepared by Yahweh devours the prophet and vomits him up again three days later, after Jonah has prayed to Yahweh (II. 1–11). At Yahweh's renewed command Jonah now goes to Nineveh and proclaims the fall of the city in forty days' time (III. 1–4). But the citizens fast and do penitence and Yahweh will not allow them to be destroyed (III. 5–10). Jonah is angry at Yahweh's kindness and resentfully wishes for death (IV. 1–3). He takes up a position outside the city in the shadow of a castor oil plant which Yahweh has specially made to grow for him, and there he awaits the fate of the city. Yahweh makes the bush wither suddenly, and when Jonah becomes annoyed again about this He reproaches him, saying: "You pity the plant . . . and should not I pity Nineveh, that great city?" (IV. 4–11).

How remote this is from reality is shown by certain small details in the story, such as the description of Nineveh as a great and legendary city, the absence of its king's name, and the fasting of all the animals. Some have seen in the Book of Jonah an allegory on the fate of Israel or on the Messiah and have tried all manner of subtle and ingenious interpretations. But the whole character of the book shows that it belongs to the literary genre of prophetic legend. These legends, filled with a deep reverence towards Yahweh, do not always show

[56] For commentaries and literature, see Bibliography.

His servants in the best light.[57] Their business is not merely to tell a story but to teach. For this reason the Jonah story has no proper ending: the narrator is interested in the story only up to the point where he can fit in his teaching—in this instance the compassion of God towards all men, even the heathen, if they will only repent.

The story has grown out of several pieces. This is quite clear from the psalm (II. 3–10) which contains the thanksgiving of the individual for his deliverance from Sheol and thus fits the particular distress in which Jonah finds himself. But the Hebrew art of storytelling loves to interrupt the course of the narrative at suitable points and weave in apparently suitable songs (cf. II. 4) or prayers. These were not specially created for a particular instance but were picked up anywhere in the tradition so long as they appeared at all relevant: the prayer of Jonah (IV. 2 f.) is also proof of this. As to the development of the psalm, it can only be stated that it will be older than its present surroundings and may even originate from pre-exilic times (II. 8). But the whole account of the sea voyage and the fish (I, II. I, 10) very probably does not originally belong to the legend, as is evident even from purely external appearances in the word-for-word repetition of I. 1–2 in III. 1–2; also, the following legend is quite different in nature and makes no reference at all to the miracle of his deliverance, although it would have ample opportunity to do so. Here in chapter I. we have old material of *Märchen* and myth, which would originally have quite a different significance from what it has here: it must have been of popular origin and was probably assimilated later to the legend. The legend itself (chs. III–IV) seeks its heroes in the distant past and arranges their stories round the prophet Jonah, son of Amittai, of Gath-hepher (cf. II Kings XIV. 25). The beginning "Then the word came" (III. 1) indicates that it was part of a larger whole at a supposedly earlier date.

There is only internal evidence for its date of origin. The principal factor is its difference from the more recent Daniel legends, in which the lines are much more roughly drawn.[58]

---

[57] This is shown by the example of the prophet Elijah (I Kings XIX. 4 ff.), the unnamed prophet (I Kings XIII. 4 ff.) and Gehazi (II Kings V. 20 ff.).

[58] Cf. Dan. II. 47, III. 28–9, IV. 34, VI. 27. Nothing is said here about Nineveh now renouncing her own gods and serving Yahweh alone.

The Jonah legend will have come into being in a period of religious exclusiveness which looked upon Yahweh as its, and only its, own national and private God; that is, in the days of Nehemiah and Ezra, about 400 B.C. If this small writing appears at first out of place among the minor prophets, it is nevertheless a real prophetic proclamation of God; not only because Jesus made special mention of the signs of Jonah in connexion with His own death and resurrection (Mt. XII. 39–40, XVI. 4), but because it makes a stand against narrow national piety, and proclaims the message of God's all-embracing love and compassion for all men and all nations.

Micah

According to the heading (I. 1), Micah,[59] short form of Micaiah (=who is like Yahweh), from Moresheth[60] near Jerusalem, was active in the reigns of Kings Jotham, Ahaz, and Hezekiah of Judah. He was therefore a somewhat younger contemporary of Isaiah, and there is a certain inner relationship between the preaching of the two men. Very little about the prophet himself can be deduced from his book. It is hardly probable that he was one of the professional prophets, even if, in spite of his sharp criticism (III. 5), he does not denounce and reject their activities (III. 7). Micah's proclamation is the announcement of doom for Israel and Judah: he meets with little response from his listeners (II. 6, 11), for he unsparingly shows up their sins (III. 8).

His utterances are gathered together in several collections, but no guiding principle can be recognised in their arrangement. Since oracles of doom (I. 5 ff., VI ff.) alternate with prophecies of salvation (IV f., VII. 8 ff.), the possibility of later additions must be considered. The individual oracles of the first compilation (chs. I–III) should certainly be ascribed to the prophet, but these in turn consist of smaller collections which are clearly separated by a post-exilic prophecy of salvation (II. 12 f.). After the powerful introduction of Yahweh as the judge

---

[59] For commentaries and literature, see Bibliography.

[60] J. Jeremias, "Moreseth-Gath, die Heimat des Propheten Micha," in *P. Jb.* 1933, pp. 42–53; K. Elliger, "Die Heimat des Propheten Micha," in *Z.D.P.V.*, LVII (1934), pp. 81–152.

(I. 2 ff.), the first collection contains a threat against the Northern Kingdom (I. 6 ff.), hence earlier than 722 B.C.; while a second portion (I. 10 ff.), in a chain of puns, presents a lament on the devastation of Judah and the threat to Jerusalem, and thus presupposes the conditions prevailing in 701 B.C. The last portion attacks the covetousness of the great (II. 1 ff.) with a call of Woe! and an oracle of doom, which is interspersed with considerations on the work of the prophet. The second, smaller collection (ch. III,) whose unusual beginning "and I said" (III. 1) indicates that it was part of a lost autobiographical account, also consists of several individual oracles, as is evident from the words of the introduction (III. 5) and the repeated beginnings "Hear you" (III. 1, 9). The theme is the bad leaders of the people who "abhor justice and pervert all equity, who build Zion with blood and Jerusalem with wrong" (III. 9–10). In their infamous and self-confident acts (III. 11) they are still supported by the prophets (III. 5 ff.). So the deserved punishment of Yahweh cannot be avoided: failure of inspiration for the prophets, Zion as a ploughed field, Jerusalem a heap of rubble, and the Temple hill covered with trees. This prophecy, a hundred years later, saved the life of Jeremiah (cf. Jer. XVIII–XIX).

A second collection (chs. VI–VII), linked by "Hear," which also goes back to Micah, contains further threats. Yahweh will have a lawsuit with His people (VI. 1–2). He has done them nothing but good (VI. 3 ff.); but they behave badly, lie, and deceive one another; their punishment has therefore already started with the calamity of war (VI. 10 ff.). Because they uphold the statute of Omri and the works of the house of Ahab—allusions whose meaning is quite obscure—they will be made a desolation and the laughing-stock of the nations (VI. 14 ff.). They will only be used for evil, so all their possessions will be consumed (VII. 1 ff.). Everywhere the bonds of confidence are loosened, even within the family there is nothing but deceit and betrayal (VII. 5 ff.). But Micah looks up towards the help of his God. So these prophecies of gloom end in faith and confidence in God. Still more important is the Torah liturgy which the prophet must recite. The real relationship of Man to God consists not in external things, not even in the cult, even were one to make the most costly sacrifices, indeed

one's firstborn son. The one thing that matters is the fundamental rule of ethics:

> He has showed you, O man, what is good;
> and what does the Lord require of you
> but to do justice, and to love kindness,
> and to walk humbly with your God?
>
> (vi. 8)

Between these two larger compilations have been inserted a
number of prophecies of salvation from exilic and post-exilic
times. These are all eschatological (iv. 1, 6, v. 9) and can hardly
be dated. They presuppose the exile (iv. 6, v. 6 ff.) and speak of
the Day of Judgment as the final victory over the enemies (iv. 13,
v. 8) and the coming of the kingdom of peace (iv. 3). They could
hardly, however, have formed a complete collection originally;
these are unconnected, individual oracles, the first of which
occurs not only here but also in Isaiah (cf. Is. ii. 2 ff.). The
first three have been inserted here (iv. 1 ff., 6 ff., 11 ff.)
because Zion plays a part in them all (iv. 2, 7, 11, 13) and iii.
12 provided the appropriate cue. Elsewhere later material of a
varied nature has crystallised round genuine Micah prophecies
like v. 1 and the Messianic Bethlehem prophecy of the Prince
of Peace (v. 2 ff.). It is possible, however, that iv. 9 and v.
10–14 are to be traced back to Micah.[61] The end of the book
(vii. 8–20) dates from the exilic or early post-exilic period. The
different parts—the song against the enemy (vii. 8 ff.), the
prophecy of salvation (vii. 11 ff.), and the prayer (vii. 14 ff.)—
belong together as a prophetic liturgy which was probably
destined for a day of mourning.

Nahum

The heading (i. 1) of the small book handed down to us under
the name Nahum (= rich in comfort) is different in many
respects from what we have seen up till now.[62] It does not give
any chronological data concerning Nahum nor the name of his

---

[61] Another solution sees in iv–vii nameless prophetic oracles, some from the
pre-exilic period (T. H. Robinson and F. Horst, *Die Zwölf Kleinen Propheten*, Hb.
A.T., 1st ser., vol. xiv, 2nd edn. Tübingen 1954), or else postulates a separation of
prophetic oracles from those of the cultic prophets (cf. G. Fohrer in *Th. R.*, xix
(1951), p. 317).

[62] For commentaries and literature, see Bibliography.

father, but restricts itself to the brief tag "the Elkoshite." No doubt this refers to his birthplace, but where exactly this is has not yet been ascertained. Moreover it is notable that the heading refers expressly to "the book," and finally that it describes the contents both as "Massah (= doom-oracle) of Nineveh" and "The book of the vision of Nahum." Corresponding with the heading, a double series of traditions is at work in the contents. The one contains prophetic oracles (I. 12 ff., II. 1 ff.) proclaiming that Yahweh will eliminate the mighty enemy (I. 14, II. 13), break his yoke (I. 13), and restore the vineyards of Israel and Judah (II. 2); in addition there are two threats (II. 13, III. 5 ff.) that Yahweh will destroy the enemy (II. 13) and make them a laughing-stock and spectacle among the nations. We are left in no doubt that the enemy is Assyria (III. 7). In the nature of these short oracles we cannot expect profound religious thoughts. These are just as rare in the other series, which contains two larger poems (II. 4 ff., III. 1 ff., 8 ff.). These present a vivid, powerful, and very realistic picture of the conquest of Nineveh which is now only receiving the punishment she deserves for her avarice towards other nations. The character of these poems is more poetic than prophetic, and by their whole nature they are on the same level as individual portions of the Massah collection in the Book of Isaiah (e.g. Is. xv) and other oracles against foreign nations. The conclusion to the whole is a song of ironical mockery in the form of a dirge (III. 18 f.). No reference whatever is made to Nahum's personal circumstances, but we may assume with some certainty that he was active in Jerusalem (II. 1) as a professional prophet.

Just as all his single oracles and songs treat of the same theme, so they all date from the same narrowly restricted period; they originated shortly before the decisive attack by the Medes and Babylonians which led to the conquest of Nineveh (612 B.C.) and thus to the fall of Assyria. Placed right at the beginning of this compilation is a portion from an alphabetical psalm which very fortunately, especially from the religious angle, supplements the poems. For in addition to a statement of confidence (I. 7) it brings in the still lacking ideas of Yahweh's majestic might and His powerful wrath, revealed both in natural phenomena (I. 3 ff.) and in His revenge against enemies (I. 2, 8); and His work is final and complete (I. 9). The whole of the psalm has not been transmitted, and only about half the letters of the alphabet can definitely be identified. Some scholars have ingeniously tried to trace its continuation in what follows, but such an attempt does not appear to be on the right lines, and not only because the text of the following verses is so corrupt that they are almost incomprehensible. In addition one must remember that when they used such songs the Old Testament writers were in the habit of only incorporating as much of the transmitted material as they required for their own purposes. That this occurred here is supported by the fact that the "M" and "N" stanzas are in reverse order. This psalm fragment was inserted by the prophet when he was compiling his oracles. Today many try to read a particular intention into his action, namely that he wanted to make his collection into a cultic and mythical liturgy[63] for the victory celebrations immediately following the destruction of Nineveh. Indeed, there is much to be said for this view; but in this event one would expect a song of thanksgiving to Yahweh, at least at the end of the book, even though the nature of the material necessarily forces the religious ideas very much into the background behind the political and national elements. Since, however, the content does not look back to events which have already taken place, but comprises threats for the future, it is more probable that this work originated before the fall of Nineveh.

Habakkuk

Both in time and content the prophecy of Habakkuk (Greek Ambakum = Assyrian name for a garden plant) is very closely related to the Book of Nahum.[64] Of his personal circumstances we learn only that he was a nabi, that is a professional prophet (I. 1, III. 1) and in contrast to the other prophets he deliberately tries to procure visionary experiences and revelations of Yahweh (II. 1 ff.); these he writes down and displays in public so that every passer-by may read them. His book consists of two distinct parts, as is evident from the new heading "A prayer of Habakkuk the prophet" (III. 1) in contrast with "The oracle of God which Habakkuk the prophet saw" (I. 1). The first book

[63] A. Haldar, *Studies in the Book of Nahum*, Uppsala 1947, on the evidence of Ugarite and Assyrian documents.
[64] For commentaries and literature, see Bibliography.

(chs. I–II) speaks mainly of the godless and the righteous, and its features are so individual that it might be taken as directed at one single person and dealing with the conditions and circumstances in the life of his own nation. The whole attitude of the oracles (I. 14, 17, II. 5), however, shows that the prophet's concern is with something quite different, namely with very closely defined matters of foreign policy. Unfortunately the references are so general that they would permit several solutions, none of which is entirely satisfactory. So their actual historical relationship is a puzzle, and the suggested solutions have ranged from the Scythians, via the Assyrians, the Babylonians, the Persians, and the Greeks, even to the Seleucids. Since, however, the Chaldeans (Babylonians) are expressly mentioned (I. 6) as the instrument of punishment raised up by Yahweh, the most probable solution is to identify the godless with Assyrian imperialism. Some, referring back to Isaiah (Is. x. 5 ff.), have then wanted to interpret the oracles which follow as referring to Babylon which had been disobedient to its master, Yahweh (I. 11). But there is no good reason for this assumption: this verse alone cannot be decisive, even less so as the comparison with the net (I. 16–17) admirably fits Assyria, as is clear from the metaphorical pictures. The stone (II. 11), in contrast with the tiles used by the Babylonians, also points to Assyria.

After clearing up these preliminary points, which is essential if they are to be understood, we can turn our attention to the content itself. The book contains two laments (I. 2–4, 12–17) about the land-hungry and brutal Assyrians, and two oracles of comfort, the first of which (I. 5–11) deals with Yahweh's instrument of punishment, the Chaldeans, who make light of every stronghold (I. 10) and whom no one can withstand.[65] The prophet's sketch of this rising military power is in general terms and does not provide us with a sharply defined picture of a great army; nor is it taken from the range of ideas based on the eschatological enemy: it is rooted rather in that other conception of Yahweh's demonic punishing forces which are absolutely invincible. Although this act of punishment has not been

---

[65] H. Schmidt, "Ein Psalm im Buche Habakuk," in *Z. alttest. W.*, LXII (1950), pp. 52–63, combines I. 2–4, 12–13 and III. 18–19 as an independent psalm, the content of which represents court proceedings.

P

completed—warns the second oracle (II. 1–5)—just wait: it will certainly come (II. 3). The righteous will live by his faith (II. 4)—a statement which was given its full meaning by the Apostle Paul (Rom. 1. 17)—but the faithless shall perish and the proud shall not endure (II. 5). II. 6 forms the transition to a series of Woe! cries (II. 6–20) which deal with the guilt and punishment of Assyria in various pictures and under different aspects. Whether the last Woe! (II. 19) is also original one cannot say: at all events the transmitted text of the book contains several glosses (II. 6, 14, 18). The individual parts, as established above, are joined in the text to form a unit which is a prophetic liturgy: lament before Yahweh, Yahweh's answer, second lament, second answer. That the repeated Woes! also belong here is clear from the cultic call: "But the Lord is in his holy temple: let all the earth keep silence before him" (II. 20; Zeph. I. 7; Zech. II. 13). A recent tendency[66] has been to separate off II. 5–20 as an independent collection of five single oracles against Babylon, extracting II. 18–20 as a polemic against the idols of the exilic period.

Headed by a new title there follows a prayer of the prophet (III. 1 ff.): it is only in its appendix (III. 17–19), however, that it assumes the character of a prayer.[67] Originally it is a vision, a "poem of trembling" (III. 1): that is, a song of triumph. Here with the colours of mythology and eschatology a powerful picture is painted of Yahweh Himself riding out to battle to the accompaniment of all the phenomena anticipated on the Last Day (storms, natural catastrophes) and annihilating the godless for the salvation of His own people. Here, it is true, the idea of salvation on the Day of Judgment is confined to "the people of Yahweh": but all the more valuable is Habakkuk's interpretation of history, whose master is Yahweh and whose ultimate meaning is realised in Yahweh's final victory. There

---

[66] Cf. K. Elliger, *Das Buch der zwölf Kleinen Propheten*, VOL. II, A.T.D. VOL. XXV, Göttingen 1950, p. 40–66.

[67] W. A. Irwin, "The Psalm of Habakkuk," in *J.N.E.S.*, I (1942), pp. 10–40; U. Cassuto, "Il capitolo 3 di Habaquq e i testi di Ras Shamra," in *Annuario di studi ebraici* 1935–37, Rome 1938; W. F. Albright, "The Psalm of Habakkuk," in *Studies in Old Testament Prophecy*, ed. Rowley, pp. 1–18, with reconstructions of the text; E. J. Evans, "The Song of Habakkuk," in *Bibliotheca Sacra*, henceforth cited as *Bibl. Sac.*, CXII (1955), pp. 62–7, 164–9; W. A. Irwin, "The mythological background of Habakkuk Chapter III," in *J.N.E.S.*, XV (1956), pp. 47–50; S. Mowinckel, "Zum Psalm des Habakuk," in *Th. Z.*, IX (1953), pp. 1–23.

are no serious objections to the unity of this whole book and its authorship by Habakkuk.[68] The date can also be fairly accurately fixed. According to the assumptions it makes, the Book of Habakkuk must have been written before the fall of Nineveh but also before the Babylonian defeat at Veste Takrit and before the unsuccessful Assyrian siege. It fits the historical situation around 615 B.C., when Nebopolassar had successfully completed his campaigns up the Euphrates and had beaten the Assyrians at Madanu.

Zephaniah

Zephaniah[69] (=Yahweh has protected; Septuagint, Sophonias), whose forefathers are listed in the heading back to his great-great-grandfather Hezekiah (I. I), belongs to a somewhat earlier period than Habakkuk. It has been concluded from the name Hezekiah that the prophet belonged to the royal house (II Kings XVIII. I), but if this were so it would certainly be specially mentioned. It is more probable that the reason for this unusual family tree is the fact that Zephaniah is described as the son of Cushi. This need not be a proper name, but can just as easily mean "son of an Ethiopian" (cf. II Sam. XVIII. 21 ff.; Jer. XIII. 23). At all events a similar list is given for Jehudi, whose grandfather was the son of Cushi (Jer. XXXVI. 14).

About Zephaniah's activities, which are quoted as taking place in the reign of King Josiah (640–609 B.C.), we learn absolutely nothing. Perhaps some of the sad experiences of the prophet are reflected in III. 5. The rigid arrangement of the book according to the familiar pattern (threats against his own people, oracles against foreign nations, prophecies of salvation) suggests a literary revision of the original oracles. The first collection (I. 4 ff.) is joined on to an apparently well-known pronouncement of judgment over the whole earth (I. 2–3), and contains a number of mostly short oracles in which Zephaniah threatens the judgment of Yahweh on princes and officials (I. 8) and on the rich (I. 11) who feel themselves so secure

[68] Lods, *Histoire de la littérature*, pp. 457–8, assumes a complicated developmental history: a prophecy (I. 5–10 and perhaps also I. 14–17) from the period around 604 was revised and extended between 597 and 550 to I. 5–II. 4; according to Lods I. 2–4; II. 12–14, 17–20 are secondary; chapter III is a still later addition.

[69] For commentaries and literature, see Bibliography.

(I. 12) with their idolatry (I. 4–5) and their deceit (I. 9). This judgment the prophet intimately connects with the Day of Yahweh (I. 7 ff.), the fearful extent of which is vividly depicted:

> A cry will be heard from the Fish Gate,
> a wail from the Second Quarter,
> a loud crash from the hills.
> Wail, O inhabitants of the Mortar!
>
> (I. 10–11)

But salvation may yet come. "Come together and hold assembly, O shameless nation" (II. 1), "seek righteousness, seek humility; perhaps you may be hidden on the day of the wrath of the Lord" (II. 3). A middle section follows in the form of a collection of oracles against foreign nations (II. 4–15). As in Jeremiah IV–VI, some have wanted to take these for warnings of an approaching Scythian storm, and have dated this portion to the period between 630 and 625 B.C.; but it is difficult to say how much, if anything at all, of this originates from Zephaniah. For the different forms of the individual oracles show that the section is not a unit. Only a few of these threat-oracles contain any reason, and where they do (II. 8–10) the conquest of Jerusalem is assumed. The oracles against the Philistines and Moab-Ammon point to the exilic (II. 9) and post-exilic (II. 7) periods; similarly the oracle against Nineveh (II. 15) with its allusions to post-exilic passages (cf. Is. XIII. 21, XXXIV. 11, XLVII. 8). The third part (III. 1 ff.) presents a threat to Jerusalem and her leaders who are disobedient to Yahweh and pay no heed to His warnings (III. 1 ff.), and also a promise of future salvation for His people (III. 9 ff.). One must reckon that there have been slight amendments and fairly large amplifications. The song of praise at the end, consisting of royal rejoicing at Yahweh's accession to His throne (III. 14 ff.), an oracle of comfort (III. 16–17), and a prophecy of salvation (III. 18 ff.) assume the circumstances prevailing after the conquest of Jerusalem.

The date of the prophecy of Zephaniah presents no great problem, for the content confirms the chronological data contained in the heading. Indeed, we can even narrow the limits and say that the oracles were spoken in the main during King Josiah's minority (I. 8), that is a number of years before the reform of the cult, about 630 B.C. Who first compiled these oracles, and when, we do not know. In any case they were arranged according to definite views and completed by the collection of oracles against foreign nations at a later stage in the redaction. The book probably reached its final form during the exile—a possibility not discounted by even later, post-exilic additions. Zephaniah is not a prophet of special importance, even though he should not be regarded as the one-sided representative of *"dies irae, dies illa."* In essence the thoughts he presents have already been proclaimed by his great predecessors Amos, Hosea, and Isaiah. But—and herein lies his great significance—he has at least faithfully followed them. Thus he became the forerunner of the approaching reform of the cult.

Haggai

The Book of Haggai takes us into the early post-exilic period.[70] Some of the Jews have already returned home. The religious tolerance shown by the Persians has restored to them some of the Temple furnishings stolen by Nebuchadnezzar, and has also made means available for the rebuilding of the Temple. For many reasons, however (Ezra iv. 1 ff.), this rebuilding never got beyond the stage of laying the foundation stone. Here, almost twenty years later (Ezra v. 1), Haggai's career begins. The sole object of the picture given of him is to present him as the driving force behind the building of the Temple. Only a few oracles have been transmitted, all of them originating in the second year of Darius's reign, that is in 520 B.C. The prophet traces the failure of the harvest and the difficult economic situation of the community back to the fact that they have been building houses for themselves and neglecting the Temple (i. 3 ff.). When work on the Temple begins, the tide turns: now Yahweh will bestow His blessings again (ii. 14 ff.). A further promise deals with the magnificence of the new Temple, which will outshine the first in its beauty (ii. 1 ff.), and with the choosing of Zerubbabel as governor by Yahweh (ii. 20 ff.). A conversation on the same day between Haggai and the priests on the subject of "clean and unclean" serves as an image of the uncleanness of the people (ii. 10 ff.).

This small book, which must have been written soon after

[70] For commentaries and literature, see Bibliography.

520 B.C., differs essentially from pre-exilic prophetic writings. In the first place, it is not the prophet himself who is writing but someone else, who certainly was very close to him and faithfully transmitted his utterances. Since he introduces each one separately in detail, and deals in even more detail with the effect of the first prophetic utterances (I. 12 ff.), the whole book gives the impression rather of being part of a chronicle of the building of the Temple than a collection of prophetic utterances. Moreover, Haggai's message reveals the great gulf between him and the pre-exilic writing prophets. While for them the coming salvation is bound up with Yahweh's judgment over all the world, this thought is only vaguely hinted at here (II. 6–7, 21–2) and is restricted to the heathen who, thus shaken, will voluntarily pay their tribute to the Temple (II. 7). Thus future salvation is very much a matter of this world and is very materially bound up with the Temple and its restoration. Herein lies the great turning point of the prophecies from the internal to the external, from the thoughts of one's own mind to the religion of the Law.

Zechariah (I–VIII)

Less strange and colourless than Haggai is the figure of his somewhat younger contemporary Zechariah (= Yahweh has remembered),[71] who belonged to the circle of priests (Neh. XII. 16). He was the son of Iddo (Ezra V. 1, VI. 14), not his grandson: the incorrect description "son of Berechiah" (I. 1, 7) contains a reminder of Isaiah (Is. VIII. 2), or else it should be considered as the title of Deutero-Zechariah (IX. 1). His oracles and visions, in so far as they are exactly dated, are from the period from 520 B.C. (I. 1) to 518 B.C. (VII. 1) but this does not mean that the prophet could not have had a longer career.

The core and basis of his book is a collection of eight visions, the so-called night visions, which are uniform in structure and contain autobiographical passages. The first (I. 7–15) deals with riders who report at the gate of Heaven on the peace and stillness prevailing on earth; soon, however, the anger of Yahweh will descend upon the nations, and with this the era of salvation will dawn. The second vision (I. 18–21), of the four

[71] See Bibliography.

horns and the four smiths, announces the defeat of Israel's enemies, while the third, (II. 1–5) of the man with the measuring line, obviously demonstrates the future greatness of Jerusalem. In the fourth (III. 1–7) the High Priest Joshua, who is being accused by Satan, is acquitted in the court of Heaven, and the fifth (IV. 1–6, 10–14) deals with the two anointed ones, the royal and the priestly, who will stand beside Yahweh like the olive trees of the vision beside the candlestick. The sixth vision, (V. 1–4) of the flying scroll which hovers as a curse over thieving and perjury, and the seventh (V. 5–11), of the removal of wickedness to Babylon, belong together, while the eighth (VI. 1–8) refers back to the first: the chariots of Yahweh set out towards the north; those that are far away will come and build the Temple. The details of these visions, all of which are based on the same idea, the coming salvation, are in part very difficult to understand with their, to us, strange allusions to mythology and religious history. The addition of a whole series of Zechariah's oracles (I. 16–17, II. 6 ff, 10 ff., III. 8, IV. 6 ff.) intended to complete the sense and make the meaning clearer, does not make it easier to understand. This collection is set between an oracle exhorting the people to repent (I. 2–6), drawing their attention to their forefathers who did not listen to the prophets, and an incomplete and much-corrected final oracle (VI. 9 ff.) concerning the coronation of Zerubbabel (Joshua, VI. 11).

A further compilation of Zechariah's oracles is presented in the so-called fasting sermon (chs. VII–VIII) which originated in the year 518 (VII. 1) and circulated independently at first. An enquiry about the fasting which was instituted because of the destruction of the Temple, is answered by the prophet to the effect that now is the time of joy. Into this episode (VII. 1–7, VIII. 18–19) has been inserted a series of individual prophetic utterances, telling of future salvation but giving expression at the same time to the old basic moral requirements of the prophets (VII. 8 ff., VIII. 16 f.).

This review of the contents has briefly outlined the evolution of the book; single visions and oracles fitted tightly together and framed as two smaller collections, the arrangement of which is governed particularly by the dates cited (I. 1, VII. 1). Whether the prophet himself moulded the two together we do not know.

Zechariah has much in common with Haggai, who regarded the neglect in building the Temple as the sole obstacle in the way of the coming of salvation. Zechariah also lives in the high tension of this expectation of salvation. Unfortunately it has not been passed on to us how this tension resolved itself when the building of the Temple had been completed: even Ezra's report, which breaks off abruptly with the consecration (Ezra vi. 22), has nothing to say on this point. Zechariah's connexion with his great predecessors among the prophets is established by his call for the proper service of God and his grave view of sin. For him, too, Yahweh is the Lord of history, who punishes the disobedient but at the same time leads back His people out of His love for them and wants to live in the midst of them. So little is said about the fate of "the nations" in these last days (I. 15, 21, II. 9) that a later writer tried to fill the gap by making a special addition (VIII. 20 ff.). For Zechariah, however, Yahweh is also the inaccessible God, who uses an intermediary even in His dealings with the prophets; this idea is quite different from the prophets of earlier times, from whom Zechariah consciously divorces himself (VII. 7, 12). His night-visions also have little of the originality and directness of the earlier visions, while even his expectation of the Messiah, with its split between a temporal and a spiritual head and its purely national limitation, does not approach that of the older prophets.

Anonymous Prophets (*Zechariah* IX–XIV)

Attached to the collection of the minor prophets there are three anonymous smaller collections, all of which carry the same heading "Massah" (= the burden of the word of Yahweh) (Zech. IX. 1, XII. 1; Mal. I. 1). These have been added since, like Zechariah, they all deal with the coming salvation. It is striking, however, even in the very first collection usually referred to as Deutero-Zechariah (second Zechariah) (Zech. IX–XI, XIII. 7–9),[72] that they contain a few smaller prophetic oracles which do not fit into this period. Examples are the song about the coming Messiah (IX. 9 f.), which has some pre-exilic features and has been explained by Jesus's entry into Jerusalem (Mt. XXI. 5); a reminder, timeless in itself (X. 1–2),

[72] For literature, see Bibliography.

that in times of drought one should turn not to seers and teraphim but to Yahweh alone; part of a mocking song (XI. 1–2)
from an old oracle against foreign nations; an oracle concerning
bad shepherds (XI. 16) from the familiar cycle of shepherd
songs and songs of self-exultation (Ezek. XXXIV. 4); and a cry of
Woe! to bad shepherds (XI. 17) which recalls similar words from
an earlier period (Jer. XXIII. 1; Ezek. XXXIV. 2). The same is
true of the two oracles (IX. 1 ff., X. 3 ff.) which refer in such a
concrete way to definite historical events of the eighth century
that they do not fit in the present context. A clue is provided
by the fact that this oracle contains prophetic words interspersed with the words of Yahweh. This shows that we are
here dealing with pre-exilic portions which have subsequently
been transferred by Deutero-Zechariah to his own contemporary conditions and to suit his own purposes—a procedure
which Jeremiah denounced (Jer. XXIII. 30): "The prophets . . .
steal my words from one another."

A clue to the development of this anonymous prophecy is
given in the symbolic tale (XI. 4 ff.), but as this is an allegory
it remains very questionable to what extent the individual
features can be interpreted. If the allusion (XI. 14) is to the
breaking away of the Samaritans, this collection would be
dated prior to 300 B.C. However, many scholars interpret the
two shepherds as Onias II and Alcimus (1 Macc. VII. 5 ff., IX.
54) and date this portion around 160 B.C.

That the rest of the book (chs. XII–XIV) does not belong to
Deutero-Zechariah is evident from the new heading and
especially from the short hymn fragment which accompanies it
(XII. 1). This third or Trito-Zechariah comprises two collections
(XII–XIII, XIV) fairly parallel in course. Both contain individual
prophecies, loosely linked together by "on that day." Nevertheless one cannot deny a certain logical sequence in their
arrangement. The nations and inhabitants of Judah are march-
ing against Jerusalem, but Yahweh protects the city; He
destroys the nations and will pour out His spirit over the house
of David and Jerusalem. The lament over him who has been
pierced (XII. 10 ff.) presents a problem; it is not known whether
it is an allusion to a martyr-Messiah or to a judicial murder.
Two threats in prose based on "uncleanness" (XIII. 2–3, 4 ff.)
are appended: these deal with the prophets who are to be

exterminated at the same time as the images and unclean spirits. The second collection (ch. XIV) lets Jerusalem be overcome and destroyed by the nations and part of the population be carried away. But then Yahweh steps forward, and now Jerusalem is blessed with final salvation in the kingdom of Yahweh, which is depicted with fantastic details; but the nations are consumed by a plague. Their fate is represented as a civil war, which is described in added prose passages (XIV. 13 ff.). The survivors, under threat of punishment, go up to Jerusalem for the celebration of the Feast of Tabernacles. A prose oracle on ritual purity (XIV. 20–1) brings this collection to an end.

The whole attitude of these prophecies, which see the kingdom of God as "a Judaised universal kingdom" with the sanctity of the ritual and Jerusalem with its cult at the centre, shows what a great gulf separates them from true prophecy with its direct experience of God; but it also shows their close relationship with apocalyptic. We can no more explain the contrast between Jerusalem and Judah than the many other contemporary allusions. Even if one does not interpret XII. 10 as a reference to the murder of the High Priest Onias III (II Macc. IV. 34) in the year 170 B.C., one must necessarily date the Trito-Zechariah compilation to this quite late period.

Malachi

The name Malachi (=my messenger) has been included in the heading as the result of misconception (from III. 1); this, like the appendixes to Zechariah, is an anonymous prophecy.[73] The whole book consists of six sections, all built on the same pattern of a dialogue. The first (I. 2–5) points out Yahweh's love for His people as illustrated in the wilderness of Edom. Several sections attack lax ideas on matrimonial fidelity (II. 10–16) and abuses in cultic matters, such as the sacrificing of imperfect animals (I, 6–II. 9), by doing which the priests hinder reverence of Yahweh, and the careless handling of the prescribed Temple dues (III. 6–12). Two oracles (II. 17–III. 5, III. 13–IV. 3) are concerned with the grumbling of the people against the justice of Yahweh. But He will soon come to judge and reveal His justice in the punishment of the wicked and the rewarding of those who fear God. The conclusion (IV. 4–6)

[73] For commentaries and literature, see Bibliography.

is probably from a later hand and gives an explanation (IV. 5 f.) of Yahweh's messenger (III. 1). Verse 4 in the Septuagint, but also in the readings in the synagogue, is placed at the end, no doubt to avoid a gloomy conclusion.

The questions of evolution are easy. Apart from small additions (I. 11 ff., II. 11–12) the whole thing is the work of one person. The Temple is rebuilt (III. 1, 10), a govenor is in the land (I. 8), but Ezra's reforms have not yet been carried out— all this points to a time shortly before Ezra. In its emphasis on ethical requirements the book belongs to the ranks of the greater prophets; with its pronounced cultic interest, however, and its judgment on the Edomites it reveals itself as a forerunner of later Judaism.

CHAPTER V

THE WRITINGS

THE PSALMS

THE LAST large section of the Old Testament, "the Writings," contains material of all types and descriptions. Poetry and prose, religious songs and wisdom sayings, didactic poems and love songs, short stories and festival legends, apocalypse and chronicles—in short, everything which could find a place neither in the Torah nor among the prophets but is nevertheless considered as "Holy Scripture." At the head of these stand the Psalms,[1] whose profound influence on the souls of men in all ages is unrivalled by any other part of the Old Testament. It is the first of the three great poetic works (along with Proverbs and Job), and presents an extensive collection of religious lyrics, the name given to which was probably also used as a label for the complete group of "the Writings" (cf. Lk. XXIV. 44). In the Talmud[2] the Psalms are immediately preceded by the Book of Ruth, because Ruth was the ancestress of David, who "satisfied the Lord with songs of praise and thanksgiving." This statement is in accordance with the Hebrew name for the collection "Telhillim" (= praises), but it is the Greek name from the Septuagint "Psalms" which has prevailed. The word psalm actually means playing on a stringed instrument, the psaltery. In all, 150 songs have been handed down: why exactly this number, we do not know. At all events we have quite often encountered psalms in the Torah and in the Prophets: the work of the Chronicler, too, and especially Maccabees, contain many psalms or psalm fragments. Despite some variation in details, the Septuagint has the same number: twice it counts two songs which belong together as one (IX–X, CXIV–CXV), but this is compensated for by its division of two others (CXVI, CXLVII) into two songs each. An additional psalm fragment is added at the end of the Psalter, but this with the

---

[1] For commentaries and literature, see Bibliography.
[2] Baba bathra 14b; cf Goldschmidt, *Talmud*, VOL. VIII, p. 55.

express observation in the title that this song "lies outside the number calculated."

Probably in accordance with the subdividing of the Pentateuch, the whole Psalter is divided into five books,[3] which are separated from one another by means of uniform, hymn-like, or liturgical passages (XLI. 13, LXXII. 18–19, LXXXIX. 52, CVI. 48). But this division, which took place before the Septuagint translation, bears no relation to such original collections as there may have been. More significant is the fact that in the second and third books the name for God "Yahweh" is almost always replaced by "Elohim." This is particularly striking in places where the word Elohim occurs twice together (e.g. XLIII. 4, XLV. 7, L. 7). Anyone who considers this too artificial or too far-fetched need only compare the titles given to God in psalms which have been transmitted more than once and in different compilations.[4] This leads to the conclusion that Pss. XLII–LXXXIII were originally an independent collection, to which Pss. LXXXIV–LXXXIX perhaps also belong as an appendix. In addition to this Elohistic group there is another smaller collection which stands out by its similar headings—the fifteen Songs of Degrees or Songs of Ascents (CXX–CXXXIV), probably a group of pilgrimage songs sung by festival pilgrims as they approached Jerusalem. Then the Hallelujah psalms (CXI–CXIV, CXVI–CXVIII, CXXXV–CXXXVI, CXLVI–CL), all of which begin with Hallelujah (= praise Yahweh), although in some cases this has been transferred to the end of the preceding psalm (CXV–CXVII). In addition there are the Korahite psalms (XLII–XLIX) with a supplement (LXXXIV–LXXXV, LXXXVII–LXXXVIII) and the psalms of Asaph (L, LXXIII–LXXXIII). Of the psalms of David, to whom almost half the Psalter has been ascribed, there must have been at least two collections (III–XLI and LI–LXXII); otherwise the note contained in the Elohistic collection that "the prayers of David, the son of Jesse, are ended" (LXII. 20) is incomprehensible.[5] The first collection of the Songs of David consists mainly of songs sung by an individual, not by the community, and these generally end in words of comfort concerning Yahweh's treatment

---

[3] Qiddusin 33a; cf. Goldschmidt, *Talmud*, VOL. VI, p. 617.

[4] Pss. XIV, cf. LIII; XL. 13–17, cf. LXX; XXXI. 2–4, cf. LXXI. 1–3; CVIII, cf. LVII. 7–11 and LX. 5–12.

[5] In all only three psalms (XVII, LXXXVI, CXLII) are transmitted expressly as "Prayers of David."

of those who believe in Him. The second Davidic collection (LI ff.) is well planned, as is evident from the different subheadings.

Of the evolution of the Psalter as it exists today we know nothing. We are solely dependent on hypotheses and probabilities. But this much can be said: the Elohistic collection is made up of three smaller collections (David, LI–LXXII; Asaph; and Korah). Clues as to the date of this compilation are provided by the accent on the guild of singers which flourished in the fourth century B.C. Moreover, attention should be drawn to the omission of the name Yahweh, which points to the collection having been corrected by a Jewish school of thought which developed in the third century. This Elohistic collection was then united with another independent, and indeed older, compilation of psalms of David (III–XLI without XXXIII) and prefaced by the added Psalm II, which is quite clearly (II. 7) related to the last song in the collection (LXXXIX. 27–30). In addition there is another group (XC–CL) from a later period: this contains religious songs of all dates, starting from Moses down to the not more exactly defined present. This group has assimilated individual smaller groups of songs like the Hallelujah psalms (CXIII–CXVI) and the psalms of degrees. Originally it must have been an independent collection, as is clear from the correspondence between some of the songs (CV, CVIII) and those in the other collection (LXXVIII, LVII, LX); also, it was available to the Chronicler (1 Chron. XVI. 8 ff.; Pss. CV, XCVI, CVI). The unification with the existing collection (II–LXXXIX), in the course of which a didactic psalm (Ps. I) was inserted as a kind of preface to the whole work, must have taken place shortly afterwards, still in the third century.

A sharp distinction must be drawn between the development of the collection of Psalms as such, and the origin of the individual psalms. It all looks very simple: more than two-thirds of all the psalms are provided with titles naming the author. In Asaph, Heman (Ps. LXXXVIII), and Ethan (LXXXIX), who in Chronicles is also called Jeduthun, we have the three chief singers of David who are named by the Chronicler[6] as the founders of the singing families in the cult of the post-exilic Temple. The "children of Korah," the gatekeepers of the Temple (1 Chron. IX. 19, XXVI. 1), also seem to have played a

<hr>

[6] 1 Chron. VI. 16 ff., XV. 19, XXV. 1 ff.; II Chron. V. 12.

part in the cult (II Chron. XX. 19). In many instances in the seventy-three psalms of David the *raison d'être* of the individual song is given. But since these explanations have been taken almost word for word from the Books of Samuel, and by no means always coincide with the content of the songs, they cannot claim to be reliable. This is particularly evident in the songs in which "David" speaks of the King (as XX, XXI, LXI), and presupposes the existence of the Temple (as V.7, XXVII. 4); similarly, references to the destruction of cities (LXIX. 35 f.) and walls (LI. 18) do not fit in with him or his age. Perhaps, however, "David" is not to be taken as a name at all but, as in Mari, as a title (dawidum = leader of troops), in which case the title of the psalm would mean "for the king." Further evidence of the insignificant value of these titles is found in the fact that the Septuagint ascribes four songs (Pss. CXLV–CXLVIII) more than the Masoretic Text to the prophets Haggai and Zechariah, and a good dozen more to David, including those which relate to the captivity (LXXI, CXXXVII) and to the rebuilding of the Temple (XCVI). The fact that it is not until Chronicles[7] that David is claimed as the originator of singing in the Temple, while the Books of Samuel are completely silent on this point, in itself speaks neither for nor against psalms by David. In any case, little reliance is to be placed on the data in the headings, and the content of every song should be specially examined to see what period it belongs to. Certainly this is a very imperfect criterion, since the statements in many of the psalms are in quite general terms; but no other course is open to us. And so, in so far as there are no serious reasons to the contrary, we must follow the transmitted text.

In addition to the name of the author many of the titles contain supplementary details about the use of the psalms in worship. So, for example, "to the choirmaster," which occurs more than fifty times (as IV, V; Hab. III. 19) and which we do not know how to treat; perhaps it means "for a suitable pitch." In addition there is a whole series of supplementary notes (as in V, VI, VIII, IX, etc.), the meaning of which is not quite certain. It is usually assumed that they contain definite instructions about the type of musical performance for the individual psalm. But we do not know whether it is a case of special melodies or

[7] I Chron. XXIII. 5, XXV. I ff.; II Chron. VII. 6.

musical keys or of the instrumental accompaniment, or whether
it is a matter of the beginnings of the songs or the designation
of certain rites. Neither do we know what "to Jeduthun"
(XXXIX, LXII, LXXVII) is supposed to mean, for it is difficult to
equate it with the name of the singers cited in Chronicles. It
even remains an open question whether the "Selah" which
occurs frequently in certain psalms is a signal for a pause or a
repeat mark.[8] At all events, these signs point to the songs
having been used in the cult. In some cases, indeed, their
particular purpose is stated—thus, for the dedication of the
Temple (XXX), a thank-offering (C), memorial offerings
(XXXVIII, LXX), or for the Sabbath day (XCII). The Septuagint
carries this even further and appoints certain psalms for the
Tamid offerings on different days of the week—Sunday (XXIV),
Monday (XLVIII), Wednesday (XCIV), and Friday (XCIII), while
the Talmud tradition[9] completes the picture by adding the
psalms for Tuesday (LXXXII) and Thursday (LXXXI) as they
were sung by the Levites in the Temple. From the Talmud we
learn further that the song of praise (CXLV–CL) was read aloud
daily at morning prayer, while the songs of ascent were
intended for the Passover and the Hallelujah psalms for feast
days—a custom which is also transmitted in the New Testament (Mt. XXVI. 30). In Chronicles (I Chron. XVI) we have an
account of the service of worship followed in the post-exilic community, and a few psalms (like CVII, CXXXVI) provide us with a
picture of the antiphonal singing in the Temple: even the Sabbath psalm *Jubilate* (LXVI) is divided up into choir and individual
voice. Ps. LXVIII is extremely difficult: a hundred years ago Ed.
Reuss described it as "a monument of exegetical difficulty and
art," and a more modern commentator has divided it up into six-
teen unconnected individual parts. Now attempts are being made
to establish that it is a list of thirty beginnings of Old Hebrew lyrics,
in which case we should have a Hebrew counterpart to the two
well-known Sumerian lists and the Assyrian hymn catalogue.[10]

[8] R. Gyllenberg, "Die Bedeutung des Wortes Sela," in *Z. alttest. W.*, LVIII (1940),
pp. 153–6; N. H. Snaith, "Selah," in *Vet. test.*, II (1952), pp. 43–56.

[9] Cf. Tamid 33*b*, Goldschmidt, *Talmud*, VOL. XII, p. 715; Sabbath 118*b*, *op. cit.*,
VOL. I, p. 799; Taanith 28*b*, *op. cit.*, VOL. III, p. 738.

[10] H. Schmidt, *Die Psalmen*, Hb. A.T., Tübingen 1934, p. 127; W. F. Albright,
"A catalogue of early Hebrew lyric poems (Psalm LXVIII)," in *H.U.C.A.*, XXIII
(1950–51), pp. 1–39; F. James, *Thirty Psalmists*, New York 1938.

The individual psalm is very close to life and indeed stems from everyday life. Some have tried to classify the psalms according to certain points of view, differentiating between songs happy, sad, and peaceful in mood, or picking out certain types of piety. No doubt the religious lyric has passed through different periods and types of religious devotion. But the material of each can be judged solely by the laws of its own type. If we compare the psalms with one another we find that many are strikingly similar in form and follow a set pattern, while at the same time somewhat vague and generalised in expression. Often, particularly in the psalms of David, the theme is the enemy. But why are no details given about this enemy; why is it never named? The only possible answer is that these songs were not to be understood as personal at all; they belonged to the liturgy and their *"Sitz im Leben"* is the cult. We must not, of course, make the mistake of thinking that all the psalms can simply be fitted into one pattern. It is in these very songs that the individual poet frequently breaks through the original pattern and reveals to us his whole being and heart with all his personal devotion. But the starting point, to which we must go back for our better understanding, is the cult.[11]

Our task is to gather together all the songs which were sung on certain occasions in the services, to work out the thoughts and moods which they have in common, and to give our attention to their linguistic form and vocabulary. This method may at first appear to be purely external and mechanical, but only in this way is it possible to find out the principles which governed the evolution of the psalms, and to recognise the

---

[11] For literature on this point, see Bibliography. N. H. Tur-Sinai, "The literary character of the Book of Psalms," in *Oudtest. St.*, VIII (1950), pp. 263–81, rejects the cultic origin of the Psalms and sees in them excerpts from historical books. A new thesis on the place of the Psalms has been advanced by A. Weiser, who, starting from the theophanies of Jahweh (Pss. XVIII. 8–16, L. 2 ff., LXVIII. 2 ff., LXXVII. 17, XCVII. 3–6), tries to trace a common cultic tradition throughout the Psalms and explains them as fragments from the ritual of the Festival of the Covenant: cf. A. Weiser, "Zur Frage nach den Beziehungen der Psalmen zum Kult: die Darstellung der Theophanie in den Psalmen und im Festkult," in *Bertholet-Festschrift*, pp. 513–31; id., *Die Psalmen*, A.T.D., VOLS. XIV–XV, 2nd edn. Göttingen 1955, pp. 11–29; cf. also his *Einleitung*, para 13. The numbers of those who reject Weiser's theory, however, are increasing: L. Grollenberg, in *Revue biblique*, henceforth cited as *Rev. bib.*, LVIII (1951), pp. 593–6; R. J. Tournay, in *Rev. bib.*, LVIII (1951), pp. 257–8; H. Buckers, "Zur Verwertung der Sinaitraditionen in den Psalmen," in *Bibl.*, XXXII (1951), pp. 401–12.

many-sided world of religious devotion which is expressed in
them. In the Hebrew lyric, just as in Egyptian and Babylonian
songs, firmly established and definite types can be recognised,
which in the earlier period were kept pure but as time went on
became more and more intermingled. The influence of the
prophets, who set so little store on everything concerned with
the cult, was especially responsible for the decisive change from
the purely cultic to the spiritual song, the best and most
valuable possession of the Psalter. But, if in the poetry of the
psalms the development is from the cultic to the cult-free,
spiritual song, the history of the compilation of the Psalms
reveals exactly the opposite trend, developing towards the cult,
as is indicated by the inclusion of instructions for music in non-
cultic songs (e.g. Pss. LI, LIV, LV, LVII). The material, however,
is so extensive that we must restrict ourselves in this account to
the most important points.

The first of the four main types is the hymn (like Pss. XCVI,
XCVIII, C, CV, CXLVII–CL), in which the liturgical connexion is
still often evident, especially in the group of hymns calling His
people to glorify and rejoice in the majesty of God. The basic
mood is reverence of God, rejoicing in Yahweh, enthusiasm for
His power and greatness, praising in varied phrases His power
in heaven and on earth, in creation and in history. One
variety of hymn is the Zion songs (LXXXIV, LXXXVII, CXXII) with
their glorification of the Temple and their desire for blessings
on this holy place. More important, however, are the songs of
accession (XCIII, XCVII, XCIX, XLVII, XCVI), which are sung with
a procession—probably at the New Year festival—to celebrate
Yahweh's accession to His throne. Their model is the coronation ceremonies of the secular monarch, and they arose either
to imitate or to rival the Babylonian New Year festival. Their
basic idea is to invite coronation rejoicing over Yahweh's deeds,
particularly over the beginning of His kingship.[12] Under the
influence of prophetic preaching, however, they have taken
on a strongly eschatological impress, and in full confidence of
victory tell of the coming of a new universal kingdom, in which
Yahweh will rule as monarch over all the nations of the earth.
The King's songs, despite their external similarity, must not be
confused with these; they were performed in the presence of

[12] For literature on this point, see Bibliography.

the king and his nobles in the sanctuary or in the palace or were spoken by the king himself. Their content is extremely varied, according to the very different circumstances of their origin. They are principally songs of accession (II, XXI, LXXII, CX)[13]; but also war songs (XVIII, XX, CXLIV), a wedding song (XLV), a dedication ceremony for Temple and kingdom (CXXXII), and a throne speech by the king (CI). Although so concerned with secular matters, they are nevertheless religious songs, matching the close connexion between the king and the God of the people. It should be noted here that nowhere in these songs is a definite political situation outlined, neither are any names quoted (apart from David and Melchizedek). Their concern is not with one particular king but more with the concept, the ideal figure of the king. Thus they too have a certain strictness of form. In details they sometimes change over into other types (songs of thanksgiving or laments, for example), and then—in comparison with the hymn—they assume a more personal tone.

The second large group is that of the national laments (XLIV, LXXIV, LXXIX–LXXX, LXXXIII): their ideal situation is a period of fasting, brought about by any kind of distress such as drought, bad harvests, or danger of war. It is a festival of lamentation, at which the community congregates in the Temple to pour out their hearts before Yahweh with sacrifices, mourning, and vows, complaining in moving tones of their distress, which was always felt to be at the same time religious and moral. Next come requests aimed at awakening Yahweh's compassion; descriptions of the people's weakness and helplessness, assertion of their innocence, but also acknowledgment of their sins and of the well-merited wrath of God. They conclude with all manner of thoughts of comfort, including revenge and reprisals against their enemies. More important, however, is the consciousness of all that Yahweh has done for His people, and confidence that He will help them even now for His

---

[13] L. Durr, *Psalm CX im Lichte der neueren altorientalischen Forschung*, Münster 1929; E. R. Hardy, "The date of Psalm CX," in *J. Bib. Lit.*, LXIV (1945), pp. 13–24. On the basis of an acrostic "Simeon" in Ps. CX. 1–4, Pfeiffer, *Introduction*, p. 630, wants to date Ps. CX in the year 141 B.C. (I. Macc. XIV. 41) and, for the same reason, Ps. II in the year 103 B.C. (mention of the wedding of Alexander Jannaeus and Alexandra); cf. also with regard to Ps. IV "Zerubbabel" Slonim, Pfeiffer, *Introduction*, p. 630.

name's sake. So these songs lead from the depths of despair
and anxiety to the victorious certainty of divine help. "May
those who sow in tears reap with shouts of joy! He that goes
forth weeping, bearing the seed for sowing, shall come home
with shouts of joy, bringing his sheaves with him" (CXXVI. 5 f.).
At times one or other thought is so much to the forefront that
we can speak of songs of confidence (CXXV), songs of innocence
and repentance (CVI).

Intimately connected with these are the laments of the
individual which occupy the most space in the Psalter and have
largely provided the models for the hymns of the Protestant
Churches. For a long time these songs were understood
allegorically, and the "I" of the worshipper was interpreted as
the post-exilic community. But this is wrong, for they have a
completely personal stamp and clearly witness to the bond
between the believer and his God. Here it is not the community
but the individual worshipper who is pouring out his heart
before God.[14] The "Sitz im Leben" of these songs is not clearly
recognisable. If sacrifices (V. 3), oracles (LXXXVI. 17, CXXX. 5),
and fasting (XXXV. 13, LXIX. 3) point to the Temple, in others
again personal privacy (IV. 8, LV. 17) or a sick-bed (VI. 6,
LXIII. 6) is assumed. In content they resemble the national
laments, only here the thoughts are turned completely away
from the political, external, and general to the personal and
heartfelt. And this is what makes these songs so valuable, and
as significant for the worshipper of today as for their first
singer: a source of comfort and strength, of inner fortification
and elevation. "Why are you cast down, O my soul, and why
are you disquieted within me? Hope in God; for I shall again
praise him, my help and my God" (Ps. XLII. f.). Such songs are
the models of true devotion in all ages. "The fortunate may do
without the eternal Helper: but the sufferer, who despairs of
Man and the world, stretches out his hands from the depths of
his distress upwards to God in heaven" (Gunkel). The sufferings which are passionately lamented in these songs are depicted in a profusion of pictures, which cannot always, however,
be taken literally. But two main motifs in particular stand out:
the one sickness, which brings the believer near to death (XXV.
16, XXXI. 9 ff., XLII. 10, LXXI. 20), down to Sheol, the underworld,

---

[14] E. Balla, *Das Ich der Psalmen*, Göttingen 1912.

where he is deserted by the help of Yahweh. The other
is the enemies who gibe at the worshipper and seek his misfortune, so that they can triumph over the bankruptcy of his
faith. Thus religious contrasts between the pious and the
wicked take up much space (III, V, VI, etc.). The reason for
some of these songs seems to lie in a lawsuit (VII. 6 f., LXIX. 4):
but the allusions are hardly extensive enough to permit
distinguishing special "songs of the accused."[15] The requests for
help point to personal distress and the shameful conduct of the
opponent, and touch on God's mercy and on the experiences
which the believer has had of His faithful assistance in the past.
They give expression to a great confidence; similarly the ideas
of consolation are supported by the same faithful trust in
Yahweh. "In God I trust without a fear. What can man do
to me?" (LVI. 11). Here, too, as in the national laments, the
emphasis varies so that one or other thought is in the foreground. So there are psalms of curses and revenge (CIX) on
one's enemies; songs of repentance (LI, CXXX), innocence (V,
VII, XVII, XXVI), and above all confidence (as IV, XI, XVI, XXIII);
and songs of thanksgiving (as VII. 18, XIII. 6, XXII. 23 ff.,
XXVII. 6).

The counterpart to the lament of the individual is found in
the songs of the thanksgivings of the individual (XVIII, XXX,
XXXII, XXXIV, etc.), but not many of these have been handed
down; for it is only human nature that requests should out-
number thanks. What the believer asked of Yahweh in the
lament has now taken place: Yahweh has helped, either in
distress or in danger. The song of thanksgiving tells in detail,
in a form corresponding to that of the laments, of the difficulties
surmounted, confesses that Yahweh is the deliverer, and offers
a thanks-offering (LXVI. 13 ff., CVII. 22, CXVI. 17). The *"Sitz
im Leben"* is quite evident here—the thanks-offering presented
to the guests at the next sacrificial meal by the one who has
been delivered, surrounded by his friends and relatives (CVI,
CVII, CXXXVI). At the centre of the celebration stands the

[15] H. Schmidt, *Das Gebet der Angeklagten*, Beihefte z. Z. alttest. W., No. 49,
Giessen 1928; H. Birkeland, *Die Feinde des Individuums in der israelitischen Psalmen-
literatur*, Oslo 1933; A. Bentzen, "Der Tod des Beters in den Psalmen," in *Festschrift Otto Eissfeldt zum 60. Geburtstage*, ed. J. Fück, Halle 1947, pp. 57–60; A. F.
Puukko, "Der Feind in den alttestamentlichen Psalmen," in *Oudtest. St.*, VIII (1950),
pp. 47–65.

thanks-offering, which on occasion has become a liturgy of thanks (XXVI. 6 f., CVII, CXVIII). The fact that these songs contain much that is uniform and impersonal follows from their liturgical origin: the result is that, especially in the earlier period, they are somewhat stereotyped. Gradually, however, they broke more and more free from the cult; and the song of the thanks-offering becomes the spiritual song of thanksgiving in which the soul, having thrown off cultic bonds, kneels alone in prayer before its God. These songs, too, reveal many points of contact with the hymn and with the lament and also clearly show the influence of the prophets.

In addition there are a number of less extensive types, of which only the most important will be mentioned briefly here. First come the blessings (I. 1 ff., II. 11b, XXXII. 1 f., XXXIII. 12) and the invocation of blessings (CXV. 12 ff., CXXI. 7 f., CXXVIII. 5 f.) with all the things that make life richer and stronger: the counterparts of these are the pronouncements or invocation of curses (I. 4 ff., CXII. 10, CXIX. 21, CXXXVII), many of which have found their way into other types. Pilgrim songs (LXXXIV, CXXII), in spite of their general nature, quite often express the feelings of the individual; victory songs are purely temporal in origin and glorify the deeds of heroes in battle, but go on to praise the victory as the work of Yahweh (XLVI. 8 f., LXVI. 5 ff., LXXVI. 3, CXVIII. 15, CXLIX. 4). In addition to these there is the legend type, telling of Yahweh's actions towards Israel (LXXVIII, CV, CVI) and showing a certain relationship with Israel's songs of thanksgiving (LXVI. 8 ff., LXVII, CXXIV, CXXIX). The latter were recited in the sanctuary on special occasions, and in other respects show parallels to the songs of thanksgiving of the individual; like the latter, they are not numerous. Torah psalms are rare (L); somewhat less rare are the Torah liturgies (XV, XXIV) and also other liturgies, which developed as mixed forms of the oracle,[16] combined chiefly with songs of lamentation (XII, LX, LXXXV, CXXI), but also with other types (CXXVI, CXXXII, CXXXIV). The prophetic element to a large extent stimulated and gave greater depth to the poetry of the Psalms,

---

[16] J. Begrich, "Das priesterliche Heilsorakel," in *Z. alttest. W.*, LII (1934), pp. 81–92; N. Nicolsky, *Spuren magischer Formeln in den Psalmen*, Beihefte z. *Z. alttest. W.*, No. 46, Giessen 1927; A. Guillaume, *Prophecy and Divination among the Hebrews and other Semites*, New York 1938.

whether with eschatological ideas (XLVI. 2 ff., LXVIII, LXXVI, XCIII, XCVIII) or in the form of prophetic liturgies (LXXV, LXXXV, CXXVI). Even the wisdom literature with its exhortations and teaching, particularly with its questioning of divine requital, has not remained without influence on the Psalms, even if wisdom sayings (CXXVII, CXXXIII) and wisdom poems (XLIX) occur only in isolated instances.

The method of considering the Psalms adopted here may at first appear strange. But only when we fit the individual song into its own particular category, the historical development of which is revealed in its individual units, can we understand how and when the individual psalm came into being. The fact that Egypt, Babylonia, and Canaan (Ugarite) produce similar songs[17] speaks only for the great age of the Hebrew lyrics, the value of which is in no way diminished by these parallels. On the contrary, it is only by comparison with these songs of other lands that the distinctive piety of Israel is brought home to us. If we review all this material, which is not restricted solely to the Psalms, we can ascertain that the various types of song go back far into the pre-exilic period. Micah's use, for instance (VI. 6 ff.), of the form of the Torah liturgy is a sign that this form must have been already known and favoured as far back as the eighth century B.C. The songs about kings and their accession are also very old, even though the exile must necessarily have modified them considerably: it would not, however, affect other types to any appreciable extent. On the question of the general line of development of the Psalms one can say that the more intact the form in which a song has been preserved, the older is the song: blending with other types points to a later period. So the Psalter contains songs from a number of different centuries, starting from brilliant kings such as David and ending up in the period after the exile, for which it had an inestimable significance as a book of prayer and of edification.

It goes without saying that, in the case of collections, everything that has been handed down is not on the same spiritual level. For us much of it, particularly in the psalms of vengeance and the invocations of curses, is alien and repulsive: we find its glowing passion offensive. But even today the ultimate

[17] For literature on this point, see Bibliography.

verdict on these "small Biblia" cannot be other than that of
Martin Luther in his "Prefaces": "But what is the greatest
thing in the Psalter but these serious speeches delivered in all
sorts of storms? Where does one find finer words of joy than
in the psalms of praise and thanksgiving? There you see into
the hearts of the devout as into a lovely, happy garden, or
heaven itself. . . . Again, where does one find more profound,
more wretched, more pitiable words of sadness than in the
psalms of lamentation? There you look into the hearts of the
devout as into death, into Hell. . . . And is it not best of all
that the speaking of such words against God and to God gives
them double weight, makes them doubly alive? . . . For this
reason the Psalter is the book of all holy men, and everyone,
in whatever circumstances he may find himself, can find
psalms and words therein which fit his situation exactly and
seem to have been made for his very purposes, so that he can
neither find better expressions for himself, nor would he wish
to do so."[18]

THE BOOK OF JOB

The Book of Job[19] belongs among the great literary works of
the world, generally being named along with Aeschylus's
Prometheus, Dante's *Divina Commedia*, and Goethe's *Faust*. It
derives its greatness not merely from the power of its language
and the richness of its images, its fine character-drawing and
the vitality of the narrative in the epic-like beginning and
conclusion, in the dramatically lifelike conversation with the
friends and the passion of its lyrics, but also from its content,
which deals with a perenially up-to-date theme. This is the
terrific tension existing between human life as it ought to be
and as it really is; the question of questions, which is as old as
mankind itself and which troubles the souls of thinking men in
all ages; the question of injustice in the life of Man. For the
course of life does not run as it should in the opinion of the
upright and pious. Experience tells us that only too often the
man who pursues his own objectives and desires without consideration or restraint gets on and achieves success and prosperity

[18] M. Luther, *Vorreden zur Heiligen Schrift*, ed. W. Heinsius, Munich 1934,
pp. 19–21.
[19] For commentaries and literature, see Bibliography.

in his lifetime. And the other, the man with a conscience, the correct and pious man who directs his life and actions by God and His commandments, nevertheless often has to follow a path of failure and poverty, sickness and suffering. How can this undeniable fact be reconciled with faith in God and in divine justice (theodicy)? The age in which the author of the Book of Job lived has its own answer to this question, an answer deeply rooted in the dogma of requital. The justice of God was a certain and unshakable fact, and so the only solution was that even the pious man must have some secret guilt or sin for which God punishes him by suffering. The Book of Job contests this view, and tries to find a better and more profound answer to the question of the suffering of the righteous.

The book consists of several parts. Even to the cursory observer a framing narrative based on the theme of the blessing of true piety is immediately distinguishable, because it is written in prose (I–II. 10, XLII. 10–17). It describes to us Job (Ijjob, Greek Iob = "attacker," or probably better "the attacked") from the land of Uz (Gen. xxxvi. 28) in the region of Edom. A model of piety, he is blessed by Yahweh for his God-fearing conduct with riches and good fortune (I, 1–5). At a council meeting in Heaven Satan, whose task it is to test the uprightness of Man, casts doubts on the unselfishness of this piety and gets permission from God to put Job's integrity to the test, but with the reservation that Job himself must not be touched (I. 6–12). Armed with this plenary authority Satan smites Job with one misfortune after another, robs him of his servants and his herds, and takes away his seven sons and three daughters. But Job suffers all these blows of fate and does not sin against God (I. 13–22). At a second heavenly council Satan reports his lack of success and expresses his doubt that Job would still remain steadfast if God removed the reservation about his personal safety. With God's permission Satan may now take action against Job himself and afflict him with illness (II. 1–7). Job suffers even this with devotion to God. Even when his wife tempts him to denounce God he remains steadfast in his belief: "Shall we receive good at the hand of God, and shall we not receive evil?" (II. 8–10). In the face of so much devotion and faithfulness God restores the fortunes of Job and rewards his piety, doubling his possessions and giving him sons and daughters again. At the end of the story Job dies, "an old man and full of days" (XLII. 10–17). It is a pious and edifying story in the style of the old patriarchal tales, from which Man should learn resignation and devotion to God, even in suffering. This is a complete, finished unit which requires no supplementation, although the important question remains whether the Satan sections (I. 6–12, II. 1–6) originally belonged to it.

Inserted into the story is a long controversial dialogue between Job and his friends, and other poetical writings. It has to be considered whether the story originally belonged with the dialogue or whether it should be regarded merely as a framework for the poetical work. The fact that Satan does not figure in the poetry is not evidence, for even in the story itself Satan only appears in the councils in Heaven; neither is the different description of Job's sickness of any help (II. 7, VII. 5, XVI. 12–22), for it is much too vaguely indicated. The fact that the references to the children (XIV. 21, XIX. 17) do not seem to fit properly into the narrative is a better proposition, but better still is the varied nature of the content. The narrative describes only the external aspect; it reports, quite objectively, on a series of events and their results; while the poem is written with passion from the depths of a deeply felt personal experience. In the story the whole course of events seems so natural and comprehensible that one really cannot expect anything else to happen; the poem, on the other hand, takes us into tremendous inner struggles and wrestles with the idea of innocence. The Job of the story is the pious man, constant and steadfast in his devotion to God, which neither external blows of Fate nor personal suffering can shake: in the poem, however, a human soul quivers in agitation, shaken to its very depths, cursing itself, attacking God bitterly as the enemy of mankind, and finally challenging Him to a lawsuit in no uncertain terms. If one further considers that the introduction of Job's three friends (II. 11–13) is not particularly apt and that they are still less relevant at the end (XLII. 7–9), these are all reasons which make a close connexion between the story and the poem highly improbable. On the other hand, it has been objected that the poem without the story would be quite incomprehensible. But this objection is based too much on the present-day point of view to be justifiable. It must be borne in mind that the author of the poem named his hero "Job." This name must have given the listeners of old a fair idea of the subject-matter of the poem and prepared them for the ideas to be expressed.[20] This we see from Ezek. XIV. 14, 20, where Noah, Daniel, and Job are assumed to be thoroughly well-known names. Recent findings have taught us that Daniel was famous from ancient times in Canaan as a model of wisdom and righteousness, and so we cannot dismiss the probability that Job also and his devoted patience were the subject of an old tale, not necessarily originating in Israel. It is fairly generally supposed that the poet used this folk-tale as a framework for his poem and indeed, in part, that he himself gave it its present written form. But the essential differences between the prose and the poetry, and the unskilful linking of the two parts (II. 11–13 and XLIII. 7–9), make both theories equally improbable. The framework was no doubt erected later round the poem.

The poem itself comprises several parts: the soliloquies of Job, the discussion with his friends, the song in praise of wisdom, the speeches of Elihu and of God. How far these belong together is much disputed. The centre of gravity is Job's conversation with his friends (chs. IV–XXVII). Of these, Eliphaz speaks sensibly and with a certain dignity; Bildad, from the first, appears somewhat sharper, and Zophar is the most passionate of all. Externally this discussion is rigid in structure and takes the form of three cycles of speeches. One after the other in the same sequence the friends take the floor and deliver their rather long expositions which, each time, are followed by Job's replies. This arrangement is abandoned in the third cycle, however, where Bildad answers very briefly while Zophar says nothing at all. It is very questionable whether this is actually a literary subtlety intended to express the idea that the friends had no answers left for Job's objections. It is much more probably a case of fairly extensive textual corruption, as is also indicated by the incongruous "These ten times you have cast reproach upon me" (XIX. 3) in the second cycle. On the whole, it is believed that parts of

[20] For us also certain names are bound up with very definite ideas, for example, names from the Greek (Heracles, Odysseus, Alexander) and German sagas (Siegfried, Parsifal, Tannhäuser).

ch. XXVI (vss. 2–4, 5–14) belong to the third speech of Bildad, while the missing third speech by Zophar is transmitted in ch. XXVII (vss. 7, 10, 13–23). On the other hand, many have gone so far as to reduce the poem to one single cycle of speeches, regarding fairly large portions as secondary[21] or else grouping the transmitted material differently.[22] Whether this is correct can be left undecided. But these attempts are instructive in so far as they show that certain parts of the discussion emanating from the mouths of his friends could equally well have been spoken by Job. In this controversial discussion, therefore, what we have is not the opposition of two different points of view, which are clarified in the course of the conversation and drawn closer together as the ideas expressed are developed or refuted, until finally a result acceptable to both parties to the discussion is achieved. Whether we compare the individual speeches or examine the train of the thought, we come to the same conclusion. Both Job and his friends are in complete agreement that in the eyes of Man suffering is a punishment by God for sins committed. Thus the expositions of the individual speakers and the course of their thoughts do not primarily increase knowledge but lead rather to a statement of the points of view which can be formulated briefly as follows. Because there is suffering, there is guilt (the friends): because he is innocent, God must take the suffering away (Job). In neither case, therefore, is an answer given to the question of the innocent suffering of the righteous. But the certainty which emanates from XIX. 25 ff. affords something like a solution to the problem.

The poet has skilfully framed these speeches with the soliloquies of Job. First of all, there are the curses on his own life which precede the discussion (ch. III): these remind us of

---

[21] Where a research worker recognises a third cycle one finds reconstruction of the third Zophar speech and padding of the third Bildad speech from textual material transmitted. Baumgartel in particular, followed by Kraeling, has greatly reduced the extent of the "genuine" textual tradition.

[22] The text has been radically rearranged by M. Buttenwieser, M. Jastrow, and M. Simon, the latter eliminating the third cycle, but for one Eliphaz speech, and working it into the first cycle. Assuming a purely fragmentary textual model, H. Torczyner, *The Book of Job*, Jerusalem 1941, has reconstructed the text (in Hebrew) forming one cycle of dialogue, with an answer from Job every time and two Divine speeches interrupted by a Job speech. With the exception of the Elihu speeches he uses all the textual material.

similar moods in Jeremiah (Jer. xx. 14 ff.) and represent a
much-favoured form of the lament. At the other end are the
descriptions of his former good fortune (ch. xxix) and his
present misery (ch. xxx), the thoughts in which are very close
to those in the laments of the individual; and a great protestation of his innocence (ch. xxxi) set out in question form and
interspersed with occasional curses upon himself (vss. 6, 8, 10,
22, 40): this reminds us of expositions in the Egyptian Book of
the Dead, but no connexion between the two can be established.
If one reads Job's speeches one after the other they can best be
characterised as the words of the "fault-finder" who wants to
"contend with the Almighty" (xl. 2). Not only the conclusion
of his protestation of innocence, but all his speeches strike this
note. Because he is conscious of his innocence he will reason
with God (xiii. 3), who denies him his rights (xxvii. 2); he is
prepared for a legal dispute and is ready to speak and answer
questions before a court (xiii. 22). In this court case God is his
adversary (xvi. 9), but at the same time his witness (xvi. 19),
his surety (xvii. 3), and advocate, who will reveal his innocence
(xix. 25)—even if not until after Job's death. The challenge to
the lawsuit with the violent remonstrance "Here is my signa-
ture! Let the Almighty answer me!" (xxxi. 35) is followed
by the notice "the words of Job are ended" (xxxi. 40).[23] This
brings Jer. li. 64 to mind and suggests that this is the end of
the original book. And so, to a large extent, it has been understood, everything that follows being explained as later additions
on the same theme. If so, the book closes with a defiant
challenge, which, however, at the same time is a confident
acknowledgment that God will see that Job gets his rights. It
has been argued that this is no solution to the problem. But
this it cannot be, any more than God's speeches are. For there
is, and there can be, no rational solution.

Whether genuine or secondary, at all events the speeches of
God (chs. xxxviii–xlii) fit in very well as a continuation to
Job's challenge. Now God for His part challenges Job to a
lawsuit (xxxviii. 2–3). In a storm theophany (xxxviii. 1) God
confronts Job with an overwhelming list of questions: "can you,
do you know, have you?" With a clever artistic touch the poet

---

[23] xxxi. 38–40 are now, as is generally admitted, in the wrong place and should
be arranged within ch. xxxi nearer the beginning.

makes God answer with questions the many questions put by Job (ch. XXXI). To the great wonders of creation and the universal kingdom Job can give no answer. Now he sees plainly in his heart the utter madness of his undertaking to reason with God. The majesty and omnipotence of God compel him to humble himself, to submit quietly to God; there is only one thing left for him—to admit the greatness of God which no man can measure or comprehend. Before the face of God Job pronounces judgment upon himself: "I had heard of thee by the hearing of the ear, but now my eye sees thee; therefore I despise myself, and repent in dust and ashes" (XLII. 5–6).

In the transmitted text God's speech is now divided into two: correspondingly, there is a dual surrender by Job (XL. 3, XLII. 1), which is certainly not in keeping with the plan or intention of the poet. This ugly and irritating split is caused by secondary additions dealing with the hippopotamus (XL. 15 ff.) and the crocodile (ch. XLI), the latter account embellished with the features of a mythical monster, leviathan.[24] But Job's first submission (XL. 3 ff.) belongs with the second (XLII. 1 ff.), and forms the answer to the conclusion of God's speech:

> Look on every one that is proud, and bring him low;
>   and tread down the wicked where they stand.
> Hide them all in the dust together;
>   bind their faces in the world below.
> Then will I also acknowledge to you
>   that your own right hand can give you victory.
>
>   (XL. 12–14)

A further supplementary insertion is the song in praise of wisdom (ch. XXVIII), a very valuable and fine poem but quite out of place in this context. Moreover, this is quite a different conception of wisdom from that on which the poem is based. It has a special lesson to impart: Man can do much, he can even raise up treasures hidden in the bowels of the earth; but he is never able to fathom the seat and origin of wisdom. God alone has known them. The words on the value of wisdom (XXVIII. 13–20) are probably even later in origin, as the repetition shows (vs. 12 = vs. 20).

[24] The description of the ostrich (XXXIX. 13–18), the form of which varies, is also to be regarded as largely secondary.

A special section, much discussed and much disputed, is formed by the Elihu speeches (chs. XXXII–XXXVII). Between Job's challenge and God's speech in reply, the transmitted text has a group of three—not four, as shown by the variation in the formula in XXXVI. 1—similarly introduced (XXXII. 6, XXXIV. 1, XXXV. 1) speeches by one Elihu, who has not previously appeared either in the framework or in the poem. Now, therefore, he is ceremoniously presented in a pompous prose introduction (XXXII. 1–6a) giving the name of his father and his family. With painful exactness he gives the reason for his presence; this alone must cast doubts on the original character of his speeches, doubts which are increased by the fact that we hear no more about him. He says at the beginning of his speeches that because of his youth he has been present at the discussion only as a silent onlooker. But this modesty is rather difficult to reconcile with his later description of himself as "perfect in knowledge" (XXXVI. 4). Since Job's friends have no more to say, he will now impart his knowledge. He turns on Job, who considers God is his enemy (XIII. 24). Suffering should be differently understood, rather as a reminder and a warning from God (XXXIII. 15 ff.). In his second speech he agrees with Job's friends that God acts justly; for God, unlike a human judge, does not require to heed position and wealth (XXXIV. 19) but punishes the wicked, and without a trial (XXXIV. 24). When God appears to act unjustly in not taking action against the wicked it is because the wicked man has in fact repented and turned again to Him (XXXIV. 31). Job's words are therefore imprudent and unjust. If God is silent in face of the vanity of evil men (XXXV. 12–13)—so the third speech runs—one must have patience (XXXVI. 2). For God is and remains just (XXXVI. 5) and punishes even kings for their sins; but if they are ready to repent and heed God's warning He will receive them to Himself again (XXXVI. 11). For this reason Job should also beware of unjust behaviour (XXXVI. 13 ff.)—here again his sufferings are represented as a test by God (XXXVI. 21). There is only one way open to men: extol the words of God and recognise His wisdom (XXXVI. 22 ff.). The speech draws to a close with a reference to God's wonderful creations in Nature, which either "for correction . . . or for love" do His will (XXXVII. 13), and ends with God's appearance in the clouds, which provides a tolerably good transition to what follows. Much can be said against the original character of these speeches; not only stylistic and linguistic considerations, not only the variation in God's name, not only the fact that the close connexion between God's speech and Job's words is interrupted and the contents of the divine speech are even anticipated to some extent. Moreover, the fact that one speaker expressly refers to certain words and thoughts of another speaker is quite out of keeping with the poet's peculiar habit of making the participants in a conversation appear at cross purposes. Also the Elihu speeches do not in fact contribute such new thoughts as the introductory words of the first speech lead one to expect; rather they reproduce what has already been said (v. 17 ff., VIII. 5, XXI. 22 ff.) in broader terms and with greater emphasis. If the poet himself had wanted to give these thoughts greater prominence he would certainly not have done so in an alleged "appendix from his later days." We must credit him with this much ability for organising his work, that he would have worked the thoughts into the speeches of Job's controversy with his friends. Thus the Elihu speeches are also to be considered as later additions to the Book of Job.

This, however, does not mean that the book, as we know it, does not represent one of the most powerful pieces of writing that try to solve the perennial problem of the innocent suffering of the righteous. Whatever Man can say on this subject, he is merely groping and stumbling, trying in vain to raise the curtain which God has drawn across His dealings with men. Jeremiah (XII. 1 ff.) touched quite lightly on this question, which is stated openly and clearly by Habakkuk (I. 13–14), while Deutero-Isaiah (LIII. 10 ff.) gives the suffering innocent a great promise of God. Where this thought arises in the Psalms, the so-called "Job Psalms" (Pss. XXXVII, XLIX, LXXIII), it is accompanied by a confession that God's treatment of us men is incomprehensible to our understanding (Ps. LXXIII. 16); but the conclusion is not renunciation, but the certainty that God will help the righteous (Ps. XXXVII. 39) and save him from the grave (Ps. XLIX. 15), and the defiant confession of faith and of trust in God:

Nevertheless I am continually with thee;
   thou dost hold my right hand.
Thou dost guide me with they counsel,
   and afterwards thou wilt receive me to glory.
(Ps. LXXIII. 23–4)

Of course, we must not overlook the fact that all this piety was conditioned by the view that for Man death means the great separation from God. Since the time of Jerome men have tried to read a hope of resurrection into Job XIX. 25–7— a passage which is textually very difficult and which, moreover, has been transmitted in a corrupt state; but the orginal sense of these words has no knowledge of a future life. And so the final answer to Job's question can only be provided by the faith which knows that neither affliction nor death can separate us from God's love and that for those who love Him God works for good in all things (Rom. VIII. 28). On this basis alone, in the light of eternity (II Cor. IV. 17), are all the questions of God's righteousness solved (Rom. IX. 14, 20).

Opinions vary greatly as to the date of origin of the book and its additions. The whole Book of Job is so timeless that it allows of no definite statement. In the light of its relationship with other Old Testament writings it must be dated in exilic or early post-exilic times. All sorts of suggestions have been made concerning the author: Talmudic tradition sees him as Moses; others seek his native land in Edom or Egypt. But there is no decisive reason why he should be a foreigner. It is common ground that the poet, who was as familiar with conditions in the wilderness as with the culture of Egypt, must have been a widely travelled and educated Jew; more, however, we cannot say about his personal circumstances.

THE PROVERBS OF SOLOMON

The Proverbs of Solomon, along with the Book of Job and Ecclesiastes, constitutes a particular group within the Old Testament, the Wisdom literature,[25] which must have been very widespread and popular in the ancient Orient. Not only in Babylon, but especially from Egypt, relatively extensive collections of wisdom sayings have been handed down from

[25] For works on the Wisdom literature, see Bibliography.

R

different periods, beginning with the sayings of Ptah-notep
(*c.* 2600 B.C.) and the teaching of King Merikarê (*c.* 2300 B.C.),
down to the sayings of Amen-em-ope (*c.* 900 B.C.) and of Ani
(*c.* 850 B.C.). In the Old Testament, in addition to a reference
in Isaiah (XIX. 11), the Book of Proverbs specifically refers to
this wisdom of Egypt; similarly the Bible tells of the wisdom of
Babylon (Jer. L. 35–6, LI. 57) and of Edom (Ob. 8 = Jer. XLIX. 7,
Job II. 11). The inclination towards wisdom teaching must
have been very old, even in Israel, although the writing
prophets make only occasional reference to it (cf. Is. XLIV. 25,
Jer. IX. 23). The first Book of Kings (chs. V, X) reports the
flourishing of Israelite wisdom under Solomon,[26] so that
friends of wisdom "from all the kings of the earth, from all
lands," even the Queen of Sheba herself, came to Jerusalem
to make the acquaintance of Solomon's all-surpassing wisdom.
For Solomon was held in Israel as the model of wisdom and,
according to the scripture, himself wrote 3000 proverbs: in
addition "the judgment of Solomon" (I Kings III. 16–28) also
achieved proverbial fame. And so it is not to be wondered at
that the collections of wisdom teaching contained in the Proverbs commanded special respect because of his name.

The Book of Proverbs[27] has an extraordinarily detailed
heading, which, in addition to the name of the author, outlines
the purpose of this collection:

> That men may know wisdom and instruction,
>   understand the words of insight,
> receive instruction in wise dealing,
>   righteousness, justice,
> that prudence may be given to the simple,
>   knowledge and discretion to the youth—
> the wise man also may hear and increase in learning,
>   and the man of understanding acquire skill,
> to understand a proverb and a figure,
>   the words of the wise and their riddles.   (I. 2–6)

This introduction is most instructive, for it tells us two things.
On the one hand we learn that these proverbs are not so much
testimonies of piety, as sober and practical rules for living

---

[26] A. Alt, "Die Weisheit Salomos," in *Th. Lz.*, LXXVI (1951), cols. 139–44.
[27] For commentaries and literature, see Bibliography.

which appeal to our reason. And on the other hand the mention of the wise men indicates that in the early days of the monarchy in Israel, as well as in other countries (Is. xxxix. 3) there must already have been a special class of wise men (Is. xxix. 14, Jer. xviii. 18) in addition to the priests and prophets. The various headings of the individual sections of the book, such as "words of the wise" (xxii. 17, xxiv. 23), "the words of Agur" (xxx. 1), and "the words of the mother of King Lemuel" (xxxi. 1), point to the inaccuracy of the initial heading. Not everything can be traced back to Solomon, whose individual collections of sayings are specially named (x. 1, xxv. 1), or even to his age.

This is particularly true of the first collection (i. 7–ix. 18), which does not contain any actual wisdom sayings at all. This part differs from the proverbs in its general form of address, its long sentences, and its fairly large sections on one particular topic, although these do not always adhere strictly to their theme. It is essentially concerned with the instructions and exhortations which an old wise man (called father) imparts to a younger man (son) based on his own knowledge and experience. This is a form quite frequently encountered in Egyptian wisdom literature. No actual grouping or classification can be discerned within the collection. General exhortations alternate with pieces of advice for practical living and recommendations to wisdom, which on several occasions is personified. Wisdom is equated with the intellectual power with which God created the world (iii. 19), and appears as a divine being which existed long before the world (viii. 22) and was God's favourite, His delight, allowed to play in His workshop during the Creation. Certain fairly extensive trains of thought stand out. First of all the warning against evil (i. 10–19), and the description of the fivefold blessing of wisdom (ii. 1–22), which leads to fear of God and correct behaviour, protects against bad company and loose women, and points out the right path to follow. Correspondingly we read of the fourfold blessing of fearing God (ch. iii), how it is based on trust in God, observance of the cult, humility, and submission to the discipline of Yahweh. The rest of the chapter (from vs. 13) speaks once more of the value and blessing of wisdom: the train of thought here, however, is interrupted by a few short bits of advice (vss. 27 ff.).

What follows is also concerned with the blessing of wisdom; how it has been passed on to the teacher from his father (IV. 1 ff.), and how its path is brightly lit (IV. 10 ff.). This leads on to warnings against the loose woman (ch. V), which frequently recur (VI. 24 ff. VII. 5 ff.), with a masterly description of her method of seduction (ch. VII): all in all it is obvious that the prostitute is given all the responsibility for broken marriages. Inserted into this sequence are several practical warnings against standing surety (VI. 1 ff.), laziness (VI. 6 ff.), and mischievousness (VI. 12 ff.), and in addition a numerical proverb (VI. 16 ff.) enumerating the seven things which are an abomination to Yahweh. Also woven in are several longer expositions in which wisdom itself speaks threateningly (I. 20 ff.) or more enticingly (VIII. 1 ff.) of its own useful consequences; and then finally wisdom (IX. 1 ff.) and folly (IX. 13 ff.) are personified as two women competing to entice men. The mixed nature of the contents is in itself sufficient to show that the collection consists of several parts; an impression which is confirmed by the various doublets (e.g. I. 8: VI. 20, II. 16: VII. 5, III. 14: VIII. 10). To try to trace the origin of the different parts would be useless: similarly the indefinite and general character of the compilation makes it difficult to ascertain its age. Comparison with the other sections shows that this is the latest of the collections united in the Book of Proverbs. Considerations of style and content lead one to assume in general that this collection (I. 7–IX. 18) dates from post-exilic times, probably from the fourth century B.C.

Quite a different impression is given by the second collection (X. 1–XXII. 16), the most extensive of the whole book. Here we have true proverbs, uniformly constructed according to the laws of Hebrew poetry; sharp and pointed couplets which always contain two statements, the second of which either supplements and expands the first or presents an antithesis in order to enhance the effect of the first statement. In all, this compilation contains 376 short proverbs, in the case of one of which (XIX. 7) only half has been transmitted. They are placed loosely side by side with no link and no inherent connexion. Nevertheless we do find, even if to only a modest extent, fairly small groups with the same theme, like the proverbs concerning the king (XVI. 10 ff.), the diligent man

(XII. 24 ff.), or the fool (XVIII. 6–7); or they may be grouped by purely external considerations, such as similar words (X. 6 f., XII. 5 ff., etc.), or even the same initial letters (XI. 9 ff., XX. 7 ff., XX. 24 ff., XXII. 2 ff.). Variations on the same proverb are numerous (e.g. XII. 14: XIII. 2: XVIII. 20, XIII. 14: XIV. 27: XIX. 23); the main reason given is that the matter is an abomination to Yahweh.[28] Due to the lack of any internal arrangement it is difficult to comprehend the content of the ideas in this collection. It has been observed that its background is the life of a people practising arable farming (X. 5: XII. 11) and a few proverbs (such as XII. 10, XIV. 4, etc.) clearly point in this direction. The images and comparisons, too, are drawn in many cases from the countryman's world (e.g. XI. 22, XIII. 23, XVI. 15): but since there are also allusions to the city (e.g. X. 15, XVIII. 19), no further conclusions can be drawn.

The proverbs of this collection are concerned with the most diverse aspects of human life. It is probably not a mere coincidence that a word on the rearing of children appears right at the beginning (X. 1). "Train up a child in the way he should go, and when he is old he will not depart from it" (XXII. 6). And so to educate one's son correctly (XIII. 1, XV. 5) one must not spare the rod (XIII. 24). For a foolish son brings shame and disgrace (XV. 20–1, XVII. 25) to his parents; he is not only wanting in proper respect for his parents (XIX. 18, 26, XX. 20) but is a complete calamity (XIX. 13), a puppet in the hands of a clever slave (XVII. 2). Women are considered both as mothers in connexion with the bringing up of children (X. 1, XVII. 25), and also as good wives (XI. 16, XIV. 1, XVIII. 22): such a one is the crown of her husband (XII. 4), a gift from God (XIX. 14). But the misfortune of a dissolute (XI. 22) and quarrelsome (XIX. 13, XXI. 9, 19) wife is not overlooked. A great deal of space is given to proverbs concerning the dangers of the tongue, which has the power of death and life (XVIII. 21). Truthful men are favoured by Yahweh (XII. 22, XIV. 25, XIX. 22, 28), but lying lips are an abomination to Him (X. 18 ff., XII. 22, XVIII. 6 ff., etc.); so false witnesses do not go unpunished (as XII. 17, XIV. 5, 25, etc.), and the bold liar shall not escape (XIX. 5). Yahweh detests partiality and unjust judgment (XVII. 5, 26, XVIII. 5); but bribery (XVII. 8, 23, XVIII. 16) is only

[28] Thus XI. 1, 20, XII. 22, XV. 8, 9, 26, XVI. 5, XVII. 15, XX. 10, 23, XXI. 27.

to be expected since a gift in secret pacifies anger (XXI. 14).
The contrast between rich and poor is treated simply as a fact
(X. 15, XVIII. 23, etc.), which must be as it is (XXII. 2). Riches
bring benefits (XIV. 20), but they also give rise to trouble
(XV. 16) and dangers (XI. 28, XIII. 11, 23, XXI. 13). For "an
inheritance gotten hastily in the beginning will in the end not
be blessed" (XX. 21). So many a man with great possessions is
poor, while another is rich in his poverty (XIII. 7). If the poor
man is despised (XIX. 7) and neglected (XIX. 4), "better is a
little with righteousness than great revenues with injustice"
(XV. 16, XVI. 8). Wisdom is better than riches (XVI. 16). But
this does not prevent poverty being considered as one's own
fault, for riches are at the same time also the reward of diligence
(X. 4, XX. 13). Thus there are many proverbs on laziness
(X. 5, XV. 19, XIX. 24, etc.), which is condemned in the same
way as haughtiness (XI. 2, XVI. 5) and pride (XXI. 4) which
comes before the fall (XVI. 18). Particular attention is drawn
to patience (XVI. 32, XIX. 11) and commercial honesty over
weights and measures (XI. 1, XVI. 11, XX. 10, 23). Several
proverbs deal with the king (XVI. 14 f., XIX. 12), who should be
treated with respect (XIV. 35). Uprightness and just decisions
are the special virtues (XVI. 10, 12 f., XX. 8, 26) which support
his throne (XX. 28). That the Israelite king is particularly in
mind here cannot, it is true, be concluded from the fact that
he can prophesy (XVI. 10), but it can from the fact that his
"heart is a stream of water in the hand of the Lord; he turns
it wherever he will" (XXI. 1).

In looking for the ethical and religious bases for these proverbs we must bear in mind that they are meant to be a
picture of practical living. " 'It is bad, it is bad,' says the
buyer; but when he goes away, then he boasts" (XX. 14).
Such is life. And it is for this life that instructions and experiences are given, sensible and to the point. They derive a
particular force from the emphasis that is laid on their useful-
ness and expediency, on the advantages and success to be
attained by applying them. He who does good, meets with
good also (XI. 27, XII. 14); "the tent of the upright will flourish"
(XIV. 11); the righteous achieves honour and prosperity (X. 3,
XXI. 21), and his children will be blessed (XX. 7). For
"righteousness exalts a nation, but sin is a reproach to any

people" (xiv. 34). And yet we must remember that about a seventh of this collection of proverbs is related in some way or other to piety and fear of Yahweh, although the connexion may be fairly loose. On many occasions, indeed, it is no more than a statement that fear of Yahweh guarantees long life (x. 27, xiv. 27, xix. 23), honour, and riches (xxii. 4), and signifies a sure refuge (x. 29, xiv. 26, xviii. 10); that Yahweh's blessing makes one rich without trouble (x. 22), and He repays the kind-hearted for his good deeds (xix. 17). But side by side with these we find more personal and profound thoughts. Quite frequently a practice is discouraged, not for fear of the consequences but because such behaviour is an abomination to Yahweh;[29] He hears the prayer of the righteous (x. 24, xv. 29) because He loves him (xv. 9). For the most part, Yahweh stands at the centre: our destiny is in His hand (xx. 24), His eyes are everywhere, on good and evil (xv. 3); He loosens the tongues of men (xvi. 1), weighs their spirits (xvi. 2, xx. 27) and their hearts (xvii. 3, xxi. 2), and fear of Him instructs them to wisdom (xv. 33). A man plans his way himself, but Yahweh directs his steps (xvi. 9, xix. 21, xx. 24). The distance separating Man from the greatness of God is aptly expressed: "Who can say 'I have made my heart clean; I am pure from my sin'?" (xx. 9). Such a proverb belongs to the lines of prophetic piety, while those on the worthlessness of sacrifices and the value of prayer (xv. 8, xxi. 27), and on moral behaviour, which is more precious to Yahweh than sacrifice (xxi. 3), take us close to Hosea (Hos. vi. 6) and Isaiah (Is. i. 11 ff.). So the man is to be praised as happy who puts his trust in Yahweh (xvi. 20).

It has been suggested that this collection is made up of two smaller ones, the first (chs. x ff.) of which, with 184 proverbs, has 169 in antithesis, while the second (chs. xvi. ff) has only 31. But perhaps this is merely a matter of arrangement rather than of different styles; for the two parts belong together both in content and in form. Comparison with the other collections in the book shows that this collection offers neither challenges nor instructions, but consists entirely of maxims as objective statements of fact. This leads to the conclusion that the collection is very old. The sayings concerning kings point to the

[29] See note 28, p. 253.

pre-exilic period, and the short and simple couplet form of the proverbs shows that we are dealing with an old collection, the oldest of the whole Book of Proverbs. Whether it goes back wholly or in part to Solomon, as the heading (x. 1) maintains, can naturally not be decided in view of the general and indefinite nature of the contents. This is, however, a possibility to be taken into account.

A first appendix to the above, from somewhat later pre-exilic times, presents as "the words of the wise" (XXII. 17) a smaller collection (XXII. 17–XXIV. 22), which, as the address (XXIII. 15) shows, consists of two parts. In the main it treats of the same themes as the "Solomon collection," and comes from the same social and religious background. But the form is completely different; for the proverbs here for the most part are four-line or longer poems, the parallel statements (except XXIV. 16) are not antithetical, and the whole section contains pieces of advice in the form of commands. The first part (XXII. 17–XXIII. 11) was the subject of much discussion some thirty years ago, when it was discovered that it corresponds more or less with the Egyptian teaching of Amen-em-ope which was published at that time: indeed it has even adopted the latter's division into thirty chapters (22 or 20 in the Hebrew text). These are instructions for a young man that he may be successful in his career as a civil servant. But the Old Testament text has not simply been copied down from the Egyptian original: it has been freely adapted and so has taken on a particular character of its own.[30] Later on a proverb (XXIII. 12 ff.) was appended which largely corresponds with the Aramaic Achikar (c. 500 B.C.): the Septuagint also includes another five verses from the same source at the

[30] A. Erman, "Eine ägyptische Quelle der Sprüche Salomos," in *Sitzungsberichte der Berliner Akademie der Wissenschaft*, 1924, pp. 86–93; H. Gressmann, "Die neugefundene Lehre des Amen-em-ope und die vorexilische Spruchdichtung Israels," in *Z. alttest., W.*, XLII (1924), pp. 272–96; P. Humbert, *Recherches sur les sources égyptiennes de la littérature sapientiale d'Israel*, Neuchâtel 1929; H. J. Cadbury, "Egyptian influences on the Book of Proverbs," in *Journal of Religion*, henceforth cited as *J. Rel.*, IX (1929), pp. 99–108. R. O. Kevin, "The Wisdom of Amen-em-apt and its possible Dependence upon the Hebrew Book of Proverbs," in *Journal of the Society of Oriental Research*, XIV (1930), pp. 115–57, tries to indicate the dependence of Amen-em-ope on the biblical Book of Proverbs, but the results are not convincing. A. Alt, "Zur literarischen Analyse der Weisheit des Amenemope," in *Vet. test.*, Suppl. III (1955), pp. 16–25.

end of the collection. This is clear proof that the limits of such collections were by no means firmly established. The second part (XXIII. 15 ff.) of this appendix contains individual exhortations to adopt the way of innocence, which is so much downtrodden, and issues special warnings against drunkenness, dissolute living, and pleasure in the misfortune of others.

A second appendix (XXIV. 23–34) which also contains "words of the wise" (XXIV. 23) supplements the first to a certain extent, dealing with judgment and sloth; the lazy man is wittily characterised. Of the developments of this collection we know nothing: but it apparently led an independent existence for a long time as is shown by its juxtaposition with the Agur proverbs (XXX. 1–14) in the Septuagint version.

A further fairly large collection (chs. XXV–XXIX) dates from the time of Hezekiah, that is, towards the end of the eighth century B.C. Its heading: "These also are proverbs of Solomon which the men of Hezekiah king of Judah copied" (XXV. 1) points beyond the appendixes to the Solomonic collection itself. It contains proverbial sayings for everyday life, mostly in couplets: and thus has much in common with the other collection both in form and in content. The existence of common features and even doublets between the two is a sign that the Hezekiah collection is not designed to supplement that of Solomon. It is characterised to a large extent by its imagery, but suppresses the ethical and religious motives. It is probably later than the Solomon collection and may perhaps have originated—or at least its basic material—in the days of Hezekiah. The threat to bad royal counsellors (XXV. 5) is believed to refer to the treasurer Shebna (1 Kings XII. 8 ff.; Is. XXII, 15 ff.).

The next collection has as little connexion with that of Hezekiah as with the actual Proverbs. It contains the words of an unknown Agur (XXX. 1–14), followed by a series of numerical proverbs (XXX. 18 ff.) of unknown origin. We know as little about the basis and development of these as about the words of Lemuel (XXXI. 1 ff.), an unknown king in northern Arabia (cf. Gen. XXV. 14–15): to a limited extent these present the image of a prince. Neither the Agur nor the Lemuel collections are in any way characteristic of Israel, nor do they contain any particular religious ideas. The final conclusion is a secular song (XXXI. 10–31) which sketches the ideal portrait of a married woman. The song is arranged alphabetically (cf. Nah. 1; Pss. IX–X, XXXIV, etc.) and, like so many other songs, is timeless.

How the Book of Proverbs evolved is far from clear. It may well be that several appendixes containing words of the wise— no doubt including the Agur and Lemuel proverbs—crystallised round the old pre-exilic Solomon collection. Into this was inserted an independent Hezekiah collection, concerned with temporal affairs and dating from pre-exilic times. A conclusion was then added to this complex, in the form of a picture of the virtuous woman, and an introduction in the form of the Wisdom collection (chs. I–IX). The compilation of the book will not be any older than the latest of these collections (chs. I–IX), that is hardly before the fourth century B.C.: and regroupings of the individual collections took place even after this date, as is shown by the different arrangement in the Septuagint.

THE FIVE MEGILLOTH

Assembled under the name Megilloth (Festival Rolls) are five quite different scriptures which nevertheless have one thing in common, namely that they were all read publicly on the occasion of great festivals—the Book of Ruth at the Feast of Weeks and the Feast of Ingathering, the Song of Solomon at the Feast of the Passover, Ecclesiastes at the Feast of Tabernacles, Lamentations at the commemoration of the destruction of Jerusalem, and the Book of Esther at the Purim Festival. Only the last of these small books has, like the Torah, preserved its roll form (Megilla) to the present day. Originally these writings were not grouped together in the Old Testament; Luther followed the order of the Septuagint. Arranging them together goes back to the Masoretic Text and is based on practical considerations of liturgical use. They stand in order of the dates of their supposed authors, for according to the Talmudic tradition Samuel was the author of Ruth, Solomon the author of the Song of Solomon and Ecclesiastes, Jeremiah the author of Lamentations, and Mordecai the author of Esther.

The Book of Ruth

The Book of Ruth[31] is one of the most beautiful stories of the Old Testament: according to Goethe it is the loveliest complete little work in the Bible, in epic and idyllic style. It is a short story, laid in the era of the judges (I. 1). But it is far removed from the crude reality of those days; and the fact that the old custom of taking off a shoe (Deut. xxv. 9) requires explanation (IV. 7) shows the interval separating it from olden times. There are no dramatic conflicts in the story; Orpah acquiesces in being sent home (I. 13–14); the heir renounces his right of inheritance (IV. 6). The story flows peacefully and evenly to its happy ending. Misfortunes (I. 3–5) and embarrassments (III. 8–9) are hinted at rather than detailed. All the main characters are good: the upright and noble Boaz, the wise Naomi, the meek and obedient Ruth who, although herself a Moabitess, remains loyal to her Israelite mother-in-law and by her piety and the grace of God becomes the ancestress of David.

What of the deeper meaning of the story? There is certainly more to it than merely the pleasure of story-telling, or extolling piety and a widow's loyalty. Many different aims have been read into this short book: for example, stressing the obligations of a kinsman towards a childless widow (levirate marriage, Deut. xxv. 5 ff.), or receiving heathen into the community (Zech. II. 11; Neh. XIII. 3; Deut. XXIII. 4), and an opposition to Ezra's ban on mixed marriages (Ezra x. 3 ff.; Neh. XIII. 23 ff.). Recently there has been a tendency to deduce from the names Elimelech (=my God is King), Boaz (which is considered synonymous with Baal), and Naomi (in which a connexion with the cult of Adonis has been sought), the existence of a vegetation cult at Bethlehem, the name of which is to be traced back to the Sumerian god Lachmu.[32] The most probable supposition, however, remains that the intention was to give some account of David's ancestors, for the Book of Samuel contains no details about them, apart from the name of his father Jesse. At any rate, this is the best background against which to explain the old connexions which David must have had with the land of Moab (cf. 1 Sam. XXII. 3–4). With

---

[31] For commentaries and literature, see Bibliography.
[32] W. E. Staples, "The Book of Ruth," in *A.J.S.L.*, LIII (1937), pp. 145–57; id., "Notes on Ruth II. 20 and III. 12," in *A.J.S.L.*, LIV (1937), pp. 62–5.

the exception of the final verses (IV. 18 ff.), which constitute a
later addition based on the family tree in 1 Chron. II. 5 ff., the
book will have come into being in the period immediately
after the exile; but the language in which it is written makes it
probable that the story circulated orally before this time.

The Song of Solomon

The most remarkable and fascinating book of the Old Testament is perhaps "the song of songs, which is Solomon's" (I. 1),
that is, the most beautiful of Solomon's songs.[33] It has inspired
much poetry, painting and music: it has a firm place in Jewish
worship as well as in Catholic liturgy, and Protestant hymnody
is full of illusions to and echoes of the Song of Songs. But yet
it is completely lacking in religious ideas; indeed, from the
first to the last line there is such an absence of God and religion
that one cannot but ask how this book could have been
accepted into the Canon and could have joined the Megilloth.
In the first and second centuries A.D. this was still a matter of
dispute, until Rabbi Akiba (d. about A.D. 137) helped to give
it some respect and recognition by saying: "The Song of Songs
is sacred." Such a verdict is only possible on the basis of
definite religious presuppositions. And so the Song of Songs
has been regarded as an allegory right up to the present day;
whether one interprets it (like the Jews) as referring to the
exodus from Egypt or other great events of the past and to the
end of the world, or whether, as in the Christian Church, one
sees it as a representation of the relationship between Christ
and His Church and between Christ and the individual human
soul.

The Song of Songs is supposed to be the work of Solomon,
who, according to the scriptures (1 Kings IV. 32), composed
1005 songs. But there is little support for this in the text; and
where we read of an unspecified king (I. 4, 12, VII. 5) there is
no special indication that this is Solomon. His female counterpart is the Shulammite (VI. 13), perhaps something like Shelo-
mith (1 Chron. III. 19); but it is not at all certain whether this
is a person's name or derived from a place-name. The book
speaks of love, the lovers' relationship being reflected in songs
of yearning and satisfaction, of jesting and boasting, of

[33] For commentaries and literature, see Bibliography.

description, of wonderment and self-portraiture, of riddle and comparison. Since, however, it is now a woman, now a man, now a group of men (VIII. 8–9) or women (III. 9 ff., VI. 13) that appears as the speaker or takes part in the dialogue (V. 2 ff., VIII. 8 ff.), some have regarded the book as some kind of drama. The Shulammite is brought from her home, where she loves a shepherd, to the court of the king, where she is to become the wife of Solomon. However, she remains constant in spite of all Solomon's wooing and all the persuasion the ladies of the court have to offer, so that Solomon is forced to let her return home, where she then marries her shepherd.

> For love is as strong as death . . .
> Many waters cannot quench love,
>   neither can floods drown it.
> If a man offered for love all the wealth of his house
>   it would be utterly scorned.
>
> (VIII. 6, 7)

But although this interpretation has persisted to the present day it is opposed by the lyrical character of the book, and further by the fact that the main requirement of a drama, namely the development of a plot, is completely lacking, and can only be read between the lines with difficulty and with the exercise of a great deal of imagination. Moreover the interpretation is based on the very doubtful assumption that the Song of Songs constitutes a complete unit.

The same objection applies to the other view, that it is a poem. True, the whole work is filled with similar thoughts and the same spirit; but it lacks the necessary progression of these thoughts, the logical conclusion of which would have to be the mutual possession of the lovers. But this is affirmed right at the beginning (ch. 1 f.) and in the middle (ch. IV f.), while the conclusion points to the awakening of a young love.

For this reason a third interpretation has come more into favour. This adopts Herder's idea of the "mounting of many pearls on one string," and sees in the Song of Songs a collection of individual love songs. A comparison with the oriental wedding custom of "the king's week," according to which the newly married couple, for the first seven days after their marriage, play the parts of king and queen in songs and dances, does indeed help to bring us nearer understanding many parts of the Song of Songs. But it does not explain everything, for a number of the songs have nothing to do with a wedding. So today the Song of Songs is widely looked upon as a collection of love songs of varying content, the basic arrangement of which is as yet unexplained. Certain repetitions and parallels lead us to suspect the presence of two smaller collections which were subsequently combined.

More recently a fourth theory has joined the other three. This looks upon the Song of Solomon as a song collection; but the songs are understood not as secular, popular poetry, but as the allegorical expression and writing down of cultic practices. This development in interpretation is the same as was noted in the Book of Ruth. The explanation is based on the fact that from the time of Darius II (419 B.C.) the Passover was combined with the Mazzoth festival which was celebrated earlier in the Northern Kingdom. The argument is that, as a festival reading, the song is related to the awakening of Nature in the spring. This has no connexion with the Passover, but the Mazzoth festival not only signified the beginning of the harvest, but was also a celebration of spring, of Nature coming to life again: thus the Song is looked upon as containing the cultic songs for this festival. This would bring them very close to the Syrian belief, popular at that time, in the rising from the dead of Tammuz, the god of spring. In addition the wedding songs would correspond to the familiar ancient idea of the weddings of the gods, which was important, particularly in Babylonian religion. The festival connexion of this old song collection has been left unbroken; but since its meaning could no longer be understood at a later date it was re-interpreted allegorically, reinforced by being attributed to Solomon, and thus, as it were, made worthy of the Canon. These ideas may at first strike us as strange; but there is much to be said in their favour. The mention of Tirzah (VI. 4), the old Israelite residence down to the time of Omri (I Kings XVI. 23–4), indicates the Northern Kingdom; further, the Song shows striking affinities with an Assyrian hymn catalogue, which leads to the conclusion that the cultic songs were based on an originally non-Israelite model. Finally, the worship of Tammuz was not very unusual, even in Israel (cf. II Kings XXI. 2 ff.; Is. XVII. 10; Ezek. VIII. 14).

But the necessary complement to and presupposition for a god rising from the dead is the myth of a dying god, and the Song makes no mention of the intimate connexion between these two sequences of thought. Whether and to what extent this mythological interpretation is valid we can only judge with difficulty in view of the paucity of comparative material and the fact that the songs which were used were "sung to death." At least, however, we can say that cultic songs and secular love songs exercised a reciprocal influence on one another.

Nothing can be said about the development of the individual songs, for such songs are timeless. But it is possible that some of them date back to the later monarchy. As to the development of the collection, the occurrence of some Persian and Greek words provide certain clues. The Song of Solomon, as a collection, is therefore to be placed in the post-exilic period, very probably in the fourth century B.C.

Ecclesiastes (*The Preacher*)

The third of the Old Testament wisdom books is Qohelet (Septuagint, Ecclesiastes).[34] Unlike Job, it is not a question of calling in wisdom to help solve a difficult problem. Nor is it, as in the Proverbs, a matter of instructions on how to obtain good fortune and success, although sayings of this nature are quite frequently introduced (such as VII. 1 ff., VIII. 16, IX. 4) and serve as a basis for the author's own opinion (I. 15, 18, II. 12, VI. 1, 6 ff.). The deliberate juxtaposition of these sayings, which throw light on different, indeed in places even contrasting viewpoints (IV. 5 f., VI. 7, 9, VIII. 1, X. 16–19), illuminates the particular intention of the Preacher. True, a high place in human life is allotted to the scholastic doctrine of wisdom, but at the bottom it is rejected and opposed. "Vanity of vanities! All is vanity. What does man gain by all the toil at which he toils under the sun?" (I. 2–3). This is the conclusion drawn by the Preacher from the vicissitudes of a long and eventful life. This is the centre round which all his thoughts revolve. And everything he has to say, general remarks and personal confessions, observations and considerations, admonitions and warnings, all these must help to throw light on and confirm this point of view.

[34] For commentaries and literature, see Bibliography.

The book has no firm structure. It is divided into thirty-two, or thirty-four, or even thirty-seven units of different length. The thoughts are not grouped or arranged in any way, but are merely set down one after another, held together only by the basic mood which finds expression throughout: "all is vanity, and a striving after wind." This is true of all human actions (I. 12 ff.), which hold their own dangers (X. 8 f.); of pleasure and luxury (II. 1 ff.), for which the rich man has no use when he is sick (V. 13 ff.); of all striving (IV. 13 ff.), the effect of which is incalculable for all one's ability and knowledge (IX. 11 f.) and which is condemned to failure (IV. 4 ff.): be it righteousness or iniquity (III. 16 f.) and unrighteousness (V. 7 ff.) —everything is vain and worth nothing under the sun. And what is to be said about wisdom in this connexion? Certainly wisdom is to be praised (VII. 1 ff., IX. 13 ff.), and that it is useful at the right time (X. 10 f.) is evident from the actions of the fool (IX. 17 f.), which do great damage (X. 4 ff., 12 ff., 16 ff.). But the verdict on wisdom is no different from the rest: it, too, is merely trying to catch the wind (I. 16 ff.). For it is not strong enough to withstand Fate (VII. 23 ff.); it has no final advantage over foolishness: "the wise man dies just like the fool" (II. 16 f.).

In the face of the inexorable fact of death all our efforts are as nothing (V. 10 ff.) and our striving is in vain. This reminds us of the German poet Matthias Claudius: "We are spinning webs of air and seeking many arts." And yet there is a fundamental difference between the two. The Christian has the certain hope of eternal life; but for the Preacher death is the irrevocable end. For Man, death is inevitable:

> the pitcher is broken at the fountain, or the wheel
> broken at the cistern, and the dust returns to the earth
> as it was, and the spirit returns to God Who gave it.
> (XII. 6 ff.)

Man has no advantage over the beasts (III. 18 ff.): both have the same destiny, the same death. Everything goes back to one place: both are of the dust and return to the dust. "Who knows whether the spirit of man goes upward?" (III. 21). The Preacher recognises God, who has given men life (V. 18, VIII. 15, XII. 7), and from whose hand everything comes (II. 24), good and evil days (VII. 10 ff.). But the Preacher's God is not

our God, neither is He the God of Israel, as is indicated by the
complete absence of the name Yahweh from the book. This
God is not the righteous God, but a distant, hidden God, who
introduces all the contradictions and tensions in life which Man
has to suffer (III. 1 ff.) in order that Man shall fear Him
(III. 14); but this not in the sense of Proverbs, that the fear of
God is the acme of wisdom. What is meant here is fear before
God, the necessary fear of the incomprehensible in God, in
whose hand lie both love and hatred (IX. 1) and who gives joy
to the man who pleases Him, but to the sinner the work of
gathering and reaping (II. 26). The Preacher has no personal
relationship with his God, and this explains his gloomy, sub-
Christian attitude, which is also far removed from the piety of
the Old Testament. And yet pessimism is not the basic mood
of the Preacher, nor renunciation of the questionable good
things of life. On the contrary, just because life is so vain and
so transitory, because God is so unfathomable, therefore—this
is the doctrine implicit in his reflexions—Man should rejoice
in (III. 18 ff., VIII. 15, XI. 7 ff.) and enjoy his life.

> For if a man lives many years, let him rejoice in them
> all; but let him remember that the days of darkness
> will be many.   (XI. 8)

Of the author we know very little. The name Qohelet
(I. 2, 12, XII. 8) is a pseudonym, as is evident from the remarkable feminine form. According to the heading "son of David,
king in Jerusalem" (I. 1), Solomon should be meant, but he
cannot be the author. The futility of this disguise, which is
intended to endow the book with great authority, is revealed
by the statements concerning kings, and especially by the
statement "I have been king" (I. 12), which appears in
Egyptian tomb inscriptions as words spoken by the dead ruler.
Moreover, what is said about this king (II. 4 ff.) is more in
keeping with the legendary fame of Solomon than with reality.
Scholars have been at pains to read allusions to specific contemporary events into some passages (e.g. IV. 13–14, IX. 13 ff.;
X. 16 ff.). But these are not so much historically accurate
recollections as textbook examples, and their value should not
be overestimated any more than that of the personal confessions which, as a description of the author's life, are of very

S

doubtful validity. These are the words of a wise old man, spoken to his pupils. This is evident from the varied exhortations and bits of advice, which draw useful lessons from recognising the irrationality of this life and in other respects too are aimed at practical living (IV. 17 ff., VIII. 2 ff.).

What the Preacher has to say cannot all be reduced to one common denominator; many contradictory and unreconciled statements stand side by side. From this some scholars have concluded that the book, as we have it, was compiled from various sources, or that we are dealing with an accidental manuscript, that is a manuscript the loose pages of which have been fastened together in the wrong order. But this occasional lack of symmetry is much more simply and naturally explained by the Preacher's struggle for knowledge, in the course of which he has not always made himself perfectly clear. Moreover, what the Preacher has to teach us is so far removed from all other religious belief that it is understandable that later additions have been made expressing orthodox teaching (such as III. 17, VIII. 5, 12–13). In spite of this, however, the value of the book has long been the subject of dispute in Jewish tradition.

Occasionally we come upon supplementary glosses by a strange hand which are intended to clarify the Preacher's thoughts (as V. 19). The appendix (XII. 9 ff.), in which the pupil gives a short appreciation of his teacher, is certainly not original. The conclusion (XII. 12 ff.) should also be ascribed to a later pen: it speaks from the standpoint of a teacher but tries to alter the theme of the book into one of scholastic wisdom.

For dating the book, only internal evidence can be cited; in particular the language, which, on the whole, has an Aramaic tinge and includes loan-words, and the subject-matter, which is closely connected with Greek culture, although there is no direct connexion with the sayings of Theogenes. Thus the book should be placed in the later post-exilic period, in the third century B.C., if not a little later.

The Lamentations of Jeremiah

The five poems gathered together under the title "Lamentations" (Threni)[35] have from time immemorial been ascribed

[35] For commentaries and literature, see Bibliography.

to Jeremiah (Jeremiades), although neither text nor content justify his authorship. Even the Septuagint introduces the songs with the words "After Israel had been led into captivity and Jerusalem had been destroyed, Jeremiah sat down and wept, mourning Jerusalem, and spoke thus." This remark, which has been adopted by the Jewish and Christian traditions, no doubt arose from the note in Chronicles (II Chron. xxxv. 25) which speaks of laments for Josiah and ascribes one of them to Jeremiah. In the Masoretic Text Lamentations does not have a special name but is designated according to the first word (I. 1) as "êka" (= Woe). With the exception of the fifth poem they are written in typical dirge verse and alphabetically arranged, although in the second, third, and fourth the placing of the letter P varies.

Each poem is one chapter in length. The third (ch. III) stands out as a characteristic lament of the individual. It depicts personal distress in detail and contains the customary expressions of trust, of which the words on God's mercy, which has no end, but is new every morning, and on His great faithfulness (III. 22–3), are particularly comforting and confident. That this song originally had nothing in common with the content of the others is evident from "I have become the laughingstock of all peoples" (III. 14) and the statement about the prisoners (III. 34), which does not necessarily refer to the exile. It is linked up to a certain extent with the situation described in the other songs by means of the inserted fragment of a national lament (III. 42–7) and by the short verses on the distress of the people (III. 48) and the mourning for the city (III. 51). As regards its development all that can be said is that it dates from the exilic period and is both the latest and the most personal of the five poems.

Parallel to it in certain respects is the fifth (ch. v), which in the first place differs from the others in form. This is a typical national lament, in which much space is devoted to describing the catastrophe which has befallen the people and its effects (v. 1–14). True, the present distress is the consequence of their own sinfulness (v. 16): but to a very much greater extent they are merely paying for the sins of their fathers (v. 7; cf. Ezek. xviii. 2). Even Zion is desolate, a playground for jackals (v. 18); but—and this is the confident ending—Yahweh reigns

for ever (v. 19) and will restore them and renew their days as
of old (v. 21). Thus it is not lamentation, but hope that has
the last word. This poem particularly matches the situation of
those left behind in the country after the destruction of Jerusalem and will date from this period, that is from the generation
after 587 B.C.

The two first and the fourth poems are more closely related,
as is evident even externally from their similar beginnings.
They share the same subject, the frightful misery of the people.
This has been brought upon them by Yahweh Himself (I. 5,
12 f., II. 1 ff., IV. 16); but it is the punishment which they
(I. 18–19, IV. 6) and their wicked leaders (II. 14, IV. 13) deserve
for their sins. If in the fourth poem the account of Yahweh's
wrath (IV. 1 ff.) ends in something approaching a thought of
consolation (IV. 22), in the first two the cry for help remains
inarticulate, being only hinted at in the request that Yahweh
will look upon the distress of His children (I. 9, 11, 20–1, II. 20).
The second poem, with its very vivid pictures (II. 8 ff., 20–1),
and the fourth with its account of experiences in circles close
to the king (IV. 17 ff.), appear to have originated immediately
after the destruction of Jerusalem. In the first poem, which is
interspersed with the thoughts of a national lament (I. 11 ff.)
there are many signs (I. 4, 9, 16, 20) which point more to the
tribulations of the siege of Jerusalem than to its conquest and
destruction. This entitles us to regard this poem as the oldest
of the five songs and to date it between 598 and 587 B.C.

The Book of Esther

The last of the five Megilloth contains the reading for the
Purim festival, the origin of which is explained by the story of
the beautiful and wise Esther.[36] At the time of Ahasuerus
(Xerxes), according to the Septuagint Artaxerxes, there lived
in Susa the young and charming Jewess Hadassah (=myrtle)
with the Persian name of Esther (=star). After the king had
expelled his disobedient wife Vashti, Esther was chosen to be
queen. By her entreaties she succeeded in preventing the
king's favourite, Haman, from doing harm: he had arranged a
persecution of the Jews, but consulted the oracle (pur) as to
the time when this massacre should be carried out. Haman

---

[36] For commentaries and literature, see Bibliography.

forfeited his own life, and his family were put into Esther's hands for punishment. In addition the king issued an order to all parts of his great kingdom that the Jews might take revenge on their enemies. So in Susa on the thirteenth day of Adar 500 enemies of the Jews were slain and on the next day a further 300, while in the provinces of the kingdom 75,000 perished (the Septuagint gives 15,000).

Woven into this story is another dealing with Esther's relative and guardian Mordecai. He had previously uncovered a plot against the King's life. Just when a dangerous conflict is brewing between Mordecai and the all-powerful Haman, to whom he refuses to do homage, the king has a sleepless night. He begins to read his court annals and in so doing is reminded of Mordecai's services: he shows his special gratitude by making Haman, his enemy, do Mordecai public honour. After Haman's execution Mordecai assumes his high position, and thanks to the grant of the king's signet ring commands the same great authority as Haman.

The end of the book (ix. 20 ff.) is a later appendix which does not appear to form a unit in itself and is different from the book in language and thought. Here the festival is instituted as a ceremony to be repeated annually, but in contrast to the story, where it appears as "a day for gladness and feasting" (ix. 19), it is characterised here in addition (ix. 22) as a festival of fasting and lamentation (ix. 31).

The Book of Esther begins with the claim that it records actual events and is credible and reliable, and seeks to prove its claim by citing dates, numbers, and names. It contains valuable material for the history of culture, with its details of the Achaemenean palace, and shows itself conversant with Persian customs and court etiquette. Its picture of Xerxes also contains certain historical features, but it must be admitted that it might just as well fit many another Oriental ruler. The narrator has a definite idea of the size of the kingdom, with its many provinces and great army of officials, and knows something of the highly developed Persian system of communications. But on closer inspection it becomes evident that his ideas of the Persian period are very vague and indefinite. Neither a Vashti nor an Esther was ever queen in Persia; moreover, by Persian law, the king was restricted in his choice of a wife to seven Persian families. Apparently Ahasuerus-Xerxes is thought of as Nebuchadnezzar's successor. How otherwise would it be possible for Mordecai, who was among those deported in 587 B.C. (II. 5–6), to have lived in the days of Xerxes (485–465)? But there are other problems. The king agrees with Haman's decree against the Jews (III. 8 ff.): why then is he so amazed and enraged at it (VII. 7)? Why the long interval of eleven months between the publication of the measures to be taken against the Jews and their actual execution (III. 7)? In spite of the secrecy they maintained (II. 10, 20) would Haman really have known nothing of the relationship between Mordecai and Esther and her Jewish faith? Further points also tell against the historicity of the story—above all the *Märchen* features in the arrangement of the festival, the boast of the queen's beauty, the levy of maidens, the choice as queen of the lowly and unknown maiden, the most beautiful in all the land, and the promotion of Mordecai. Typical also is the delight in large numbers: 127 provinces (I, 1), a feast of 180 days (I. 4), 10,000 talents (III. 9), 75,000 massacred (IX. 16). And above all the understandable wishful thinking of a downtrodden nation: a Jewess adorned with a royal crown, a Jew as the Grand Vizier of the whole kingdom, with unrestricted authority to take revenge, as he thinks fit, for all the injustice and oppression his people have suffered. This is no historical account; it has as little connexion with history as the stories in the Book of Daniel.

What we have here is an historical novel, but nevertheless a masterly composition. The author is an excellent and exciting storyteller and has the gift of constructing and contrasting the individual scenes of the fast-moving plot vividly and with much artistic skill. Whether and how far historical features are present is difficult to say with such stories. Despite the religious tolerance of the Persians, it is quite possible that there were occasional pogroms against the Jews. At all events the Book of Esther is separated by a wide interval from the period of which it tells. It will not originate earlier than the third century B.C. On the basis of IX, 20 Mordecai was long considered to be the author of the book.

The main point of the story is found in the appendix, which

aims at explaining the origin of the Purim festival. The festival is derived from the word "pur," which is supposed to correspond to a Hebrew word for "lot," but is unknown in Persian. It occurs in Babylonian, however, with the meaning of "lot-oracle" in connexion with the New Year Festival. For this reason attention has been drawn to the obvious similarities with the names of Babylonian (Marduk, Ishtar) and Elamite (Vashti, Humman) divinities; thus it has been presumed that a myth dealing with the supplanting of Elamite by Babylonian gods is the basis of the Book of Esther. But apart from the similarity in the names there are no grounds at all for this suspicion: moreover the name Mordecai occurs elsewhere (cf. Ezra II. 2; Neh. VII. 7). The fact that the Purim festival, under the name Mordecai's Day, is first mentioned in II Maccabees (xv. 36) in conjunction with Nicanor's Day, leads us to conclude that it was of late origin. It will be a case of an originally heathen festival taken over by the Diaspora Jews of the east— a view corroborated by the complete absence of everything religious from the Book of Esther. Even in places where it would undoubtedly be expected the naming of God is avoided: "relief and deliverance will rise for the Jews from another quarter" (IV. 14). The Septuagint felt this want and tried to give the book something of a religious air by making several insertions.[37] Jewish tradition has it that people had to drink so much at the Purim festival that they could not differentiate between the songs "Cursed be Haman" and "Praised be Mordecai".[38] The Book of Esther was disputed for a long time on account of its purely secular character, but gradually it became a great favourite. It is a testimony of narrow-minded and fanatical nationalism. We can understand why Luther in his heart rejected this scripture with its "heathen tricks" and so disliked it that he would have preferred it not to have existed at all. From the point of view of religion the Book of Esther has nothing to say to the Protestant believer.

[37] Septuagint additions: A (before I. 1) Mordecai's dream XI. 2–XII. 6; B (after III. 13) Artaxerxes' edict concerning the Jews XIII. 1–7; C (after IV. 17) Mordecai's prayer XIII. 8–XIV. 9; D (following after C) Esther's prayer XV. 4–19; E (after VIII. 12) Artaxerxes' edict for the Jews XVI. 1–24; F (at the end of the book) interpretation of Mordecai's dream X. 4–XI. 1.

[38] Megilla Fol. 7b; cf. Goldschmidt, *Talmud*, VOL. IV, p. 27.

THE BOOK OF DANIEL

Like the Book of Esther, the Book of Daniel[39] has no heading
but begins with a date and plunges immediately into what it
has to say. It obviously consists of two different parts: the first
(chs. I–VI) contains stories, and the second (chs. VII–XII) dreams
and visions in the form of autobiographical accounts. The
individual stories are held together by the time, place and
literary material they have in common. The setting is Babylon
and the royal court; the period is the exile; and the centre of
interest is the fate of Daniel and his three companions in their
relations with the pagan state.

Chapter I tells how, in the third year of Jehoiakim's reign
(605 B.C.), Daniel and his friends are chosen along with other
exiles to be trained for service at the court. As pages they
receive their food from the king's table, but since they do not
want to be defiled by it, a kind-hearted overseer, after a
remarkable test, allows them to live as vegetarians. After three
years of training they are presented to King Nebuchadnezzar,
who has to acknowledge that they have ten times more wisdom
and understanding than all the wise men and astrologers of
his kingdom. In addition Daniel has received from God the
gift of interpreting visions and dreams.

In the second year of his reign Nebuchadnezzar has a terrifying dream (ch. II), which the wise men and astrologers are
unable not only to interpret, but even to recount to him. He
threatens to punish them with death for their failure. Daniel
prays to God for wisdom and strength and thus is able to
recount to the King his dream of the colossus with the feet of
clay which falls over a stone and is smashed to pieces. He is
also able to interpret the monster as the four kingdoms and the
stone as the "God of Heaven and earth," who will crush all
kingdoms and set up His own eternal one. The King acknowledges this God and wants to reward Daniel richly; but the
latter renounces the governorship offered to him in favour of
his three companions, and remains at the court.

Chapter III tells the story of Nebuchadnezzar's enormous
golden image, which everyone must worship. The three devout
companions refuse, are denounced before the King, but remain
steadfast even during their trial and are thrown into a blazing

[39] For commentaries and literature, see Bibliography.

furnace. But an angel comes and protects them so that the fire cannot do them the slightest harm. Overpowered by this miracle, Nebuchadnezzar joins in a song of praise to God and forbids, on pain of severe punishment, any word to be spoken against Him. The three faithful Jews are richly rewarded.

In the form of a decree (letter) to all the peoples of the earth (ch. IV) Nebuchadnezzar reports a dream in which he saw a mighty tree which was a blessing to all living things. But a watcher from heaven came and hewed it down. Daniel is the only person able to interpret this dream and equates the tree with the King, who is to be cast out for seven years; but the kingdom will be assured to him, when he has acknowledged the power of heaven. After a year Nebuchadnezzar loses his reason, but is later cured and restored to his kingdom. Therefore he praises and blesses "the King of Heaven."

The next story (ch. V) describes how, at a banquet where Belshazzar and his lords are sacrilegiously drinking from the Temple vessels stolen from Jerusalem, an inscription which no one can read appears on the wall. At the instigation of the queen-mother Daniel is sent for: he appeals to the King's conscience and prophesies the coming invasion by the Medes and Persians. The King rewards Daniel and gives him one of the highest official posts. During the night Belshazzar is slain and Darius takes possession of his kingdom.

In chapter VI Darius wants to set Daniel over the whole kingdom. Envy and intrigues to prevent this miscarry in the face of Daniel's integrity and loyalty. So his enemies get the King to forbid the practice of foreign cults for one month. Daniel, however, in his devotion, continues to pray to his God and is promptly accused. The King would fain save him, but there is no possibility of annulling his own orders. So Daniel is thrown into a den of lions which is closed and sealed off with a stone. The next day the King finds the pious Daniel alive and unharmed, "because he had trusted in his God." Daniel is taken out of the den: in his place his informers and all their families are thrown to the lions and are immediately torn to pieces. At the royal command Daniel's God is to be worshipped henceforth throughout the kingdom.

So much for the content of these stories, several of which show internal parallels (II, IV; III, VI). The subject-matter of the conflicts, and the outcome, are also uniform to some extent. The presentation of the material shows little of the power of the old art of storytelling; the characters are shadowy and unreal; they do not impress us as human beings. But the narrator is not interested in so doing. Moreover, what we said about the Book of Esther is also true here. The historical data are full of mistakes: Jerusalem was not conquered in the third year of Jehoiakim's reign; Nabonaid, not Belshazzar, was the last Babylonian king; there was no Darius "of the Medes," etc. For all their claims to exactness and reliability these stories contain so many impossibilities and improbabilities, are so rich in exaggerations and features of the *Märchen* that their historical importance is very slight. The driving forces here are not a sense of history, but the desire to see the devout emerge triumphant and a longing for things to be changed. This is the great value and special significance of these stories: they sketch for us the ideal picture of the pious Jew who is ready to make any sacrifice, even that of his own life, rather than be induced by pleading, threats, or punishment to break faith with his own God. Thus they present us with models of the noblest in Jewry at that time, from which the devout man can derive support and strength. The religious life is constantly confronted with the same conflicts and has to prove itself by suffering. Thus one seeks comfort and edification from the past and its great examples of faith.

If we scan this group we see clearly that we are dealing here with individual, independent stories, each with its own conflict and happy solution. The story of the three men (ch. III) makes no mention of Daniel, while in the dream of the four kingdoms, on the other hand, the three companions are dragged in with no good reason (II. 13, 17–18, 49): at Belshazzar's banquet Daniel himself is introduced as a completely strange and unknown figure (v. 10 ff.): also the edicts of tolerance (III. 28–9, VI. 26 ff.) parallel each other in so many respects that the two stories must originally have been completely independent. They circulated independently and singly and were later gathered together into a story cycle. To this an introduction was added (ch. I) to explain the heroes' presence in Babylonia and their connexion with the court, and to complete the equation of Shadrach, Meshach, and Abed-nego with Azariah,

Mishael, and Hananiah. The date of this compilation cannot be ascertained. From internal evidence it can only be concluded that the individual stories came into being in the third century B.C. and were later extended and brought up to date with the addition of the visionary passages, as is evident, for example, from a comparison of dream and interpretation (II. 41 ff.).

With the second part of the Book of Daniel (chs. VII–XII) we step into quite a different world. Here we have not stories, simple in construction and readily comprehensible in meaning, but dreams and visions. But these are completely different from what we have examined under the same name in the case of the prophets. These were short visions which came upon the prophet suddenly and are easy to understand with their allegorical character. Here on the other hand we have rather long and very difficult expositions of self-induced experiences, for which Daniel prepared himself inwardly by prayer, fasting, and mortification (IX. 3, 20 ff., X. 12), and which correspondingly result in fear, horror, and fainting fits from which the angel has to awaken him (VII. 15, VIII. 17–18, X. 9, 15–16). In the Temple vision in particular (Ezek. XL–XLII) we noted the transition from the vision as an inner experience to the literary form: here we have only this literary genre. And as in Zechariah it is no longer Yahweh Himself who explains the vision to the prophet, but an intermediary, an angel; so here we find an angel in every case as interpreter (*angelus interpres;* X. 11, 18, VII. 16, VIII. 16). But we are in the same position as Daniel (VII. 28, VIII. 27, XII. 8): we are equally unable at first to understand both the interpretation and the vision itself with its strange descriptions. Everything is dark and mysterious, and, in spite of all its details the account is more allusive than expressive. The theme is supposed to be the future, "what is to befall you people in the latter days. For the vision is for many days yet to come" (X. 14). But the future is concealed from Man, "shut up and sealed until the time of the end" (XII, 9). But for men who have eyes the hidden can be seen and the veiled future uncovered. For this reason they are called apocalyptists (uncoverers). Their writings must have enjoyed great popularity, for they form a very extensive literature. Some of them, such as the apocalypses in Isaiah, Daniel and the Revelation of John, have been included in the biblical Canon.

Chapter VII contains one of Daniel's dreams from the first year of Belshazzar's reign. Four fantastic beasts rise up out of the sea: the last is particularly horrible to look at with its great iron teeth and its ten horns. Between these an eleventh, smaller horn emerges, tearing out three other horns as it does so and having "eyes like the eyes of a man and a mouth speaking great things." Another picture: in His majesty, surrounded by hosts of angels, God pronounces judgment on the beast, which is slain and thrown into the fire. A new scene: one like the Son of Man, to whom God has granted power over all nations, descends on the clouds of heaven. At Daniel's request an angel gives him an interpretation, but this is still very vague and requires intimate historical knowledge for the understanding of its details. The four beasts are four kingdoms, no doubt those of the Babylonians, Medes, Persians, and Seleucids. The ten horns are ten kings (from Seleucos I, 312–280 B.C. to Seleucos IV, 187–175 B.C.); the small horn is a king (Antiochus IV Epiphanes, 175–164 B.C.), who will subdue three others, i.e. set aside three candidates for the throne, whose names can be historically established. His rule is characterised in some detail: "He shall speak words against the Most High, and shall wear out the saints of the Most High, and shall think to change the times and law [meaning the cult and piety]; and they shall be given into his hand for a time, two times, and half a time." These vague time references occur again in another context (XII. 7; cf. Rev. XIII. 5–6). When God's judgment goes against him, his kingdom, power, and greatness "under the whole heaven shall be given to the people of the saints of the most High." It is evident that the "son of man"—a concept which has achieved great importance through Jesus's description of himself as the Son of Man (Lk. XXI. 27 and *passim*)—apparently does not relate in this instance to an individual such as the Messiah, but to the whole nation (vss. 18, 27).

Very similar to this is the vision in chapter VIII, from the third year of Belshazzar's reign, of the ram with the two horns, interpreted as the Medes and Persians, and the goat, interpreted as the kingdom of Alexander the Great. When the goat's horn broke, four new horns appeared in its place (the Diadochean kingdoms): out of one of these grew the small horn (again Antiochus IV Epiphanes) which hindered the Jews in

the practice of their religion, forbade daily sacrifices and dese-
crated the Temple, by erecting—we can add—a heathen altar
to Zeus. But his activities, as Daniel learns from the conversation of two saints (cf. VII. 25), are restricted to 1150 days, after
which he will be crushed. The angel Gabriel—this is the first
reference in literature to him—interprets this vision, but
Daniel does not quite understand it.

In the first year of Darius's reign (ch. IX) Daniel is studying
the scriptures and comes on Jeremiah's prophecy of the seventy
years (Jer. XXV. 11–12): he prays to God for an explanation,
which is given to him through the angel Gabriel. It really
means seventy times seven years (weeks of years) with subsections of seven weeks (=490 years)—the "anointed one"
refers to the reinstatement of a High Priest; and sixty-two
weeks (=434 years), counting from then until the extermina-
tion of the anointed one, that is until the murder of the High
Priest Onias III in the year 171 B.C. (cf. II Macc. IV. 27 ff.). In
any event the first span is too short and the second too long.
The last week of years (171–164 B.C.) covers the destruction of
city and sanctuary; in the middle of this period (25 Kislev
168 B.C.; cf. I Macc. I. 20 ff.) sacrifice to Yahweh is abolished.
The prince who is to come is once more Antiochus IV Epiphanes
the desolator, upon whom the destruction already determined
by God shall be poured. That these calculations do not quite
fit the older period is not particularly surprising, for historical
information on this period is altogether unsatisfactory (cf. IX. 1).
According to the starting-point chosen for the calculation, the
seventy weeks have been differently understood: the commonest
interpretations are the eschatological, taken to refer to the
destruction of Jerusalem by Titus (A.D. 70), and the messianic,
referring to the second coming of Christ. On the cue of the word
"prayer" (IX. 3), a prayer has been inserted (IX. 4–20) which
from its national lament character is quite evidently a later
interpolation.

The fourth and last vision (chs. X–XII) claims to date from
the third year of Cyrus's reign. After he has been fasting for
three weeks an angel appears before Daniel. This angel is
described in detail (X. 5–6) and has come to reveal the future
to him. For twenty-one days he has been hindered by the prince
(=guardian angel) of the Persians, but has finally overcome

him (x. 1–19) with the help of the prince Michael "who
has charge of your people" (xii. 1). He and Michael will have
to fight on, first of all against the prince of the Persians, over
whom there will be another three kings (no doubt meaning
Darius i, 521–486 B.C., Xerxes, 485–465 B.C., and Artaxerxes,
464–424 B.C.), and then against the prince of Greece, where a
mighty king (= Alexander the Great, 336–323 B.C.) shall rule.
But at the zenith of its power this kingdom will collapse and
will be divided towards the four winds of Heaven (x. 20–xi. 4).
The resulting kingdoms (= Diadochean kingdoms) are represented in the vision as the kingdom of the south (Ptolemies in
Egypt) and the kingdom of the north (Seleucids in Syria) in
their peaceful and warlike inter-relationships. The details
given here are so accurate that the numerous historical events
can immediately be pin-pointed (xi. 5–20). Then, as usual,
there is a portrait of Antiochus iv Epiphanes, "to whom royal
majesty has not been given . . . he shall obtain the kingdom by
flatteries" (xi. 21). In addition, his disputes with the king of
the south and his defeat in the Mediterranean (ships from
Kittim) are described in uncertain terms (xi. 21–30), and then
his measures against the Jewish religion: the Temple dese-
crated, daily sacrifice forbidden, the horror of devastation,
causing the pious to fall by the sword, fire, captivity, and
plunder for a time. He will speak terrible things against the
God of gods (= Yahweh) and will respect neither the favourite
of women (= Adonis = Tammuz) nor any other god; for he
will set himself up above everything and will honour the God of
fortresses (= Zeus Olympios) (xi. 31–9). But at the end—and
now the solid ground of history is abandoned and the events
which are reported from this point to the end (xi. 40–5) are
prophecies, foretelling the future, which do not agree at all with
actual historical events. In these last days the great prince
Michael will deliver the people and set up God's kingdom
(xii. 1–3), and this prophecy, which Daniel is to keep secret,
will be fulfilled for "a time, two times, and half a time" (xii. 7)
—1290 days after the prohibition of daily sacrifice. The change
to 1335 days and the final advice to Daniel (xii. 12 f.) were
probably added later.

All these visions—and this is what is typical of them—end
up with Antiochus iv Epiphanes and his harsh measures of

religious *Gleichschaltung* by which he hoped to weld his kingdom together. The visions claim to date from the sixth century B.C. and start in the distant past. But their very vague historical presentation proves that they are far removed in time from that period. On the other hand they are historically very correct and very reliable for the reign of Antiochus IV, from which they must date. It is in the nature of this literary form that they should claim to emanate from ancient times; also that they should describe past and present under the guise of prophecies of the future in order to give more weight and credibility to their actual prophecies of the end of suffering and the coming of salvation. They were written by a contemporary of Antiochus IV, in the period between 168 and 164 B.C., and have wrapped themselves in the authority of one Daniel, who has certainly no connexion with the Daniel in Ezekiel (Ezek. XIV. 14, 20) but is probably synonymous with the Daniel in the book of that name (Dan. I. 6). They are grouped together with the stories (chs. I–VI) because they all have the same aim in view and because of the similarity between the dream of the colossus (ch. II) and the visions. A special difficulty is presented by the change in language—II. 4 to VII. 28 is transmitted in Aramaic—for which no intelligible explanation has been found to this day.

The historical outlook of these visions is much freer and more comprehensive than in the case of the prophets. It sees a number of temporal kingdoms following one another as determined by God, and finally overcome by the kingdom of God. The time when this will take place is exactly defined. Human curiosity, which would like to penetrate God's hidden thoughts and fathom His plan of salvation, has throughout the history of the Church down to the present day repeatedly made feverish attempts to interpret these mysterious figures for the future. But "of that day and hour no one knows, not even the angels of heaven, nor the Son, but the Father only" (Mt. XXIV. 36). It is not in these figures that the great value of the Book of Daniel lies, but in the basic attitude of a firm and confident faith which is most beautifully expressed in visions and stories alike. Amid all the religious oppression and persecution of the present they exhort men to perseverance and faithfulness, whether by examples of real devotion or by pointing out that all the sufferings of today are merely the first steps towards future salvation. Thus they serve to edify and sustain tempted and weak souls: they are an acknowledgment of God and a witness to the unshakable certainty of His help.

EZRA AND NEHEMIAH

Originally the Books of Ezra and Nehemiah were a single book, known as the Book of Ezra. This was only separated into two, first and second Ezra, from the time of Origen. Following the precedent of the Vulgate the Hebrew manuscripts adopted this division from 1448 onwards, and Luther, on the basis of Nehemiah I. 1, gave second Ezra the particular name of Nehemiah. In the Masoretic Text Ezra-Nehemiah is not in the correct place for its content and date; for, as the repetition of the last two verses of Chronicles (II Chron. XXXVI. 22–3) at the beginning of the Book of Ezra (Ezra I. 1 ff.) shows, Ezra-Nehemiah is actually the immediate continuation of the great work of the Chronicler. Its position before Chronicles in the Hebrew text may be due to the fact that it was accepted into the Canon earlier than Chronicles. Ezra-Nehemiah[40] is of special importance because it is our only historical source for the period from the return from exile (538 B.C.) down to Nehemiah's second sojourn in Jerusalem (432 B.C.). It does not, however, record all the events, but omits large periods of time: neither is the historical sequence always maintained.

The first part (Ezra I–VI) deals with the period from the return until the rebuilding of the Temple (516 B.C.). The section begins with a reference to Cyrus's decree (I. 1–4) which allowed the Jews to return home and which, because of its importance, is reported several times over in the text (V. 13–15, VI. 3–5); it then goes on to report the distribution of the Temple treasures which Nebuchadnezzar had taken away, and the return home of the first of the captives under a Jewish prince Sheshbazzar (Babylonian: Sin-ab-usur), of whom we learn no more (II. 63, V. 14, 16). Perhaps he is to be identified with the grandson of King Jehoiakim, Shenazzar the son of Jeconiah, mentioned in Chronicles (I Chron. III. 18);[41] but in no event is he identical, as the text would lead one to believe,

---

[40] For commentaries and literature, see Bibliography.
[41] Cf. W. F. Albright, *The Biblical Period*, Pittsburg 1950, p. 49.

with Zerubbabel who, with Jeshua (Joshua), comes forward as leader of the people (II. 2, III. 2). There follows a somewhat isolated list of the returned exiles (II. 1–(67) 69), which is also contained in a different form in Neh. VII. 5 ff. and which does not make it clear whether we are here dealing with the first contingent of returned captives.[42] To this are appended short reports on contributions towards the building of the Temple (II. 68 ff.), the erection of the altar (III. 1 ff.), the celebration of the Feast of Tabernacles (III. 4 ff.), and the laying of the foundation stone for the Temple (III. 7–13) "in the second year of their coming" (III. 8). But the Samaritans, whose aid in building the Temple the Jews declined, put difficulties in the way of the effort (IV. 1–5, 24). Further proof of the Samaritans' hostile attitude from an earlier period is added, as shown in accusations sent to Xerxes (=Ahasuerus, IV. 6) and to Artaxerxes (IV. 7), and also in an intimation sent to the latter of the building of the walls (IV. 8–23). This account belongs to the period shortly before 445 B.C., when Nehemiah (Neh. II. 1, 8), in the twentieth year of Artaxerxes' reign, obtained permission for the building of the walls of Jerusalem. These passages, like what follows (V. 1–VI. 18), are transmitted in Aramaic and therefore belong with it.[43] Originally, however, they would come after Ezra VI. 18, where they belong in time. In the second year of Darius's reign (520 B.C.) the building of the Temple, which had come to a standstill, is resumed at the instigation of the prophets Haggai and Zechariah in particular, and is not interrupted even by the application of the new governor Tattenai to the King (V. 6–17). When the records have been consulted Cyrus's decree permitting the building of the Temple is confirmed, and instructions are given for state

[42] Cf. K. Galling, "The 'Gola List' according to Ezra II/Nehemiah VII," in *J. Bib. Lit.*, LXX (1951) pp. 149–58; A. L. Allrik, "The lists of Zerubbabel (Neh. VII and Ezra II) and the Hebrew numeral notation," in *B.A.S.O.R.*, CXXXVI (1954) pp. 21–7.

[43] Klostermann's thesis, repeated by Schaeder, *Esra der Schreiber*, Tübingen 1930, p. 27 f., that this was not a case of an accusation against the Jews but a request by the Jew Tabeel (cf. Ezra IV. 7) to Artaxerxes seeking the latter's approval of the building of the wall, would certainly eliminate the chronological difficulties of the Aramaic portion of the text; but this Tabeel theory is contradicted by certain verses, to which even Schaeder objects, namely Ezra V. 1–2, VI. 14, 16–18, the Aramaic language of which is very unlikely to be a Chronicler's addition. cf. also W. Rudolph, *Esra and Nehemiah mit 3. Esra*, Hb. A.T., 1st ser., VOL. XX, Tübingen 1949, pp. 37–40.

T

help for the building (VI. 3–12), so that it may be quickly completed and the Temple consecreated and made ready for the regular worship of God (VI. 13–18). A report, in Hebrew, of the celebration of the Passover is appended (VI. 19–22).

Starting with a time reference which tells us nothing—"now after this" (VII. 1)—and without any firm connexion, there follows the second main section (Ezra VII–X; Neh. VIII–IX), a report on the activities of Ezra, the priest and "scribe skilled in the law of Moses which the Lord God of Israel had given," which, in modern terms, would mean something like "adviser on Jewish religious affairs to the Persian Government." But in this report, too, all the information does not come from the same source. The statement at the beginning concerning Ezra's lineage (VII. 1b–5) interrupts the continuity and has been taken over from the more detailed genealogical list in Chronicles (1 Chron. v. 29 ff.). Then follows, briefly anticipated, his journey to Jerusalem (VII. 6–10). From another, and that an Aramaic, source we have the text of Ezra's authority from Artaxerxes (VII. 11–26). Then again in Hebrew, there is an autobiographical passage by Ezra (VII. 27–IX. 15), in which we sadly miss any exact time reference. After a short, hymn-like prayer vs. 6 is taken up again in VII. 28b, and Ezra gives us a list of those who are returning home with him (VIII. 1–14) and have gathered for the return journey at the river that runs to Ahava. It transpires that there are no Levites among them. This is quite understandable, since the majority of them, belonging as they did to a non-propertied class, would have remained behind in Palestine, and those who were deported would have shown no outstanding desire to return to their old homeland. Nevertheless Ezra succeeds in gathering together thirty-eight Levites and two hundred temple servants from an unknown place called Casiphia (VIII. 15–20). A list of these was also made; it is not included here but is merely alluded to with the words: "These were all mentioned by name" (VIII. 20). Ezra then goes on to describe the preparations for the journey with prayer and fasting. He declines the military escort offered by the King, trusting in God's gracious protection. Particular importance is attached (in the report also) to the transport of the costly votive offerings the exiles have been given. It is surprising that Ezra makes no

reference to the duration of the return journey, which from
other data (VII. 7–9) is to be estimated at three and a half
months. When the exiles reach their destination, unharmed
and happy, they rest for three days and then deliver the votive
offerings as they were commanded, entering them all in a
register (VIII. 31–4). The content of the appended description
of the returned exiles' first days in the city (VIII. 35–6) fits in
here, but it is surprising that it is not transmitted in the personal
report which continues in IX. 1. In any case the link provided
by the general statement "after these things had been done"
does not give the impression of an immediate continuation,
but indicates rather that something is missing—and the main
point of Ezra's mission at that. Thus it is almost generally
assumed that parts of the Book of Nehemiah (Neh. VII. 72–IX)
belong here, especially as these portions deal exclusively with
Ezra—the name Nehemiah was not added until later in Neh.
VIII. 9; likewise the name Ezra in Neh. XII. 36*b*—and therefore
do not fit in properly in Nehemiah, and also as the text of
Neh. VII is continued in Neh. XI–XII. The apocryphal 1 Esdras
also includes Neh. VIII in the Book of Ezra, even if he places it,
incorrectly, after Ezra X (1 Esdr. IX. 37–55). The housing of
the returned exiles would take some time (Neh. VII. 73), for it
would certainly not be without difficulty that one could
accommodate the servants in the vicinity of the Temple. On
the first day of the seventh month (New Year's Day) all the
people congregated in the square in front of the water gate,
and at the request of the people Ezra read aloud to them from
"the law of God which was in his hand" (Ezra VII. 14, 25–6),
the "law of Moses which the Lord the God of Israel had given"
(Ezra VII. 6; Neh. VIII. 1). As is clear from these descriptions,
this cannot be a new Law written by Ezra: it must be the Torah,
in so far as he had it in exile. We cannot draw any conclusion
about the extent of the law from the fact that the reading
lasted six hours; for Ezra—the Levites in Neh. VIII. 7, 11 are
a supplement—was translating from the page before him into
Aramaic so that everyone could understand. The effect on
this excited and attentive audience must have been shattering
—"all the people wept"; but Ezra knew how to turn it into a
day of celebration (Neh. VIII. 1–12). The next day he read
further portions from the Law to a smaller circle of those who

were specially concerned, with the result that the Feast of Tabernacles was kept for seven days with a final solemn assembly on the eighth day (Neh. VIII. 13–18). As the continuation shows (Ezra IX), the object now was to put an end to troublesome mixed marriages. From the way the text is transmitted it must strike us that Ezra had only just begun to concern himself with this question. But the note on the advice he now gave (Ezra X. 3) shows that he had already attempted to regulate it. Since he had no success, however, the matter was probably not mentioned further. Now, however, a solution must be achieved (IX. 1–5). Ezra utters here a great prayer of repentance, which in many ways assumes the character of a sermon of repentance to the people (IX. 6–15). This is followed immediately, though not in autobiographical form, by the account of the effects on the people of Ezra's prayer and the lessons they learned from it (X. 1–6). A special commission is set up which, in the course of its three months' activity, makes all the men pledge themselves to repudiate their non-Jewish wives. A list of those affected is appended (X. 18–44); but it is so short that it can hardly have been transmitted in full. The accepted obligation is carried out on the twenty-fourth day of the month with a day of fasting (Neh. IX. 1–2): here again it seems strange that these measures, which cut deeply into family life and therefore into the life of the community, should be so briefly disposed of. Following this is a song of thanksgiving (Neh. IX. 5–37), taken, as usual, from available traditional material and therefore not quite in keeping with the actual situation. Taking the history of the people (cf. Pss. LXXVIII, CV, CVI), it reviews their sinfulness and the mercy shown by Yahweh and concludes with a national lament on the present political distress: "Behold, we are slaves this day in the land that thou gavest to our fathers to enjoy its fruit and its good gifts, behold, we are slaves. And its rich yield goes to the kings whom thou hast set over us because of our sins; they have power also over our bodies and over our cattle at their pleasure, and we are in great distress" (Neh. IX. 32–7). But these thoughts do not seem at all appropriate to a representative of the Persian Government, and so we can regard this as the contribution of a reviser. With this the sources of Ezra are exhausted; anything else said about him elsewhere (Neh. XII.

26, 36) comes from a different hand which was trying to construct simultaneous activity for Ezra and Nehemiah.

The source which contains Ezra's autobiographical account is generally described as the Ezra Memoirs. But this name does not quite do justice to its character. "Memoirs" would be bound to say something about the long journey which cannot have been absolutely free from danger, especially as it was undertaken without military protection. Moreover Ezra was in Jerusalem in an official capacity. Thus the gifts to the Temple, for example, are reported in elaborate detail, revealing the official interest of a government servant. The source appears to have been some kind of official report which, we must immediately add, the author of the Book of Ezra-Nehemiah has taken over word for word only in part. It is surprising that nothing is said about the appointing of clerks and judges as the King had commanded (Ezra VII. 25). Also we miss more details about the first attack launched in the mixed marriage question: as soon as a decision is imminent the report suddenly becomes very reticent. We can imagine only too well that a conflict arose, and it is not improbable that Ezra may have been unequal to the difficulty of his task. But the author has selected for his account only what turned out favourably and showed Ezra in the best light; less pleasant matters are passed over in silence or replaced by prayers or lists. Thus the picture we are given of Ezra's activities is incomplete and one-sided.

A third large section (Neh. I–VII. 72), separated expressly from the remainder by its special heading, is formed by the "words of Nehemiah the son of Hacaliah," which comprise one long, connected autobiographical account. In this Nehemiah, the cup-bearer at the court of Artaxerxes, recounts how he was told by his brother Hanani of the plight of the returned exiles and the sorry state (cf. Ezra IV. 23) of the walls of Jerusalem (Neh. I. 1–3). He fasts in his grief and prays to Yahweh that "the God of heaven" may change the attitude of the Persian King (Neh. I. 4–11), at whose command the building of the walls was stopped (cf. Ezra IV. 19 ff.). When Artaxerxes hears of his concern, Nehemiah, no doubt due to the queen's influence, is given leave and sets out, accompanied by a military escort, with full powers to restart the building of the walls and with an authorisation to obtain wood for the purpose. His welcome from the governor of Samaria, Sanballat, and his "servant," the Persian official Tobiah, is not exactly friendly (Neh. II. 1–10). Nehemiah makes his initial preparations with great secrecy in Jerusalem; ascertains, in the course of an inspection by night, the extent of the destruction of the walls; and secures the co-operation of the leading Jewish families (Neh. II. 11–18) before he begins his repairs to the city walls in the face of the derision of Sanballat and his officials (II. 19–20). Since the people's heart is in their work, although the working song inserted in IV. 4 would tend to give the opposite impression, it goes ahead well (IV. 6) and is completed in fifty-two days (VI. 15). True, there were difficulties in plenty to be overcome—from the Samarian governor (IV. 1 ff., 7 ff.), who tries to sabotage the work with his agents, among whom there are even some prophets (VI. 10 ff.), plots political intrigues against Nehemiah and even has designs upon his life (VI. 1 ff.). But there is opposition on the Jewish side also, for the poorer people are further impoverished by working on the walls without pay. With much diplomatic skill Nehemiah succeeds in persuading the rulers to return mortgaged land and to renounce outstanding debts. He immediately binds them with an oath, to which he gives special weight by his symbolic curse on those who may violate it (V. 1–13). He himself sets a laudable example. He renounces his income as governor, which means a considerable sacrifice for him, even if he does not stress the point (V. 14–19). He gives charge of the city to his brother Hanani, already known to us (cf. I. 2), and to Hananiah, the politically reliable and devout captain of the Temple stronghold, and appoints gatekeepers and watchmen (VII. 1–3).

But before the consecration of the walls is described (XII. 27–43), Nehemiah tells first of another important step: the settlement of the depopulated city by immigrants from the country (VII. 4–5, XI. 1–2, 20–1). As a basis for this he uses an old list of returned exiles (VII. 6 ff.; cf. Ezra II). The continuity is further interrupted by the list of inhabitants of the "holy city" (XI. 3–19), which has also found its way into Chronicles (I Chron. IX. 2 ff.), by supplements to this list (XI. 21–4) based on good information, and by a list, from a later period, of villages where the people of Judah lived (XI. 25 ff.). Starting with "on that day," observations are added concerning the overseers of stores (XII. 44–7) and the separation of the foreigners (XIII. 1–3).

In another autobiographical passage from the period of his second sojourn in Jerusalem (after 433 B.C.) Nehemiah deals with the sorting out of a few grievances (XIII. 4 ff.), in which personal opposition to Sanballat (XIII. 28) and Tobiah (XIII. 7 ff.) plays a part. The conclusion takes the form of a list of those members of the community who pledged themselves in the covenant (Neh. X. 1, 28–39): this is written in the first person plural, but has been included by the author of the book in the context of Ezra's activities.

The Nehemiah Memoirs, like those of Ezra, are one-sided and make much that is unfavourable appear in a better light. They also represent a memorial. But they are in no way an official report prepared for the King or for the Jews. On the contrary, peculiarities of style, especially the pious wishes for himself which are always appearing (V. 19, XIII. 14, 22, 31), and the very impious wishes for his opponents (IV. 5, VI. 14, XIII. 29), show that this document was intended as a sort of consecration gift for the Temple.

The relationship in time between Ezra and Nehemiah presents a special problem. According to the text Ezra must have been the elder; but the one date quoted (458 B.C., Ezra VII. 7–8) stands on very insecure ground. Also, it is surprising that despite the decisive steps taken in the matter of the mixed marriages Nehemiah had to intervene again. For these and other reasons the conclusion has been reached[44] that Nehemiah was active in Jerusalem, first from 445 to 433 B.C. and for a second (Neh. XIII. 6–7), shorter period, and then Ezra, perhaps in the thirty-seventh year of Artaxerxes' reign (428 B.C.).

As we have seen, the author of the Book Ezra–Nehemiah used

[44] A. Van Hoonacker in various works, the last in *Rev. bib.*, XXXII (1923), pp. 481–94, XXXIII (1924), pp. 33–64, cf. in particular the summary of the arguments on p. 44–47; H. H. Rowley, "The chronological order of Ezra and Nehemiah" in *Memorial I. Goldhizer*, VOL. I, Budapest 1948, pp. 117–49; E. Johannesen, *Studier over Ezras og Nehemjas Historie*, Copenhagen 1946; W. M. F. Scott, "Nehemia —Ezra?" in *Ex. Times*, LVIII (1946–47), pp. 263–7; N. H. Snaith, "The date of Ezra's arrival in Jerusalem," in *Z. alttest. W.*, LXIII (1952), pp. 53–66; H. H. Rowley, "Nehemiah's mission and its background," in *Bulletin of the John Rylands Library*, henceforth cited as *B.J.R.L.*, XXXVII (1955), pp. 528–61.

a number of sources for his account: Aramaic documents and reports, original notes made by Ezra and Nehemiah, all manner of lists and registers which, in spite of many later amplifications, contain good and reliable material. In the details there is much that can be disputed. Thus opinion varies as to whether Neh. x is to be related to Ezra or Nehemiah, or whether and how far the lists (especially Neh. vii. 6–72 and xi. 25–xii. 25) belong to the original text. Opinion varies most, however, on the extent of the literary activity of the Chronicler. While this is generally considered of much less importance than the source material, there is very strong support for a more extensive narrative contribution by the Chronicler, denying completely the existence of the Ezra Memoirs but recognising those of Nehemiah.[45] Be that as it may, we have here an account of the important events of the early post-exilic period: the return, the building of the Temple and the walls, reform laws, and a combined view of the two great men Nehemiah and Ezra, whose importance for the Jews cannot be sufficiently highly estimated. Thus for our knowledge of post-exilic Jewish piety and the Jewish religious community as a whole this work forms a source of very great value. It should be dated around the middle of the fourth century B.C. or even a little later. As peculiarities of style, the quite special type of the author and not least the repetition of the end of Chronicles at the beginning of Ezra show, Ezra–Nehemiah and Chronicles belong together, the former deriving from the same pen as the second part of the so-called Chronistic work.

THE BOOKS OF CHRONICLES

Like Samuel and Kings, the two Books of Chronicles[46] originally formed only one book. The title which has been used for this work since the time of Jerome corresponds well with the Hebrew expression "events [literally, words] of the days," while the Septuagint description "Paraleipomena" (= passed over, omitted) gives a false impression, as of supplements or appendixes to the older historical books. But this is not the

---

[45] Noth, *Überlief. Stud.*, pp. 144–50, considers Ezra i. 9–11a, iv. 6–vi. 18, vii. 12–26, viii. 1–14 and Neh. i. 1–vii. 5, xi. 1–2 as sources and describes as secondary Ezra ii. 1–67 (69), vii. 1–5, 7–9; x. 18. 20–44; Neh. i. 5–11a, vii. 6–72, x. 2–28, x. 38b–40a, xii. 1–26, 27–29, xiii. 1–3, (xi. 3–19, 20–36).

[46] For commentaries and literature, see Bibliography.

nature of Chronicles, nor its aim. Here we have one single, large historical account starting with David—or, if one likes, with Adam—and finishing with the last king of Judah. To a large extent it is parallel to the records from Genesis to II Kings, but it is something other than a repetition or shorter edition of the historical work of the Deuteronomist. Even if a great deal has been taken over word for word, a general comparison shows how very far Chronicles has pursued its own path, especially in what it has omitted, or added or changed. Its account begins with David.

The preceding material is not an historical report but merely a series of genealogical tables (I Chron. I–IX): the genealogical tree of Judah (chs. I–II) with a list, alien to the present context, of the Edomite kings and tribes (I. 43–54) and a place register of the descendants of Caleb (II, 42–55); a review of the family of David down to several generations after the exile (ch. III); a list of the individual Israelite tribes (chs. IV–VIII), in which there are no data concerning Dan and Zebulon and which is incomplete in other respects also. Levi in particular is dealt with in some detail (ch. VI), lists being given of the high priests and of the forefathers of the families of singers (VI. 31 ff.), with Levite and priestly services, a list of Aaron's descendants (VI. 49–54; cf. VI. 3 ff.), and an enumeration of the Levite cities (VI. 54–81). The account of Judah contains details about the places which were important in post-exilic times (IV. 1–23; cf. II. 1 ff.), and that of Benjamin (ch. VIII) refers particularly to the descendants of Saul (VIII. 33 ff. = IX. 35 ff.). Inserted between these, no doubt at a later date, is a part of the list of the families dwelling in Jerusalem (IX. 1 ff.) with which we are already familiar from Neh. XI. 3 ff. and which is very much out of place here; as well as details of gatekeepers and Levites (IX. 17 ff.) of which we have, in part, a better parallel account in XXIII. 28 ff. It is noticeable that the character of this section, with its dry cataloguing of names, is altered here and there by quite short historical notes (IV. 39 ff., V. 1 ff., 18 ff., 25 f.). For his tribal lists the author of Chronicles used selected portions of Num. XXVI and perhaps also of Gen. XLVI. 8–27. In this whole complex, however, we may reckon on very many secondary additions and proliferations.

After this genealogical introduction there follows the actual historical account of the Israelite kingdom in three large sections. The death of Saul is reported (ch. x), and then we come to the political history of David (chs. XI–XXI). This is an idealised account ignoring all the less pleasant episodes of his family history (I Sam. IX–XX). On the other hand, the story of the Ark of the Covenant (I Chron. XIII. 11 ff.) is more extensive than in the older report (II Sam. VI); and among the various lists (chs. XI–XII, XVIII) the register of warriors who associated themselves with David even in Saul's lifetime (XII. 24–40) is peculiar to Chronicles. But in the light of XI. 10–47 this passage must be secondary, as must XII. 1–23, which belongs to the story of the rise of David which the Chronicler does not deal with elsewhere. In the hands of the Deuteronomist David had many very human characteristics and a number of weaknesses, but the picture which is drawn here is of David as he lived on in the minds of posterity—the ruler without fault or failing. The one black spot on this picture is the census of the people (ch. XXI), but as this is intimately connected with the acquisition of the threshing floor of Ornan (Araunah), the site of the altar of burnt offerings, it could not be overlooked.

Almost the same space is given to details of David as the pioneer of the building of the Temple and organiser of the cult (chs. XXII–XXIX). Apart from the short notice of David's death (XXIX. 26 ff.; cf. I Kings II. 11–12) this large section has nothing in common with the old historical books. Here all the interest is concentrated on the Temple and the cult. So it is reported how David, in view of Solomon's youth and inexperience (I Chron. XXII. 5), made preparations to the last detail for the building of the Temple, got the building materials ready, and even went so far as to commission the craftsmen. It only remained for the work to be carried out, and this David left to his son (ch. XXII). This theme is continued in the account of the last assembly called by David, in which he presents Solomon as his successor and solemnly entrusts him with the building of the Temple (XXVIII. 1 ff.). He hands over to Solomon detailed building plans and ordinances for the priests and Levites (XXVIII. 13, 21), to which a later hand has appended instructions regarding the holy furnishings (XXVIII. 14 ff.). From Solomon David now turns to the assembly as a whole, which—

on his example—is now contributing generously to the Temple building (xxix. 1 ff.). All present join in the King's prayer of thanksgiving with a hymn. The assembly concludes with the offering of sacrifices and a sacrificial feast, at which Solomon was made "king the second time" and recognised (xxix. 20 ff.). A note is appended on David's death, and the source of his history is quoted (xxix. 26 ff.).

The thread of the otherwise fairly unitary narrative is interrupted by a series of lists (chs. xxiii–xxvi) based on the ordinances laid down (xxviii. 13). Also somewhat out of place here are lists of army captains (xxvii. 2–15; cf. xi. 11 ff.), tribal princes omitting Gad (xxvii. 16–24), overseers of the King's personal property (xxvii. 25–31), and the King's counsellors (xxvii. 32–4). There is much that is difficult in this, such as the naming of Asahel as a captain (xxvii. 7) although he had fallen in battle a long time before (ii Sam. ii. 18 ff.), and the fourteen names (xxv. 4; cf. xxv. 23–31), which are here certainly meant as names but which in origin represent a rhythmical psalm fragment.

> Be gracious to me, Yahweh, be gracious!
>   Thou are my God, whom I praise and extol,
> Thou are my help in the time of need.
>   Ah, give to me many of Thy visions!

These lists probably contain good and old material; but they have no doubt been revised to conform to later conditions, if they are not (like the arrangement of the various classes participating in the cult) completely secondary.

The subject of the second large section (ii Chron. i–ix) is David's son and successor: in structure and content this is fairly parallel to the report in i Kings. Here, as there, the centre of interest is the building of the Temple (ii Chron. ii ff.), the moving of the Ark (ch. v), and the consecration of the Temple (chs. vi–vii). This is set between an account of Solomon's sacrifice at Gibeon (i, 1 ff.) and a note about his chariots and horsemen (i. 14 ff.) at the beginning, and details of the organisation of the kingdom (ch. viii) at the end. The section concludes with the visit of the Queen of Sheba (ix. 1 ff.), a description of Solomon's wealth (ix. 13 ff.), and a note on the historical sources and Solomon's death (ix. 29 ff.). Although

similar, the structure is not identical with that of the model in
I Kings. The cultic aspect is given greater emphasis by extensions (v. I ff., VII. 6), the most important of which, along with
the greater detail of the promise (VII. 12 ff.), is Yahweh's
permanent miracle at the consecration of the Temple (VII. I ff.).
On the other hand, anything which might belittle Solomon in
the eyes of a religious assessor is omitted. For instance, no
mention is made of the setting aside and removal of his
opponents (I Kings I f.); the building of the royal palace
(II Chron. II. I, VIII. I), as well as his marriage with Pharaoh's
daughter (II Chron. VIII. 11), are only vaguely alluded to,
while nothing at all is said about his large harem (cf. I Kings XI.
1–13). The difficulties with external and internal enemies
(I Kings XI. 14–40) are also passed over. Solomon is to appear
as the great and peaceful ruler whose whole interest is centred
in the cult and the worship of God. For this reason even his
wisdom is left in the background (cf. I Kings III. 16 ff., IV. 29 ff.);
even the special preference for lists of all kind is curbed when
these concern court officials and overseers (I Kings IV) or the
King's household (I Kings IV, 29 ff.). In order that Solomon's
portrait may be an unblemished unity the threefold sacrifice
(I Kings IX. 25) is converted into a daily act (II Chron. VIII.
12 ff.), and any offence which might be given by Solomon's
sacrifice at the "high place" at Gibeon is forestalled by the
observation that the Ark stood there (II Chron. I. 3–4). Indeed
the facts are completely reversed, so that it is not Solomon (as
I Kings IX. 11 ff.) but the King of Tyre who cedes twenty cities
(II Chron. VIII. 2). But it would be wrong to accuse the
Chronicler of falsifying the facts: the idea that the kingdom of
David might have forfeited any of its greatness under Solomon
was impossible and incompatible with his whole spiritual
attitude. More detailed comparison with the account in
I Kings might bring even more variations to light, but the
examples mentioned are sufficient to characterise the Chroni-
cler and his conception of history.

The third and last section (chs. X–XXXVI) deals with the
history of the southern kingdom of Judah from Solomon's
death until its fall. Here also the contents are essentially in
agreement with those of the Books of Kings. But in keeping
with the particular attitude of the Chronicler there is a series

of additions concerned with the priests and Levites, the organisation of the cult, and the restoration of the pure worship of Yahweh. Since he sees and judges everything from the angle of the Temple and the cult, it is readily understandable that the Chronicler pays no attention to the history of the Northern kingdom, Israel. For Israel had its own sanctuaries and its own special cult which had no connexion with the Temple at Jerusalem. Thus the Chronicler includes the history of Israel only so far as seems necessary for the understanding of the history of the Southern Kingdom. Naturally the breaking away of the Northern Kingdom, which led to the perpetual division of the great kingdom united under David and Solomon, must be dealt with (ch. x), but not its decline, the political consequences of which did not affect Judah at once or directly. The relations between the two kingdoms, whether as enemies or friendly neighbours, are not seen in the light of political necessities and events, but are considered solely from the religious point of view, from the standpoint of cultic piety. Even the wreck of Jehoshaphat's ships when he tried to revive Solomon's maritime trade is traced back to the deeper reason of his alliance with the King of Israel (II Chron. xx. 35). The Chronicler follows his Deuteronomistic model in taking fortune and misfortune as the measure of piety (cf. II Chron. xxxi. 21, XII. 2, 5). The kings, therefore, are not idealised like David and Solomon but portrayed in their relationship to Yahweh, their faithfulness and piety, but also their weaknesses and sins. With his special knowledge of the facts, the Chronicler does not overlook the defection of Joash (xxiv. 18 ff.) and Jehoram's fratricide (xxi. 2 ff.). The revolt of Libnah and the Edomites in the reign of Jehoram has its basis in the sins of the King: "because he had forsaken the Lord, the God of his fathers" (xxi. 8 ff.). Thus in the end every defeat is a punishment from Yahweh for sins of the ruler (e.g. xxi. 16, xxiv. 24, xxv. 20), while God gives victory to the pious king (XIII. 14 ff., XIV. 10–11, xx. 27). On this basis it seems to be an offence against Yahweh for Amaziah to reinforce his army with Israelite mercenaries (xxv. 6 ff.). Although it is Yahweh who defeats the enemy (xIV. 12), the Chronicler has no hesitation in providing a good deal of information about military rearmament and the creation and strengthening of defence posts;[47] and he transmits more about the incidents of war, victories and defeats than is contained in the Books of Kings.[48]   In addition the Chronicler gives a review of Rehoboam's family (XI. 18 ff.) with certainly old and valuable material; he reports the appointment of judges and courts in the reign of Jehoshaphat (XIX. 5 ff.) and a special commission to give instruction in the Law of Yahweh in the cities (XVII. 7 ff.).

Much of the additional material is devoted to the activities of prophets who are not mentioned elsewhere: Eliezer (XX. 37), Hanani (XVI. 7), Jahaziel (XX. 14), Oded (XXVIII. 9), Zechariah (XXIV. 20, XXVI. 5) and an unknown prophet of the time of Amaziah (XXV. 7 ff., 15 ff.).   As regards prophets who are named elsewhere, the threatening writings of Elijah (XXI. 12 ff.) and the words of Jehu (XIX. 2 ff.) and Shemaiah (XII. 5) are peculiar to Chronicles.   In addition to their speeches some short prayers of kings of Judah are scattered throughout the account (XIII. 4 ff., XIV. 11, XX. 5 ff., etc.): these, like the exaggerated numbers quoted for the sacrifices (e.g. XV. 11, XXIX. 33) and for military forces (e.g. XIII. 3, 17, XIV. 8, XVII. 14 ff.), are designed for edification.   On the same lines is the report that the people are so happy at the Feast of the Passover that they decide there and then to repeat the celebration (XXX. 23).   The report of the threat to Jerusalem in the days of Hezekiah is much abbreviated compared to Kings (II Kings XVIII. 13–XX. 19), but Hezekiah's cultic reforms (II Kings XVIII. 4–6) are described in much more detail (II Chron. XXIX. 3–XXXI. 21).   If on the other hand the account of Josiah's reforms is significantly shorter than in the Book of Kings, the explanation is that the Chronicler could not bear to admit that the King did not abandon the worship of idols until the eighteenth year of his reign.   Thus he makes it appear as if Josiah had carried out his reforms in the twelfth year of his reign (i.e. when he was twenty years old) and merely supplemented them in the eighteenth year (II Chron. XXXIV. 3).

If we look at the whole historical work of the Chronicler

---

[47] II Chron. XIV. 7, XVII. 12 ff., XXVI. 1 ff., XXXIII. 14; creation and strengthening of defences: II Chron. XI. 5 ff., XIV. 6 ff., XXVI. 9–10, XXVII. 4, XXXII. 5, XXXIII. 14.
[48] Victories: II Chron. XIII. 13 ff., XIV. 8 ff., XX. 1 ff., XXV. 11, XXVII. 5; Defeats: II Chron. XXIV. 23 ff., XXVIII. 17 ff.

(1 Chron. to Nehemiah) we see that his account is supported by a profound piety which centres round his belief in divine recompense. We have already indicated that according to this doctrine of recompense Yahweh intervened directly in the various wars, and that victory or defeat was the direct result of the king's and people's pious or godless existence. How can one reconcile with this belief the fact that such a pattern of devotion as Josiah should die in battle? Because, in disobedience to Yahweh, he had opposed Pharaoh Neco in battle (xxxv. 22). Or how did it happen that so godless a king as Manasseh could reign for fifty-five years? The Chronicler's answer is that Manasseh cannot have been so godless, or at least that he must have turned back to Yahweh later. And so he tells that Manasseh was brought to Babylon as a prisoner— the reliability of this information cannot be checked—and because he "humbled himself greatly before the God of his fathers . . . God . . . heard his supplication and brought him again to Jerusalem into his kingdom" (xxxiii. 11–13). It is not fitting to make Yahweh's anger the reason for the census of the people (as II Sam. xxiv. 1), so the Chronicler alters the instigator to the old opponent Satan (1 Chron. xxi. 1). Uzziah's leprosy is a judgment of God (II Chron. xxvi. 16): it therefore offends the Chronicler to see the leprous king buried with his fathers (II Kings xv. 7), and so he has him buried in a field near the royal graves (II Chron. xxvi. 23). Many more such details could be cited: they all give us the same picture, the picture of a piety which is finally and most profoundly expressed in the worship of the Temple and the observance of the cult. And so a path is opened up which the writing prophets (especially in the older period) always opposed, a path which was bound to lead in the end to belief becoming rigid and to fulfilment of the letter of the law being raised as the ideal of true piety pleasing to God; to a Jewish legalism which took its faith with tremendous seriousness but could not penetrate from the letter to the spirit of the Law. To it, therefore, the Gospel remained a closed book.

But the aim of the Chronicler is less limited than is generally supposed. If the lists and family trees of the Levites are a secondary component of the work, it cannot have been the Chronicler's intention to justify Levite claims in the service of

the Temple. Recent research has stressed his polemic against
the Samaritans—particularly emphatic in the speech of Abijah
(II Chron. XIII. 4–12). This has led to the opinion that the
Chronicler's main aim was to show the legitimacy of the kingdom of David and of the Temple at Jerusalem as the true place
of worship of Yahweh, and that, for him, the cultic community
in Jerusalem was the successor of the old, legitimate "Israel."[49]

Since the thoughts and views of Chronicles have a uniform
basic attitude, the whole should be looked upon as the work
of a single author. This unity, however, naturally does not
make it impossible for later extensions to have accrued to the
original text. Indeed, many often go further and suspect that
a later hand revised the whole work. As to sources, the
Chronicler used the Pentateuch (or at least the Priestly Code)
and, as his main source, the Deuteronomic history, with which
he is in agreement for long stretches. This is particularly
evident in the fact that the Chronicler has left out the remark,
most depressing to the Southern Kingdom and the dynasty of
David, that all the people, with the exception of the tribe of
Judah, made Jeroboam king over the whole kingdom (I Kings
XII. 20). But besides these he used other sources, as is shown
by the amount of material which does not appear in the Books
of Samuel and Kings and is peculiar to Chronicles. At least he
refers several times to a "Book of the Kings of Israel and
Judah" (II Chron. XXVII. 7, XXXV. 27, XXXVI. 8), which is no
doubt the same as others he mentions with a similar title[50] but
which cannot be identified with our canonical Books of Kings,
since many of the stories quoted[51] are not found in the latter.
Whether this source also includes the Midrash (= commentary)
on the book of kings (II Chron. XXIV. 27) we cannot say with
certainty; nevertheless this does seem probable, for the peculiarly Chronistic material is of a predominantly edifying
character. In addition, he quotes a series of prophetic sources[52]
of which we know nothing. From the remark on the history of
Jehu (II Chron. XX. 34) it is to be assumed that these formed
parts of the Book of the Kings of Israel and Judah; but the

---

[49] Cf. Noth, *Überlief. Stud.*, p. 174.

[50] I Chron. IX. 1; II Chron. XVI. 11, XX. 34, XXV. 26, XXVIII. 26, XXXII. 32,
XXXIII. 18.

[51] I Chron. IX. 1, II Chron. XX. 34, XXVII. 7, XXXIII. 18, XXXVI. 8.

[52] I Chron. XXIX. 29; II Chron. IX. 29, XII. 15, XIII. 22, XXVI. 22, XXXII. 32.

possibility remains that they formed—perhaps in combination—
an independent document (cf. II Chron. XXXIII. 18) of Midrashic
character (II Chron. XIII. 22). The Chronicler refers to a few
other sources, which we must mention merely for the sake of
completeness.[53] But modern scholars are very sceptical about
these references, and are seriously asking whether they are in
fact genuine sources or whether the Chronicler is here merely
imitating the Deuteronomist. The second possibility is supported by the fact that the Chronicler expressly cites the
Israelite source (I Chron. IX. 1; II Chron. XXXIII. 18), although
he is reporting about the kingdom of Judah. But on the other
hand comparison of the precise details of the Siloah tunnel in
II Chron. XXXII. 30 with the very general remarks in XXXII. 3-4
(cf. II Kings XX. 20), and the statements in II Chron. XXXV.
20-2 (cf. II Kings XXIII. 29), point to the existence of a special
unknown source of the Chronicler's, to which perhaps the
individual notes concerning defences and war reports should
also be attributed.[54] As regards the date of writing, the tracing
of David's descendants to several generations after Zerubbabel
(I Chron. III. 19 ff.) is decisive, as is the close connexion between
the Books of Chronicles and their sequel in the Book of Ezra-
Nehemiah.

[53] I Chron. v. 17, XXVII. 24, XXVIII. 19; II Chron. XXXV. 25.
[54] Cf. Noth, *Überlief. Stud.*, pp. 141-3, where attention is drawn to the following: II Chron. XI. 5b-10a, XXVI. 9, 15a, XXXIII. 14a, XI. 10a-12a, XIV. 5-7, XVII.
2a, 12b-19, XXV. 5, XXVI. 11–14, XXVII. 3b-4, XXXII. 3-6a, XXXIII. 14b, XXVI. 6–8a,
XXVII. 5, XXVIII. 18; perhaps the basis of XIII. 3-20 and XIV. 8-14 should also be
included here.

CONCLUSION

THE STUDENT of the growth of the Old Testament has a long and difficult road to travel. The story of the rise and fall of a people over a period of more than a thousand years has its literary record in the Old Testament. But the same detail and clarity do not attend every period of this long span of time. If there is a relative abundance of material concerning the Israelite monarchy and the exile, the literary sources for the period before the formation of the state of Israel and for post-exilic Judaism are but meagre and for long stretches indeed are altogether lacking. Our task has been determined first and foremost by considerations of history and literary criticism. It is a case of analysing the books and collections, distinguishing the individual literary units and investigating their development so as to provide a base from which to advance towards better literary and historical understanding. For only when one has succeeded in placing the individual material within its correct historical framework can it be judged and understood. This is particularly evident in the words of the prophets and in the individual stories from the most ancient times; but it is also true of the historical books and the Writings. Admittedly we have often had to acknowledge diverse opinions among scholars as regards the date of writing and interpretation of the details. Much of what is offered as the results of research is mere hypothesis with a more or less high degree of probability; in other cases it is sheer nonsense. By the very nature and limited compass of Old Testament tradition much must remain uncertain and unexplained. But on the whole it is possible to arrive at a fairly clear picture of the growth of the Old Testament and the composition of its individual parts, and to gain some knowledge of authorship, chronological relationships, and historical, cultural, and other circumstances. Just as a mighty river is a combination of several sources and many tributaries, here too many sources, both oral and written, have joined together. And much of the tradition was added later: different hands have been at work at different periods combining and editing the various collections and books or parts of books. In many instances a later pen has glossed or interpreted the original text with his own additions, or tried to bring it up to date for his own age. Nowadays less and less attention is paid to the question of authenticity, which previously played a large part in Old Testament research. A new conception has arisen concerned with finding out what was the purpose behind these additions and with understanding the composition as such. Why did the redactor arrange the parts as we now find them— sometimes so unreconciled and so contradictory that the transitions and breaks are immediately recognisable? Was this really mere literary incompetence? Or is there a definite purpose behind it? We are touching here on a problem on which little work has been done but which may well put a better complexion on the activities of the redactors, previously such objects of derision. The individual books and collections have not only a prehistory but a post-history. One line, drawn by the faith and piety of those involved in the work, extends from what is original to the last touch added by the reviser.

This immediately gives rise to a second consideration. The Old Testament is not merely literature but a testimony of piety. Thus our next task has been to work out what is of lasting significance above everything governed by man and by time— the theological ideas contained in the various parts of the Old Testament. This, it is true, is particularly the task of the discipline described as "the theology of the Old Testament," but we cannot altogether overlook it in this present connexion. There was a time when the Old Testament occupied an isolated and special place: thanks to the knowledge produced by research in the last century it has become more and more a part of the Ancient Near East, its culture, its history, and its piety. But in spite of all the points of contact, relationships, and common features, it is and remains something completely unique and independent, differing fundamentally from all else in its particular view of things and events as deriving from God. The Old Testament is a religious book, not one among many but *the* book which in a special way provides evidence of how God, the one almighty God, spoke "in many and various ways" (Heb. I. I) to men in different ages and under all sorts of circumstances. Thus the Old Testament is a document of

God's revelation: it is "holy scripture." We must not, of course, overlook the fact that the rays of this revelation are always visible to us merely as fragments, that divine and human are bound up together in the Old Testament. But at no time and in no place is the main point found among men: it is located solely in God. Even what men today find strange in reading the Old Testament, all the details of the Law and the cult, only takes on its true meaning from the particular religious attitude which is documented within it. The deciding factor is always and in all places the evidence of the one God who has revealed Himself in the workings of history and in the direction of the individual human life.

At the same time, however, the Old Testament is "holy scripture" for the Christian; a testimony of faith and revelation intimately connected with the New Testament and obtaining its final and deepest meaning only in its relationship to Christ. The God of the Old Testament is at the same time the God of the New. Thus a strong connecting link unites the two parts of the Bible; the theology of the New Testament is rooted in that of the Old. Certainly one must not be misled, as frequently happens today, into regarding the Old and New Testaments as on the same level, and erasing the differences between them. Martin Luther warned against this with all the conviction with which he elsewhere supported the testimony of Christ in the New Testament. The Old Testament is the start and beginning, not the goal and end of the path of salvation. Christ does not stand at the beginning of the Law: He is the end of the Law. And the Law is the schoolmaster (Gal. III. 24) to lead and to educate us for Christ. Thus the Old Testament has the character of "not yet," of the conditional, the incompleted: complete fulfilment is accomplished by the Gospel.

The Apostle Paul once spoke of the Gospel as "a treasure in earthen vessels" (II Cor. IV. 7). This is true of the Old Testament also. In studying the Old Testament we should always remember these earthen vessels: then we will not take offence at the things in it which refer only to the time when they were written or the parts which are often very human. In addition, however, may we be able to recognise the "treasure" which God has given to mankind with and through the Old Testament.

THE APOCRYPHA

THE NAME Apocrypha,[1] which into the fourth century was applied to the reprehensible books, was transferred by Jerome to all the books not included in the Canon, and was later applied also to the scriptures in the Septuagint additional to the Hebrew Canon. This label is not quite correct in so far as some of these scriptures should be described as pseudepigrapha. A short résumé is given here of the books in the order in which they appear in English Bibles.

I ESDRAS

From the days of Jerome the name III Esdras was adopted for the short Greek writing which the Septuagint places before Ezra and which is therefore described as I Esdras. To a large extent it corresponds with a portion of the Hebrew–Aramaic historical writings of the Chronicler (II Chron. xxxv–Ezra x. 44, and Neh. VII. 73–VIII. 13a, Ezra IV. 7–24 preceding Ezra II), and is evidently an independent translation of the original. Apart from minor insertions (I. 21–2, V. 4–6), the major addition (III. 1–V. 3) is of particular importance, and it is to this that the book owes its popularity. It tells the story of the contest between the three members of the bodyguard of King Darius of Persia to decide what is the strongest thing on earth (III. 1–IV. 32)—one of those "superlative" questions so frequently encountered in popular Greek literature (cf. Solon and Croesus). The narrative, however, is not a unit. It is evident from III. 18–20 that the original sequence of the answers was "King, wine, women"; but a fourth answer—"truth" (IV. 33–42)—was added later.

The whole story was taken over by a Jew and inserted here because the action takes place at the Persian court and because the statement "Ask what you wish, even beyond what is written" (IV. 42) offered a welcome opportunity for explaining

---

[1] See Chap. V, note 39. For commentaries and literature, see Bibliography.

the favours granted to the Jews by the King of Persia as the reward given to the winner of the contest—Zerubbabel, according to a gloss (IV. 13). This explanation is mere fiction and has no historical value whatever.

The abrupt conclusion of the book (IX. 55) should probably be taken as a reference to Neh. VIII. 13. The purpose of the writing is no doubt to show how the worship of the Jews and their religious organisation were established under Josiah, Zerubbabel, and Ezra. No exact date can be given for its writing; but it will be later than Daniel (c. 160 B.C.), and it was widely used by Josephus (c. A.D. 37–100). It is generally assumed, therefore, to have originated at the end of the second or the beginning of the first century B.C.

THE BOOK OF TOBIT

This is an edifying story of a Jew, a model of piety, Tobit of Nineveh, who goes blind, and of his son Tobias, who is protected on a journey to Ecbatana by the angel Raphael and on his return home is able, with the angel's help, to restore his father's sight. The story shows certain connexions with that of the god Chonsu of Thebes, with the Aramaic Achikar novel, Persian demonology (Aêshma Daêva: Asmodaeus), and the *Märchen* of the grateful corpse; but all these motifs have been freely worked on. The Greek text is available in several editions, the more detailed form in the Codex Sinaiticus no doubt approaching most nearly to the supposedly Aramaic original (according to Jerome). This assumption is confirmed by the recent findings of the Dead Sea scrolls, which include fragments of the Book of Tobit in Hebrew and Aramaic. The popularity of this edifying story is evident from the very numerous translations. The book was probably written by a Jew of the Diaspora in Egypt in the second century B.C., before the Maccabean rising.

THE BOOK OF JUDITH

When Nebuchadnezzar's commander-in-chief Holofernes is besieging the Jewish city of Bethulia in the course of his successful punitive expedition against the refractory west, Judith, a beautiful and devout Jewish widow, goes into the enemy camp and wins the favour of the commander. Left alone with him, she cuts off his head and takes it back with her to the city. The besieging forces, disheartened by the death of their leader, are defeated; Judith is greatly revered, sought after by many to be their wife, but remains a widow and dies at a great age. This is an historical novel, full of fanaticism and passion, placing extraordinarily great emphasis on piety as expressed in the Law. Some have tried to attach the name to historical personages of the Maccabean period, or have suggested the generals Bagoas and Orofernes in the Syrian campaign of Artaxerxes Ochus (*c.* 350 B.C.). The novel, however, has no historical value of any kind. The Greek text is evidently—the mistakes alone prove it—a translation from a Hebrew or Aramaic original which is no longer preserved and which was written in the period after the Maccabean rising and in the early days of the prominence of the Pharisaic movement, that is about 150 B.C. or somewhat later.

ADDITIONS TO ESTHER

The Additions to Esther, that is, all the passages in the Septuagint to which nothing corresponds in the Masoretic Text,[1] have been placed since the time of Jerome at the end of the canonical Book of Esther and form chapters x. 4–13, xi–xvi of the Vulgate text. Luther divided them in a different sequence into seven chapters. The additions consist of prayers, to give the Book of Esther at least something of a religious tone; decrees, designed to make the story more authentic; and a third group (e.g. Mordecai's dream) which is probably purely literary in origin. Many scholars believe that there was an original Hebrew text, but arguments against it include the absence of these additions from the Masoretic Text, the Greek style, which does not give the impression of being a translation, and certain variants (cf. xvi. 1–4 with the addition of 5, 8). The date quoted in the subscription, "in the fourth year of the reign of Ptolemy," is important for the date of composition; but since we do not know whether it is Ptolemy VIII or IX, the date can be either 114 B.C. or 48 B.C. Nothing more exact can be agreed on.

THE WISDOM OF SOLOMON

The Wisdom of Solomon, which is placed after Job in the

Septuagint, contains an apologia of the Jewish belief in God and is addressed primarily to unfaithful Jews. From an orthodox outlook the reward of piety is represented as wisdom (chs. I–V), which is praised in a song (chs. VI–IX); a weaker third part describes the wonderful sway of wisdom in Israel's history from Adam to Moses (chs. X–XIX), interrupted by a fairly long discourse on the folly of idolatry (chs. XIII–XV). The author was a pious Jew, probably in Alexandria, who, according to the literary custom of his day, published his book under a respected pseudonym (Solomon): even Origen, Jerome, and Augustine denied the authorship of Solomon. In his expositions the author reveals a good Hellenist education and shows himself to be familiar with Plato and Xenophon, the teachings of the Epicureans and Stoics, and above all with the philosophy of Heraclitus, which had become especially popular in Alexandria. Even though the *parallelismus membrorum* is well maintained, especially in the first two parts of the book, a tendency away from individual sayings towards longer discourses and poems is pronounced in comparison with the older, canonical, wisdom literature. The idea of a second author whose work starts at XI. 5 is not convincing. In spite of many Hebraisms in the first part, there is no doubt that the whole book was originally written in Greek; even Jerome testified to the fact that this book, "whose whole style is redolent of Greek eloquence," is not to be found among the Hebrew scriptures. Next to Philo, Wisdom is the most important product of the Hellenist Jews, and was well known to Paul as well as to the authors of the Epistle to the Hebrews and the First Epistle of Peter. Luther, like Jerome, ascribed it to Philo, but it differs from Philo in its teaching and language and will be older than the latter, dating from the first century B.C.

ECCLESIASTICUS

The most extensive book in wisdom literature is the Book of Jesus ben Sirach (Vulgate, Ecclesiasticus). It bears many similarities to Proverbs and presents its sayings in couplets in accordance with *parallelismus membrorum*. It embraces, however, the most varied aspects of human life and thus forms an important document of the culture of its time. But in contrast to Proverbs, the utterances here are all arranged according to certain points of view, and in some instances the individual sections carry special headings. Seen from the theological standpoint, Ecclesiasticus suppresses the generally human in favour of the specifically Jewish; to this author wisdom is not fear of God (Job xxviii. 28) but observance of the Law and the cult, the "wise man" being a learned scholar (xxxviii. 25 ff.). In addition to proverbs the book contains poems on wisdom, hymns and songs of thanksgiving, prayers, and an alphabetic song (li. 13-30). Of special significance is the "praise of the fathers" from Enoch to Nehemiah (chs. xliv-xlix) and the appreciation of the High Priest Simon II (*d.* 199 b.c.; l. 1-21), with the closing praise, "And now bless the God of all" (l. 22-4), the model for Martin Rinckart's well-known hymn "Now thank we all our God." The book itself supplies valuable information concerning its origin and authorship. According to the preface, the author's grandson, when he came to Alexandria in the thirty-eighth year of the reign of Ptolemy Euergetes (132 b.c.), translated his grandfather's book from the Hebrew, describing him in a concluding passage as "Jesus, the son of Sirach, son of Eleazar, of Jerusalem" (l. 27). Fortunate discoveries since 1896 have presented us with several Hebrew manuscripts of the text of chapters iii-xvi and xxx-li, that is about one-third of the whole. Even though these manuscripts date only from the tenth and eleventh centruies a.d., the form of text they offer is better in several respects than that in the Septuagint. The original Hebrew text should be placed about 190 b.c.

The Book of Baruch

The small collection of writings grouped together under the name "Book of Baruch," which in the Septuagint follows immediately after the Book of Jeremiah, contains in the first place a long prayer of repentance (i. 15- iii. 8), very similar to the prayer in Daniel ix, from which part of it has been taken word for word (i. 16-18). As is evident from the historical section which accompanies it (i. 1-14), the "Book" was intended as a festival lesson for the Temple. When Baruch reads it in Babylon to King Jeconiah and his fellow prisoners, its effect is so powerful that considerable sums of money are immediately forthcoming and are sent, along with the book, to

Jerusalem to provide sacrifices. Nebuchadnezzar and the
exiles are recommended for intercession in the Temple. The
historical impossibilities of this report (vs. 8 is a gloss) show that
the book has no connexion with Baruch, the disciple and scribe
of Jeremiah. The mistakes in translation suggest a Hebrew (or
Aramaic) model with some certainty. The original, however,
must be later than Dan. IX. A few scholars see in Nebuchadnezzar and Belshazzar disguises for Vespasian and Titus, and
thus date the book around A.D. 70. Distinct from the foregoing,
both in content and in style, is a didactic poem on wisdom
(III. 9–IV. 4), the true source of which is considered to be
faithful observance of the Law. Along with this goes a small
group of seven songs (IV. 5–V. 9) containing thoughts of consolation in the style of Deutero-Isaiah and Lamentations.
Whether there is a Hebrew basis here also, we cannot prove
beyond doubt. A clue to the date of origin is provided by the
partial verbal agreement between v. 5–9 and Ps. Sol. XI, 2–7
(c. 63 B.C.). Priority should, however, no doubt be given
to the Baruch portion, which would then have to be dated
at the beginning of the first century B.C. There follows the
"Letter of Jeremiah," which in the Septuagint comes after
Lamentations but in the Vulgate is counted as the sixth
chapter of the Book of Baruch. The letter, the external form
of which is suggested by Jer. XXIX, contains a homily on Jer. X,
a warning against idolatry (cf. also Is. XLIV. 9–20), with
particular reference to the worship of Tammuz. Like Baruch
and Lamentations, this must have had a cultic origin, in this
instance the fast on the seventeenth day of the fourth month.
A Hebrew basis is very probable and is confirmed by the
evidence of Origen. II Macc. II. 2 appears already to assume
the existence of this epistle, which should be placed at least in
the second or at the end of the third century B.C.

THE PRAYER OF AZARIAH

In the story of the three friends of Daniel who were thrown into
the furnace by Nebuchadnezzar for their loyalty to their faith
(Dan. III) the Septuagint has inserted a fairly large addition
where it considered there was an omission in the text (after
vs. 23), for the religious susceptibilities of an author or copyist
must have been offended by the fact that the heathen king

offers up a prayer but the faithful martyrs do not. So the Prayer of Azariah has been inserted from the store of popular tradition, since the hymn that had already been added (see below) did not seem sufficient. The prayer is a typical national lament, by no means suited to the situation described in the story (cf. vss. 4–6, 13). The portrayal of contemporary distress in the lament is, it is true, fairly vague and in general terms, but it seems to refer to the oppression of Antiochus IV Epiphanes, in which case the song should be placed in the middle of the second century B.C. A certain roughness of style in the Greek version, plus the fact that its translation into Hebrew produces a rhythmic text beyond reproach, makes the assumption of a Hebrew original very probable.

THE SONG OF THE THREE HOLY CHILDREN

The prose section (vss. 23–8), the contents of which do not quite fit in here and spoil the artistic construction of the legend in Dan. III, forms the transition from the Prayer of Azariah to the song of the three men in the furnace. This song consists of a litany-like hymn fragment (vss. 29–34) stylised in the form of a prayer, to which is appended another expanded hymn, also like a litany in form. This hymn has preserved undamaged the characteristics of its literary genre. The essential in the hymn is its form, the artistic, architectural construction which is meticulously carried out to the last detail, better than in the shortened version of Psalm CXLVIII. The key passage (vs. 66b–d), which contains the reason for the invitation to give praise, is very unassuming—perhaps it has not been transmitted in its entirety—but does fit the situation to some extent at least with the "flame" and "fire" and with the introduction of the Hebrew names of the three friends and the "furnace." Here again a Hebrew original is very probable. The hymn will originate from the second century B.C., but should be older than the Prayer of Azariah.

SUSANNA

Two Jewish elders pursue Susanna, the beautiful, God-fearing wife of a certain Joakim, and when she will not yield to them they accuse her of adultery, distorting the facts of the case. On their evidence she is condemned to death. All her protestations of innocence are in vain, because appearances are against her. But God hears her prayer and sends a young man called Daniel (= my judge is God). Daniel contests the verdict and conducts a separate hearing of each witness, when their statements do not agree. Thus Susanna is saved and her slanderers punished with death. The absence of an historical framework, the way in which Daniel is introduced, the arrangement of the story in Theodotion before, and in the Septuagint after, the Book of Daniel instead of after Dan. I, as well as the content itself, show that there is no connexion between this and the stories in the Book of Daniel. The theme there is a loyalty to the faith which triumphs over all heathen persecution; but here it is a slandered woman and a wise judge, a secular story, the material for which has been borrowed from elsewhere and given a Jewish colouring. It owes its popularity to the allegorical interpretation of Susanna as referring to the persecutions of the Christian Church. But the concern of the story is less with Susanna and Daniel than with the value of witnesses. It is directed against the statement: "On the evidence of two witnesses or of three witnesses he that is to die shall be put to death" (Deut. XVII. 6), and the intention is to support the efforts of the Pharisees to have this law reformed. This also provides a clue for the date of the story's origin. It would be written by a Pharisee in Jerusalem at the beginning of the first century B.C. Arguments against a Hebrew original are the play on words (vss. 54 f., 58 f.) to which there is nothing to correspond in Hebrew, and the evidence of Julius Africanus in his controversy with Origen. It is just as probable, however, that a Hebrew original was suppressed by the Jews. Perhaps the Theodotion version and the shorter account in the Septuagint go back to different Hebrew models.

BEL AND THE DRAGON

The two additions after the story of Susanna (Septuagint) or at the end of the Book of Daniel (Theodotion) belong together in subject-matter. The one deals with a bronze idol, the other with a living dragon. The king maintains that both are alive, because they accept food and drink. As regards the Bel statue. Daniel, by means of a ruse, uncovers the fraud of the seventy priests who secretly remove the sacrifices from the altar and use them for themselves and their families. The king has the priests killed and Daniel is allowed to destroy Bel and his temple. In the second case the king's assertion is disproved by Daniel's throwing small cakes made of pitch, fat, and hair into the jaws of the dragon until it finally bursts. A riot threatens because of the king's religious attitude, and so he delivers Daniel to the crowd. He is thrown into a pit with seven hungry lions, but they do him no harm. After seven days the king comes sadly in to mourn Daniel—the rest of the story is analogous to that told in Dan. VI. To no purpose a passage of prophetic legend has been inserted into this story (vss. 33–9) telling how the prophet Habakkuk in Judea saves Daniel from dying of starvation in the lion's den at the command and with the assistance of an angel. Since the Septuagint in the heading adds the sub-title "from the prophecy of Habbakuk, son of Jesus of the tribe of Levi," it is possible that these additions belonged originally to the history of a prophet. Like Susanna, the story has a purpose, in this case to ridicule the worship of heathen gods. The time reference in Theodotion to Cyrus of Persia is worthless. Nevertheless there is an echo of Bel-Marduk and Tiamat; but the dragon might just as well refer to the serpent of the Aesclepios of Epidaurua which was worshipped in Oriental and Greek cults at a later period. Nothing more exact can be gleaned about the time of origin. Hypothesis places both stories at the end of the second or the beginning of the first century B.C. Theodotion and the Septuagint differ considerably in details. Again like Susanna, it may or may not have been originally written in Hebrew.

THE PRAYER OF MANASSEH

The short, lovely lament of an individual known as the Prayer of Manasseh occurs in only a few manuscripts of the Septuagint from the fifth to the tenth centuries. It is found among the so-called Odes, together with ten songs of the Old, two of the New Testament, and a Christian song of praise. Its first appearance is in the Didaskale and the so-called Apostolic Constitutions, both of which date from the third century A.D. In the Vulgate it was originally placed after Chronicles, but since the Council of Trent it has stood with III and IV (I and II) Esdras at the end of the Bible, after the New Testament. It owes its inclusion in the Apocrypha to Martin Luther. The account of Manasseh peculiar to Chronicles mentions a prayer of his (II Chron. XXXIII. 12 f.), and the source containing this prayer is quoted (vs. 18). The connexion between our apocryphal lament and II Chronicles is established by vss. 9 and 10 in particular (cf. II Chron. XXXIII. 11). But the whole account of the deportation and return of Manasseh remains very problematical, and so the question of where our song belongs is still very doubtful. Some scholars are of the opinion that the Prayer of Manasseh is an excerpt from the Didaskale. But the one is mere hypothesis as much as the other, and so nothing can be said about the date of origin of this song.

THE FIRST BOOK OF THE MACCABEES

The First Book of the Maccabees, called after the surname of Judas (II. 4, 66), reports the events from 137 to 177 by the Syrian calendar (175–135 B.C.). It describes the oppression of the Jews by Antiochus IV Epiphanes and the struggle for freedom of the Maccabeans, the priest Mattathias from Modein and his sons Judas, Jonathan, and Simon. It forms a very important and in general reliable historical source for this period, even if the value of parts of the letters scattered through it (especially VIII. 22–32, X. 22–47, XII. 1–23) is disputed. The final chapters (XIV–XVI) are certainly an appendix from a later period; not only because Josephus did not incorporate them, but above all because of their contradictory chronological arrangement and the decision of the Senate, reported in XV, 16–21 and dating from the year 47 B.C. In addition to the letters, the verses included from contemporary laments and psalms are characteristic. As Jerome stated and the Hebraisms confirm, the book is probably a translation from a Hebrew or Aramaic original which is no longer preserved. For the first part (chs. I–IX) it is possible that the great work of Jason of Cyrene, of whom no more is known, was used as a source (cf. II Macc. II. 24). As the words "to this day" (XIII. 30) suggest that a considerable time has elapsed since the erection of the monument (141 B.C.), the book should be dated between 100 and 70 B.C.

THE SECOND BOOK OF THE MACCABEES

For the period between 175 and 160 B.C. the Second Book of

the Maccabees forms an important parallel to the First, to which it bears the same relationship as Chronicles to the Books of Kings. It purports to be a shortened version of the five-volume historical work by Jason of Cyrene (II. 23); but the author himself states that he is offering "wine mixed with water" (XV. 39). Thus the narrative is characterised by a strong belief in miracles; and unlike I Maccabees reflects a particular theology on the part of the author—a belief in resurrection and the conception of divine requital and punishment, faithfulness to the Law and, closely connected with it, respect for the Temple. The style of the writing points to a Hellenist Jew (probably from Alexandria). The book was known to Philo of Alexandria (d. A.D. 40) and to the author of the Epistle to the Hebrews (cf. XI. 35) but probably not to Josephus. Opinions vary as to the date of origin, but it would probably be soon after the First Book of Maccabees, that is about the middle of the first century B.C.

CHRONOLOGICAL TABLE

REVIEW OF THE PERIODS IN OLD TESTAMENT LITERATURE

Pre-Mosaic and Mosaic period (to *c.* 1200 B.C.)

Song of Lamech (Gen. IV. 23–4). Miriam's victory song (Ex. XV. 21). The sites of Moab (Num. XXI. 14–15). The Song of the Well (Num. XXI. 17–18). Song of Sihon (Num. XXI. 27–9). Aaron's Blessing (Num. VI. 24–6). Canaanite mishpat of the Book of the Covenant (Ex. XXI. 2–11, 18–22, XXI. 28–XXII. 26). Oath against Amalek (Ex. XVII. 16). Ark Formula (Num. X. 35–6). Oracles of Noah (Gen. IX. 25–7). Patriarchal oracles (Gen. XII. 2, 3, 7, XIII. 14–17, XXVI. 11, XXVIII. 13–14, XLVIII. 22). Song of Deborah (Jg. V). List of unconquered cities (Jg. I. 21, 27–35). List of Judges (Jg. X. 1–5, XII. 7–15). Sources of J and E. Family and heroic sagas of Joshua and Judges. Historical basis of Judges (Jg. III. 16 ff., IV, VIII. 4 ff., XI. 1–11, 29, 32–3). Israelite nucleus of the Book of the Covenant. Decalogue (Ex. XX. 1–17).

Era of David (*c.* 1000 B.C.)

Song of the Bow (II Sam. I. 17–27). Collections of the Book of the Righteous and the Book of the Wars of Yahweh. Oldest Psalms. Story of the Ark (I Sam. IV–VII; II Sam. VI). War of the Kings (Gen. XIV; or late Midrash?). Nucleus of the war reports (I Sam. XIII–XV). Nathan's prophecy (oldest form of II Sam. VII). Report on Ammonite War (II Sam. X. 6–II. 1, XII. 26–31). Story of Saul (I Sam. VII–XV, XXVIII, XXXI). List of David's officials (II Sam. XX. 23–6). Heroes and deeds (II Sam. XXI. 15–22, XXIII. 8–23, 24–39). Development of the Yahwistic source document.

Era of Solomon (*c.* 950 B.C.)

Collection of the older oracles of the Jacob blessing (Gen. XLIX. 3–7, 13–27). Individual oracles of the blessing of Moses (Deut. XXXIII). Oldest Proverb collection (Prov. X. 1–XXII. 16). Beginning of recording of royal annals. Biography of Samuel. Assembly at Shechem (Josh. XXIV). Development of the Elohistic source document.

Oldest period of the separate kingdoms (922–800 B.C.)

Esau oracles (Gen. XXV. 22–3, XXVII. 39–40). Blessing of Jacob (Gen. XXVII. 27–9). Ob. 1–IX. Words of the Wise (Prov. XXII. 17–XXIV. 22); Agur (Prov. XXX. 1–14) and Lemuel Collections (Prov. XXI. 1–9). Ahab's Ammonite War (I Kings XXII. 5–28). Collection of the Elijah stories.

Earlier
monarchical
period
(800–700 B.C.)

Amos (before 760: basic material of I–II; soon after 760: collection of threat oracles (III–VI) and visions (VII–IX). Hosea (750–725). First part-collection (I–III). Zech. IX, I ff., X. 3ff. Isaiah (742–700: beginning of his career (VI); before the Syro-Ephraimitish wars: II. I–IV. 6, V. 8–24, X. I–4?; during these wars: VII, XVII. I–II; latter part of his career 713–701: XXVIII–XXXII (XXVIII. I–4 before 713), XIV. 24–7, 29 ff., XVIII. I ff., XX. I ff., XXII, I, 2–31; of indefinite period: V. I–7, 24–30, IX. 8–X. 4). Micah (735–700). Hezekiah collection (Prov. XXV–XXIX). Solomon's biography (I Kings III–XI). Unification of J and E. Collection of the Elisha stories.

Later
monarchical
period
(700–598 B.C.)

Foreign oracles (Is. XIX). David's Song of Praise (II Sam. XXII). Image of a ruler (II Sam. XXIII. I–7). Zephaniah (c. 630). Psalm (Nah. I. 2–11; Jon. II. 3–10?). Jeremiah (628–622: I, II. I–IV. 4, IV. 5–VI. 30. 605–598: rhythmic oracles from VII–XX and autobiographical passages XI. 18 ff., XIII. I ff.). Passover cantata (c. 622: Ex. XV. I–18). Habakkuk (c. 615). Nahum (before 612). Foreign prophecies (Ezek. XXV–XXVI. 5, XXVIII. 20–23). Isaiah collection (Is. I–XII). Conclusion of the Hosea collection. Isaiah stories (Is. XXXVI–XXXIX=II Kings XVIII. 13, 17–XX. 19). Final editing of the Book of the Covenant (before 622: Ex. XX. 22–XXIII. 33). Original Deuteronomy. Memoir (c. 622: II Kings XXII. 3–XXIII. 3). Excerpt from the report on Josiah's reforms (after 622: II Kings XXIII. 4–20a). Josiah's district list (Josh.). First Deuteronomist? (c. 600).

Period of
the decline
(598–587 B.C.)

Jeremiah (Threats: X. 17–21, XIII. 15 ff., XV. 5–9, XXII. 20 ff., XXI. I ff., XXIII. 9 ff., XXIII. 34 ff.; autobiographical passages: XXIV, XXV. 15 ff., XXVII, XXXII. 5 ff.). Ezekiel (until 593: threats IV–XXIV). Egyptian oracles (Ezek. XXIX–XXXII). Lamentations (I). Zech. IX. 9–10. Baruch source of the Book of Jeremiah (594 onwards).

Period of the
exile
(587–538 B.C.)

Lam. II, IV. Ezekiel (Comfort oracles: XXXIII–XXXVII). Lam. V, III. Song of Hannah (I Sam. II. I–10). Deutero-Isaiah (546–538). Trito-Isaiah (Is. LXIII. 7–64). Appendixes to Hosea and other prophetic writings: Jer. X. I–18, XVI. 19–27; Hab. II. 18–20; Mic. VII. 8–20. Ob. 10–14. 15b. Job (or early post-exilic). Historical work of the Deuteronomist (c. 550). Deuteronomistic editing of Jeremiah. Priestly Code of the Pentateuch. Draft of a constitution (Ezek. XL–XLVIII). Conclusion of the Law of Holiness.

Restoration period (538–400 B.C.)	Zech. I–VIII (520–518). Haggai (after 520). Last formation of Zephaniah. Song of Moses (Deut. XXXII. 1–43). Additions to the prophets (Is. XI. 11–16, XXVIII. 5–6, XXX. 19 ff., XXIV–XXVII, XXXII, XXXIII, XXXIV–XXXV; Jer. IX. 11–15, XXIII. 33 ff., LII; Am. IX. 8–15; Mic. II. 12–13). Trito-Isaiah (Is. LVII. 14–18; collection LX–LXII). Framing of the Blessing of Moses (Deut. XXXIII. 2–5, 26–9). Malachi (before 445 without the later additions I. 11 ff., II. 11–12; III. 23–4). Trito-Isaiah (before 445: Isaiah LVI. 9–LVII. 21).
End of the Persian and Macedonian period (400–300 B.C.)	Joel (without III. 1–5, IV. 4–8). Is. XXIII. From Trito-Isaiah: repentance liturgy Is. LXIII. 7–LXV. 25; Temple oracle: Is. LXVI. 1–4. Collections of the Psalms. Song of Solomon. Prov. I–IX. Image of virtue (Prov. XXXI. 10–31). Final editing of the Pentateuch. Chronicler's historical work (Chron., Ezra, Neh.). Completion of Pentateuch canon (before 330).
Seleucid period (300–200 B.C.)	Deutero-Zechariah (IX–XI, XIII. 7–9). Ecclesiastes. Tyre oracle (c. 274: Is. XXIII. 15–18). Stories of the Book of Daniel (Dan. I, II–VI). Book of Esther. Jeremiah's Epistle (Baruch VI). Septuagint translation of the Torah. Conclusion of the second stage of the Canon (c. 200).
Period of oppression and revolt (200–100 B.C.)	Hebrew Ecclesiasticus (c. 190). Trito-Zechariah (c. 170: Zech. XII–XIII, XIV). Baruch III. 9–V. 9. Song of the Three Young Men. Prayer of Azariah. Dreams and visions of Daniel (168–164: Dan. VII–XII). Book of Tobit. Book of Judith (c. 150). Translation of Ecclesiasticus (c. 132). Baruch I–III. 8. Translation of the Septuagint completed (before 130). Rest of Esther (c. 114?).
Period of Pharisaism (from 100 B.C.)	Susanna, Bel and the Dragon. I Maccabees (before 70). II Maccabees (c. 50). Rest of Esther (c. 48?). The Wisdom of Solomon.
c. A.D. 90	Canonisation of the Old Testament completed.

LIST OF WORKS COMMONLY CITED IN NOTES

ALT, A. *Staatenbildung* = *Die Staatenbildung der Israeliten in Palästina.* Leipzig 1930.

—— *Ursprünge* = *Die Ursprünge des israelitischen Rechts.* Leipzig 1934.

BEER, G. *Exodus.* Tübingen 1939.

B. Heb. = *Biblia Hebraica.* 7th edn. ed. R. Kittel. Stuttgart 1951.

Bertholet-Festschrift = *Festschrift für Alfred Bertholet zum 80. Geburtstag gewidmet,* edd. W. Baumgartner, O. Eissfeldt, K. Elliger, and L. Rost. Tübingen 1950.

DELITZSCH, L. *Lese- und Schreibfehler* = *Die Lese- und Schreibfehler im Alten Testament.* Berlin 1920.

EISSFELDT, O. *Einleitung* = *Einleitung in das Alte Testament.* 2nd edn. Tübingen 1956.

FOHRER, G. "Ezechielglossen" = "Die Glossen im Buche Ezechiel," in *Z. alttest. W.,* LXIII (1951), pp. 33–53.

GOLDSCHMIDT, L. *Talmud* = *Der babylonische Talmud neu übertragen.* 12 vols. Berlin 1930–6.

HALDAR, A. *Cult Prophets* = *Associations of Cult Prophets among the Ancient Semites.* Uppsala 1945.

HEMPEL, J. *Alt-hebräische Literatur* = *Die alt-hebräische Literatur und ihr hellenistisch-jüdisches Nachleben.* Potsdam-Wildpark 1930.

HERTZBERG, H. W. *Nachgeschichte* = *Die Nachgeschichte alttestamentlicher Texte innerhalb des Alten Testaments.* Beihefte z. *Z. alttest. W.* No. 66. Berlin 1936.

LODS, A. *Histoire de la littérature* = *Histoire de la littérature hébraïque et juive des origines à la ruine de l'état juif.* Paris 1950.

MENES, A. *Die vorexilischen Gesetze* = *Die vorexilischen Gesetze Israels in Zusammenhang seiner Kulturgeschichtlichen Entwicklung.* Beihefte z. *Z. alttest. W.* No. 50. Giessen 1928.

MOWINCKEL, S. *Psalmenstudien III. Kultprophetie und prophetische Psalmen.* Kristiania 1923.

—— *Two Sources* = *The Two Sources of the Pre-Deuteronomic primeval History (JE) in Gen. I-XI.* Oslo 1937.

NOTH, M. *Die Geschichte Israels.* Göttingen 1950. Eng. trans. *The History of Israel.* 2nd edn., revised by P. R. Ackroyd. London 1960.

—— *Josua* = *Das Buch Josua.* Hb. A.T. VOL. VII. 2nd edn. Tübingen 1953.

—— *System der Stämme* = *Das System der zwölf Stämme Israels.* Stuttgart 1930.

—— *Überlieferungsgeschichte* = *Die Überlieferungsgeschichte des Pentateuchs.* Stuttgart 1948.

—— *Überlief. Stud.* = *Überlieferungsgeschichtliche Studien I.* Halle 1943.

PFEIFFER, R. H. *Introduction* = *Introduction to the Old Testament.* New York 1941.

RAD, G. VON. *Das erste Buch Mose.* A.T.D. 4th edn. Göttingen 1956.

—— *Die Priesterschrift im Hexateuch.* Stuttgart 1934.

—— *Deut.-Studien* = *Deuteronomium-Studien.* 2nd edn. Göttingen 1948. Eng. trans. *Studies in Deuteronomy,* tr. D. M. G. Stalker. London 1953.

RUDOLPH, W. *Jeremia.* Hb. A.T. 1st ser. VOL. XII. Tübingen 1947.

SELLIN, E. *Einleitung* = *Einleitung in das Alte Testament.* 8th edn., ed. L. Rost. Heidelberg 1950.

Studies in Old Testament Prophecy presented to Professor Theodore H. Robinson, ed. H. H. Rowley. Edinburgh 1950.

WEISER, A. *Einleitung* = *Einleitung in das Alte Testament.* 2nd edn. Göttingen 1949.

ABBREVIATED TITLES OF SERIES AND PERIODICALS

Act. Or. = *Acta Orientalia.* Budapest.

Arch. Or. = *Archiv für Orientforschung.* Berlin.

A.J.S.L. = *American Journal of Semitic Languages and Literatures.* Chicago.

A.T.D. = Das Alte Testament Deutsch, edd. V. Herntrich and A. Weiser. Göttingen.

B.A.S.O.R. = *Bulletin of the American Schools of Oriental Research.* Baltimore.

B. Cent. = *La Bible du Centénaire,* ed. Société biblique de Paris. Paris.

Beihefte z. *Z. alttest. W.* = Beihefte zur *Zeitschrift für die alttestamentliche Wissenschaft.* Giessen, later Berlin.

Bibl. = *Biblica.* Rome.

Bibl. Komm. A.T. = Biblischer Kommentar, Altes Testament, ed M. Noth. Neukirchen.

Bibl. Sac. = *Bibliotheca Sacra.* Dallas, Texas.

B. Jérus. = La Sainte Bible, ed École biblique de Jérusalem. Paris.

Camb. Bible = The Cambridge Bible, ed J. J. S. Perowne. Cambridge.

C.B.Q. = *Catholic Biblical Quarterly.* Washington.

Cent. Bible = The Century Bible, ed. W. F. Adeney. Edinburgh.

C.Q.R. = *Church Quarterly Review.* London.

Echter-Bibel = Die Heilige Schrift in deutscher Übersetzung (Echter-Bibel), ed. F. Nötscher. Würzburg.

Ev. Theol. = *Evangelische Theologie.* Munich.

Ex. Times = *Expository Times.* Edinburgh.

Hb. A.T. = Handbuch zum Alten Testament, ed O. Eissfeldt. Tübingen.

Heil. Schr. A.T. = Die Heilige Schrift des Alten Testaments, edd. F. Feldmann and H. Herkenne. Bonn.

Hk. A.T. = Handkommentar zum Alten Testament, ed. W. Nowack. Göttingen.

H.T.R. = *Harvard Theological Review.* Cambridge, Mass.

H.U.C.A. = *Hebrew Union College Annual.* Cincinnati.

I.C.C. = International Critical Commentary on the Old and New Testaments, edd. S. R. Driver, A. Plummer, and C. A. Briggs. Edinburgh.

Int. = *Interpretation.* Richmond.

Int. Bible = *The Interpreter's Bible,* ed. G. A. Buttrick. New York and Nashville.

J. Bib. Lit. = *Journal of Biblical Literature and Exegesis.* Philadelphia.

J. Bib. Rel. = *Journal of Bible and Religion.* Wolcott, later Garden City, N.Y.

J.N.E.S. = *Journal of Near Eastern Studies.* Chicago.

J. Rel. = *Journal of Religion.* Chicago.

Komm. A.T. = Kommentar zum Alten Testament, ed E. Sellin. Leipzig.

Oudtest. St. = *Oudtestamentische Studien.* Leiden.

P. Jb. = *Palästina-Jahrbuch.* Berlin.

Rev. bib. = *Revue biblique.* Paris.

R.h.p.r. = *Revue d'histoire et de philosophie religieuses.* Strasbourg.

R. th. ph. = *Revue de theologie et de philosophie.* Lausanne.

St. th. = *Studia theologica cura ordinum theologorum Scandinavicorum edita.* Lund.

Th. Bl. = *Theologische Blätter.* Leipzig.

Theol. Stud. u. Krit. = *Theologische Studien und Kritiken.* Gotha, Stuttgart.

Th. Lz. = *Theologische Literaturzeitung.* Leipzig.

Th. R. = *Theologische Rundschau.* Tübingen.

Th. Z. = *Theologische Zeitschrift.* Basel.

Torch Comm. = Torch Bible Commentaries, edd. H. Marsh, A. Richardson, and R. G. Smith. London.

Vet. test. = *Vetus testamentum.* Leiden.

West. Comm. = Westminster Commentaries, edd. W. Lock and D. C. Simpson. London.

Z. alttest. W. = *Zeitschrift für die alttestamentliche Wissenschaft.* Giessen, later Berlin.

Z.D.M.G. = *Zeitschrift der deutschen morgenländischen Gesellschaft.* Leipzig.

Z.D.P.V. = *Zeitschrift des deutschen Palästina Vereins.* Leipzig.

Z. Th. K. = *Zeitschrift für Theologie und Kirche.* Tübingen and Leipzig.

BIBLIOGRAPHY

Headings in this bibliography are arranged in the order
in which the subjects are discussed in the text.

CHAPTER I
THE DEAD SEA SCROLLS

ALLEGRO, J. M. *The Dead Sea Scrolls*. Harmondsworth 1956.
BARDTKE, H. *Die Handschriftenfunde am Toten Meer*. 2nd edn. Berlin 1953.
BAUMGARTNER, W. "Der palästinische Handschriftenfund," in *Th. R.*,
   XVII (1948) and XIX (1951).
BRUCE, F. F. *Second Thoughts on the Dead Sea Scrolls*. London 1956.
BURROWS, MILLAR. *The Dead Sea Scrolls*. London 1956.
—— *More Light on the Dead Sea Scrolls*. London 1958.
CROSS, F. N. *The Ancient Library of Qumrân and Modern Biblical Studies*.
   London 1958.
DUPONT-SOMMER, A. *Aperçus préliminaires sur les manuscrits de la Mer Morte*.
   Paris 1950. Eng. trans. *The Dead Sea Scrolls, A Preliminary Survey*,
   tr. E. M. Rowley. Oxford 1952.
—— *Nouveaux aperçus sur les manuscrits de la Mer Morte*. Paris 1953. Eng.
   trans. *The Jewish Sect of Qumrân and the Essenes: New Studies on the
   Dead Sea Scrolls*, tr. R. D. Barnett. London 1954.
—— *Les Écrits esséniens découverts près de la Mer Morte*. Paris 1959.
GASTER, T. H. *The Scriptures of the Dead Sea Sect in English Translation*.
   London 1957.
MILIK, J. T. *Dix ans de découvertes dans le désert de Juda*. Paris 1957. Eng.
   trans. *Ten Years of Discovery in the Wilderness of Judaea*. London 1959.
ROBERTS, B. J. "The Dead Sea Scrolls and the Old Testament Scriptures,"
   in *B.J.R.L.*, XXXV (1953).
ROWLEY, H. H. *The Zadokite Fragments and the Dead Sea Scrolls*. Oxford 1952.

DEVELOPMENT OF THE OLD TESTAMENT

ANDERSON, G. W. *A Critical Introduction to the Old Testament*. London 1959.
BENTZEN, A. *Introduction to the Old Testament*. 2nd edn. Copenhagen and
   London 1952.
BEWER, J. A. *The Literature of the Old Testament in its Historical Development*.
   Revised edn. New York 1948.
DRIVER, S. R. *An Introduction to the Literature of the Old Testament*. 9th edn.
   Edinburgh 1913.
EISSFELDT, O. *Einleitung in das Alte Testament*. 2nd edn. Tübingen 1956.
MOORE, G. F. *The Literature of the Old Testament*, revised by L. H.
   Brockington. London 1948.

OESTERLEY, W. O. E. and ROBINSON, T. H. *An Introduction to the Books of the Old Testament.* 5th reprint. London 1949.
PFEIFFER, R. H. *Introduction to the Old Testament.* New York 1941.
ROWLEY, H. H. *The Growth of the Old Testament.* London 1950.
SELLIN, E. *Einleitung in das Alte Testament.* 8th edn., ed. L. Rost. Heidelberg 1950.
WEISER, A. *Einleitung in das Alte Testament.* 2nd edn. Göttingen 1949.
YOUNG, E. J. *An Introduction to the Old Testament.* Grand Rapids 1949.

TEXTS AND COMMENTARIES

A. Series

Biblischer Kommentar, Altes Testament, ed. M. Noth. Neukirchen 1956– .
Das Alte Testament Deutsch, edd. V. Herntrich and A. Weiser. Göttingen 1949– .
Die Heilige Schrift des Alten Testaments, edd. F. Feldmann and H. Herkenne. Bonn 1923– .
Die Heilige Schrift in deutscher Übersetzung (Echter-Bibel). Das Alte Testament, ed. F. Nötscher. 15 vols. Würzburg 1947–53.
Handbuch zum Alten Testament, ed. O. Eissfeldt. Tübingen 1935– .
Handkommentar zum Alten Testament, ed. W. Nowack. Göttingen 1892– .
Kommentar zum Alten Testament, ed. S. Sellin. Leipzig 1913– .
La Bible du Centénaire, ed. Société biblique de Paris. 4 vols. Paris 1916–47.
La Sainte Bible, ed. Société biblique de Jérusalem. Paris 1948– .
The Cambridge Bible, ed. J. J. S. Perowne. Cambridge 1877– .
The Century Bible, ed. W. F. Adeney. 33 vols. Edinburgh 1901–13.
The International Critical Commentary on the Old and New Testaments, edd. S. R. Driver, A. Plummer, and C. A. Briggs. Edinburgh 1895– .
The Interpreter's Bible, ed. G. A. Buttrick. 6 vols. New York and Nashville 1952–6.
The Soncino Books of the Bible, ed. A. Cohen. Hindhead, London, Bournemouth 1945–51.
Torch Bible Commentaries, edd. H. Marsh, A. Richardson, and R. G. Smith. London 1952– .
Westminster Commentaries, edd. W. Lock and D. C. Simpson. London 1899– .

B. Single Works

A Catholic Commentary on Holy Scripture, edd. B. Orchard, E. F. Sutcliffe, R. C. Fuller, and R. Russell. Edinburgh 1953.
A New Commentary on Holy Scripture, edd. C. Gore, H. L. Goudge, and A. Guillaume. New edn. London 1943.
CLARKE, W. K. L. *Concise Bible Commentary.* London 1952.
KAUTZSCH, E. and A. BERTHOLET. *Die Heilige Schrift des Alten Testaments.* 2 vols. 4th edn. Tübingen 1922.

The Abingdon Bible Commentary, edd. F. C. Eiselen, E. Lewis, and D. G. Downey. New York and Nashville 1929.

The Teachers' Commentary, edd. G. H. Davies and A. Richardson. Revised edn. London 1955.

CHAPTER II

PENTATEUCH CRITICISM

A. General

BAUMGARTNER, W. "Alttestamentliche Einleitung und Literaturgeschichte," in *Th. R.*, VIII (1936), pp. 179–222.

—— "Wellhausen un die heutige Stand der alttestamentlichen Wissenschaft," in *Th. R.*, II (1930), pp. 287–307.

EISSFELDT, O. "Die literarkritische Arbeit am Alten Testament in den letzten 12 Jahren," in *Th. R.*, x (1938), pp. 255–91.

—— "Die neueste Phase in der Entwicklung der Pentateuchkritik," in *Th. R.*, XVIII (1950), pp. 91–112, 179–215, 267–87.

HUMBERT, P. "Die neurere Genesisforschung," in *Th. R.*, VI (1934), pp. 147–60.

NORTH, C. R. "Pentateuch Criticism," in *The Old Testament and Modern Study*, ed. H. H. Rowley. Oxford 1951.

WRIGHT, G. E. "Recent European study in the Pentateuch," in *J. Bib. Rel.*, XVIII (1950).

B. Special Problems

COPPENS, J. *Histoire critique des livres de l'Ancien Testament.* 3rd edn. Bruges 1942.

EISSFELDT, O. *Hexateuchsynopse.* Leipzig 1922.

ENGNELL, I. *Gamla Testamentet. En traditionshistorisk inledning.* Stockholm 1945.

GRAY, G. B. *Old Testament Criticism, its Rise and Progress.* London 1923.

MOWINCKEL, S. *The Two Sources of the Pre-Deuteronomic Primeval History (JE) in Genesis I–XI.* Oslo 1937.

NOTH, M. *Die Gesetze im Pentateuch, ihre Voraussetzungen und ihr Sinn.* Halle 1940.

—— *Überlieferungsgeschichte des Pentateuchs.* Stuttgart 1948.

—— *Überlieferungsgeschichtliche Studien I.* Halle 1943.

RAD, G. VON. *Das formgeschichtliche Problem des Hexateuchs.* Stuttgart 1938. Reprinted in G. von Rad, *Gesammelte Studien zum Alten Testament.* Munich 1958.

ROST, L. "Zum geschichtlichen Ort der Pentateuchquellen," in *Z. Th. K.*, LIII (1936), pp. 1–10.

WELLHAUSEN, J. *Israelitische und jüdische Geschichte.* 8th edn. Berlin 1921.

—— *Prologomena zur Geschichte Israels und der historischen Bücher des Alten*

Testaments. 3rd edn. Berlin 1899. Eng. trans. *Prologomena to the History of Israel,* tr. J. S. Black and A. Menzies. Edinburgh 1885. *See also books mentioned in note* 11, *p.* 53.

COMMENTARIES

Genesis

A.T.D. (G. von Rad, 4th edn. 1956). *B. Cent.* (VOL. I, L. Aubert, 1916). Echter-Bibel (H. Junker, 2nd and 3rd edns. 1955). Heil. Schr. A.T. (P. Heinisch, 1930). I.C.C. (J. Skinner, 2nd edn. 1920). *Int. Bible* (VOL. I, 1952, C. R. Simpson). Komm. A.T. (O. Procksch, 2nd and 3rd edns. 1923). Torch Comm. (A. Richardson, 1953). West. Comm. (S. R. Driver, 2nd edn. 1909).

Exodus

A.T.D. (M. Noth, 1959). Camb. Bible (S. R. Driver, 1911, reprinted 1929). Echter-Bibel (H. Schneider, 2nd and 3rd edns. 1955). Hb. A.T. (G. Beer and K. Galling, 1939). Heil. Schr. A.T. (P. Heinisch, 1934). Hk. A.T. (B. Baentsch, 1903). *Int. Bible* (VOL. I, 1952, J. C. Rylaarsdam). West. Comm. (A. H. McNeile, 2nd edn. 1931).

Leviticus

B. Jérus. (H. Cazelles, 1951). Camb. Bible (A. J. Chapman and A. W. Streane, 1914). Cent. Bible (A. R. S. Kennedy, n.d.). Echter-Bibel (H. Schneider, 2nd and 3rd edns. 1955). Heil. Schr. A.T. (P. Heinisch, 1935). *Int. Bible* (VOL. II, 1953, N. Micklem).

Numbers

B. Jérus. (H. Cazelles, 1952). Camb. Bible (A. H. McNeile, 1911, reprinted 1931). Echter-Bibel (H. Schneider, 2nd and 3rd edns. 1955). Heil. Schr. A.T. (P. Heinisch, 1936). Hk. A.T. (B. Baentsch, 1903). I.C.C. (G. B. Gray, 1903). *Int. Bible* (VOL. II, 1953, J. Marsh). West. Comm. (L. E. Binns, 1927).

Deuteronomy

B. Jérus. (H. Cazelles, 1950). Camb. Bible (G. A. Smith, 1918). Cent. Bible (H. W. Robinson, 1907). Echter-Bibel (H. Junker, 2nd and 3rd edns. 1955). Heil. Schr. A.T. (H. Junker, 1933). Hk. A.T. (K. Steurnagel, 2nd edn. 1923). I.C.C. (S. R. Driver, 1895). *Int. Bible* (VOL. II, 1953, G. E. Wright). Komm. A.T. (E. König, 1917). Torch Comm. (H. Cunliffe-Jones, 1951).

P

AUERBACH, E. "Die babylonische Datierung im Pentateuch and das Alter des Priesterkodex," in *Vet. test.,* II (1952), pp. 334–42.
BUDDE, K. "Ellä toledoth," in *Z. altest. W.,* XXXIV (1914), pp. 241–53, XXXVI (1916), pp. 1–7.
ELLIGER, K. "Sinn und Ursprung der priestlichen Geschichtserzählung," in *Z. Th. K.,* XLIX (1952), pp. 121–43.

GRELOT, P. "La dernière étape de la rédaction sacerdotale," in *Vet. test.*, VI (1956), pp. 174–89.

HEMPEL, J. "Priesterkodex," in *Paulys Realencyclopädie der classischen Wissenschaft*, VOL XLIV, Stuttgart 1954, cols. 1943–67.

JEPSEN, A. "Zur Chronologie des Priesterkodex," in *Z. alttest. W.*, XLVI (1929), pp. 251–5.

KAUFMANN, J. "Der Kalendar und das Alter des Priesterkodex," in *Vet. test.*, IV (1954), pp. 307–13.

—— "Probleme der israelitisch-jüdischen Religionsgeschichte," in *Z. alttest. W.*, XLVIII (1930), pp. 23–42, LI (1933), pp. 35–7.

LÖHR, M. *Untersuchungen zum Hexateuchproblem. I: der Priesterkodex in der Genesis.* Beihefte z. *Z. alttest. W.* No. 38. Giessen 1924.

RAD, G. VON. *Die Priesterschrift im Hexateuch.* Stuttgart 1934.

ROST, L. *Vorstufen von Kirche und Synagoge.* Stuttgart 1938.

VOLZ, P. *P ist kein Erzähler.* Beihefte z. *Z. alttest. W.* No. 63. Giessen 1933.

D

ALT, A. *Kleine Schriften zur Geschichte des Volkes Israel.* VOL. II. Munich 1953. Pp. 250–75: "Die Heimat des Deuteronomiums."

BAUMGARTNER, W. "Der Kampf um das Deuteronomium," in *Th. R.*, I (1929), pp. 7–25.

BEWER, J. A., G. DAHL, and L. B. PATTEN. "The case for the early date of Deuteronomy," "The case for the currently accepted date of Deuteronomy," "The case for the post-exilic date of Deuteronomy," in *J. Bib. Rel.*, XLVII (1928), pp. 305–21, 322–56, 358–79.

BREIT, H. *Die Predigt des Deuteronomisten.* Munich 1938.

CAUSSE, A. "L'idéal politique et social du Deutéronome," in *R.h.p.r.*, XIII (1933), pp. 289–323.

EISSFELDT, O. "Die Umrahmung des Mose-Liedes Dtn. XXXII. 1–42 und des Mose-Gesetzes Dtn. I–XXX in Dtn. XXXI. 9–XXXII. 47," in *Wissenschaftliche Zeitschrift der Halle Gesellschaft für Sprachwissenschaft*, 4th ser. (1954–5), pp. 411–17.

HORST, F. *Das Privilegrecht Jahwes. Rechtsgeschichtliche Untersuchungen zum Deuteronomium.* Göttingen 1930.

KÖNIG, E. "Deuteronomische Hauptfragen," in *Z. alttest. W.*, XLVIII (1930), pp. 43–66.

KRAUSE, H. *Das Deuteronomium in der wissenschaftlichen Bearbeitung des 19. und 20. Jahrhunderts.* Breslau 1931.

KUYPER, L. J. "The Book of Deuteronomy," in *Int.*, VI (1952), pp. 321–40.

NOTH, M. *Die Gesetze im Pentateuch, ihre Voraussetzung und ihr Sinn.* Schriften der Königsberger gelehrten Gesellschaft, VOL. XVII, No. 2. Halle 1940.

OESTERREICHER, T. *Das deuteronomische Grundgesetz.* Gutersloh 1930.

RAD, G. VON. *Das Gottesvolk im Deuteronomium.* Stuttgart 1929.

—— *Deuteronomium-Studien.* 2nd edn. Göttingen 1948. Eng. trans. *Studies in Deuteronomy*, tr. D. M. G. Stalker. London 1953.

SCHMIDT, H. "Das deuteronomische Problem," in *Th. Bl.*, VI (1927), pp. 40–8.

SIEBENS, A. R. *L'Origine du code deutéronomique*. Paris 1929.
WELCH, A. C. *Deuteronomy: the Framework to the Code*. Oxford 1932.
—— *The Code of Deuteronomy*. London 1924.
WRIGHT, G. E. "The Levites in Deuteronomy," in *Vet. test.*, IV (1954), pp. 325-30.

BOOK OF THE COVENANT

ALT, A. *Die Ursprünge des israelitischen Rechts*. Leipzig 1934.
CAZELLES, H. *Études sur le code de l'alliance*. Paris 1946.
JEPSEN, A. *Untersuchungen zum Bundesbuch*. Stuttgart 1927.
JIRKU, A. *Das weltliche Recht im Alten Testament*. Gutersloh 1927.
MENES, A. *Die vorexilischen Gesetze Israels im Zusammenhang seiner kultur-geschichtlichen Entwicklung*. Beihefte z. *Z. alttest. W.* No. 50. Giessen 1928.
MORGENSTERN, J. "The Book of the Covenant," in *H.U.C.A.*, v (1928), pp. 1-151, VII (1930), pp. 19-258, VIII-IX (1931-2), pp. 1-150, 741-6.
PFEIFFER, R. H. "The transmission of the Book of the Covenant," in *H.T.R.*, XXIV (1931), pp. 99-109.
SMITH, J. M. P. *The Origin and History of Hebrew Law*. Chicago 1931.

THE DECALOGUE

KESSLER, W. "Die literarische, historische, und theologische Problematik des Dekalogs," in *Vet. test.*, VII (1957), pp. 1-16.
KOHLER, L. "Der Dekalog," in *Th. R.*, I (1929), pp. 161-84.
MOWINCKEL, S. *Le Décalogue*. Paris 1927.
—— "Zur Geschichte des Dekalogs," in *Z. alttest. W.*, LV (1937), pp. 218-35.
PFEIFFER, R. H. "The oldest decalogue," in *J. Bib. Lit.*, XLIII (1924), pp. 294-310.
ROWLEY, H. H. *Moses and the Decalogue*. Manchester 1951. Reprinted from *B.J.R.L.*, XXXIV (1951).
SPIEGEL, S. "A prophetic attestation of the Decalogue: Hos. VI. 5, with some observations on Psalms XV and XXIV," in *H.T.R.*, XXVII (1934), pp. 105-44.

CHAPTER III

JOSHUA

A. Commentaries

A.T.D. (H. W. Hertzberg, 1933). B. Jérus. (F. M. Abel, 1950). Echter-Bibel (F. Nötscher, 2nd and 3rd edns. 1955). Hb. A.T. (M. Noth, 1953). Hk. A.T. (C. Steuernagel, 1923). *Int. Bible* (VOL. II, 1953, J. Bright).

B. Literature

ABEL, R. P. "Les stratagèmes dans le livre de Josué," in *Rev. bib.*, LVI (1949), pp. 321–39.

ALT, A. *Josua.* Beihefte z. *Z. alttest. W.* No. 66. Berlin 1936.

ELLIGER, K. "Josua in Judäa," in *P. Jb.*, XXX (1934), pp. 47–71.

GARSTANG, J. *Foundations of Bible History: Josua and Judges.* London 1937.

MOHLENBRINK, M. "Die Landnahmesagen des Buches Josua," in *Z. alttest. W.*, LVI (1938), pp. 238–68.

MOWINKEL, S. *Zur Frage nach dokumentarischen Quellen in Josua 13–19.* Oslo 1946.

NOTH, M. "Überlieferungsgeschichtliches zur zweiten Hälfte des Josua-buches," in *Alttestamentliche Studien. Friedrich Nötscher Festschrift*, edd. H. Junker and J. Botterweek. VOL. I. Bonn 1950.

SMEND, R. "JE in den geschichtlichen Büchern des Alten Testaments," in *Z. alttest. W.*, XXXIX (1921), pp. 181–217.

WRIGHT, G. E. "The literary and historical problem of Joshua X and Judges I," in *J.N.E.S.*, V (1946).

JUDGES

A. Commentaries

A.T.D. (H. W. Hertzberg, 1953). *B. Cent.* (VOL. II, A. Lods, 1923). B. Jérus. (A. Vincent, 1952). Echter-Bibel (F. Nötscher, 2nd and 3rd edns. 1955). Hk. A.T. (W. Nowack, 1900). *Int. Bible* (VOL. II, 1953, J. M. Myers).

B. Literature

AUERBACH, E. "Untersuchungen zum Richtersbuch," in *Z. alttest. W.*, XLVIII (1930), pp. 286–95.

BURNEY, C. F. *The Book of Judges with Introduction and Notes.* London 1918.

DORNSEIFF, F. "Das Buch Richter," in *Arch. Or.*, XIV (1944), pp. 319–28.

EISSFELDT, O. *Die Quellen des Richterbuches.* Leipzig 1925.

JENNI, E. "Vom Zeugnis des Richterbuches," in *Th. Z.*, XII (1956), pp. 257–76.

ROBERTSON, E. "The period of Judges: a mystery period in the history of Israel," in *B.J.R.L.*, XXX (1946), pp. 3–26.

RUDOLPH, W. "Textkritische Anmerkungen zum Richterbuch," in *Festschrift Otto Eissfeldt zum 60. Geburtstage 1 September 1947 dargebracht von Freunden und Verehren*, ed. J. Fück. Halle 1947.

WHITLEY, C. W. "The sources of the Gideon stories," in *Vet. test.*, VII (1957), pp. 157–64.

SAMUEL

A. Commentaries

A.T.D. (H. W. Hertzberg, 1956). *B. Cent.* (VOL II, J. A. Maynard and A. Lods, 1944) B. Jérus. (R. de Vaux, 1953). Cent. Bible (A. R. S. Kennedy, n.d.). Echter-Bibel (M. Rehm, 1949). Hk. A.T. (W.

Nowack, 1902). I.C.C. (H. P. Smith, 1899). *Int. Bible* (VOL. II, 1953, G. B. Caird). Komm. A.T. (W. Caspari, 1926).

B. Literature

BOER, P. A. H. DE. *Research into the Text of I Sam. 1–16.* Amsterdam 1948.
—— "Research into the text of I Sam. XVIII–XXXI," in *Oudtest. St.*, VI (1949), pp. 1–100.
BRIGHT, J. "I and II Samuel," in *Int.*, V (1951), pp. 450–60.
BRUNO, A. *Das hebräische Epos. Eine rhythmische und textkritische Untersuchung der Bücher Samuelis und Könige.* Uppsala 1935.
BUBER, M. "Die Erzählung von Sauls Königswahl," in *Vet. test.*, VI (1956), pp. 113–73.
DRIVER, S. R. *Notes on the Hebrew Text and the Topography of the Books of Samuel.* 2nd edn. London 1913.
EISSFELDT, O. *Die Komposition der Samuelisbücher.* Leipzig 1931.
ELLIGER, K. "Die dreissig Helden Davids," in *P. Jb.*, XXXI (1935), pp. 29–74.
HYLANDER, I. *Der literarische Samuel-Saul-Komplex (I Sam. 1–15) traditionsgeschichtlich untersucht.* Uppsala 1932.
IRWIN, W. A. "Samuel and the rise of the monarchy," in *A.J.S.L.*, LVIII (1941), pp. 113–34.
PFEIFFER, R. H. "Midrash in the books of Samuel," in *Quantulacumque. Studies presented to Kirsopp Lake*, edd. R. P. Casey, S. T. Lake, and A. K. Lake. London 1938.
ROST, L. *Die Überlieferung von der Thronnachfolge Davids.* Stuttgart 1926.
SIMON, M. "La prophétie de Nathan et le temple," in *R.h.p.r.*, XXXII (1952), pp. 41–58.

KINGS

A. Commentaries

B. Cent. (VOL. II, A. Causse, C. Jaeger, and A. Lods, 1944). B. Jérus. (R. de Vaux, 1949). Cent. Bible (J. Skinner, n.d.). Echter-Bibel (M. Rehm, 1949). Hk. A.T. (R. Kittel, 1900). *Int. Bible* (VOL III, 1954, N. H. Snaith).

B. Literature

ALBRIGHT, W. F. "Further light on synchronismus between Egypt and Asia in the period 935–685 B.C.," in *B.A.S.O.R.*, CXLI (1956), pp. 23–7.
—— "The chronology of the divided monarchy of Israel," in *B.A.S.O.R.*, C (1945), pp. 16–22.
BEGRICH, J. *Die Chronologie der Könige von Israel und Juda.* Tübingen 1929.
BENZINGER, I. *Jahwist und Elohist in den Königsbüchern.* Stuttgart 1921.
BURNEY, C. F. *Notes on the Hebrew Text of the Books of Kings.* London 1903.
CARLIER, F. *La Chronologie des rois de Juda et d'Israël.* Paris 1953.
HÖLSCHER, G. "Das Buch der Könige; seine Quellen und seine Redaktion," in *Eucharisterion. Festschrift für Hermann Gunkel*, ed H. Schmidt. Göttingen 1923.

JEPSEN, A. *Die Quellen des Königsbuches.* 2nd edn. Halle 1956.

LEWY, J. *Die Chronologie der Könige von Israel und Juda.* Giessen 1927.

MOWINCKEL, S. "Die Chronologie der israelitischen und jüdischen Könige," in *Act. Or.*, x (1932), pp. 161–277.

ROBINSON, T. H. *The Decline and Fall of the Hebrew Kingdoms. Israel in the Eighth and Seventh Centuries B.C.* Oxford 1926.

RUDOLPH, W. "Zum Text der Königsbücher," in *Z. alttest. W.*, LXIII (1951), pp. 201–15.

SMEND, R. "JE in den geschichtlichen Bücher des Alten Testaments," in *Z. alttest. W.*, XXXIX (1921), pp. 181–217.

THEILE, R. "A comparison of the chronological dates of Israel and Judah," in *Vet. test.*, IV (1954), pp. 185–95.

—— "The chronology of the kings of Judah and Israel," in *J.N.E.S.*, III (1944), pp. 137–86.

—— *The Mysterious Numbers of the Hebrew Kings.* Chicago 1951.

VOGT, E. "Die neubabylonische Chronik über die Schlacht bei Karkemisch und die Einnahme von Jerusalem," in *Vet. test.*, Suppl. IV (1957), pp. 67–96.

WISEMAN, D. T. *Chronicles of Chaldaean Kings (626–556 B.C.) in the British Museum.* London 1956.

CHAPTER IV

GENERAL

EISSFELDT, O. "The prophetic literature," in *The Old Testament and Modern Study*, ed. H. H. Rowley. Oxford 1951.

FOHRER, G. "Neuere Literatur zur alttestamentlichen Prophetie," in *Th. R.*, XIX (1951), pp. 277–344, XX (1952), pp. 193–271.

GUNKEL, H. "Die geheimen Erfahrungen der Propheten" und "Die Propheten als Schriftsteller und Dichter," in *Die grossen Propheten*, ed. H. Schmidt. 2 vols. Göttingen 1923.

HEMPEL, J. *Worte der Propheten in neuer Übertragung und mit Erläuterungen.* Berlin 1949.

HYATT, J. C. *Prophetic Religion.* New York 1947.

JEPSEN, A. *Nabi.* Munich 1934.

JOHNSON, A. R. *The Cultic Prophet in Ancient Israel.* Cardiff 1944.

KUHL, C. *Israels Propheten.* Munich and Bern 1956. Eng. trans. *The Prophets of Israel*, tr. R. J. Ehrlich and J. P. Smith. Edinburgh 1960.

NEHER, A. *L'Essence du prophétisme.* Paris 1955.

ROBINSON, T. H. "Neuere Propheten-Forschung," in *Th. R.*, III (1931), pp. 75–103.

—— *Prophecy and the Prophets in Ancient Israel.* 2nd edn. London 1953.

ROWLEY, H. H. *Prophecy and Religion in Ancient China and Israel.* London 1956.

—— "The nature of prophecy in the light of recent study," in *H.T.R.*, XXXVIII (1945), pp. 1–38.
SCOTT, R. B. Y. *The Relevance of the Prophets.* New York 1947.
WELCH, A. C. *Kings and Prophets of Israel.* London 1951.
—— *Prophet and Priest in Old Israel.* London 1936, Oxford 1953.
—— *The Religion of Israel under the Kingdom.* Edinburgh 1912.

ISAIAH

A. *Commentaries*

A.T.D. (V. Herntrich, 1950). Camb. Bible (I–XXXIX, J. Skinner, 1915). Cent. Bible (I–XXXIX, O. C. Whitehouse, 1905). Echter-Bibel (J. Ziegler, 2nd edn. 1953). Hk. A.T. (B. Duhm, 4th edn. 1922). I.C.C. (G. B. Gray, 1912). *Int. Bible* (VOL. V, 1956, R. B. Y. Scott). Komm. A.T. (O. Procksch, 1930). West. Comm. (G. W. Wade, 2nd edn. 1929).

B. *Literature*

BENTZEN, A. *Jesaja.* 2 vols. Copenhagen 1943–4.
BOUTFLOWER, C. *The Book of Isaiah, Chs. I–XXXIX, in the Light of Assyrian Monuments.* London 1930.
BUDDE, K. "Das Immanuelzeichen und die Ahaz-Begegnung Jes. VII," in *J. Bib. Lit.*, LII (1933), pp. 22–54.
FOHRER, G. "Zu Jes. VII. 14 in Zusammenhang von Jes. VII. 10–22," in *Z. alttest. W.*, LXVIII (1956), pp. 54–6.
GRESSMANN, H. *Der Messias.* Göttingen 1929. Pp. 235–46, 462–78.
HAMMERSHAIMB, E. "The Immanuel sign," in *St. th.*, III (1951), pp. 124–42.
JOHN, D. "The tradition of the oracles of Isaiah of Jerusalem," in *Z. alttest. W.*, LXVII (1955), pp. 226–46.
JUNKER, H. "Ursprung und Grundzüge des Messiasbildes bei Isajas," in *Vet. test.*, Suppl. IV (1957), pp. 181–96.
KISSANE, J. *The Book of Isaiah translated from a critically revised Hebrew text with Commentary.* 2 vols. Dublin 1943.
KÖHLER, E. "Zum Verständnis von Jes. VII. 14," in *Z. alttest. W.*, LXVII (1955), pp. 48–50.
KRAELING, E. G. "The Immanuel prophecy," in *J. Bib. Lit.*, LII (1933), pp. 177–97.
LIEBREICH, L. "The composition of the Book of Isaiah: I. The divisions of the book," in *Jewish Quarterly Review*, XLVI (1955–6), pp. 259–77.
MOWINCKEL, S. "Die Komposition des Jesajabuches Kapitel I–XXXIX," in *Act. Or.*, XI (1933), pp. 167–92.
—— *Jesaja.* Oslo 1949.
NORDEN, E. *Die Geburt des Kindes.* Leipzig and Berlin 1924.
SCOTT, R. B. Y. "The literary structure of Isaiah's oracles," in *Studies in Old Testament Prophecy presented to Professor T. H. Robinson*, ed. H. H. Rowley. Edinburgh 1950.
SMITH, G. A. *The Book of Isaiah.* 2 vols. Revised edn. London 1927.
STAMM, J. J. "Die Immanuelweissagung, ein Gespräch mit E. Hammershaimb," in *Vet. test.*, IV (1954), pp. 20–33.

—— "La prophétie d'Emmanuel," in *R.h.p.r.*, XXIII (1943), pp. 1–25.
—— "Neuere Arbeiten zum Immanuel-Problem," in *Z. alttest. W.*, LXIII (1956), pp. 46–53.
VISCHER, W. *Die Immanuel-Botschaft im Rahmen des königlichen Zionsfestes.* Zollikon-Zürich 1955.
WILDBERGER, H. "Die Völkerwallfahrt zum Zion, Jes. II. 1–5," in *Vet. test.*, VII (1957), pp. 62–81.
WÜRTHWEIN, K. "Jesaja VII. 1–9. Ein Beitrag zum Thema: Prophetie und Politik," in *Theologie als Glaubenswagnis. Festschrift zum 80. Geburtstag von Karl Heim.* Hamburg 1954.

DEUTERO-ISAIAH

A. Commentaries

B. Cent. (VOL. II, P. Humbert, 1945). Cent. Bible (XL–LXVI, O. C. White-house, n.d.). *Int. Bible* (VOL. V, 1956, J. Muilenberg). Komm. A.T. (P. Volz, 1932). Torch Comm. (C. R. North, 1952).

B. Literature

BEGRICH, J. *Studien zum Deuterojesaja.* Stuttgart 1938.
FOHRER, G. "Zum Text von Jes. XLI. 8–13," in *Vet. test.*, V (1955), pp. 239–49.
KÖHLER, L. *Deuterojesaja (Jes. 40–55) stilkritisch untersucht.* Beifehte z. *Z. alttest. W.* No. 37. Giessen 1923.
MOWINKEL, S. "Die Komposition des deuterojesajanischen Buches," in *Z. alttest. W.*, XLIX (1931), pp. 87–112, 242–60.
NORTH, C. R. *The Suffering Servant in Deutero-Isaiah.* London 1948.
RIGNELL, L. G. *A Study of Isaiah, Chapters 40–55.* Lund 1956.
SIMON, U.E. *A Theology of Salvation. A Commentary on Isaiah 40–55.* London 1953.
SMITH, S. *Isaiah Chapters XL–LV. Literary Criticism and History.* Oxford 1944.
TORREY, C. C. *The Second Isaiah.* Edinburgh 1928.
See also above, ISAIAH, *for commentaries and literature on the whole book.*

TRITO-ISAIAH

A. Commentaries

B. Cent. (VOL. II, J. Marty, 1945).

B. Literature

ABRAMOWSKI, R. "Zum literarischen Problem des Tritojesajas," in *Theol. Stud. u. Krit.*, XCVI–XCVII (1925), pp. 90–143.
ELLIGER, K. "Der Prophet Tritojesaja," in *Z. alttest. W.*, XLIX (1931), pp. 112–41.
—— *Deuterojesaja und sein Verhältnis zu Tritojesaja.* Stuttgart 1933.
—— *Die Einheit des Tritojesaja.* Stuttgart 1928.
KESSLER, W. "Zur Auslegung von Jesaja 56–66," in *Th. Lz.*, LXXXI (1956), cols. 335–8.

Y

McCullough, W. S. "A re-examination of Isaiah LVI–LXVI," in *J. Bib. Lit.*, LXVII (1948), pp. 27–36.

Mowinckel, S. "Neuere Forschungen zu Deuterojesaja, Tritojesaja, und dem Abäd-Jahwä-Problem," in *Act. Or.*, XV (1937), pp. 1–40.

Morgenstern, J. "Two prophecies from the fourth century B.C. and the evolution of Yom Kippur," in *H.U.C.A.*, XXIV (1952–3), pp. 1–74.

Odeberg, H. *Trito-Isaiah (Isaiah 56-66)*. Uppsala 1931.

Sellin, E. "Tritojesaja, Deuterojesaja, und das Gottesknechtproblem," in *Neue kirchliche Zeitschrift*, XLI (1930), pp. 73–93, 145–73.
  See also above, Isaiah and Deutero-Isaiah.

Jeremiah

A. Commentaries

A.T.D. (A. Weiser, 152–3). Cent. Bible (A. S. Peake, 1910–11). Echter-Bibel (F. Nötscher, 1947). Hb. A.T. (W. Rudolph, 2nd edn. 1958). Hk. A.T. (F. Giesebrecht, 2nd edn. 1907). *Int. Bible* (VOL. IV, 1956, J. P. Hyatt). Komm. A.T. (P. Volz, 2nd edn. 1928). West. Comm. (L. E. Binns, 1919).

B. Literature

Augustin, F. "Baruch und das Buch Jeremia," in *Z. alttest. W.*, LXVII (1955), pp. 50–6.

Hertzberg, H. W. *Prophet und Gott. Eine Studie Religiosität des vorexilischen Prophetentums.* Gutersloh 1923.

Horst, F. "Die Anfänge des Propheten Jeremia," in *Z. alttest. W.*, XLI (1923), pp. 94–153.

Hyatt, J. P. "Jeremiah and Deuteronomy," in *J.N.E.S.*, I (1942), pp. 156–73.

—— "The Deuteronomic edition of Jeremiah," in *Vanderbilt Studies in the Humanities*, ed. R. C. Beatty. VOL. I. Nashville 1951.

May, H. G. "The chronology of Jeremiah's oracles," in *J.N.E.S.*, IV (1945), pp. 217–27.

—— "Toward an objective approach to the Book of Jeremiah. The biographer," in *J. Bib. Lit.*, LXI (1942), pp. 139–55.

Podechard, E. "Le livre de Jérémie: structure et formation," in *Rev. bib.*, XXXVII (1928), pp. 181–97.

Rendtorff, R. "Zum Gebrauch der Formel *ne'um jahwe* im Jeremiabuch," in *Z. alttest. W.*, LXVI (1954), pp. 26–37.

Robinson, T. H. "Baruch's roll," in *Z. alttest. W.*, XLII (1924), pp. 209-21.

Rowley, H. H. "The prophet Jeremiah and the Book of Deuteronomy," in *Studies in Old Testament Prophecy presented to Professor T. H. Robinson*, ed. H. H. Rowley. Edinburgh 1950.

Skinner, J. *Prophecy and Religion. Studies in the life of Jeremiah.* 2nd edn. Cambridge 1926.

Smith, G. A. *Jeremiah.* 4th edn. London 1929.

Torrey, C. C. "The background of Jeremiah 1–x," in *J. Bib. Lit.*, LVI (1937), pp. 193–216.

VOGT, E. "Jeremias-Literatur," in *Bibl.*, XXXV (1954), pp. 357–65.
VOLZ, P. *Der Prophet Jeremia.* 3rd edn. Tübingen 1931.
WELCH, A. C. *Jeremiah: His Time and His Work.* 2nd edn. Oxford 1951.

EZEKIEL

A. Commentaries

A.T.D. (W. Eichrodt, 1959). *B. Cent.* (VOL. II, E. Bruston, 1947). Bibl.
Komm. A.T. (W. Zimmerli, 1955–). Echter-Bibel (J. Ziegler, 1948).
Hb. A.T. (A. Bertholet and K. Galling, 1936; G. Fohrer and K.
Galling, 1955). Hk. A.T. (R. Kraetzschmar, 1900). I.C.C. (G. A.
Cooke, 1936). *Int. Bible* (VOL. VI, 1956, H. G. May). Komm. A.T.
(J. Herrmann, 1924). West. Comm. (H. A. Redpath, 1907).

B. Literature

IRWIN, W. A. "Ezekiel research since 1943," in *Vet. test.*, III (1953),
pp. 54–66.
KUHL, C. "Neuere Hesekielliteratur," in *Th. R.*, XX (1952), pp. 1–26.
—— "Zum Stand der Hesekielforschung," in *Th. R.*, XXXV (1957).
—— "Zur Geschichte der Hesekielforschung," in *Th. R.*, V (1933),
pp. 92–118.
OESTERLEY, W. O. E. "The Book of Ezekiel: a survey of recent literature,"
in *C.Q.R.*, CCXXXII (1933), pp. 187–200.
ROWLEY, H. H. *The Book of Ezekiel in Modern Study.* Manchester 1953.
Reprinted from *B.J.R.L.*, XXXV (1953), pp. 146–90.

THE MINOR PROPHETS

A. Commentaries

A.T.D. (2 vols. K. Elliger, A. Weiser, 1951). Echter-Bibel (F. Nötscher,
1948). Hb. A.T. (T. H. Robinson and F. Horst, 2nd edn. 1954).
Heil. Schr. A.T. (2 vols. J. Lippl and J. Theis, H. Junker, 1937–8).
Int. Bible (VOL. VI, 1956, various authors). Komm. A.T. (E. Sellin,
2nd and 3rd edns. 1929–30).

B. Literature

BRUNO, A. *Das Buch der Zwölf: Eine rhythmische und textkritische Untersuchung.*
Stockholm 1957.
CALKINS, R. *The Modern Message of the Minor Prophets.* New York and
London 1947.
COPPENS, J. *Les Douze Petits Prophètes: Bréviare du prophétisme.* Bruges and
Louvain 1950.
GASTER, T. H. *Thespis, Ritual, Myth, and Drama in the Ancient Near East.*
New York 1950.
WOLFE, E. "The editing of the Book of the Twelve," in *Z. alttest. W.*, LIII
(1935), pp. 90–129.

HOSEA

A. Commentaries

B. *Cent.* (VOL. II, A. Baumgartner, 1947). I.C.C. (W. R. Harper, 2nd edn. 1936). Torch Comm. (G. A. F. Knight, 1960). West. Comm. (S. L. Brown, 1932). See also under MINOR PROPHETS.

B. Literature

BATTEN, L. W. "Hosea's message and marriage," in *J. Bib. Lit.*, XLVIII (1929), pp. 257–73.

BAUMANN, E. "Wissen um Gott bei Hosea als Urform der Theologie?" in *Ev. Theol.*, XV (1955), pp. 416–25.

BUDDE, K. Articles in *Theol. Stud. u. Krit.*, Sonderheft 1925, pp. 1–85; *J. Bib. Lit.*, XLV (1926), pp. 250–97, LIII (1934), pp. 118–33; in *Journal of the Palestine Oriental Society*, XLV (1934), pp. 1–41.

GORDIS, R. "Hosea's marriage and message: a new approach," in *H.U.C.A.*, XXV (1954), pp. 9–35.

LINDBLOM, J. *Hosea literarisch untersucht.* Abö 1927.

MACKENZIE, J. "Knowledge of God in Hosea," in *J. Bib. Lit.*, LXXIV (1955), pp. 22–7.

MAY, H. G. "The fertility cult in Hosea," in *A.J.S.L.*, XLVIII (1932), pp. 73–98.

NYBERG, H. S. *Hoseaboken.* Uppsala 1931.

—— *Studien zum Hoseabuche.* Uppsala 1935.

ROBINSON, H. W. *Two Hebrew Prophets: Studies in Hosea and Ezekiel.* London 1948.

ROBINSON, T. H. "Die Ehe des Hosea," in *Theol. Stud. u. Krit.*, CVI (1935), pp. 301–13.

ROWLEY, H. H. *The Marriage of Hosea.* Manchester 1956. Reprinted from *B.J.R.L.*, XXXIX (1956), pp. 198–233.

SNAITH, N. H. *Mercy and Sacrifice: A Study of the Book of Hosea.* London 1953.

VRIEZEN, T. C. *Hosea: profeet en cultur.* Groningen 1941.

WATERMAN, L. "Hosea, chapters I–III in retrospect and prospect," in *J.N.E.S.*, XIV (1955), pp. 100–9.

WOLFF, H. W. "Erkenntnis Gottes im Alten Testament," in *Ev. Theol.*, XII (1952–3), pp. 533-54.

JOEL

A. Commentaries

I.C.C. (J. M. P. Smith *et al.*, 1912). West. Comm. (G. W. Wade, 1925). See also under MINOR PROPHETS.

B. Literature

CANNON, W. W. "'The Day of the Lord' in Joel," in *C.Q.R.*, CIII (1927), pp. 32–63.

DENNEFELD, L. "Les problèmes du livre de Joel," in *Recherches de science religieuse*, XV (1925), pp. 33–57, 591–608.

JEPSEN, A. "Kleine Beiträge zum Zwölfprophetenbuch: I. Joel," in *Z. alttest. W.*, LVI (1938), pp. 85–96.

KAPELRUD, A. S. *Joel Studies*. Uppsala and Leipzig 1948.

THOMPSON, J. A. "Joel's locusts in the light of Near Eastern parallels," in *J.N.E.S.*, XIV (1955), pp. 52–5.

TREVES, M. "The date of Joel," in *Vet. test.*, VII (1957), pp. 149–56.

AMOS

A. Commentaries

I.C.C. (W. R. Harper, 2nd edn. 1936). Torch Comm. (J. Marsh, 1959). West. Comm. (G. A. Cooke, 2nd edn. 1926). See also under MINOR PROPHETS.

B. Literature

BALLA, E. *Die Droh- und Scheltworte des Amos*. Leipzig 1926.

BEEK, M. A. "The religious background of Amos II. 6–8," in *Oudtest. St.*, V (1948), pp. 132–41.

BENTZEN, A. "The ritual background of Amos I. 2–II. 16," in *Oudtest. St.*, VII (1950), pp. 85–99.

BUDDE, K. "Zu Text und Auslegung des Buches Amos," in *J. Bib. Lit.*, XLIII (1924), pp. 46–131, XLIV (1925), pp. 63–122.

CRAMER, K. *Amos: Versuch einer theologischen Interpretation*. Stuttgart 1930.

CRIPPS, R. S. *A Critical and Exegetical Commentary on the Book of Amos*. 2nd edn. London 1955.

HAMMERSHAIMB, E. *Amos*. Copenhagen 1946.

HYATT, J. P. "The translation and meaning of Amos V. 23–24," in *Z. alttest. W.*, LXVIII (1956), pp. 17–24.

KAPELRUD, A. S. *Central Ideas in Amos*. Oslo 1956.

KOHLER, L. "Amos-Forschung von 1917 bis 1932," in *Th. R.*, IV (1932), pp. 195–213.

MAAG, V. *Text, Wortschatz, und Begriffswelt des Buches Amos*. Leiden 1951.

McCULLOUGH, W. S. "Some suggestions about Amos," in *J. Bib. Lit.*, LXXII (1953), pp. 147–54.

MORGENSTERN, J. *Amos Studies*. VOL. I. Cincinnati 1941.

ROWLEY, H. H. "Was Amos a nabi?" in *Festschrift Otto Eissfeldt zum 60. Geburtstage 1 September 1947 dargebracht von Freunden und Verehren*, ed. J. Fück. Halle 1947.

SPEIER, S. "Bemerkungen zu Amos," in *Vet. test.*, III (1953), pp. 305–10.

WATTS, J. D. W. "An old hymn preserved in the Book of Amos," in *J.N.E.S.*, XV (1956), pp. 33–4.

—— "The origin of the Book of Amos," in *Ex. Times*, LXVI (1954–5), pp. 109–12.

—— *Vision and Prophecy in Amos*. Leiden 1958.

WEISER, A. *Die Profetie des Amos*. Beihefte z. *Z. alttest. W.* No. 53. Giessen 1929.

WÜRTHWEIN, E. "Amos V. 21–7," in *Th. Lz.*, LXXXII (1947), cols. 144–52.

—— "Amosstudien," in *Z. alttest. W.*, LXII (1950), pp. 10–52.

OBADIAH

A. Commentaries

B. Jérus. (J. Trinquet, 1953). I.C.C. (J. M. P. Smith *et al.*, 1912), West. Comm. (G. W. Wade, 1925). See also under MINOR PROPHETS.

B. Literature

BIČ, M. "Zur Problematik des Buches Obedja," in *Vet. test.*, Suppl. 1 (1953), pp. 11–25.

CANNON, W. W. "Israel and Edom, the oracle of Obadiah," in *Theology* (1927), pp. 129–40, 191–200.

GRAY, J. "The diaspora of Israel and Judah in Obadiah verse 20," in *Z. alttest. W.*, LXV (1953), pp. 53–9.

RUDOLPH, W. "Obadja," in *Z. alttest. W.*, XLIX (1931), pp. 222–31.

JONAH

A. Commentaries

B. Cent. (VOL. II, A. Lods, 1947). I.C.C. (H. G. Mitchell, J. M. P. Smith, and J. A. Bewer, 1912). Torch Comm. (G. A. F. Knight, 1950). West. Comm. (G. W. Wade, 1925). See also under MINOR PROPHETS.

B. Literature

FEUILLET, A. "Le sens du livre de Jonas," in *Rev. bib.*, LIV (1947), pp. 340–61.

—— "Les sources du livre de Jonas," in *Rev. bib.*, LIV (1947), pp. 161–86.

JOHNSON, A. R. "Jonah II. 3–10: a study in cultic phantasy," in *Studies in Old Testament Prophecy, presented to Professor T. H. Robinson*, ed. H. H. Rowley. Edinburgh 1950.

RAD, G. VON. *Der Prophet Jona*. Nuremberg 1950.

SCHMIDT, H. *Jona: Eine Untersuchung zur vergleichenden Religionsgeschichte*. Göttingen 1907.

MICAH

A. Commentaries

I.C.C. (J. M. P. Smith *et al.*, 1912). Torch Comm. (J. Marsh, 1959). West. Comm. (G. W. Wade, 1925). See also under MINOR PROPHETS.

B. Literature

BRUNO, A. *Micah und der Herrscher aus der Vorzeit*. Leipzig 1923.

BUDDE, K. "Verfasser und Stella von Micha IV. 1–4 (Jes. II. 2–4)," in *Z.D.M.G.*, LXXXI (1927), pp. 152–8.

EDELKOORT, A. H. "Prophet and prophet (Micah II. 6–11, III. 5–8)," in *Oudtest. St.*, V (1948), pp. 179–89.

GUNKEL, H. "Der Micha-Schluss," in *Zeitschrift für Semistik und verwandte Gebiete*, II (1924), pp. 145–78.

JEPSEN, A. "Kleine Beiträge zum Zwölfprophetenbuch: 2. Micha," in *Z. alttest. W.*, LVI (1938), pp. 96–100.

LINDBLOM, J. *Micha literansch. untersucht.* Abô 1929.

MILIK, J. T. "Fragments d'un midrasch de Michée dans les manuscrits de Qumran," in *Rev. bib.*, LIX (1952), pp. 412–8.

NAHUM
A. Commentaries

B. Cent. (VOL. II, P. Humbert, 1947). B. Jérus. (A. George, 1952). I.C.C. (J. M. P. Smith *et al.*, 1912). West. Comm. (G. V. Stonehouse and G. W. Wade, 1929). See also under MINOR PROPHETS.

B. Literature

HALDAR, A. *Studies in the Book of Nahum.* Uppsala 1947.

HUMBERT, P. "Essai d'analyse de Nahoum I. 2–II. 3," in *Z. alttest. W.*, XLIV (1926), pp. 266–80.

—— "La vision de Nahoum II. 4–11," in *Arch. Or.*, V (1928), pp. 14–19.

—— "Le problème du livre de Nahoum," in *R.h.p.r.*, XII (1932), pp. 1–15.

MIHELIC, J. "The concept of God in the Book of Nahum," in *Int.*, II (1948), pp. 199–207.

HABAKKUK
A. Commentaries

B. Cent. (VOL. II, P. Humbert, 1947), I.C.C. (J. M. P. Smith *et al.*, 1912). West. Comm. (G. V. Stonehouse and G. W. Wade, 1929). See also under MINOR PROPHETS.

B. Literature

BEVENOT, H. "Le cantique d'Habacuc," in *Rev. bib.*, XLII (1933), pp. 499–525.

HUMBERT, P. *Problèmes du livre d'Habacuc.* Neuchâtel 1944.

NIEBEN, E. "The righteous and the wicked in Habaqquq," in *St. th.*, VI (1953), pp. 54–78.

TORREY, C. C. "The prophecy of Habakkuk," in *Jewish Studies in Memory of G. A. Kohut.* New York 1935.

WALKER, H. H. and N. W. LUND. "The literary structure of the Book of Habakkuk," in *J. Bib. Lit.*, LIII (1934), pp. 355–70.

ZEPHANIAH
A. Commentaries

B. Cent. (VOL. II, P. Humbert, 1947). I.C.C. (J. M. P. Smith *et al.*, 1912). West. Comm. (G. V. Stonehouse and G. W. Wade, 1929). See also under MINOR PROPHETS.

B. Literature

GERLEMAN, G. *Zephaniah textkritisch und literarisch untersucht.* Lund 1942.

HYATT, J. P. "The date and background of Zephaniah," in *J.N.E.S.*, VII (1948), pp. 156–73.

SMITH, L. P. and E. L. LACHEMAN. "The authorship of the Book of Zephaniah," in *J.N.E.S.*, IX (1950), pp. 137–42.

HAGGAI

A. Commentaries

I.C.C. (H. G. Mitchell, J. M. P. Smith, and J. A. Bewer, 1912). See also under MINOR PROPHETS.

B. Literature

ACKROYD, P. R. "Studies in the Book of Haggai," in *Journal of Jewish Studies*, II (1951), pp. 163–76, III (1952), pp. 1–13.
—— "The Book of Haggai and Zechariah I–VIII," in *Journal of Jewish Studies*, III (1952), pp. 151–6.
ALT, A. "Die Rolle Samarias bei der Entstehung des Judentums," in *Festschrift Otto Procksch zum* 60. *Geburtstag überreicht*. Leipzig 1934. Reprinted in A. Alt, *Kleine Schriften zur Geschichte des Volkes Israel*, VOL. II. Munich 1953.
BENTZEN, A. "Quelques remarques sur le mouvement messianique parmi les juifs aux environs de l'an 520," in *R.h.p.r.*, X (1930), pp. 493–503.
BLOOMHARDT, P. F. "The poems of Haggai," in *H.U.C.A.*, V (1928), pp. 153–95.
NORTH, F. S. "Critical analysis of the Book of Haggai," in *Z. alttest. W.*, LXVIII (1956), pp. 25–46.
WATERMAN, L. "The camouflage purge of three Messianic conspirators," in *J.N.E.S.*, XIII (1954), pp. 73–8.

ZECHARIAH

A. Commentaries

I.C.C. (H. G. Mitchell, J. M. P. Smith, and J. A. Bewer, 1912). See also under MINOR PROPHETS.

B. Literature

GALLING, K. "Die Exilswende in der Sicht des Propheten Sacharja," in *Vet. test.*, II (1952), pp. 18–36.
HERTZBERG, H. W. "Grüne Pferde," in *Z.D.P.V.*, LXIX (1953), pp. 177–80.
JEPSEN, A. "Kleine Beiträge zum Zwolfprophetenbuch: 4. Sacharja," in *Z. alttest. W.*, LXI (1945–8), pp. 95–114.
LE BAS, E. E. "Zechariah's enigmatical contribution to the cornerstone," in *Palestine Exploration Quarterly*, LXXXII (1950), pp. 102–22.
PRESS, R. "Das erste Nachtgesicht des Propheten Sacharja," in *Z. alttest. W.*, LIV (1936), pp. 43–8.
RIGNELL, L. G. *Die Nachtgesichte des Sacharja: eine exegetische Studie*. Lund 1950.
ROST, L. "Bemerkungen zu Sacharja 4," in *Z. alttest. W.*, LXIII (1952), pp. 216–21.
—— "Erwägungen zu Sacharjas 7. Nachtgesicht," in *Z. alttest. W.*, LVIII (1940–1), pp. 223–8.
SCHMIDT, H. "Das vierte Nachtgesicht des Propheten Sacharja," in *Z. alttest. W.*, LIV (1936), pp. 48–60.

DEUTERO-ZECHARIAH

For commentaries, see ZECHARIAH

Literature

CANNON, W. W. "Some notes on Zechariah ch. 11," in *Act. Or.*, IV (1927), pp. 139–46.

DELCOR, L. "Deux passages difficiles, Zach. XII. 11 et XI. 13," in *Vet. test.*, III (1953), pp. 67–77.

HELLER, B. "Die letzten Kapitel des Buches Sacharja im Licht des späteren Judentums," in *Z. alttest. W.*, XLV (1927), pp. 151–5.

HOFTIJZER, J. "À propos d'une interprétation récente de deux passages difficiles: Zach. XII. 1 et Zach. XI. 13," in *Vet. test.*, III (1953), pp. 407–9.

JEPSEN, A. "Kleine Beiträge zum Zwolfprophetenbuch: 3. Der Aufbau des deuterosacharjarischen Buches," in *Z. alttest. W.*, LVII (1939), pp. 242–55.

KRAELING, E. G. "The historical situation in Zechariah IX. 1–10," in *A.J.S.L.*, XLI (1924–5), pp. 24–33.

MALACHI

A. Commentaries

I.C.C. (H. G. Mitchell, J. M. P. Smith, and J. A. Bewer, 1912). See also under MINOR PROPHETS.

B. Literature

BULMERINCQ, A. VON. *Der Prophet Maleachi.* 2 vols. Dorpat 1926–32.

CAMERON, D. "A study of Malachi," in *Transactions of the Glasgow University Oriental Society*, VIII (1938), pp. 9–12.

HOLTZMANN, O. "Der Prophet Maleachi und der Ursprung des Pharisäertums," in *Archiv für Religionswissenschaft*, XXIX (1930), pp. 1–21.

LATTEY, C. *The Book of Malachy.* London 1935.

CHAPTER V

PSALMS

A. Commentaries

A.T.D. (A. Weiser, 4th edn. 1959). Bibl. Komm. A.T. (H. J. Kraus, 1958–). Echter-Bibel (F. Nötscher, 4th edn. 1953). Hb. A.T. (H. Schmidt, 1934). Heil. Schr. A.T. (H. Herkenne, 1936). Hk. A.T. (H. Gunkel, 4th edn. 1926). I.C.C. (C. A. Briggs, 1906–7). *Int. Bible* (VOL. IV, 1955, W. S. McCullough). Komm. A.T. (R. Kittel, 5th and 6th edns. 1929). West. Comm. (W. E. Barnes, 1931).

B. General Literature

BARTH, C. *Die Errettung vom Tode in den individuellen Klage- und Dankliedern des Alten Testaments.* Zollikon 1947.

BAUMANN, E. "Strukturuntersuchungen im Psalter," in *Z. alttest. W.*, LXI (1945–8), pp. 114–76, LXII (1950, pp. 115–52.

BIRKELAND, H. *āru und ānāw in den Psalmen.* Oslo 1933.

—— *Die Feinde des Individuums in der israelitischen Psalmentliteratur.* Oslo 1933.

BUTTENWEISER, M. *The Psalms chronologically treated.* Chicago 1938.

CALÈS, J. *Le Livre des psaumes.* Paris 1936.

EERDMANS, B. D. "The Hebrew Book of Psalms," in *Oudtest. St.*, IV (1947).

HALLER, M. "Ein Jahrzehnt Psalmenforschung," in *Th. R.*, I (1929), pp. 377–402.

JAMES, F. *Thirty Psalmists.* New York 1938.

JOHNSON, A. R. "The Psalms," in *The Old Testament and Modern Study*, ed. H. H. Rowley. Oxford 1951.

KIRKPATRICK, A. E. *The Book of Psalms.* Cambridge 1903.

KISSANE, E. J. *The Book of Psalms translated from a critically revised Hebrew Text.* 2 vols. Dublin 1953–4.

KOHLER, L. "Psalm 23," in *Z. alttest. W.*, LXVIII (1956), pp. 227–34.

KÖNIG, E. *Die Psalmen.* Gutersloh 1927.

LESLIE, E. A. *The Psalms translated and interpreted in the Light of Hebrew Life and Worship.* New York 1949.

MONTGOMERY, J. A. "Recent developments in the study of the Psalter," in *Anglican Theological Review*, XVI (1934), pp. 185–98.

MOWINCKEL, S. "Psalm criticism between 1900 and 1935," in *Vet. test.*, V (1955), pp. 13–33.

—— *Psalmenstudien I–VI.* Kristiania 1921–4.

OESTERLEY, W. O. E. *A Fresh Approach to the Psalms.* London 1937.

—— *The Psalms.* London 1939.

PATERSON, J. *The Praises of Israel: Studies Literary and Religious in the Psalms.* New York 1950.

PETERS, N. *Das Buch der Psalmen (Psalmi).* Paderborn 1940.

PODECHARD, E. *Le Psautier.* 3 vols. Lyons 1949–54.

SCHMIDT, H. *Das Gebet des Angeklagten im Alten Testament.* Beihefte z. *Z. alttest. W.* No. 49. Giessen 1928.

SNAITH, N. H. *Studies in the Psalter.* London 1934.

STAMM, J. J. "Ein Vierteljahrhundert Psalmenforschung," in *Th. R.*, XXIII (1955), pp. 1–68.

WELCH, A. C. *The Psalter in Life, Worship, and History.* Oxford 1926.

WEVERS, J. "A study in the form criticism of individual omplaint psalms," in *Vet. test.*, VI (1956), pp. 80–96.

WÜRTHWEIN, E. "Erwägungen zu Psalm 139," in *Vet. test.*, VII (1957), pp. 165–82.

WUTZ, F. *Die Psalmen textkritisch untersucht.* Munich 1925.

C. The Psalms and the Cult

CAUSSE, A. "L'ancienne poésie culturelle d'Israël et l'origine du Psautier," in *R.h.p.r.*, VI (1926), pp. 1–37.

GUNKEL, H. and J. BEGRICH. *Einleitung in die Psalmen.* Göttingen 1933.
MOWINCKEL, S. *Offersang og Sangoffer: Salmediktning i Bibelen.* Oslo 1951.
PETERS, J. P. *The Psalms as Liturgies.* New York 1922.
QUELL, G. *Das kultische Problem der Psalmen.* Stuttgart 1926.
SNAITH, N. H. *Hymns of the Temple.* London 1951.

D. *The Accession Songs*

BENTZEN, A. *Det sakrale kongedømme.* Copenhagen 1945.
—— "King ideology—'Urmensch'—Troonbestijgingsfeest," in *St. th.*, III
(1949–51), pp. 143 ff.
—— *Messias—Moses redivivus—Menschensohn: Skizzen zum Thema Weissagung
und Erfüllung.* Zürich 1948. Eng. trans. *King and Messiah.* London 1955.
EISSFELDT, O. "Jahwe als König," in *Z. alttest. W.*, XLVI (1928), pp. 81–105.
ENGNELL, I. *Studies in Divine Kingship in the Ancient Near East.* Uppsala 1943.
JOHNSON, A. R. "Divine kingship and the Old Testament," in *Ex. Times*,
LXII (1950), pp. 36–42.
—— *The Rôle of the King in the Jerusalem Cultus* in the *Labyrinth*, ed. S. H.
Hooke, London 1935.
KRAUS, H. J. *Die Königsherrschaft Gottes im Alten Testament.* Tübingen 1951.
MICHEL, D. "Studien zu den sogenannten Thronbesteigspsalmen," in
Vet. test., VI (1956), pp. 40–68.
MOWINCKEL, S. *Psalmenstudien II.* Kristiania 1922.
SCHMIDT, H. *Die Thronfahrt Jahwes.* Giessen 1927.
SNAITH, N. H. *The Jewish New Year Festival: its Origin and Development.*
London 1947.

E. *The Psalms and the Literature of Neighbouring Countries*

BEGRICH, J. "Die Vertrauensäusserungen im israeliteschen Klagelied des
Einzelnen und in seinen babylonischen Gegenstück," in *Z. alttest. W.*,
XLVI (1928), pp. 221–60.
COPPENS, J. *Les Parallèles du Psautier avec les textes de Ras Shamra-Ugarit.*
Louvain 1946.
CUMMINGS, C. G. *Assyrian and Hebrew Hymns of Praise.* New York 1934.
FALKENSTEIN, A. and A. VON SODEN. *Sumerische und Akkadische Hymnen und
Gebete.* Zürich and Stuttgart 1953.
FEINBERG, C. L. "Parallels to the Psalms in Near Eastern Literature," in
Bibl Sac., CIV (1947), pp. 290–321.
O'CALLAGHAN, R. T. "Echoes of Canaanite literature in the Psalms," in
Vet. test., IV (1954), pp. 164–76.
PATTON, J. H. *Canaanite Parallels to the Book of Psalms.* Baltimore 1944.
STUMMER, F. *Sumerisch-akkadische Parallelen zum Aufbau alttestamentlicher
Psalmen.* Paderborn 1922.
The Psalmists, ed D. C. Simpson, Oxford 1926. See essays by W. F.
Blackman, G. R. Driver, and H. Gressmann.
WIDENGREN, G. *The Akkadian and Hebrew Psalms of Lamentation as Religious
Documents.* Uppsala 1936.

Job

A. Commentaries

A.T.D. (A. Weiser, 2nd edn. 1956). Cent. Bible (A. S. Peake, 1904). Echter-Bibel (H. Junker, 2nd edn. 1952). Hb. A.T. (G. Hölscher, 2nd edn. 1952). Hk. A.T. (K. Budde, 2nd edn. 1913). I.C.C. (S. R. Driver and G. B. Gray, 1921). *Int. Bible* (VOL. III, 1953, S. Terrien). Torch Comm. (A. and M. Hanson, 1953). West. Comm. (E. C. S. Gibson, 3rd edn. 1919).

B. Literature

BALL, C. J. *The Book of Job.* Oxford 1922.

DHORME, P. *Le Livre de Job.* 2nd edn. Paris 1926.

EISSFELDT, O. "Modern criticism," in *Record and Revelation,* ed. H. W. Robinson. Oxford 1938.

FOHRER, G. "Zur Vorgeschichte und Komposition des Buches Hiob," in *Vet. test.,* VI (1956), pp. 249–67.

KISSANE, E. J. *The Book of Job translated from a criticially revised Hebrew Text with Commentary.* Dublin 1939.

KRAELING, E. G. *The Book of the Ways of God.* London 1938.

KRAMER, S. N. "Man and his God. A Sumerian variation on the 'Job' motif," in *Vet. test.,* Suppl. III (1955), pp. 170–82.

KUHL, C. "Neuere literarkritik des Buches Hiob," in *Th. R.,* XXI (1953), pp. 163–205, 257–317.

——— "Vom Hiobbuche und seinen Problemen," in *Th. R.,* XXII (1954), pp. 261–316.

LINDBLOM, J. *La Composition du livre de Job.* Lund 1945.

LODS, A. "Recherches récentes (1920–34) sur le livre de Job," in *R.h.p.r.,* XIV (1934), pp. 501–33.

McKECHNIE, J. *Job: Moral Hero, Religious Egoist and Mystic.* Greenock 1925.

MEEK, T. J. "Job XIX. 15–17," in *Vet. test.,* VI (1956), pp. 100–3.

STEVENSON, W. P. *The Poem of Job.* London 1947.

STRAHAN, J. *The Book of Job Interpreted.* Edinburgh 1913.

WESTERMAN, C. *Der Aufbau des Buches Hiob.* Tübingen 1956.

WISDOM LITERATURE

BAUMGARTNER, W. "Die israelitischen Weisheitsliteratur," in *Th. R.,* V (1933), pp. 259–88.

——— *Israelitische und orientalische Weisheit.* Tübingen 1933.

——— "The Wisdom literature," in *The Old Testament and Modern Study,* ed. H. H. Rowley. Oxford 1951.

FICHTNER, J. *Die altorientalische Weisheit in ihrer israelitisch-jüdischen Ausprägung.* Beihefte z. Z. alttest. W. No. 62. Giessen 1933.

GRESSMANN, H. *Israels Spruchweisheit im Zusammenhang der Weltliteratur.* Kunst und Altertum VOL. VI. Berlin 1925.

MACDONALD, D. B. *The Hebrew Philosophical Genius.* Princeton 1936.

RANKIN, O. S. *Israel's Wisdom Literature.* Edinburgh 1936.

RANSTON, H. *The Old Testament Wisdom Books and their Teachings.* London 1930.

RYLAARSDAM, J. C. *Revelation in Jewish Wisdom Literature.* Chicago 1946.

TOOMBS, L. E. "Old Testament theology and the Wisdom literature," in *J. Bib. Rel.*, XXIII (1955), pp. 193–6.

PROVERBS

A. Commentaries

Echter-Bibel (V. Hamp, 1949). Hb. A.T. (B. Gemser, 1937). Hk. A.T. (W. Frankenberg, 1898). I.C.C. (C. H. Toy, 1899). *Int. Bible* (VOL. IV, 1955, C. T. Fritsch and R. W. Schloerb). West. Comm. (W. O. E. Oesterley, 1929).

B. Literature

BALSCHEIT, B. "Die Weisheit Israels," in *Neue Wege*, XLV (1951), pp. 60–71.

BOSTRÖM, G. *Proverbiasstudien. Die Weisheit und das fremde Weib in Sprüche 1–9.* Lund 1935.

EISSFELDT, O. *Der Maschal im Alten Testament.* Beihefte z. *Z. alttest. W.* No. 24. Giessen 1913.

ELMSLIE, W. A. L. *Studies in Life from Jewish Proverbs.* London 1917.

KRAUS, H. J. *Die Verkündigung der Weisheit: Eine Auslegung des Kapitels Sprüche 8.* Neukirchen 1951.

KUHN, G. *Beiträge zur Erklärung des Salomonischen Spruchbuches.* Stuttgart 1931.

RINGGREN, H. *Word and Wisdom: Studies in the Hypostatization of Divine Qualities and Functions in the Ancient Near East.* Uppsala 1947.

ROBERT, A. "Les attaches littéraires bibliques de Proverbes I–IX," in *Rev. bib.*, XLIII (1934), pp. 42–68, 172–204, 374–84.

SAVIGNAC, J. DE. "Note sur le sens du verse VIII. 22 des Proverbes," in *Vet. test.* IV (1954), pp. 429–32.

ZIMMERLI, W. "Zur Struktur der alttestamentlichen Weisheit," in *Z. alttest. W.*, LI (1933), pp. 177–204.

RUTH

A. Commentaries

A.T.D. (H. W. Hertzberg, 1953), B. Jérus. (A. Vincent, 1952). Echter-Bibel (J. Fischer, 2nd and 3rd edns. 1955). Hb. A.T. (M. Haller and K. Galling, 1940). Hk. A.T. (W. Nowack, 1900). *Int. Bible* (VOL. II, 1953, L. P. Smith). Komm. A.T. (W. Rudolph, 1939). Torch Comm. (G. A. F. Knight, 1950).

B. Literature

BURROWS, M. "The marriage of Boas and Ruth," in *J. Bib. Lit.*, LVIII (1939), pp. 445–54.

CANNON, W. W. "The Book of Ruth," in *Theology*, XVI (1928), pp. 310–9.

CROOK, M. B. "The Book of Ruth, a new solution," in *J. Bib. Rel.*, XVI (1948), pp. 155–60.

GUNKEL, H. *Reden und Aufsätze.* Göttingen 1913: pp. 65–92, "Ruth."

HUMBERT, P. "Art et leçon de l'histoire de Ruth," in *R.th.ph.*, XXVI (1938), pp. 257–86.

JEPSEN, A. "Das Buch Ruth," in *Theol. Stud. u. Krit.*, CVIII (1937–8), pp. 416–22.

ROBERTSON, E. "The plot of the Book of Ruth," in *B.J.R.L.*, XXXII (1950), pp. 207–8.

ROWLEY, H. H. "The marriage of Ruth," in *H.T.R.*, XL (1947), pp. 77–99.

VRIEZEN, T. H. "Two old cruces; (a) Ruth IV. 5," in *Oudtest. St.*, V (1948), pp. 80–8.

THE SONG OF SOLOMON

A. Commentaries

A.T.D. (H. Ringgren and A. Weiser, 1958). Echter-Bibel (J. Fischer, 2nd and 3rd edns. 1955). Hb. A.T. (M. Haller and K. Galling, 1940). Hk. A.T. (K. Siegfried, 1898). *Int. Bible* (VOL. V, 1956), T. J. Meek and H. T. Kerr). Torch Comm. (G. A. F. Knight, 1955).

B. Literature

AUDET, J. P. "Le sens du Cantique des Cantiques," in *Rev. bib.*, LXII (1955), pp. 197–221.

BENTZEN, A. "Remarks on the canonisation of the Song of Solomon," in *Studia orientalia Ioanni Pedersen septuagenario a.d. VII Id. Nov. anno MCMLIII a collegis discipulis amicis dicata.* Copenhagen 1953.

BUZY, D. "La composition littéraire du Cantique des Cantiques," in *Rev. bib.*, XLIX (1940), pp. 169–94.

DORNSEIFF, F. "Ägyptische Liebeslieder, Sappho, Theokrit," in *Z.D.M.G.*, XCVI (1936), pp. 589–601.

KUHL, C. "Das Hohelied und seine Deutung," in *Th. R.*, IX (1937), pp. 137–67.

LANDSBERGER, A. "Poetic units within the Song of Songs," in *J. Bib. Lit.*, LXXIII (1954), pp. 203–16.

MURPHY, R. E. "Recent literature on the Canticle of Canticles," in *C.B.Q.*, XVI (1954), pp. 1–11.

RINGGREN, K. V. H. "Hohes Lied und hieros gamos," in *Z. alttest. W.*, LXV (1953), pp. 300–2.

ROWLEY, H. H. "The interpretation of the Song of Songs," in *Journal of Theological Studies*, XXXVIII (1937), pp. 337–63.

—— "The meaning of the Shulamite," in *A.J.S.L.*, LVI (1939), pp. 84–91.

RUDOLPH, W. "Das Hohelied im Kanon," in *Z. alttest. W.*, LIX (1941), pp. 189–99.

SCHMÖKEL, H. *Heilige Hochzeit und Hohes Lied.* Wiesbaden 1956.

—— "Zur kultischen Deutung des Hohenliedes," in *Z. alttest. W.*, LXIV (1953), pp. 148–55.

WATERMAN, L. *The Song of Songs translated and interpreted as a Dramatic Poem.* Ann Arbor (Mich.) 1948.

WUTZ, F. *Das Hohelied.* Stuttgart 1940.

ECCLESIASTES

A. Commentaries

Echter-Bibel (F. Nötscher, 1948). Hb. A.T. (M. Haller and K. Galling, 1940). Heil. Schr. A.T. (A. Allgeier, 1925). Hk. A.T. (K. Siegfried, 1898). I.C.C. (G. A. Barton, 1908). *Int. Bible* (VOL. V, 1956, O. S. Rankin). Komm. A.T. (H. W. Hertzberg, 1932).

B. Literature

DAHOOD, M. J. "Canaanite-Phoenician influence in Qoheleth," in *Bibl.*, XXXIII (1952), pp. 30–52.

—— "The language of Qoheleth," in *C.B.Q.*, XIV (1952), pp. 227–32.

DORNSEIFF, F. "Das Buch Prediger," in *Z.D.M.G.*, LXXXIX (1935), pp. 43–249.

GALLING, K. "Kohelet-Studien," in *Z. alttest. W.*, L (1932), pp. 276–99.

—— "Stand und Aufgabe des Koheletforschung," in *Th. R.*, VI (1934), pp. 355–73.

GINSBERG, H. L. *Studies in Koheleth*. New York 1950.

—— "The structure and contents of the Book of Kohelet," in *Vet. test.*, Suppl. III (1955), pp. 138–49.

GORDIS, R. "Koheleth—Hebrew or Aramaic?" in *J. Bib. Lit.*, LXXI (1952), pp. 93–109.

—— *Koheleth: The Man and his World.* New York 1951.

—— *The Wisdom of Ecclesiastes.* New York 1945.

LAUHA, A. "Die Krise des religiösen Glaubens bei Kohelet," in *Vet. test.*, Suppl. III (1955), pp. 183–91.

MUILENBERG, J. "A Qoheleth scroll from Qumran," in *B.A.S.O.R.*, CXXXV (1954), pp. 20–8.

REINES, C. W. "Koheleth on wisdom and wealth," in *Journal of Jewish Studies*, V (1954) pp. 80–4.

ROWLEY, H. H. "The Problem of Ecclesiastes," in *Jewish Quarterly Review*, XLII (1951–2), pp. 87–90.

STAPLES, W. E. " 'Profit' in Ecclesiastes," in *J.N.E.S.*, IV (1945), pp. 87–96.

—— "The 'vanity' of Ecclesiastes," in *J.N.E.S.*, II (1943), pp. 95–104.

ZIMMERLI, W. *Die Weisheit des Predigers Salomo.* Berlin 1936.

LAMENTATIONS

A. Commentaries

A.T.D. (H. Ringgren and A. Weiser, 1958). Bib. Komm. A.T. (H. J. Kraus, 1956). Echter-Bibel (F. Nötscher, 1947). Hb. A.T. (M. Haller and K. Galling, 1940). Hk. A.T. (M. Löhr, 2nd edn. 1906). *Int. Bible* (VOL. VI, 1956, T. J. Meek). Komm. A.T. (W. Rudolph, 1939). Torch Comm. (G. A. F. Knight, 1955).

B. Literature

GOTTWALD, N. K. *Studies in the Book of Lamentations.* London 1954.

JAHNOW, H. *Das hebräische Leichenlied im Rahmen der Völkerdichtung.* Beihefte z. Z. alttest. W. No. 36. Giessen 1923.

WIESMANN, H. *Die Klagelieder übersetzt und erklärt*, ed. W. Koester. Frankfurt 1954.

—— Articles in *Bonner Zeitschrift für Theologie und Seelsorge*, V (1928), pp. 97–118; in *Th. Q.*, CX (1929), pp. 381–428; *Biblische Zeitschrift*, XXII (1934), pp. 20–43; *Bibl.*, XVII (1936), pp. 71–84.

ESTHER

A. Commentaries

A.T.D. (H. Ringgren and A. Weiser, 1958). Echter-Bibel (F. Stummer and V. Hamp, 1950). Hb. A.T. (M. Haller and K. Galling, 1940). Hk. A.T. (K. Siegfried, 1901). I.C.C. (L. B. Paton 1908). *Int. Bible* (VOL. III, 1954, B. W. Anderson). Torch Comm. (G. A. F. Knight, 1955).

B. Literature

ANDERSON, B. W. "The place of the Book of Esther in the Christian Bible," in *J. Rel.*, XXX (1950), pp. 32–43.

LEWY, J. "The feast of the fourteenth day of Adar," in *H.U.C.A.*, XIV (1937), pp. 124–8.

MORRIS, W. D. "The purpose of the Book of Esther," in *Ex. Times*, XLII (1930–1), pp. 124–8.

RUDOLPH, W. "Textkritisches zum Estherbuch," in *Vet. test.*, IV (1954), pp. 89–90.

DANIEL

A. Commentaries

B. Jérus. (P. de Menasce, 1954). Camb. Bible (S. R. Driver, 1912). Cent. Bible (R. H. Charles, 1929). Echter-Bibel (J. Ziegler and F. Nötscher, 1948). Hb. A.T. (A. Bentzen, 2nd edn. 1952). Hk. A.T. (G. Behrmann, 1894). I.C.C. (J. A. Montgomery, 1927). *Int. Bible*, (VOL. VI, 1956, A. Jeffery). Torch Comm. (E. W. Heaton, 1956).

B. Literature

ALT, A. "Zur Menetekel-Inschrift," in *Vet. test.*, IV (1954), pp. 303–5.

BAUMGARTNER, W. *Das Buch Daniel*. Giessen 1926.

—— "Ein Vierteljahrhundert Danielforschung," in *Th. R.*, XI (1939), pp. 59–83. 125–43, 201–28.

—— "Zu den vier Reichen von Daniel XI," in *Th. Z.*, I (1945), pp. 17–22.

BENTZEN, A. "Daniel VI. Ein Versuch zur Vorgeschichte der Martyrlegende," in *Festschrift für Alfred Bertholet zum 80. Geburtstag gewidmet*, edd. W. Baumgartner, O. Eissfeldt, K. Elliger, and L. Rost. Tübingen 1950.

CHARLES, R. H. *A Critical and Exegetical Commentary on the Book of Daniel*. London 1929.

EISSFELDT, O. "Die Menetekel-Inschrift und ihre Deutung," in *Z. alttest. W.*, LXIII (1951), pp. 105–14.

FEUILLET, A. "Le Fils de l'Homme de Daniel et la tradition biblique," in *Rev. bib.*, LX (1953), pp. 170–202, 321–46.

GINSBERG, H. L. *Studies in Daniel.* New York 1948.

—— "The composition of the Book of Daniel," in *Vet. test.*, IV (1954), pp. 246–75.

KUHL, C. *Die drei Männer im Feuer (Daniel Kapitel 3 und seine Zusätze).* Beihefte z. Z. *alttest. W.*, No. 55. Giessen 1930.

LATTEY, C. C. *The Book of Daniel.* Dublin 1948.

MANSON, T. W. *The Son of Man in Daniel, Enoch, and the Gospels.* Manchester 1950. Reprinted from *B.J.R.L.*, XXXII (1950).

ROWLEY, H. H. "The composition of the Book of Daniel," in *Vet. test.*, V (1955), pp. 272–6.

—— "The unity of the Book of Daniel," in *H.U.C.A.*, I (1952), pp. 233–73.

ZIMMERMAN, F. "Some verses in Daniel in the light of a translation hypothesis," in *J. Bib. Lit.*, LVIII (1939), pp. 349–54.

EZRA AND NEHEMIAH

A. Commentaries

A.T.D. (K. Galling, 1954). Echter-Bibel (M. Rehm, 1950). Hb. A.T. (W. Rudolph, 1949). Heil. Schr. A.T. (H. Schneider, 1959). Hk. A.T. (K. Siegfried, 1901). I.C.C. (L. W. Batten, 1913). *Int. Bible* (VOL. III, 1954, R. A. Bowman).

B. Literature

AHLEMANN, F. "Zur Esra-Quelle," in Z. *alttest. W.*, LIX (1942), pp. 77–98.

BICKERMANN, E. J. "The edict of Cyrus in Ezra I," in *J. Bib. Lit.*, LXV (1948), pp. 249–75.

CAZELLES, H. "La mission d'Esdras," in *Vet. test.*, IV (1954), pp. 113–40.

GALLING, K. "Der Tempelschatz nach Berichten und Urkunden im Buche Esra," in *Z.D.P.V.*, LX (1937), pp. 177–83.

JEPSEN, A. "Nehemia x," in Z. *alttest. W.*, LXVI (1954), pp. 86–106.

KAPELRUD, A. *The Question of Authorship in the Ezra Narrative.* Oslo 1944.

MEINHOLD, J. *Esra der Schriftgelehrte.* Beihefte z. Z. *alttest. W.* No. 41. Giessen 1925.

ROWLEY, H. H. *Sanballat and the Samaritan Temple.* Manchester 1955. Reprinted from *B.J.R.L.*, XXXVIII (1955), pp. 166–98.

SCHRAEDER, H. H. *Ezra der Schreiber.* Tübingen 1930.

VAUX, R. DE. "Les décrets de Cyrus et de Darius sur la réconstruction du temple," in *Rev. bib.*, XLVI (1937), pp. 29–57.

WRIGHT, J. S. *The Date of Ezra's Coming to Jerusalem.* London 1947.

CHRONICLES

A. Commentaries

A.T.D. (K. Galling, 1954). Camb. Bible (W. A. L. Elmslie, 1916). Hk. A.T. (R. Kittel, 1902). I.C.C. (E. L. Curtis and A. A. Madsen, 1910). *Int. Bible* (VOL. III, 1954, W. R. Elmslie). Komm. A.T. (J. W. Rothstein and J. Hänel, 1927).

B. Literature

BEA, A. "Neuere Arbeiten zum Problem der Chronikbucher," in *Bibl.*, XXII (1941), pp. 46–58.

BENTZEN, A. "Sirach, der Chronist, und Nehemia," in *St. th.*, III (1949), pp. 158–61.

BRANET, A. M. "Le Chroniste et ses sources," in *Rev. bib.*, LX (1953), pp. 481–508, LXI (1954), pp. 349–86.

RAD, G. VON. *Das Geschichtsbild des chronistischen Werkes*. Stuttgart 1930.

RUDOLPH, W. "Problems of the Book of Chronicles," in *Vet. test.*, IV (1954), pp. 401–9.

TORREY, E. C. *The Chronicler's History of Israel: Chronicles—Ezra—Nehemiah restored to its Original Form*. New Haven and London 1954.

WELCH, A. C. *The Work of the Chronicler, its Purpose and Date*. Oxford 1939.

THE APOCRYPHA

Texts and Literature

Die Apokryphen und Pseudepigraphen des Alten Testaments, ed E. Kautzsch. 2 vols. Tübingen 1900.

FRITZCHE, O. *Libri apocryphi veteris testamenti graece*. Leipzig 1871.

—— and W. GRIMM. *Kurzgefasstes exegetisches Handbuch zu den Apokryphen des Alten Testaments*. 3 vols. Leipzig 1851–3.

GOODSPEED, E. J. *The Apocrypha. An American Translation*. 6th imp. Chicago 1938.

Jewish Apocryphal Literature. Series published by Dropsie College, Philadelphia from 1950.

OESTERLEY, W. O. E. *An Introduction to the Books of the Apocrypha*. London 1935.

PFEIFFER, R. H. *History of New Testament Times with an Introduction to the Apocrypha*. New York 1949.

RIESSLER, P. *Altjüdisches Schrifttum ausserhalb der Bibel*. Augsburg 1928.

The Apocrypha and Pseudepigrapha in English, ed. R. H. Charles. 2 vols. Oxford 1913.

TORREY, C. C. *The Apocryphal Literature. A Brief Introduction*. New Haven 1945.

APOCALYPTIC

FROST, S. B. *Old Testament Apocalyptic, its Origin and Growth*. London 1952.

ROWLEY, H. H. *The Relevance of Apocalyptic*. London 1947. 2nd edn. New York 1950.

TOBIT

A. Commentaries

Echter-Bibel (F. Stummer and V. Hamp, 1950).

B. Literature

ZIMMERMAN, F. *The Book of Tobit, An English Translation with Introduction and Commentary.* Dropsie College, Philadelphia, Jewish Apocryphal Literature. New York 1958.

JUDITH

A. Commentaries

Echter-Bibel (F. Stummer and V. Hamp, 1950).

B. Literature

STEINMANN, J. *Lecture de Judith.* Paris 1953.

WISDOM

A. Commentaries

Camb. Bible (J. A. F. Gregg, 1922). Echter-Bibel (J. Fischer, 1950). Hb. A.T. (J. Fichtner, 1938).

ECCLESIASTICUS

Commentaries

Camb. Bible (W. O. E. Oesterley, 1912). Echter-Bibel (V. Hamp, 2nd edn. 1952).

BARUCH

Commentaries

Echter-Bibel (F. Stummer and V. Hamp, 1950).

MACCABEES

A. Commentaries

Camb. Bible (W. Fairweather and J. S. Black, 1936). Echter-Bibel (D. Schötz, 1948).

B. Literature

DANCY, J. C. *A Commentary on I Maccabees.* Oxford 1954.

TEDESCHE, S., and S. ZEITLIN. *The First Book of the Maccabees. An English Translation with Introduction and Commentary.* Dropsie College, Philadelphia, Jewish Apocryphal Literature. New York 1950.

For the "additions" see the Roman Catholic commentaries on Esther and Daniel.

X*

INDEX

Abraham oracles: 90.

accession songs: 39, 235, 239.

accusations: 36, 245.

Achikar novel: 256, 302.

acrostic: 215, 235, 257, 267, 305.

additions, later: 57, 96, 108, 119, 129, 135, 150f., 173, 187, 192, 196, 198ff., 209f., 214, 224, 225ff., 230, 246f., 266, 275, 283, 303, 308f.

allegory: 8, 42, 210, 225, 236, 260, 262.

Amalek, oath against: 90.

Amalekites: 47, 69, 124, 126.

Ammon, Ammonites: 113, 115, 123, 130, 134, 148, 194, 199, 220.

Amorites: 75, 103.

Amos; Book of, 144, 158, 159, 169, 202ff., 206–9; prophet, 158, 162, 165, 168, 206f., 221.

amphictyon (sacral union of tribes): 97f., 105f., 108, 114.

annals: of the kings of Israel and Judah, 35, 148; of Byblos, 36; Persian, 269.

antiphonal songs: 37, 232, 307.

apocalyptic literature: 33, 175f., 226, 228, 275.

Apocrypha: 33, 283, 301–11; Hebrew or Aramaic sources of, 301, 302, 306, 307, 309.

appendix (to the original text): 45, 59, 63, 105, 117ff., 127, 129, 133, 136, 151, 172, 175, 176f., 182, 192, 200, 205, 209f., 218, 219f., 256f., 259, 269ff., 310.

Aristea's letters: 24.

Ark: formula, 39, 89; story, 120ff., 129, 134.

Assyria: 12, 36, 103, 117f., 141–7, 168, 171–3, 177, 186, 203, 215ff.; parallels to the Psalms, 239; Wisdom literature, 249.

audition: 160, 164.

autobiographical accounts: singular, 164, 171, 187ff., 191, 194, 203f., 213, 222, 272, 282f., 285–7; plural, 287.

Babylon: 12, 36, 97, 145ff., 157, 163, 166, 174, 177, 179f., 181, 186, 189, 193, 197, 199f., 215, 217, 271ff., 276, 280, 295, 302, 305–9; songs, 234, 239, 276; Wisdom, 249; religion, 262.

Baruch: 35, 188f.; source, 189ff.; Book of, 305f.

Bel and the Dragon: 308f.

blasphemer of God: 96.

Boghazkoi: 12.

Book of the Covenant: 47, 54, 83, 95–8.

Book of Jashar: 35, 103, 127, 136.

Book of the Law: 27f., 64, 80, 89, 148, 283.

Book of the Song: 136.

Book of the Wars of Yahweh: 35.

book rolls: 18, 47, 167, 195, 223.

Canaan, Canaanite: 36, 48f., 69, 90, 97, 108, 110, 155, 203, 243; memoir, 94; Mishpat, 98; songs, 239.

canon, canonical: 154, 260, 262, 275, 280, 301, 303.

canonisation: 9, 20, 27–33.

catch phrases: 16, 161, 196.

Chronicler, historical work of the: 152, 280, 288–97; material peculiar to, 294ff.; sources, 296; date, 297.

Chronicles: 17, 35, 141, 144, 148, 177, 230ff., 260, 267, 280, 288–97, 309f.

Fable: 41f., 115, 196.
feasts, calendar of: 96.
festival cantata: 92, 176.
festival legend: 228, 238.
festival rolls (Megilloth): 258.
foreign nations: oracles against, 157f.,
    166, 171–4, 192, 198f., 201, 209, 215,
    219ff., 224f.; poems against, 162,
    199, 208; prose threats against, 205.
fragments: 64, 66, 69f., 75, 87, 101ff.,
    106, 113, 129, 168, 170, 197, 204f.,
    208, 215f., 222f., 228, 233, 284, 307.
fulfilment of Old Testament: 2ff.
funeral laments: 38, 127, 128, 135,
    162, 199, 215, 267.

Generations, Book of: see THOLEDOTH.
glosses: 12, 20, 107, 166, 192, 218, 306.
God, name given to: in Septuagint,
    24; in Pentateuch, 52–5, 64, 73;
    in Psalms, 229.
Greeks: 217, 276, 278.

Habakkuk: 35, 158, 216–9, 248;
    commentary from Dead Sea, 23;
    prophetic legend of, 309.
Haggai: 158, 221f., 224, 231.
Hammurabi: 92f.; Code of, 45, 97.
Hananiah, Prophet: 157, 163.
Hannah, Song of: 135.
headings: 167, 173, 194, 202, 204, 209,
    212, 214, 216, 218f., 222, 224ff.,
    231f., 250, 265, 272, 285, 305, 309.
Hexapla: 9, 25.
Hexateuch: 50, 52, 59, 63, 71, 106, 117.
historical tales: 115, 166, 191, 228,
    290.
history: of Uzziah, 35; of Saul, 122ff.,
    134; of the rise of David, 124ff.,
    134; of Solomon, 138; of Jehu, 148;
    of Samuel, 153; of the kings of
    Israel and Judah, 153.
Hittites: 93.
Holiness, Law of: 49, 63, 81, 95f., 200.

Hosea: 9, 99, 119, 160, 162f., 165,
    210–4, 221, 255.
hymns: 121, 135, 291, 305, 307;
    fragments, 178f., 208, 225, 307;
    Assyrian catalogue of, 232, 262;
    hymn-like prayer, 282.

Innocence and repentance, songs of:
    236, 237.
inserts of older material: 63, 82f., 86f.,
    95f., 98, 104, 110, 114f., 123, 128f.,
    133, 135, 215, 284, 293f.
interpretation of scriptures: 4ff., 7f.;
    fourfold, 8.
Isaac oracles: 90.
Itala (Vetus Latina): 26.
Isaiah: Book of, 2, 3, 17, 19, 22, 24,
    32, 35, 115, 150, 167–77, 182, 192,
    214f., 217, 221f., 250; prophet, 19,
    146, 160, 163, 167, 183, 193, 212,
    255; date, 168; small collection,
    169f.; Assyrian collection, 172ff.;
    Massah collection, 174; apocalypse,
    175f.; prophetic liturgy, 176;
    historical supplement, 177; Psalm
    of Hezekiah, 177.

Jacob: Blessing of, 87, 90f.; oracles,
    90.
Jehovist: 54f., 75ff.
Jeremiah: prophet, 31, 34f., 82, 84,
    86, 147, 157, 160, 163, 183–90, 193,
    195, 199, 204, 213, 225, 245, 248,
    277, 305; Book of Consolation, 35,
    186, 191; Deuteronomistic source
    and, 188, 190f.; Baruch source,
    189f.; original roll, 191; oracles
    against foreign nations, 192; appen-
    dix to, 192; Letter of (apocryphal),
    306.
Jesus Sirach: 17, 24, 28f.
Job: 20, 240–9, 263, 303, 305;
    framing narrative, 241ff.; contro-
    versial dialogue, 242ff.; soliloquies,

With great care, Curt Kuhl analyzes each book in the Old Testament according to composition, date, and authorship. He presents in a compact, readable manner the complicated process through which the Old Testament has passed. Very thorough in his treatment, Kuhl aims to bring the best of biblical scholarship within the reach of the average pastor and student.

Introductory material increases the value of the book. In the introduction, Kuhl gives a short survey of the authority of the Old Testament, the critical methods applied to its study, the formation of the canon, its transmission and literary character. At the end of the book he includes a discussion of the Apocrypha, a chronological table, bibliography, and indexes.

Kuhl's treatment is fresh and stimulating and has the added strength of direct reference to the text. Although he is involved in critical processes, Kuhl endeavors to define the religious value of a passage and to discover its moral and spiritual content.

CURT KUHL

A German theologian and Old Testament scholar, Curt Kuhl was born in the village of Gaudenz, East Prussia, in 1890.

He is the author of *The Prophets of Israel*, and among his other published works European bibliographies list *The Library Unity of Ezekiel*.